NO SHORTCUTS
TO THE TOP

BROADWAY BOOKS ▲ New York

NO
SHORTCUTS
to the
TOP

CLIMBING THE WORLD'S
14 HIGHEST PEAKS

▲

ED VIESTURS
with
DAVID ROBERTS

PUBLISHED BY BROADWAY BOOKS

Published in the United States by Broadway Books, an imprint of
The Doubleday Broadway Publishing Group, a division of Random
House, Inc., New York.
www.broadwaybooks.com

BROADWAY BOOKS and its logo, a letter B bisected on the diagonal,
are trademarks of Random House, Inc.

Book design by Maria Carella

Photograph on title page and chapter openings courtesy of
Jennifer Ann Daddio and Joseph Duraes

Map reprinted with permission of the National Geographic Society
from the book *Himalayan Quest: Ed Viesturs on the 8,000-Meter Giants*
by Ed Viesturs with Peter Potterfield. Copyright © 2003 Ed
Viesturs. Maps copyright © 2003 National Geographic.

Library of Congress Cataloging-in-Publication Data
Viesturs, Ed.
   No shortcuts to the top : climbing the world's 14 highest peaks /
Ed Viesturs with David Roberts.
      p. cm.
   1. Viesturs, Ed. 2. Mountaineers—Biography. 3. Mountaineering.
I. Roberts, David, 1943– II. Title.
GV199.92.V54A3 2006
796.52'209—dc22
[B]   2006042604

ISBN-13: 978-0-7679-2470-2
ISBN-10: 0-7679-2470-3

PRINTED IN THE UNITED STATES OF AMERICA

10 9 8 7 6 5 4 3 2 1

First Edition

For Paula, Gilbert, Ella, and Anabel—
the best reasons in the world for coming home

And in memory of my great partners
Rob Hall, Scott Fischer, and Jean-Christophe Lafaille

CONTENTS

CONTENTS

viii

NO SHORTCUTS TO THE TOP

Self-Arrest

At last things seemed to be going our way. Inside our Camp III tent, at 24,300 feet, Scott Fischer and I crawled into our sleeping bags and turned off our headlamps. The next day, we planned to climb up to Camp IV, at 26,000 feet. On the day after, we would get up in the middle of the night, put on all our clothing, grab our gear and a little food, and set off for the summit of K2, at 28,250 feet the second-highest mountain in the world. From Camp IV, the 2,250 vertical feet of snow, ice, and rock that would stretch between us and the top could take as long as twelve hours to climb, since neither Scott nor I was using supplemental oxygen. We had agreed that if we hadn't reached the summit by two P.M., we'd turn around—no matter what. ▲ It was the evening of August 3, 1992. Fifty-four days earlier, we had started our hike in to base camp on the Bal-

2

toro Glacier, which we had reached on June 21. Before the trip, even in my most pessimistic scenario I had never imagined that it could take us more than six weeks just to get in position for a summit push. But this expedition had seemed jinxed from the start—by hideous weather, by minor but consequential accidents, by an almost chaotic state of disorganization within our team.

As usual in the midst of a several-day summit push at high altitude, Scott and I were too keyed up to fall asleep. We tossed and turned in our sleeping bags. Then suddenly, around ten P.M., the radio in our tent crackled to life. I turned on my headlamp, grabbed the walkie-talkie, and listened intently. The voice on the radio was that of Thor Kieser, another American, calling from Camp IV, 1,700 feet above us. "Hey, guys," Thor blurted out, his voice tense with alarm. "Chantal and Alex aren't back. I don't know where they are."

I sighed in pure frustration. In the beam of my headlamp, I saw a kindred expression on Scott's face. Without exchanging a word, we knew what this meant. Our summit push was now on indefinite hold. Instead of moving up to Camp IV to get into position, the next day we would find ourselves caught up in a search—and possibly a rescue. The jinx was alive and well.

On August 3, as Scott and I had made the long haul from base camp up to Camp III (a grueling 7,000 feet of altitude gain), Thor Kieser, Chantal Mauduit, and Aleksei Nikiforov had gone for the summit from Camp IV. Chantal, a very ambitious French alpinist, had originally been part of a Swiss team independent from ours. When all of her partners had thrown in the towel on the mountain and left for home, she had stayed on (illegally, in terms of the permit system) and in effect grafted herself onto our group. She was now the only woman on the mountain. Aleksei—or Alex, as we called him—was a Ukrainian member of the Russian quintet that made up the core of our team.

That morning, Alex and Thor had set out at five-thirty A.M., Chantal not until seven. These starting times were much later than Scott and I would have been comfortable with, but the threesome had been delayed because of high winds. Remarkably, climbing without bottled oxygen, Chantal caught up with the men and surged past them. Struggling in the thin air, Thor turned back a few hundred feet below the summit, unwilling to get caught out in the dark. Chantal summited at five P.M., becoming only the fourth woman ever to climb K2. Alex topped out only after dark, at seven P.M.

The proverbial two P.M. turn-around time isn't an iron-clad rule on K2 (or on Everest, for that matter), but to reach the summit as late as Chantal and Alex did was asking for trouble. And trouble had now arrived.

On the morning of August 4, as Scott and I readied ourselves for the search and/or rescue mission that would cancel our own summit bid, we got another radio call from Thor. The two missing climbers had finally showed up at Camp IV, at seven in the morning, but they were in really bad shape. Chantal had been afraid to push her descent in the night and had bivouacked in the open at 27,500 feet. Three hours later, Alex had found her and talked her into continuing the descent with him—possibly saving her life.

Staggering through the night, the pair had managed to stay on route (no mean feat in the dark, given the confusing topography of K2's dome-shaped summit). But by the time they reached the tents at Camp IV, Chantal was suffering from snow blindness, a painful condition caused by leaving your goggles off for too long, even in cloudy weather. Ultraviolet rays burn the cornea, temporarily robbing you of your vision. Chantal was also utterly exhausted, and she thought she had frostbitten feet. In only marginally better shape, but determined to get down as fast as possible, Alex abandoned Chantal to Thor's safekeeping and pushed on toward our Camp III. He just said, "Bye-bye" and took off.

Thor himself was close to exhaustion from his previous day's effort, but on August 4 he gamely set out to shepherd a played-out Chantal down the mountain. It's an almost impossible and incredibly dangerous task to get a person in that kind of shape down slopes and ridges that are no child's play for even the freshest climber. Thor had scrounged a ten-foot hank of rope from somewhere—that's all he had to belay Chantal with, and maybe to rappel.

Over the radio to us, Thor had pleaded, "Hey, you guys, I might need some help to get her down." So Scott and I had made the only conscionable decision: to go up and help.

As we were getting ready, we watched as Alex haltingly worked his way down the slope above, eventually stumbling toward camp. We went up a short distance to assist him, then helped him get into one of the tents, where we plied and plied him with liquids, since he was severely dehydrated. Meanwhile, surprisingly, he didn't show any concern for Chantal.

Going to the summit, both he and Chantal had pushed themselves over the edge, driven themselves to their very limits. It happens all the time on the highest mountains, but it's kind of ridiculous.

To make matters worse, on August 4 the snow conditions were atrocious. Same with the weather: zero visibility. Scott and I tried to go, made it up the slope for a couple of hours, then had to turn around and head back to camp. We made plans for another attempt the following day.

We were in radio communication with Thor. He'd started to bring Chantal down to Camp III, but he only got partway. They had to camp right in the middle of a steep slope, almost a bivouac, though Thor had been smart enough to bring a tent with him.

The next day, August 5, Scott and I got up, packed our gear, and started up again, hoping we could meet up with Thor and Chantal and help them back to our camp. At some point, we could see them through the mist and clouds, two little dots above. It was blowing hard, and little spindrift avalanches were coming down the slope we were climbing. Part of it was stuff Thor and Chantal were kicking off from way above, stuff that by the time it got to us was a little bigger. But no really big slides. I'd scrounged a fifty-foot length of rope, with which Scott and I were tied together, because of the crevasses that riddled the slope.

At one point, Scott was above me. Something just didn't feel right. I yelled up to Scott, "Wait a minute, this is not a good slope." It was loaded, ready to avalanche. If you've done enough climbing, you can feel the load on a slope. I attribute that sense to the years of guiding I'd done by that point in my life. At that time, Scott hadn't done as much guiding as I had.

We stopped in our tracks. I said, "Man, let's not get ourselves killed doing this. Let's discuss this." Scott sat down facing out, looking down at me. I figured, if a big spindrift slide comes down now, we're going to get washed off the face.

I started digging a hole with my ice ax, thinking I might protect myself if a slide came from above. After a few moments, I looked up just in time to see Scott engulfed by a wave of powder. He disappeared from sight. At once I tucked into my hole and anchored myself, lying on top of my ax, the pick dug into the slope. Bracing myself for impact, I thought, *Here it comes*.

It got dark; it got quiet. I felt snow wash over my back. The lights literally went out. I hung on and hung on. And then, the avalanche seemed to subside. I thought I'd saved myself. I thought, *Wow, my little trick worked*.

But the fact was, Scott had been blindsided. He was tumbling with the snow, getting swept down the face. He hurtled past me, out of control. Scott was a big guy, maybe 225 pounds. I weigh 165.

The rope came tight. Boom! There was no way I could hold both of us. I got yanked out of my hole, like getting yanked out of bed. I knew instantly what had happened. Scott was plummeting down the mountain, with me in tow, connected by what should have been our lifeline. And there were 8,000 vertical feet of cliff below us.

If you're caught in an avalanche and careening down the slope, there are several ways of trying to save yourself. One of the ways is called a self-arrest. The idea is to get your ice ax underneath your body, lie on it with all your weight, hold on to the head, and try to dig the pick into the slope, like a brake.

I'd learned the self-arrest when I'd started climbing, and as a guide I'd taught it to countless clients. So the instinct was automatic. It ran through my head even as I was getting jerked and pummeled around by the avalanche: "Number one: Never let go of your ax. Number two: Arrest! Arrest! Arrest!" I kept jabbing with the pick of the ax, but the snow beneath me was so dry, the pick just kept slicing through. I'd reach and dig, reach and dig.

Yet I wasn't frantic. Everything seemed to be happening in slow motion, and it was as if sound had been turned off. We probably fell a couple of hundred feet. For whatever reason, Scott couldn't even begin to perform his own self-arrest.

Then, as I was still desperately attempting to get a purchase in the snow with my ice ax, suddenly I stopped. A few seconds later, just as I expected, the rope came tight again, with a tremendous jolt. But my pick held. With my self-arrest, I'd stopped both of us.

"Scott, are you okay?" I yelled down.

His answer was almost comical. "My nuts are killing me!" he screamed. The leg loops of his waist harness had had the unfortunate effect, when my arrest slammed him to a sudden stop, of jamming his testicles halfway up to his stomach. If that was the first thing Scott had to complain about, I knew that he'd escaped more serious harm.

Yet our roped-together plunge in the avalanche had been a really close call. If it hadn't been for the fact that two other mountaineers were in desperate straits, there's no way Scott or I would ever have tried to climb in those conditions.

Meanwhile, somewhere up above, Thor and Chantal still needed our help—more urgently with each passing half hour.

In mountaineering, 8,000 meters—26,247 feet—has come to signify a magical barrier. There are only fourteen peaks in the world that exceed that altitude above sea level, all of them in the Himalaya of Nepal and Tibet or the Karakoram of Pakistan. They range from Everest, at 8,850 meters (29,035 feet) down to Shishapangma, at 8,012 meters (26,286 feet).

During what has often been called the golden age of Himalayan mountaineering, the first ascents of all fourteen were accomplished, beginning with the French on Annapurna in 1950 and ending with the Chinese on Shishapangma in 1964. The stamp of the expeditions that waged that fourteen-year campaign was typically massive—with tons of supplies, hundreds of porters and Sherpas, and a dozen or more principal climbers—as well as fiercely nationalistic, as the French, Swiss, Germans, Austrians, Italians, British, Americans, Japanese, and Chinese vied to knock off the prizes. (If any country can be said to have "won" that competition, it would be Austria, whose leading climbers claimed the first ascents of Cho Oyu, Dhaulagiri, Nanga Parbat, and Broad Peak—two more mountains than any other nation's climbers would bag.)

Given the gear and technique of the day, it was considered cricket to throw all available means into the assault on an 8,000er. There were experts, after all, who doubted that Everest would ever be climbed. So teams strung miles of fixed ropes up the slopes of the highest peaks, allowing those tons of gear to be safely ferried from camp to camp. They bridged crevasses and short cliffs with metal ladders. And they routinely used bottled oxygen to tame the ravages of thin air in the "Death Zone" above 26,000 feet. (It was long assumed that any attempt to climb Everest without supplemental oxygen would prove fatal.)

Only one of the fourteen 8,000ers was climbed on the initial attempt. Remarkably enough, that was Annapurna, the first of all the fourteen to be ascended, thanks to an utterly brilliant effort spearheaded by the Parisian alpinist Maurice Herzog and three Chamonix guides, Louis Lachenal, Lionel Terray, and Gaston Rébuffat. So heroic was the ascent of a single 8,000er considered that each such deed accrued a seemingly limitless fund of national glory. The fiftieth anniversary of the triumph on K2 in 1954 was recently celebrated in Italy with much pomp and circumstance. The first ascent of Everest by the British the year before—news of which arrived in England at the very moment of Queen Elizabeth II's coronation—has been called, with no apparent irony, "the last great day in the British Empire." Sir Edmund Hillary remains the most famous mountaineer in history. (Alas, his more experienced partner, the Sherpa Tenzing Norgay, does not even rank a close second.)

So hard-won were those early successes on the 8,000-meter peaks that only two men—the Austrians Hermann Buhl and Kurt Diemberger—participated in more than a single triumph. At the cost of losing several toes to frostbite, Buhl pushed on to the summit of Nanga Parbat in a now legendary solo ascent in 1953, after all his teammates had faltered. Diemberger topped out on Dhaulagiri in 1960. And the two men joined forces on an admirably light, small-party first ascent of Broad Peak in 1957. Only eighteen days later, Buhl fell to his death on a neighboring peak when a cornice broke beneath his feet. His body has never been found.

By the mid-1970s, the most ambitious Himalayan mountaineers were attempting the 8,000ers by routes that were far more technically difficult than those followed on the first ascents. Difficulty for its own sake became, in fact, the ultimate cachet. Meanwhile, the first ascent lines, while not exactly being reduced to the humdrum status of "trade routes," were proving less fearsome than the pioneers had found them. By 1975, for instance, thirty-five different climbers, including the first woman, Junko Tabei from Japan, had successfully climbed Everest by the South Col route opened by Hillary and Tenzing.

Yet it would take one of the most visionary mountaineers of all time—Reinhold Messner, who grew up in the German-speaking Dolomites of northern Italy—to define, and then to realize, the ultimate high-altitude challenge of our time. Messner climbed his first 8,000er, Nanga Parbat, by a very long and very hard new route in 1970. In 1978, with his friend the Austrian mountaineer Peter Habeler, Messner proved the skeptics wrong by reaching the summit of Everest without bottled oxygen. Two years later, Messner repeated the feat—solo, by a new route! That 1980 ascent is rightly enshrined as one of the most extraordinary deeds ever accomplished in the mountains.

As I started my own climbing career in the late 1970s, the example Messner had set had a huge influence on me. It wouldn't be going too far to call him one of my mountaineering heroes. What especially impressed me was Messner's insistence on climbing the highest peaks by what he called "fair means"—without supplemental oxygen, refusing the support of porters and Sherpas, and going what we call "alpine-style," fast and light, with no fixed ropes and no stocked camps.

In 1975, having climbed Manaslu and Gasherbrum I as well as Nanga Parbat, Messner became the first person to top out on three different 8,000ers. By then a world-famous climber with lavish commercial sponsorship, Messner kept going back to the Himalaya and Karakoram, collecting yet other 8,000-meter peaks. Yet he would later claim that the idea of trying to be the first person to reach the summit of all fourteen 8,000ers didn't occur to him until 1982. By that date, however, the ultimate high-altitude challenge had become a flat-out race between Messner and the redoubtable Pole Jerzy Kukuczka.

In the end, Messner won the race, completing his quest in 1986, just a year before Kukuczka nailed his own last 8,000er. Some insiders felt that the Pole's achievement actually surpassed Messner's, since Kukuczka often climbed his peaks by routes far more difficult than the *voies normales* Messner favored. Just two years after rounding out his own quest, Kukuczka died attempting a very bold new line on the south face of Lhotse, the world's fourth-highest mountain.

By 1992, I hadn't seriously thought of trying to climb all fourteen 8,000ers myself. But in 1989 I'd made it to the top of Kangchenjunga, at 28,209 feet the third-highest mountain in the world, and the following year I reached the summit of Everest on my third try. In aiming for K2, I was very much aware that if I succeeded, I'd be the first American—and one of only a handful of climbers worldwide—to reach the tops of the three highest mountains.

That summer I was thirty-three years old, struggling to make a living as a guide on Mount Rainier in the summers, working as a carpenter building houses in the winter. In my twenties, I'd gotten my doctorate in veterinary medicine, then worked as a vet in several Seattle-area clinics. By 1992, though, I'd given up my vet practice, because mountaineering was starting to take over my life. I lived in a cheap basement apartment in West Seattle, just scraping by. I had yet to attract any sponsors, but I'd been a member of five Himalayan expeditions. At that date, any thought of going for all fourteen 8,000ers seemed way beyond the pale, if for no other reason than that I couldn't imagine how I could afford to pay my way onto so many expeditions. Besides, by 1992 Messner and Kukuczka were still the only guys who had completed the fourteen, though others were closing in. One of them, the Frenchman Benoît Chamoux, disappeared just below the summit of Kangchenjunga on what would have been his fourteenth 8,000er. As it turned out, the strong Swiss alpinist Erhard Loretan became the third man to complete the quest, in 1995.

In 1991, I guided Mount Everest for a client named Hall Wendel, who'd gotten the climbing bug relatively late in life. We've since become great friends. During that expedition someone asked what I had in mind for the following year. I mentioned that I had a desire to attempt K2, the second-highest peak in the world. This guy happened to know a fellow Seattleite, Scott Fischer, who had plans to attempt K2 the following summer. By chance Scott was at the moment climbing Baruntse, a lower peak near Everest, and I thought that with a little luck I might bump into him after our respective expeditions in Kathmandu. The capital of Nepal is the hub of Himalayan mountaineering, still a small enough city that it's not hard to meet up with old friends and make new ones.

Sure enough, I met Scott there on our way out of Nepal. Introducing myself, I suggested we get together for a few beers. After we'd had a few cold ones and started to get to know each other, I asked if I could join his K2 team.

He frowned and said, "Well, I've already got a team. I guess I could put you on a standby list. But I'd have to ask the other members about you coming along."

In those days getting a permit for K2 wasn't easy, and to have one was a big deal. Plus, Scott's permit was for the north side of K2, a harder route than the Abruzzi Ridge on the southeast, by which the mountain was first climbed by the Italians in 1954.

Back in Seattle, I kept the ball rolling, asking Scott every few weeks where I stood. By the end of the summer, I was on the team. Now we had to organize our logistics and raise the money for the expedition. Between plane tickets, permit fees, hiring porters, and buying food and gear, it would cost each of us $8,000, and I sure as hell didn't have that kind of money in my savings account.

Through the fall and winter, one by one the other members fell by the wayside. Some of them had regular jobs; others just didn't have the time or desire to scrape up the money and work on logistics. I was single and had plenty of free time, energy, and desire. One day Scott told me, "Ed, it's you and me. We're the sole survivors." So now Scott had to sell his permit. It was far too expensive for just the two of us. The only way to get to K2 now would be to find some other team with a permit and see if we could buy our way on board by paying for our share of the logistical support.

A bit of history here. Back in the golden age of the 1950s and early '60s, the choice of a team for Everest or K2 or Annapurna was a matter of national concern, rife with mountaineering politics. In 1950, the Comité de l'Himalaya of the Club Alpin Français chose Maurice Herzog to lead the French expedition to Annapurna. Herzog was far from the strongest climber in France, and he had never led an expedition before, but he had the right connections. To their surprise and chagrin, before leaving Paris the three great Chamonix guides, Lachenal, Terray, and Rébuffat—all three far more talented and experienced than Herzog—had to swear a formal oath of un-questioning obedience to their leader on the mountain.

Similarly, not long before the launching of the British 1953 Everest expedition, the Himalayan Committee of the Alpine Club and the Royal Geographic Society fired Eric Shipton as leader and replaced him with Colonel John Hunt. Already a mountaineering legend, Shipton had been on five previous Everest expeditions or reconnaissances, leading two of them. But the committee thought his style too casual, compared to the military ef-ficiency Hunt would bring to the trip, and scuttlebutt had it that Shipton's reputation as a charming womanizer might tarnish the propriety of the un-dertaking. (To his credit, Hunt, with no Everest experience before 1953, did a splendid job leading a team of thirteen highly competitive members. It was during this expedition that Hillary and Tenzing became the first men to reach the highest point in the world.)

In some cases during the golden age, training retreats were held in the Alps before expeditions, to pit candidates against one another in trials of skill and endurance aimed at weeding out the "losers." In this fashion, Ric-cardo Cassin, the finest Italian climber of his day and one of the greatest of all time, was dismissed from the 1954 K2 expedition. This time the scuttle-butt had it that the fanatically autocratic team leader, Ardito Desio, was afraid Cassin might steal the limelight and maybe even the de facto leadership from himself.

By the early 1990s, however, militaristic nationalism of this sort had been pretty much divorced from Himalayan expeditions. Mountaineering politics were still involved in the business of getting permits to climb the 8,000ers, but now it was mainly a matter of applying for the right route at the right time with the right amount of money in hand, since the number of permits granted in any given year was still limited. In the mid-1990s, though, the governments of Nepal, China, and Pakistan began selling permits like free-market commodities, making no effort to determine the skill levels of the applicants—which is one of the reasons that during the disastrous spring 1996 season on Everest, there were so many people on the mountain, some of whom had barely enough experience to be there. Nepal, in particular, seemed interested mainly in squeezing the greatest possible revenue out of the dozens of teams elbowing one another aside to get up Everest.

This plethora of available permits had both positive and negative consequences. On the one hand, you could obtain a permit on short notice, instead of having to apply years in advance and wait with bated breath to be "granted permission." On the other hand, the absence of restrictions created the potential for overcrowding on the big-name peaks—particularly Everest and Cho Oyu, which was the easiest of the 8,000ers.

A by-product of this state of affairs was that it became increasingly common for a leader who had obtained a permit to turn around and sell places on his team, like seats on a bus—often to complete strangers. In some cases, the strangers would try to join together as a "team," using a common base camp and sharing supplies. Often, though, without cohesive leadership or a bond of trust between friends, these expeditions would fail. Another approach—one I would eventually employ—was to purchase slots on a permit but climb autonomously with my own partners, using only our own supplies, following our own strategies.

In 1992, the only way Scott and I could get to K2 was to purchase places on somebody else's permit. This was the first time that I bought my way onto an 8,000-meter peak, but it would not be my last.

Another American told us that there was a Russian team with a permit that was looking to sell slots. It was led by Vladimir Balyberdin, a famous climber in his own country. He'd already gotten up Kangchenjunga and Everest, so, like me, he was going for the Big Three. Balyberdin's permit was for the Abruzzi Ridge, the route of the 1954 first ascent, which was still unclimbed by Americans. And in the previous six years, the Abruzzi had turned back no fewer than twenty expeditions, without a single success. By the time Scott and I heard about the Russian permit, six or seven other Americans had bought places, but there were still two slots left. That's how the Russians would do it: get the permit, arrange the logistics, then use American dollars to pay for it all. So the expedition came together as this mishmash of people who chipped in and showed up in Pakistan.

Scott and I spent the whole autumn and winter trying to figure out how to raise the money for the trip. He was married, with two kids, and was running his own guiding service, Mountain Madness, but it wasn't very lucrative. He was as broke as I was.

I spent my days working as a carpenter, building houses, while Scott tended to his business. Every night at eight, after he'd put his kids to bed and I'd run my seven miles, we'd meet at his office to scheme and plan. We wrote letters begging for money. We pleaded with companies to sponsor us. Finally, around eleven or twelve each night, we'd say, "Screw this, let's go drink beer." We'd hang out at the Alki Tavern, a biker bar on the beach in West Seattle, and commiserate: "Man, how're we ever gonna raise the dough?" Each session would begin in a depressed funk, but after a few pitchers of Red Hook, things started to look brighter.

We came up with the idea of printing and selling T-shirts. I was friends with the founder of the pack company JanSport, which also made and printed T-shirts. The company was great—it charged us six dollars wholesale per T-shirt, and we'd sell them retail for twelve dollars. We even made up our own logo. And JanSport gave us all the T-shirts we wanted, on credit, no interest. We sold them to friends and family, we put up flyers at REI, and Scott had his mailing list.

The big mistake was that when we sold each T-shirt, we immediately spent the twelve dollars. We never saved half of it to pay JanSport back. One day I said, "Scott, we're digging our hole deeper and deeper. We owe JanSport a ton of dough!" He wanted to keep ordering more, but at this point I told him to stop.

In the end, we owed JanSport $7,000, but we'd raised only enough money for one of us to go on the expedition. We were sitting at the Alki Tavern one night, frustrated, sad, really bummed out. We decided only one of us could go. "Okay," I said. "We've just got to flip a coin to see who it'll be." I actually had the quarter out when Scott stopped me. "Nah," he said, "after all this work, we gotta go together."

Somehow we scraped and borrowed the rest of the money. When we left the States, we were massively in debt, but we figured that we could worry about that later. We simply ignored our financial troubles and fled to Pakistan.

If this seemed like a jinxed expedition, the pattern was set from the minute we landed in Islamabad in early June. The other Americans were there, but the Russians hadn't arrived. They were driving overland to save money and had been plagued with problems and delays. To help pay for his portion of the trip, Scott had recruited two women trekkers through Mountain Madness who wanted to hike to base camp, so he took off, having to keep to his scheduled trekking itinerary. But I was stuck in Islamabad with the other Americans, waiting for the Russians. After a week of this, I started to go crazy.

Finally Thor Kieser, whom I'd met there for the first time, said, "Ed, let's just go." He'd been up the Baltoro Glacier toward K2 before. We managed to get a trekking permit, so at last we could start moving.

We couldn't afford the one-hour flight from Islamabad to Skardu, the high town that's the jumping-off point for all expeditions to the Karakoram. So we took the twenty-four-hour ride from hell, the first half crammed in a sweltering minibus. Among the passengers was a pregnant Pakistani woman who spent a good portion of the ride vomiting out the window. It was all I could do not to blow lunch myself. The second half was in the back of a Toyota truck—twelve hours sitting on a hard bench under a canvas roof that barely covered the back. When we got to Skardu, we were black with dust and grime.

To my surprise, Scott was still there with his trekkers. For some reason having to do with the proper permits and logistics, he had been delayed. Now, seeing us, he suggested that Thor and I trek with his small group to the base camp. Alone with his two women clients, he was longing for our company. In effect, we'd already paid the Russians for our porters, but I was so impatient to get to base camp that I joined up with Scott. This meant that Thor and I had to hire our own porters. I had four loads of gear but so little dough that, in the end, I had to carry one of my own seventy-pound loads all the way up the Baltoro, a ten-day march. I couldn't afford one additional porter. It was a grim task, but I was young and strong.

At base camp, we met the Swiss team, which included Chantal Mauduit, the talented French climber. They'd been there since May, working their way up and down the hill, placing a few fixed ropes and putting in camps. They were trying to climb light and fast, but the conditions had so far been atrocious, and they were struggling to make any progress.

Besides being a good mountaineer, Chantal was a gorgeous woman. She had long, wavy brown hair. She always seemed vibrant and happy, even carefree. Everybody liked her. She was very flirtatious. She had this way of laughing as she looked at you, and you'd wonder, Is she giving me the eye or is she this way with everybody?

The Swiss were very nice to us. All we had for food was a big sack of potatoes and some eggs—the rest of our rations were coming in with the Russians. So occasionally the Swiss invited us to eat with them, and their cook would fix us lunch when his team was off climbing and he was lonely. Other than those few precious meals, Scott and I subsisted on potatoes, eggs, and our one luxury: freshly brewed coffee.

With Chantal, attractive as she was, I didn't flirt at all. For one thing, we knew that Thor had had a previous relationship with her. I guessed that she had ended it. We thought that maybe one reason Thor had wanted to come in early was to try to reconnect with her. He acted like a puppy dog around her. Every time we'd get to a camp, he'd make sure to be close to her. He did everything he could, but she ignored him. He seemed desperate.

Chantal was always amazingly composed. When her team came down after several days on the hill, the Swiss guys looked all bedraggled, but she was perfect—she looked like she'd just stepped out of the shower. You can bet every guy had his eye on her.

Anyway, Scott and I decided to start climbing. But Scott didn't have his mountain boots; most of his gear was coming in with the Russians. We made several carries to Camp I, at 20,000 feet, Scott in his trekking shoes, wearing an extra pair of crampons we happened to have. We were determined to get the expedition going for our team, carrying loads, fixing rope, and acclimatizing as we went.

Then, even before the Russians got to base camp, another team showed up. They were a party of two Swedes and three Mexicans, led by the well-known New Zealand guides Rob Hall and Gary Ball. "Hall and Ball," everybody called them. It was their second or third time on K2. Scott had told me all about these famous Kiwis. Through meticulous planning and crafty fundraising, they had succeeded in climbing the Seven Summits (the highest peaks on all seven continents) in only seven months. They were also renowned for their wealth of big-mountain experience. At first I was a bit starstruck.

It was getting crowded on the Abruzzi Ridge, but I was used to such scenes on Everest. Finally, nine days after we'd reached base camp, the Russians and the rest of the Americans arrived. By that point, Scott and I had already been up to Camp I and down again several times. Now it took a few days to get the cook tent and the dining tent set up, and to sort out the mass of gear that had just arrived. We were determined to work with the Russians, but nobody seemed to assert any leadership. People would go up the ridge carrying the wrong stuff, or carrying nothing at all. It began to seem as though it was every man for himself, with no logistical plan in force.

Somehow I was voted into the role of climbing leader. I tried to put some organization into this circus: who goes up tomorrow, who carries the tents, who carries the ropes.... But the Russians had their own style. They'd just do their own thing. They'd go up in the worst conditions. We Americans weren't about to follow them. So they would talk down to us: "Why do you not go yesterday?"

"Because it was snowing and the avalanche danger was tremendous," I would answer.

"Oh, you Americans—"

I'd say to myself, *Okay, you do your thing and we'll do ours.* A natural schism started to divide our so-called team.

For some of our members, this was their first Himalayan expedition. They didn't know what to expect, and some of them were pretty much blown away. In the end, Hall and Ball and Scott and I did more than our share of the fixing of ropes for our teams.

Since the first attempt by an Italian party under the Duke of the Abruzzi in 1909, the southeast ridge route has been notorious for poor tent sites. The places available to pitch tents are small at best, and typically slanting, so it's hard to excavate a level floor, and sometimes dangerously exposed. With all these teams on the mountain, things got kind of tense. People thought we were racing to nab the best tent sites. But even though we arrived at Camp I days before the Kiwi team, Scott and I chose a less desirable spot to pitch our tent. By leaving Hall and Ball the best site, we hoped to squelch any notion that we were snatching the prime tent locations.

We actually got a pretty quick start, once everybody was at base camp. But then the terrible weather came. We'd be able to climb for a day or two, then have to go down for five days to wait out a storm. We'd go back up, breaking trail the whole way through fresh snow, only to find the tents completely buried by drifts. Then we'd have to dig them out—it was almost like starting from scratch again.

And our team was chaos personified. Lots of guys were planning to use supplemental oxygen on their summit days, so they'd have to carry their bottles up the ridge in addition to their other gear. Whether overburdened or incapable, they'd make it only halfway up to the next camp. They'd just drop their loads between, say, Camps II and III. There was stuff strewn all over the mountain. Scott and I would have to pick up the scattered loads and carry them up in addition to our own. I willingly carried group gear, but I refused to lug anybody else's oxygen bottles. My belief was that if a climber couldn't get his own bottles to Camp IV at 26,000 feet, he had no reason to go for the summit.

People on our team would say they were going to do things they didn't end up doing. I remember one guy's excuse: "I'm not carrying a load today—the rocks are a little too icy." There wasn't a lot of motivation on certain members' parts.

Then, as if things weren't going badly enough, one day Scott and I were making a routine carry from base camp up to Camp I. At the foot of the Abruzzi Ridge, you have to hike through a little icefall. We were roped up, Scott in the lead. He stepped on an ice block wedged in a small crevasse. The ice block shifted, he fell, and he put out his arms to catch himself on the edges of the crevasse. The rope came tight, and I held him—it seemed like no big deal. But Scott was screaming in pain: "Shit, I've dislocated my shoulder again!" He'd done it before on some previous climb, so he was more susceptible to a new dislocation.

I got him out of the crevasse. We left our packs and started to backtrack the two hours to base camp, but Scott was in such pain, he kept nearly passing out. Finally he said, "Ed, I can't keep going. You gotta go get help."

I raced back to base camp to find the Russian doctor. He was quite a character (he seemed to be using some of the more interesting drugs he'd brought on the expedition for himself), but he knew what he was doing medically. We went back up to Scott with several other guys—for all I knew, we might have to carry Scott down. The doctor gave him morphine and a muscle relaxant, then relocated his shoulder. Scott was a pretty muscular guy, so the doctor had to really manhandle his arm to get the shoulder back in.

Scott could walk now. The doctor told him, "You must go home. The expedition is over for you."

Scott said, "No, give me a week. I'll be back up on the hill."

Scott was an incredibly tough guy. Powerfully built, maybe six foot two, ruggedly handsome, with a mustache and short blond hair. Later he'd grow it out and sport a ponytail. He had Robert Redford looks.

He was a great guy—he'd do anything for anybody. And he was inspiring. He was always so positive, he'd get people excited. If you happened to be in his company, within minutes you'd be as jazzed about life as Scott was. But on the mountain, he wasn't very detail-oriented; nor was he the greatest organizer. His motto for Mountain Madness was "Make it happen." Later, we would jokingly change the motto to "How the hell did it happen?" Scott thought that if he surrounded himself with the right people, things would come together. And they usually did.

At the same time, especially before he got married, he was, by his own admission, a somewhat reckless climber. In his early days, he'd push it to the limit. He wasn't afraid to take falls while climbing something desperately difficult.

Now, with Scott out of commission, I started climbing with some of the other Americans. I hoped Scott would recover, but honestly. I did not know if or when. In the meantime, I felt I had to keep things moving on the mountain and stay acclimatized. Once the opportunity arose, I wanted to be ready for a summit attempt.

But Scott proved true to his word. He rested a week at base camp, then got back on the route with a special restraining rig we helped design for him so that as he jumared up the fixed ropes, he never had to raise his bad arm above chest height. To acclimatize, he even made a solo trip to Camp I. I felt immensely relieved to have my partner back in action.

By the end of July, Scott and I were at last ready for our summit bid. We pulled off the long, ten-hour haul—7,000 feet of altitude gain from base camp to Camp III—like clockwork. We settled into our sleeping bags, planning to push on to Camp IV the next day and to go for the top on the following morning.

Then came Thor's ominous radio call in the night, and our aborted attempt in the storm the next day to help him and Chantal. And then, on August 5, in the middle of our second rescue attempt, the avalanche swept Scott off his feet, pulled me out of the little hole I had frantically excavated, and, by all rights, should have carried us 8,000 feet down the mountain, to our deaths.

⋏
⋏
⋏

My self-arrest had kept us both from taking that long ride, but as we pulled ourselves together and checked that we weren't seriously hurt, we realized we were still in the middle of a huge slope ready to avalanche again. Urgently, I told Scott, "Let's try to get to a safer area." Off to the right, I saw a small ice cliff. It looked like a possible refuge, so we traversed that way as quickly as we could.

Normally, after such a brush with death, we would immediately have retreated to Camp III. But Thor and Chantal still needed our help. We could see them up above, heading right down toward the slope where we'd been avalanched.

I got Thor on the radio. "Don't come down that way," I insisted. "Go over to your left, toward this ice-cliffy area, and maybe rappel. It's steeper and icier, but a lot safer." I voiced my concern that the slope was unstable, but all I told Thor about the avalanche was that Scott and I had just had a "bad experience."

Thor followed my advice. With his short hank of rope, he would belay Chantal, then downclimb himself, or do very short rappels off ice screws or snow bollards. Just as Scott and I reached the ice cliff, Chantal staggered into sight from above, followed by Thor. Thor said, "Man, am I glad to see you guys!" He'd been two days with this exhausted, snowblind woman, desperately trying to get her to Camp III.

We laid Chantal down on her back. I'd brought anesthetic eyedrops to treat her with, but first I had to pry her eyelids open. Snow blindness is extremely painful—the feeling is like having sand rubbed constantly across your pupils.

Then we roped up all four together, Chantal and Thor in the middle, Scott leading the way back to Camp III, me at the top as anchor. It wasn't that far to camp. There were two tents there, so we put Thor and Chantal inside one. We checked her toes—it turned out they weren't frostbitten, just very cold. And we melted pot after pot of snow to make hot water for them to drink. Otherwise, however, they took care of themselves through the night.

All through this retreat, Chantal never thanked us. Instead, she said, "Oh, we made it! We made the summit! I'm so happy!"

We spent the night at Camp III. Scott and I knew that the next day we'd have to help get Thor and Chantal the rest of the way down the mountain. Both of us realized that our summit attempt had turned to ashes.

By the next morning Chantal could see a bit, but she was really exhausted. She could slide down the fixed ropes with her figure-eight device attaching her waist harness to the line, but at some of the anchors she'd just stand there. We had to take the figure eight off one rope and attach it to the next. Sometimes she'd actually fall asleep standing up.

We got Chantal and Thor all the way down to Camp I the next day. There, other climbers took over, while Scott and I blew on down to base camp. We'd left all our gear at Camp III, since we weren't ready to quit yet, hoping to go back up later. But even if we had wanted to, we couldn't have carried our gear down at the same time as we were taking care of Chantal.

By the next day, at base camp, Chantal had recovered. That night she had a little drinking party with the Russians. The day before Chantal and Aleksei Nikiforov had reached the summit, the Russian leader, Vladimir Balyberdin, and his teammate Gennadi Kopeika had also topped out. They'd pulled it off only by climbing in conditions that we Americans thought insanely dangerous. Even so, their summit push had taken them eighteen hours. Gennadi got back to Camp IV that night, but Vlad had to bivouac. He survived the night, then came down the mountain as Thor, Chantal, and Aleksei were heading up for their own attempt.

So now Chantal was celebrating with the Russians. We'd hear their cheers and revelry as we lay silent in our own tents. Scott and I hadn't been invited to the party. I just said to myself, *Whatever...*

I stayed by myself all the next day. Scott and I had decided we'd rest, go back up, and give it one more try.

That night in the dining tent, Vlad suddenly announced that the expedition was over. Everybody on his permit would have to go home. He said that we Americans had wasted our time, that we weren't fast enough, and so on.

I just stared at him. I didn't say anything, but I was thinking, Buddy, we've been busy! It's not for lack of trying that we haven't gotten to the summit yet. And about the Russians' climbing style, I thought, *Dude, we're not suicidal like you!*

Legally, though, Vlad was holding all the cards. In Pakistan, once the leader leaves the mountain, the expedition is officially over.

I was incredibly pissed off. I got up, left the dining tent, and went back to my own tent. I never said a word to Vlad, but I couldn't believe the Russians could be that selfish.

Chantal was packing up, planning to leave the next day. If Chantal was leaving, so was Thor, because he was still chasing her. And the Russians were getting ready to go home, too.

I wasn't mad about having had to rescue Chantal. I thought that morally, that's what we'd had to do. I was just fuming at Vlad for pulling the rug out from under us.

I went to bed, lying in my bag with my Walkman headphones on, listening to Little Feat, Bonnie Raitt, and Ry Cooder. It got to be eight, nine, ten P.M. I was so pissed, I couldn't sleep.

All of a sudden, I felt somebody pulling on my foot. Unbeknownst to me, Chantal had been wandering around base camp in the dark, trying to find my tent. She'd found Scott's and asked him, "Where's Ed's tent?"

Scott said, "Right over there."

Now I roused myself. "Hi," I said. "What's up?"

"Oh, I just wanted to come and say good-bye," Chantal answered. "I'm leaving tomorrow." Meanwhile, she was crawling farther and farther inside my tent, so I kind of knew what was going on. But at the same time, I thought, When does something like this ever happen?

I was still dazzled by it all the next day. As I wrote in my diary, "How could I refuse such a beautiful woman?!... Anyway, it was a fun night and she reluctantly left at 5 A.M. Whew, what a gorgeous woman!"

It was all very hush-hush. Chantal didn't want the whole camp to know. That's why she left my tent before dawn. And nobody did know, except Scott. I saw him at breakfast. He looked at me and said, "So, Ed. Big tits or little tits?" I just cracked up. With all that clothing on, you can't really tell.

All through breakfast, I kept surreptitiously plucking Chantal's long brown hairs off my fleece jacket, which we had used as a pillow. Nobody noticed. I wondered if I'd ever see her again.

▲
▲ ▲
▲

As I dwelt on Vlad's pronouncement, part of me wanted to say to him, *Fuck you, buddy, I'm going to climb the mountain anyway.* Meanwhile, Rob Hall and Gary Ball, the two experienced Kiwi guides, were still on the mountain, along with their Swedish and Mexican teammates. And five of us from Vlad's team wanted to stick around. Others had job commitments or were simply ready to bail. Working with our liaison officer as well as Hall and Ball's, we crafted an arrangement that turned Dan Mazur, one of our Americans, into the nominal leader of what was left of our party. This meant that technically we still had a legitimate right to be on K2.

Now Scott and I simply had to wait for the right conditions. When the weather broke, we'd go all the way up to Camp III again in one day. We'd reach Camp IV the next day, the summit the day after—we hoped.

But while we'd been recuperating at base camp, a huge storm had blasted the upper part of the mountain. We suspected that everything that had been left at Camp IV might have been blown away. Through binoculars, we scoured the mountainside for any traces of that camp, in vain. Scott and I knew that we'd have to carry Camp III up to 26,000 feet to establish Camp IV all over again.

To do this, we'd have to go super-light. We were going to take only a five-pound bivouac tent, one sleeping bag between us, and a fifty-foot piece of rope. For our summit attempt, we would carry only a couple of candy bars and one liter of water apiece. You simply can't carry much more of anything, because it will only slow you down.

24

Climbing at high altitudes, especially without bottled oxygen, severely dehydrates you, but drinking enough takes enormous effort. So Scott and I had established a routine: each evening in the high camps, we'd melt pot after pot of snow. We'd have drinking contests: I'd drink a cup of soup, he'd drink a cup of soup; I'd drink a cup of tea, he'd drink a cup of tea. It's like downing beers or shots in a bar. Eating was out of the question, since we had no appetite.

Some of the others didn't think they could climb the 7,000 feet from base camp to Camp III in one day, so they planned to break the push up with a layover at Camp I. On August 12, five of us got to Camp III. I arrived first and dug the camp out of the new snowdrifts. Then came Scott and Charley Mace, another American. But Hall and Ball, who'd also climbed directly from base camp, didn't arrive until dusk, very tired and on the verge of hypothermia. I helped set up their tents, while Scott brewed drinks for them. And the Mexicans and Swedes arrived in the early evening. For them, it had been a very long day.

My picture of Hall and Ball had been one of really powerful, experienced climbers. That day my estimation of them got bumped down a few notches. Even though they'd done all these expeditions, they weren't superhumans—and this mountain was kicking ass.

Still, the weather was clear and cold, and we had high hopes. The next morning, there was a bit of jockeying for position. No one seemed to want to go first, breaking trail through the deep new snow. Scott and I ended up taking the lead, even though we didn't head out until nine A.M.—rather late, but nobody else was ready. Hall and Ball, the Swedes, and the Mexicans were toast, after getting in so late the night before. We hoisted our forty-five-pound packs and headed slowly up the slope, breaking trail through deep snow.

At such altitudes, lethargy creeps into your system. Every action becomes physically harder than it is lower on the mountain, and even thinking about those actions seems daunting. The prospect of crawling out of your tent into subzero temperatures, with hours of uphill trail breaking to come, can be overwhelming at 24,000 feet.

That morning, there was also some weather building up to the south—cloud caps on the surrounding peaks. Some of the hesitation in getting out of Camp III may have been due to that: nobody wanted to go up again for naught. K2 seemed never to let down her guard. We needed to be constantly on our toes. The only way we stood a chance for the summit, we figured, was to get into position at Camp IV and wait for the right opportunity.

Scott and I finally reached the section on the ridge where we'd been avalanched off. This time we went farther right, where it was steeper but safer.

It had now been sixty-three days since we'd started hiking in from Skardu, fifty-three since we'd arrived at base camp, but as we emerged on the shoulder of the ridge at 26,000 feet, for the first time during the whole expedition we saw the summit pyramid, the last 2,250 vertical feet of snow slopes and rock bands. It was a huge adrenaline rush.

Sure enough, when we got to the site of the former Camp IV, there was almost nothing left of it. Scott and I chopped out a platform and set up our bivvy tent. Not an easy job—the terrain was still very steep up there. Our tent was small, and Scott was so big, he took up two-thirds of it. And we had to share the one sleeping bag by zipping it open like a blanket.

We had a formula: "Spooning is allowed, forking is not." When Scott rolled one way, I had to roll the same way. And vice versa.

Charley Mace arrived a bit later; at eight P.M., Hall, Ball, the two Swedes, and the three Mexicans got in. Once their tents were erected, we had a crowded little village at 26,000 feet.

Scott and I planned to be out the door and climbing by one A.M. I was adamant that no matter where we were, at two P.M. we needed to turn around. We would get up at eleven P.M. just to launch the process of getting ready to go.

The night before a summit push on the highest peaks, you're excited, nervous, anxious. You can't sleep at all. I kept wondering, Am I going to be strong enough tomorrow, after all this work? Will we have what it takes to climb 2,250 feet of terrain, without bottled oxygen?

The alarm went off at eleven P.M. It took us two hours just to brew up hot drinks, get dressed in our confined space, and sort out our gear. A storm had sneaked in during the night. Outside the tent it was blowing and snowing. We did everything to get ready, but then waited, checking every half hour until five A.M., hoping for some break in the weather. After that, we knew there was no way—it was too late to start, and we couldn't go up in those conditions. But we weren't going down either. We recognized that if we went down one more time, we'd never get back up. We'd be out of time, out of energy. Instead, we would have to hole up at Camp IV and be patient but stubborn.

That day, two of the Mexicans decided to go down. If you're not physically and mentally capable, existence is simply too tenuous at 26,000 feet. Hall and Ball's Swedish and Mexican teammates were pretty experienced climbers, so nobody thought they needed to be shepherded down the mountain.

The two Mexicans who bailed had actually climbed Everest before, but they weren't that skilled technically. On the steep slope above Camp III, to the right of where Scott and I had gotten avalanched, they made a huge mistake.

As we'd climbed that slope the day before, I'd known that Scott and I could downclimb it. That day, one of the Mexicans set up a rappel, using a ski pole as an anchor—not buried in the slope, like a dead man anchor, but just stuck in vertically. When I learned what had happened, I couldn't believe it. You don't rappel off a ski pole!

The one who'd placed the anchor managed to rappel safely, but when his partner, Adrián Benítez, put his weight on the rope, the ski pole pulled. He fell 3,000 feet to his death. Two of our team members who were still at Camp III could see his body, hung up on a slope to the left of the Abruzzi Ridge, but there was no way they could get to it without risking their own lives. We learned about the accident from them over the radio. By that evening, we knew that Adrián was dead. I thought, *Come on! What is going on with this mountain?*

Charley Mace had been paired up in a tent with the third Mexican, Hector Ponce de Leon. After Adrián's death, Hector went down to console his surviving teammate. Thus Charley was "orphaned," so eventually he teamed up with Scott and me.

We waited all day through August 14. We were bored out of our minds. We'd carried no books to read. Scott and I had been together for almost three months by now, so we had nothing left to talk about. At the same time, we started worrying: Are we in danger of getting trapped up here in the storm? Will we be given a chance to make an attempt? If so, will we be strong enough, after barely hanging on at 26,000 feet?

Just six years earlier, in 1986, in the most disastrous season in K2's history, thirteen climbers had died on the mountain. Four of them had gotten trapped by a storm right here at Camp IV, including Alan Rouse, an extremely savvy and experienced British mountaineer.

The one thing that gave me confidence now was that we had wanded the route leading up to Camp IV. I was always the guy on every expedition who insisted on wanding.

Willow wands are actually green garden stakes, very thin wooden dowels about three feet long. We'd put a bit of red tape on the head of each one, to make a kind of flag. The idea is that on a snow slope where you don't lay fixed ropes to indicate the route, you plant a wand every so many yards. It may be a beautiful, clear day on the way up, but who knows what it'll be like on the way down. In a whiteout, the wands can keep you on route and save your life.

I'd wanded the slopes between Camps III and IV, above the upper end of the fixed ropes, so I was pretty sure we could get down even in a storm. We'd started out on the mountain with hundreds of wands; now we were down to a bundle. We had to place them farther apart than normal, and we were eventually reduced to breaking them in half, which didn't leave a lot of stake protruding above the snow.

We got up early on the morning of August 15, only to find that the weather was no better. So we reconciled ourselves to more waiting. Every two hours, we had to get up and dig the drifts away from the tent. That day the Swedes were running out of bottled oxygen, which they'd been trying to use sparingly through the previous two days, so they decided to go down.

Now there were only Hall and Ball, Charley Mace, and Scott and I left at Camp IV.

While we were waiting, we weren't eating much. You have no appetite at that altitude. Scott and I would share a Pop-Tart for breakfast. In the afternoon, I'd ask Scott, "Are you hungry?" "Nah," he'd answer. So we'd wait, or maybe share a Snickers bar for lunch. One package of Top Ramen for dinner. That was about it. We were steadily losing weight.

Meanwhile, though we didn't know it, Gary Ball was coughing, spewing gunk out of his lungs. He was slowly developing pulmonary edema. He'd had the problem before, but he'd always shrugged it off. He'd survived all these high mountains, but he'd had several close calls because of his altitude problem. He and Rob were planning to go for the top with supplemental oxygen (Scott, Charley, and I would go without). They were just eking it out, sleeping on oxygen but saving a few bottles for the summit push.

Scott and I knew that people said you couldn't survive very long at 26,000 feet without supplemental oxygen. But we thought it was just mind over matter. That had become one of my mottoes: "Mind over matter. If you don't mind, it doesn't matter." Yes, it was hard, but it wasn't killing us. We thought, This is part of the deal. If you want it, you've got to wait. If the weather clears, you want to be *here,* not down below.

But we realized that if it didn't happen the next day, we would have to go down. We were just barely hanging in there.

That night it finally cleared off. At one A.M. on August 16, Scott and I were the first out of camp. We took turns kicking steps in the snow. After a while, since we were breaking trail, Charley Mace caught up to us. Then, perhaps two hours after we'd left camp, we saw Rob and Gary's headlamps as they slowly started up. Their late departure disturbed us, but we thought that with supplemental oxygen they might make up for lost time. As we climbed we watched their progress. It appeared to be agonizingly slow. Eventually we saw the headlamps turn around and start back toward camp. We didn't really know what had caused them to quit.

Just above a steep gully of snow and ice called the Bottleneck Couloir, we had to make a delicate concave traverse to the left on downsloping rock mixed with very loose snow, into which we could barely get our crampons to bite. The Russians had fixed a rope here, but it was anchored only at either end, sagging in the middle. You had to pull tight on the rope as you traversed. We didn't say anything, but the injunction was obvious: *Don't fall.*

We worked our way up the final slope. It was crevassed, so we stayed roped together. All three of us took turns breaking trail.

When we'd left camp, we'd seen a thick sea of clouds far below us. Slowly but steadily through the morning, the clouds rose. By six or seven A.M., the clouds had engulfed us.

It was very warm—so warm I took my hat off. No wind. Then huge flakes of snow started to fall. With every breath, I'd swallow half a dozen flakes. At the time it seemed both comical and irritating.

Then I began to be deeply concerned. I calculated that we still had four or five hours to go before the summit. A lot of snow was falling; the accumulation after so many hours might well reach deadly proportions. We would still face some steep terrain to descend and traverse on descent. How much new snow would there be on those slopes on our way down, hours from now?

I stopped and said, "What do you guys think?" They just looked at me. "Whaddya mean?" Scott answered. "We're going up." Charley agreed.

To me, the two of them hadn't started processing. As we were going up, I was already processing going down. That's my training as a guide: to think, This is happening now—what are the consequences for later?

I felt that we were making a big mistake. I even thought, *I should unrope right now and go down on my own. Let them go on up if they want to.* My instincts were telling me to turn back before things got out of hand.

In the next moment, though, I decided to go just a little farther—ten more minutes, to see if conditions would change. By now I had a knot in my gut. With every step, it got worse. Dread. I knew I was making a bad mistake.

Yet for some reason, I kept putting off the decision. I started to question my own judgment. Was I overprocessing? Were the conditions really not as bad as I thought they were?

I've always said, "You don't know you've made the wrong decision until you get yourself killed doing it." Then, just before the lights go out, you realize, *Oops, I was wrong.* Whereas if you turn around early, you may never know whether you made the right decision or not.

We kept climbing, roped together, taking turns breaking trail. At last we reached the final bit of ridge. I was in the lead, and I could see the summit, in the sun! We'd actually climbed out of the clouds.

We reached the top around noon. Good time, plenty of daylight left for the descent. We hugged each other, slapped each other on the back. We were utterly elated.

But when I looked down and saw how dark and black it was in that sea of clouds below us, the dread returned in full force. I knew that moments after leaving the summit, we'd be plunged into this maelstrom.

We spent only thirty minutes on the summit before starting down. Scott was in the lead. We'd long since run out of wands, so nothing marked our route, but on the way up I'd tried to memorize landmarks: this rock here, that plume of snow there. On the ascent, I'd also looked down often, so that I would remember the view as we would see it descending. I'd been out with too many climbers who were so focused on looking up that they couldn't recognize the same terrain on the way down.

Scott headed down the top of a gully. It just didn't look right to me. If you start off by only a few degrees in the wrong direction, you end up way off course. As it turns out, if we'd followed Scott's lead, we'd have ended up lost somewhere on the east face, instead of on the Abruzzi Ridge.

"No, no, no!" I shouted. "Wrong way, Scott! Wrong way! Farther to the right!"

He corrected his course. Soon I was seeing landmarks I recognized from the way up. But the new snow was thigh-deep by now, and I kept kicking loose slabs of snow that careened down the slope below us. I was saying to myself, *Ed, you've just made the last mistake you'll ever make.* I thought for sure we were going to get avalanched off. I was so mad at myself. I wasn't mad at

Scott and Charley; it wasn't their fault. They hadn't made me go up. It was my own choice.

But in the midst of this anger and despair, I told myself that we had nothing to lose now. We would probably die, but we might live. *We've just got to keep going down, but at the same time, we have to be extremely careful.*

The traverse across the cliff of loose snow and downsloping rocks was too difficult to reverse. Instead, we rappelled down the fixed rope till we hit the sagging midpoint, then jumared up the other end. In those conditions, that was pretty intimidating, but we had no alternative. Then we down-climbed the Bottleneck Couloir, facing in, kicking our crampon points and planting our axes in the steep gully.

Below the couloir, the angle eased off. We'd regained the plateau where we'd pitched Camp IV. The whiteout was so thick, though, that we couldn't see much of anything. So we spread out three abreast, going very slowly, hoping to find camp. And we started to shout for Rob and Gary: "Hey, you guys, where are you?"

They heard our shouts, called back, and led us into camp. Turned out we were pretty much right on course. We got to our tents about five P.M. We'd been gone for sixteen hours.

I remember sitting down outside my tent. I was so angry with what I'd done. I wasn't happy we'd climbed K2. I knew I had made a terrible mistake, even though we'd gotten away with it.

Years later, Charley told me, "I knew we'd be screwed on the descent, but I thought it was an acceptable risk. I always felt we had things under control."

It's not my style to second-guess others. We'll never know how close we really came to dying that afternoon in the storm. The point is simply that Charley's notion of "acceptable risk" was different from mine. I'd never say, however, that he was wrong or that I was right.

As soon as we arrived at Camp IV, we asked Rob, "What happened to you guys?"

His answer was chilling. "Gary's pretty sick," Rob said quietly. "We'd barely got moving this morning when he started having breathing problems. I got him back to camp." Rob paused. "We're going to need your help getting out of here tomorrow."

I sighed heavily. Could anything else possibly go wrong on this jinxed expedition?

Now the weather was turning even worse. The storm became violent, and at one point in the night, a spindrift avalanche hit our tent. I was startled awake by Scott's shout of "Avalanche!" At once our already claustrophobic tent space became half the size. After donning boots, crampons, and headlamp, I got out and shoveled away the snow, but shortly after that another spindrift slide hit us. We decided to leave things as they were, hoping that the worst was over.

In the morning, with the weather even worse, we had to pack everything up and take it down with us. Camp III was whatever we were carrying on our backs. At this point, Gary could still walk. But Scott, Charley, and I had to go in front to break trail in zero visibility.

It was here that the wands made all the difference, even though most of them were now sticking out of the new snow only an inch or two, with the little red-tape flag on top. I would sit down to belay Charley with our fifty-foot piece of rope. When he got to the end of it, he'd sweep right and left until he could see the next wand. Then one by one, Scott, Rob, and Gary would use the rope as a hand line, with me sitting there to anchor it. Then I'd downclimb to join them, and we'd start the process over again.

On this big open shoulder of K2, without the wands, you could easily go off in the wrong direction. In 1986, the four climbers who died at Camp IV were effectively trapped there because they knew that without wands to mark the route, they couldn't find their way down the shoulder in a storm. Of the five climbers who tried to force their way down, three Austrians collapsed and died somewhere near where we were now.

Gary was slowly deteriorating, getting weaker and weaker. Yet he was perfectly lucid. He knew exactly what was going on, since it had happened to him before.

At last we reached the site of Camp III. Here, we were at the upper end of the fixed ropes. Scott, Charley, and I decided to go on down to Camp

II. We figured Rob could handle Gary on the fixed ropes. As it was, however, they had a fierce struggle, and got into camp only very late. By now, Gary was exhausted. We had to help him into his tent, and we brewed up hot chocolate for him and Rob.

Unable to carry it, Gary had left his pack somewhere up above, so Scott and I gave him one of our sleeping bags. That night the weather worsened. Scott and I huddled, sleepless, beneath our remaining bag, the tent half-collapsed around us. We had hardly slept or eaten much at all during the last five days.

In the morning, Gary was completely out of it. At one point, he pleaded with us to leave him there. Scott yelled at him, "We're not leaving you! Get your shit together!" Meanwhile, Rob got on the radio and contacted a doctor in New Zealand, who advised him about what medications to give Gary. And we radioed base camp, where the two Swedes and the other two members of our team were waiting. They agreed to carry bottled oxygen up to Camp I and meet us later that day.

On August 18, we started down the fixed ropes again. Gary could barely walk. We had to switch over his figure-eight device for him at every anchor, just as we had with Chantal. Whatever oxygen Hall and Ball had left, Gary was on it now. And still the weather was getting worse: snowing, blowing, deep powder. I thought, How can this get any worse?

I was carrying the five-pound bivvy tent. We decided I should go ahead to Camp I and set it up, so that when he got there, Gary could crawl into the tent and collapse. When I reached that camp, the guys hadn't yet arrived from base camp with the extra oxygen. That afternoon I sat in the tent and cradled Gary in my lap. It was now two P.M.—six hours after we'd left Camp II. He was coughing up phlegm, green gobs, and splattering the tent walls with blood. He looked ghostly pale. His lungs were full of fluid, so that his breathing came in deep, rasping gasps. That night I wrote in my diary, "Gary looks 90 years old and ready to die."

Two hours later, our friends from base camp arrived with the oxygen. By this point, Gary could no longer walk. But now we had enough manpower to get him the rest of the way down. Below Camp I, the slope is steep, but it opens up in a broad fan. We put Gary in a sleeping bag, and wrapped him up like a mummy with our ropes. Then five or six of us each attached a separate rope to him. One of the Swedes went below, guiding the "sled," as it were. With our ropes, we simply slid Gary down the slope, using gravity to our advantage.

At midnight, we finally arrived at the base of the Abruzzi Ridge. Here we stopped at a place where in other years certain teams had established an advance base camp. We set up a tent and got Gary inside it; then Rob told Scott, Charley, and me that he and the others could handle things—we should just head on down to base camp.

At three A.M., we reached the Kiwis' base camp, where the cook invited us in for some food and drink. After six horrendous days on the mountain, it was so nice to just sit there and have somebody feed us. My diary entry was an outburst of relief more than joy: "We're done!" I wrote. "Alive! Summited! No frostbite! Saved 2 people!"

The next day, summoned by radio, a Pakistani military helicopter landed at the old advance base camp, picked up Rob and Gary, and whisked them from the mountain. Gary was flown to a hospital in Islamabad; later, he recovered in New Zealand.

Only a few days afterward, in the luxury of base camp, could I write a passage in my diary that gave voice to real pride and joy: "Got the Big 3 under my belt. Only American to do so, and only one of a few in the world. Yahoo!" I can't remember for sure, but perhaps in that moment I had the germ of the idea of going for all fourteen 8,000ers.

Yet nothing would ever convince me that pushing on to the summit of K2 on August 16, 1992, had been anything other than a mistake. Today, I regard it as the biggest mistake of my climbing career. What I learned from that episode has stayed with me for good. It can be summed up in a few words: *Your instincts are telling you something. Trust them and listen to them.*

From Rockford to Rainier

In December, less than four months after we got back from K2, at the American Alpine Club meeting in Framingham, Massachusetts, I was granted the David A. Sowles Memorial Award for my part in rescuing Chantal and Gary in the summer of 1992. The award is named after a young climber who was killed by lightning in the Alps in 1963, and it's given, according to the club's official language, to "mountaineers who have distinguished themselves, with unselfish devotion at personal risk or sacrifice of a major objective, in going to the assistance of fellow climbers imperiled in the mountains." It's the AAC's most prestigious award, given not yearly but only on special occasions. ▲ The club keeps its awards a secret from the winners-to-be. Ideally, the recipient happens to attend the annual meeting, where, in the middle of the Friday evening banquet, he or she is suddenly shocked and delighted to be announced as the award winner. Sometimes members of the awards committees will make a phone call or two to nudge the potential recipient into coming to the meeting—all without letting the cat out of the bag.

That year, however, I never got any encouraging phone calls, and besides, there's no way I could have afforded a trip in December from Seattle to New England. It was a few days after the meeting that H. Adams Carter, the editor of the *American Alpine Journal,* called me up to tell me I'd won the Sowles award.

I was honored, of course, but my first reaction was a kind of embarrassment. Had I been present at the ceremony, I would have insisted that the award should have been shared with others—especially Scott Fischer, Rob Hall, Thor Kieser, and Charley Mace. I asked Ad why I'd been singled out. He said that because I'd been instrumental in both rescues, and because the award could go to only one recipient, the committee had chosen me. Even today, I have a lingering sense of chagrin that the other guys didn't share the award.

In the Himalaya or the Karakoram, plenty of climbers have been happy to undertake only a single expedition to a single 8,000-meter peak. For others of us, though, the pursuit of 8,000ers became a passion in its own right, bordering on an addiction. At least five of us on that 1992 K2 expedition would fit into this latter category: Gary Ball, Rob Hall, Scott Fischer, Chantal Mauduit, and myself.

By 1992, Hall and Ball had already devised a joint career that revolved around taking clients to the highest peaks in the world. Their company, Adventure Consultants, was one of the first to secure commercial permits for guiding on Everest. Scott would soon follow suit, as his own company, Mountain Madness, went mainstream. Several times over the years, I would guide less experienced climbers on Everest, but I never intended to make that sort of thing my livelihood—it was just one more way to make ends meet. From the start, with my first Everest attempt in 1987, my ultimate ambition was to set my own goals in the high Himalaya and Karakoram.

The practice of professionals taking clients to the highest mountains of the world dates only from 1985, when noted climber and filmmaker David Breashears successfully guided Texas oilman Dick Bass to the summit of Everest. From the early years of climbing in the Alps, in the first half of the nineteenth century, the standard ascent of Mont Blanc, say, or the Jungfrau paired local guides with "amateurs" (as they were quaintly called), many of them passionate devotees from Great Britain. For a long while, even into the first decade of the twentieth century, a debate raged as to whether it was irresponsible for even the most competent "amateur" to climb in the Alps without a guide.

In the Himalaya, however, for more than thirty years after the first ascent of Everest, the notion that a client could get up an 8,000-meter peak seemed too radical. After Bass performed quite creditably (for a relative beginner) on Everest, the fad was launched, leading to such professional guiding outfits as Hall and Ball's Adventure Consultants. Jon Krakauer's *Into Thin Air*—with its vignettes of clients on Everest in 1996 so clueless they couldn't put on their own crampons, after having shelled out as much as $65,000 apiece in the hopes of getting "dragged" up the mountain—indelibly coined the image of the affluent yuppie trying to buy his or her way up Everest. Because of the success of Krakauer's book, the very term *client* has taken on a negative connotation. This bothers me, because it tends to demean the amateur climber who hires a guide to organize his expedition and lead him on the mountain. I've been in the company of many very experienced clients and have had thoroughly enjoyable experiences guiding them all over the world.

The fact is, money can't buy you a summit. Sadly, there are outfits today that will take almost any client's dough in exchange for the vague promise of bagging an 8,000er. But the reputable companies screen out clients who shouldn't be there. In my own commercial guiding, I've evaluated each client every step of the way, and there are ones I've had to tell, "Sorry, this is as high as you're going." I feel that it's my responsibility to make sure not that they get to the top but that they get home. Everything else is secondary. They're hiring me for my leadership and judgment, not for a double-your-money-back summit guarantee.

▲
▲ ▲
▲

An addiction to 8,000ers is a perilous business. Within only six years after we survived our near misses on K2, fate would cut a brutal swath through our quintet of mountaineers: Ball, Hall, Fischer, Maudit, and me. By the summer of 1998, I would be the sole survivor.

After his several brushes with death by pulmonary edema, culminating in the really close call on K2, Gary Ball should perhaps have turned his ambitions toward climbing peaks lower than 8,000 meters. But it's all too easy to second-guess in hindsight. Gary made his living guiding the 8,000ers, in large part because he loved the challenge of those mountains and was not about to give up on them. By 1992, despite failing to summit on K2, Hall and Ball had become New Zealand's two most famous active mountaineers (Sir Edmund Hillary being the most celebrated Kiwi climber ever). Climbing the Seven Summits in seven months was both an unprecedented mountaineering achievement and a great marketing opportunity, and as a result, their company, Adventure Consultants, was going great guns. Both Rob and Gary were, in a sense, locked by their very success into an ongoing game in the Death Zone.

They returned to the Himalaya in the fall of 1993 on an expedition to 26,795-foot Dhaulagiri, the world's seventh-highest mountain. The third member of their team, a Finnish climber named Veikka Gustafsson, had originally been an Adventure Consultants client on Everest; when he summited, he became the first Finn to accomplish that feat, which launched him to national stardom. On Everest, Veikka had proved so strong that he was now regarded by Hall and Ball as their equal on Dhaulagiri. Ironically, Veikka, whom I had yet to meet in 1993, would eventually become a great friend of mine and my favorite and most regular partner of all on the 8,000-meter peaks.

By October 1, 1993, the three men were established in a camp at 21,300 feet on Dhaulagiri's northeast ridge. There, despite the relatively modest altitude, Gary's old nemesis struck once more. On an attempt to push on to the next camp, Gary lagged far behind Veikka and Rob, eventually waving his arms in a plea for help. Veikka carried Gary's pack up to Camp IV, at 24,100 feet, where Gary collapsed in the tent. Rob suspected at once that his old friend had again contracted pulmonary edema. He also knew the only cure was to get Gary down low as fast as possible, but he vetoed a descent in the night, judging it too dangerous.

In the tent at Camp IV, Gary deteriorated with alarming rapidity. By October 5, he was almost incapable of standing on his own two feet, and he was, in Rob's phrase, no longer compos mentis. Even breathing bottled oxygen, Gary sank into a more and more desperate state. The next day, Veikka and Rob performed a heroic job of virtually carrying Gary down to the 21,300-foot camp. Yet before they could reach the tents, Gary simply stopped breathing.

Cruelly enough, at base camp, Rob's wife, Jan Arnold, and Gary's girlfriend, Helen Wood, were monitoring the drama by radio. At five P.M. on October 6, in a shattered voice, Rob reported that Gary had died. Two days later, Helen climbed up to the descending team, who, with the aid of Japanese climbers, were trying to sledge Gary's body down the mountain. On the spot, Rob conducted an impromptu funeral service. According to Hall and Ball's biographer, Colin Monteath,

> *Somehow, [Rob] knew he had to honour his long-standing agreement with Gary to bury him in the mountains should he die while climbing. Sobbing, he forced himself to commit Gary's body to a deep crevasse.... Rob and Helen held the rope together, then, doing what climbers are trained not to do, let it slip through their fingers. Rob said later, "Letting go of that rope was one of the most difficult things I've ever had to do."*

Helen wrote in her diary, "I didn't want him going down into the crevasse. I didn't want to let go of the rope. I needed more time..."

After I returned home from K2 in the fall of 1992, I got a phone call from Chantal. She invited me to come to Chamonix and climb with her, and

I accepted. I wanted to see whether our fling was going to go anywhere. So far, it had been one of those glamorous relationships where you briefly hook up with somebody in an exotic place, and then you go your separate ways. I was left wondering, Is this real, or is it make-believe?

So I went to Chamonix that winter, and we climbed and hung out together for two weeks. The night she had crept into my tent at K2 base camp, Chantal had told me, "From the minute I met you, Ed, I was attracted to you."

My reaction had been "Whoa! Really?" There were all these guys around. Why would she zero in on me? I thought Scott would have been a more likely target: he was movie-star handsome, with a Superman physique. But Scott was married. And there was Thor, who seemed unable to get over the end of his former affair with Chantal. Had Thor not been there, I might have approached Chantal, but at the same time, I was so focused on the climb, I didn't want anything to distract me.

I'd seen it before. If you get into a relationship like that on a mountain, you lose focus. I just didn't want to go there.

Anyway, Chantal and I climbed together in winter conditions on some famous routes in the Mont Blanc massif, and we hung out in Chamonix. I enjoyed her company; she was very attractive, and she was a good climber. But I was realistic. Did I want to move to France? No. Was she about to move to the United States? No.

I was smitten, but I wasn't in love. I knew that our relationship wasn't headed toward something like marriage. *C'est la vie.*

During the following years, I'd see Chantal several times in the Himalaya. Our relations were always cordial; we managed to stay friends. I wasn't at all bitter about our fling not progressing to something more serious. Everybody liked Chantal.

▲
▲
▲

With Gary's death, Rob needed someone else to help guide clients on the South Col route on Everest. He asked me, so I served as his assistant guide on Everest in both 1994 and 1995.

In the latter year, Chantal signed onto Rob's permit as a client. For the most part she was self-sufficient, but in some ways she was indeed a client, relying on our Sherpas and Rob and me to establish camps, carry loads, and fix ropes. Her goal was to climb Everest without supplemental oxygen, a feat no woman had yet performed, and she was saving her strength for the summit push.

At base camp, Chantal asked me, "Ed, how do I do this? What are your tactics for getting up Everest without oxygen?"

By then, I'd climbed six of the fourteen 8,000ers. I answered, "First of all, don't get yourself killed doing it. It's not worth it. On summit day, you have to start early enough to give yourself plenty of time. And even if you start at midnight, make sure that by two P.M., if you're not in striking distance of the top, you turn around and go down. And make sure you still have the energy to get down. Don't use up everything you've got going up."

Chantal seemed to get it. "Yes, yes," she said. "Thank you."

The morning of our summit day, we were all camped on the South Col, at 26,000 feet. Chantal left camp before us, since she was going without oxygen. She was accompanied by two Sherpas, who would help set her pace and also break trail for her. Sometime that morning, we caught up with her and passed her. Although I've made it an ironclad rule to climb the 8,000ers without bottled oxygen on my own expeditions, when I've guided, I've always used oxygen. For the clients' sake, not for mine: in a pinch, I can help them down more efficiently if I'm sucking oxygen myself. This very question would become a huge point of contention during the 1996 Everest disaster.

When we got to the South Summit, at 28,700 feet, Rob and I and Guy Cotter, a very strong guide from New Zealand, saw at once that we weren't going to make it to the top. It took only a telepathic glance between Rob and me for us to agree to turn around and go down. The weather was deteriorating, and the snow conditions along the ridge leading to the Hillary Step were not safe.

I was bringing the first wave of clients down, in the lead, while Rob and Guy took up the rear. On the radio, somebody said, "Chantal's still heading up." It was after one P.M. when we crossed paths. She was moving slowly, with the two Sherpas breaking trail for her. I said, "Chantal, you might think about not going any farther. Look at your watch. Remember what you asked me down at base camp."

She waved my worries off: "No, no, I'm fine."

I had my hands full getting our clients down, particularly Doug Hansen, who was near exhaustion. It had reached the point where I had to yell at him to keep him moving. I had lost my voice from breathing cold, dry air, so I had to put my face just inches from Doug's for him to hear me. Even when I bellowed, what came out was more a squeak than a roar.

Doug was an impressive and a likable guy, but by now he needed extra stimulus to keep him moving. Shouting at him like a drill sergeant seemed to do the trick.

Then I got a call over the radio from Rob, who was still on the South Summit. "Hang on, Ed," he said. "Chantal's collapsed. She's completely out of gas. We're going to have to start bringing her down."

That put the brakes on everybody. Now I had to stop and wait, even though Doug needed badly to get down to the South Col.

It turned out that Chantal had used up everything she had getting to the South Summit. Now she couldn't even walk. So she just sat there, while Guy, Rob, and the two Sherpas hauled her down, as Guy later put it, "like a sack of spuds." When they reached my position on the ridge, I helped out. Soon I was holding on to Chantal's boots, backing down, pulling on her, while the Sherpas pushed from above. She was breathing bottled oxygen by then, but she was still completely out of it.

At one point, though, I heard her say to Rob, "I signed up for your trip. You're responsible for me, Rob. You have to get me down."

It was very hard work, on top of just having climbed to within 300 feet of the summit, but we hauled her to the South Col at the end of a very long day. Guy got her through the night, though at times he thought he was going to lose her. Then the next morning—bing! She'd completely recovered. She made her way down the rest of the mountain without assistance.

Chantal had her own knack for getting away with this stuff. She'd use up everything she had getting up, and then there was nothing left. But at the moment of collapse, she'd manage to be around other climbers who were capable of helping her down the mountain.

One thing that puzzled a lot of us was that later Chantal didn't acknowledge that others had saved her life, or even offer much in the way of thanks. You don't perform a rescue, of course, to win thanks: on the mountain, it's a simple moral obligation. But in 1997, Chantal told an American journalist who interviewed her that on K2 in 1992, she had not needed to be rescued. She glossed over Scott's and my giving up our summit attempt to help Thor Kieser get her down the mountain, saying, "They helped a little. I was going down. It was nice to see them."

Similarly, about being hauled down Everest "like a sack of spuds" in '95, she told the journalist, "No, I didn't collapse. I arrived later than the others. I waited for help to go down."

Whether Chantal didn't really understand what had happened on K2 and Everest or just couldn't admit it, I'll never know. As a climber with multiple sponsors, she had a high profile in France. It wouldn't have been good for her image to admit to being rescued.

I saw Chantal again in 1996 as we climbed Everest, and she climbed Lhotse. Then I didn't see her for another two years, until we both happened to be on the northeast ridge of Dhaulagiri at the same time, in the spring of 1998. I was climbing with Veikka Gustafsson and Guy Cotter; she was paired with a Sherpa, Ang Tshering, with whom she had climbed on several previous expeditions. Our base camps were a long distance apart, so I saw her only on occasion, as we moved up and down the mountain, crossing paths.

Camp II, at 21,500 feet, lay in a tricky spot, in a kind of hollow below a steep face. The slope and prevailing winds funneled snowdrifts down from above—not true avalanches, just a lot of loose snow—so that during the course of an expedition any tent erected there would tend to get buried. Knowing this fact from the accounts of previous climbers on the northeast ridge, Veikka, Guy, and I built a snow cave there instead of pitching a tent. Chantal and Ang Tshering pitched their tent a little above our cave, and there were also several tents from other expeditions nearby.

On May 7, we could see bad weather coming in, so we decided to head all the way back to base camp and sit it out. On the way down, we ran into Chantal and Tshering coming up. She said, "We're just going to go up to Camp II and wait." I said, "Okay, be safe."

By a few days later, the grapevine on the mountain was buzzing with a mystery: "Where's Chantal?" No one had seen her since our brief meeting with her below Camp II. We weren't keeping tabs on each other's base camps, so somebody speculated that Chantal and her Sherpa partner might have wandered off down the valley, just to take a break from Dhaulagiri.

By this point, the three of us were headed back up the mountain, so we offered to keep an eye out for Chantal. But a group of Spanish climbers told us, "Don't bother looking at Camp II—we've already checked. They're not there."

When we got back up to our snow cave, we saw Chantal's tent, nearly completely buried in drifted snow. We figured maybe she'd gone up to Camp III. After a night in the snow cave, we pushed on upward. At Camp III, there was not a sign of Chantal—no tent, nothing. We radioed the news down to the other teams. At that point we realized that Chantal and Tshering had not gotten up to Camp III. Where in God's name could they be?

At last, only on May 14—seven days after the pair had last been seen—an Italian climber shook the snow loose from the tent at Camp II and tried to unzip the door. The drifts pressing against the walls were so heavy that he couldn't really get the door open. The next day, a teammate shoveled loose the drifts and fully opened the door. Inside, he found Chantal and Ang Tshering lying in their sleeping bags, dead. At Camp III, we heard the news over the radio.

In my mind, I ran through the possible scenarios. The most obvious was that they had been suffocated in their tent—either by falling asleep as the drifts covered it and cut off the air supply, or by poisoning themselves with carbon monoxide as they burned their stove with all the zippers closed tight against a storm. In both fashions, a number of experienced explorers and climbers have died over the years.

Some Sherpas managed to sledge the bodies down to Camp I. There, a helicopter retrieved them. Chantal's body was flown to France. After some sort of medical inquiry, followed by a funeral, her family announced that Chantal's neck had been broken. They speculated that an avalanche or a block of ice had jumped a rock band and crashed into the tent, killing Chantal instantly. Whether Ang Tshering had suffocated or also been killed by a block of ice or avalanche, no one knew.

This was the "official" story, but the explanation didn't make much sense to me. When we'd seen Chantal's tent on our way back up the mountain, it had looked drifted over, not smashed by an avalanche, which surely would have dislodged it from its platform. And the Italian who first tried to open the tent reported that it was slumped under drifted snow, not avalanche debris.

It would have taken extraordinary circumstances for a block of ice to strike Chantal, inside the tent, in exactly the right place to break her neck, without wrenching the tent loose from its platform. But it could be true. It was not our right to question the report. I'll never know for sure what happened. Ironically, Chantal died very close to the place on Dhaulagiri where Gary Ball had succumbed to pulmonary edema five years before.

Until 1998, Chantal had always seemed to get away with pushing herself beyond her limits, then having the good fortune to have other climbers nearby who could get her down safely. But at last her luck had run out.

No matter how she met her end, all of us on the mountain were shocked. We all liked Chantal. She was a beautiful woman and a free spirit. And despite the fact that nothing had come of our brief affair, I was deeply saddened by her death.

▲
▲
▲

My own life's trajectory toward an obsession with the 8,000-meter peaks was a long and circuitous one. Growing up in one of the flattest places in the Midwest, I had, as a kid, only a vague idea of what a mountain looked like. From age three on, I lived in Rockford, Illinois. It's a town of about 150,000 today, a center of light industry, particularly machine-tool factories. Ninety miles northwest of Chicago, eight miles from the Wisconsin border.

Both my parents were immigrants from Europe. My father, Elmars Harry Viesturs, came from Riga, Latvia. During World War II, along with a lot of other Latvians, he fled his native country when the Russians invaded it. With his family, he traveled to Germany, where they lived in a refugee camp. As grim as that was, it was better than living under Russian communism.

After the war, my dad, his sister, and his mother came to America as part of a U.S. sponsorship program to resettle refugees. The family ended up on a farm in Kansas, my dad working as a ranch hand. Later, during the Korean War, he joined the army and was stationed in Germany.

That's where he met my mom, Ingrid Giesela Lorenz. She'd grown up in Stettin, East Germany—today, thanks to the border adjustments after the war, it's part of Poland. She remembers her neighborhood getting bombed by the Allies, literally waiting in the rubble to be dug out. After my father's tour of duty ended, he brought her back to the States. Once my parents were married, they settled down in Fort Wayne, Indiana, because Dad had gotten accepted at Indiana Tech. He put himself through college, working various jobs while he attended classes, and my mom worked, too—in a cannery, a photo lab, all kinds of jobs. My sister, Velta, was born in 1957 in Fort Wayne, and I came along on June 22, 1959.

When I was three, Dad got a job in a machine-tool company in Rockford, where he worked as a mechanical engineer. He was part of a team that designed massive machines that either cut or formed metal. These machine "tools" would transform some form of sheet metal into ductwork, or into blocks of steel, by drilling, cutting, and milling the sheets, producing parts for engines, printing presses, or countless other products. Mom worked her usual series of jobs. They still live in Rockford today, as does Velta, who's married with two young girls; she earns her living as a real estate agent.

I think my work ethic comes from my parents. What I learned was, above all, Don't complain. Hard work isn't going to kill you. It's going to take hard work to succeed. I like things that are difficult to achieve—things that can't get done in a day but take much more time and effort.

As a kid, I didn't care much for organized sports. Instead, in our neighborhood we played games of pickup tackle football every fall. I had a garage-sale helmet and pair of shoulder pads. I loved sandlot football, even though kids would get hurt now and then. In the spring, we'd play baseball. In winter, some of the fathers would flood the local park so that the water would freeze, creating a makeshift ice rink. There we'd play hockey until it was almost too dark to see the puck. I wore hand-me-down white figure skates. Out of embarrassment, I painted them black.

But more than sports, I just loved to be outside. A block away from our house, there was a creek. A buddy of mine and I would spend a whole Sunday journeying as far up the creek as we could, without worrying about when we had to get home for dinner. We pretended to be explorers. The creek wasn't out in the country—it ran right through Rockford. There were culverts draining from the streets into the creek. We'd crawl into these underground pipes that ran beneath the streets. They were about four feet in diameter, so we could walk up the tunnels slightly stooped over. We'd go for miles. There'd be a grate every block or so to admit rainfall runoff, though you couldn't get out there. The grate would give us a blast of light; then we'd head back into the darkness. We never found anything in the culverts, but it was still an adventure.

Often I'd go up the creek alone. Even in winter—I'd go out and break the ice, goof around for hours, then come home wet, dirty, and muddy. The creek was my true adventure place.

And I loved animals. We always had a dog, some kind of midsized mutt, and we had a cat. But I'd also go out and bring back bugs, injured birds, and rabbits—you name it. I kept gerbils and hamsters and tropical fish. I had a terrarium in my bedroom, which soon was full of things like snakes and tent caterpillars. When the terrarium got overloaded with caterpillars crawling around, my parents would yell, "Get that out of here!"—but they never actually forced me to get rid of it.

By junior high, for sure—maybe even when I was still in grade school—I knew I wanted to be a veterinarian. I'd always been a good student, but now I worked really hard on my grades, because I understood how difficult it was to get into vet school.

In Cub Scouts and Boy Scouts, I did a little hiking, backpacking, and camping, though nothing extensive. After a while, I quit the Boy Scouts because it got too regimented for me. I'd joined mainly so I could go hiking and camping, but you also had to do inspection, you had to earn merit badges, and you had to wear a uniform. I just wanted to go camping.

Mom and Dad encouraged my interest in the outdoors. They weren't at all controlling. In fact, they were enthusiastic about whatever I was interested in.

When I was in the sixth grade, Mom signed Velta and me up for competitive swimming classes at the YMCA. I really got into it. In junior high, I swam on the team, and I did so in high school, too, where the season stretched over seven months. I also swam all summer for a club.

Swimming became my life. I swam, I ate, I slept. Two hours of practice in the morning, an hour and a half at night. There was a small group of us who were serious about and dedicated to the sport. If there was anything extra to learn from a coach—how to start faster, how to turn faster—we'd stay after practice to learn it. I even trained myself to stay streamlined by breathing as little as possible. In a fifty-yard race, I would take just one breath, near the finish line.

We spent hours and hours in the pool, working with the hardest coaches, the ones who drove us: "You're not finished yet—do ten more laps!" We'd get out of the pool just wiped. But the ones who were willing to work that hard got good at swimming.

As a high school junior, I formed a relay squad with three teammates. Soon, we'd broken a long-standing school relay record, and we bested several other team and individual marks. These three were also my best friends—we goofed off and went to parties together. In the winter, after practice we indulged in the fine art of "skitching." On ice-glazed roads, we'd hang on to the back bumper of a friend's car as he pullled us around the block, skidding on our boots as if they were skis. These high jinks came to an abrupt halt one night when the driver fishtailed out of a curve and slammed into a telephone pole. We were fine, but the car was totaled.

In my senior year, the financially strapped Rockford school board cut the budget for all extracurricular activities, including varsity sports. One of the best coaches took a job at the YMCA in Belvidere. Several of us really dedicated swimmers followed him there, even though it was an hour-long commute. Now our former rivals from other high schools became our teammates. At the Y, we formed a dream relay team, with me swimming the anchor leg. At the district championships that year, we set a new national record for the 200-yard medley relay.

That feat won us a trip to the national YMCA championships in Fort Lauderdale. To prep for our races, we shaved off all our body hair with electric razors. Then, after the races were over, we tied the razors' electric cords together to hoist six-packs of beer up to the windows of our hotel rooms, dodging the chaperones who patrolled the hallways.

We did well enough at Fort Lauderdale, but we were humbled by slightly faster teams. Still, we'd had a great season and a great experience together.

I think the athleticism I gained from competitive swimming helped me later as a climber, both physically and mentally. Having suffered through countless swimming workouts gave me the strength and resolve to suffer through high-altitude ordeals in the mountains. And I learned that working hard and training hard paid off, just as it would for me in the mountains. I was extremely competitive as a swimmer. I wanted to win. My best friend, Richard King, swam for another high school. When we had to swim against each other in a meet, I wouldn't talk to him; I wouldn't even look at him. He'd do the same to me. You had to put your game face on, trying to gain even the slightest psychological edge. Afterward, Richard and I could hang out and be pals again.

But there's an irony: I don't think of myself as a competitive climber. Or if I am, I'm competitive only with myself. On K2, for instance, I set myself the challenge of climbing the 7,000 feet from base camp to Camp III in ten hours. It wasn't to beat the other guys up there—just to do it in the time I set for myself.

I'll go even further and say that competitiveness in mountaineering is wrong. It's dangerous. Climbing should be personally motivated.

It's significant, I think, that the single sport I got serious about was an individual one, not a team sport. I was a shy kid, something of a loner. I was always happy being alone, reading in my room for hours or hiking up the creek. I was an introvert. I could hang with anyone, but I was usually the quietest person in any crowd.

In high school, for the first time I became aware of a tension between my parents. The minute I walked in the door after swimming practice I could feel it. At the dinner table, the tension would build. Mom and Dad would be superficially cordial in front of us, but both Velta and I knew something was up.

Then, when we kids were in bed and they thought we were asleep, they'd argue. Not real yelling and screaming, just loud, angry conversations. For us, that was devastating. We didn't know what they were fighting about. Parents try to hide that stuff from their kids, but the kids usually know.

I hated having to get through dinner with that tension hovering over the room. And I resolved that I'd never do that when I got married—I didn't want to live that kind of life with my own wife. And I wanted to get out—not to escape my family but to get away from the tension. Once I graduated from high school, I knew, I could leave home and go to college. I couldn't wait.

Mom and Dad finally separated when I was in college. Dad took the initiative and moved out. Mom, I think, was surprised. They got divorced five years later. Today, thank God, they're on good speaking terms. Mom remarried, but her second husband died of cancer. Dad has never remarried.

▲
▲
▲

In junior year of high school, I read lots of adventure books. Scott, Amundsen, Alfred Lansing's *Endurance*—I would escape the flatlands of Illinois by reading stories of strength and suffering. The Arctic, the Antarctic, high mountains: the colder it was, the cooler it was.

When I was sixteen, I read Maurice Herzog's *Annapurna,* the account of the first 8,000-meter peak ever climbed. I was inspired. I thought, Wow, would I love to go to the Himalaya with guys like that and do something like that.

On the face of it, it's odd that that book should seem inspiring, because it tells a grim tale: in the aftermath of the expedition, Herzog lost all his fingers and toes to frostbite, Louis Lachenal all his toes. Yet *Annapurna* is not only the best-selling mountaineering book of all time, it's the book that caused a whole generation of young men and women to become mountaineers.

It's the achievement on Annapurna that inspires, not the aftermath. How for a month the team couldn't even find the mountain, the maps were so bad. How in the last two weeks before the monsoon hit, they put it all together and blazed up the hill. How everybody helped everybody else down, carrying each other almost like victims from a battlefield. It's a story of a band of brothers, of bonding and friendship and camaraderie. Something to do with the complex mixture of hardship and perseverance that Annapurna elicited from those gutsy French climbers fired my imagination.

In retrospect, more than fifty years afterward, that triumph seems all the more extraordinary: not only would Annapurna be the only 8,000er to be climbed on the first attempt, but the mountain would turn out to be the most dangerous of all the fourteen 8,000ers. And of course I had no inkling when I was still in high school that Annapurna would end up being the last of my own 8,000ers, and the hardest of all to knock off.

Reading about Scott and Amundsen's struggles to reach the South Pole, I didn't immediately dream of going to Antarctica. But as soon as I finished *Annapurna,* I knew that going on a Himalayan expedition was something that I really wanted to do. How could I get to that point, to be invited on a Himalayan expedition? I realized that to get there, I'd have to climb a lot of smaller, lower peaks first.

I also sensed how much I needed to learn. It's like carpentry—you don't just pick up a hammer and build a house. I would need years of apprenticeship before heading off to the Himalaya. I'd have to move to somewhere where there were mountains, so that I could climb, not just read about climbing. I'd have to work my way up the ladder. It was still the era of nationally sponsored expeditions, like the 1963 American Everest assault, in which a leader put together a team on behalf of the United States. So:

what would I have to do to get myself in position to be invited on such an expedition?

Eventually, I put up posters of my mountaineering heroes on my bedroom wall: Jim Whittaker, the first American to climb Everest, in 1963, and Nawang Gombu, Whittaker's partner, who became the first person to climb Everest twice. I subscribed to *Climbing* and *Outside* and read them cover to cover. I even consumed catalogs from equipment companies.

In 1976, during my junior year of high school, my swimming rival and best friend, Richard King, and I went to Devils Lake, a small quartzite crag in Wisconsin, to teach ourselves to rock climb, driving three hours each way as often as we could get away. We'd bought a 150-foot Goldline rope. Our textbook was Royal Robbins's *Basic Rockcraft*. At first, we mostly top-roped: you pass the rope through an anchor (often a sling looped around a tree) at the top of the cliff, then dangle both ends to the base, so that you can belay from the ground; that way the climber's always secured from above and can't fall more than a few feet.

We'd go even in the dead of winter, wearing wool balaclavas over our faces, climbing in snowstorms. We'd pretend we were Doug Scott and Chris Bonington on Ben Nevis—legendary Brits we'd read about who were always having epics on gnarly winter climbs. Those guys were our heroes: what they were doing in the Himalaya seemed incomprehensible to us.

Finally we got up the nerve to try our first lead. It was only one pitch, rated 5.3, but all we had for protection was a handful of hex nuts, and we were climbing in these big, clunky hiking boots, whereas what we needed were good rock shoes. When one of us would pause on a small foothold, he'd develop sewing-machine leg, his calf muscles cramping so much that his leg went into uncontrollable up-and-down spasms. It felt desperate, but we ultimately started to get the hang of it and became fairly competent on rock.

The next summer, Richard and I and another friend, Ken Henry, took our first trip west. We rode the train to Glacier National Park, then backpacked for two weeks. We wanted to play around on snow slopes, so we knew we had to have an ice ax. We bought the longest one we could find in a catalog—it must have been three and a half feet long, almost like some Victorian alpenstock. (The ice tools I use today are much shorter and are specially devised for attacking steep ice.) We brought along our Goldline rope, but never used it. Basically, we just cavorted on the snow slopes, glissading, pretending we were climbers.

We had eighty-pound packs, because we'd brought food like canned bacon, clothing like extra Levi's and Converse tennis shoes, gear like the rope we never uncoiled. Even so, we didn't have nearly enough to eat. We'd bought all our food beforehand and stored it in the basement of Ken's house. Turns out his little brother had eaten a lot of our rations. In Glacier, we'd open our boxes and say, "Where's the freeze-dried stuff? Where are the Pop-Tarts?" We ended up eating rice with syrup three times a day.

We were often in grizzly country. On the map, certain trails were off-limits because of the bears. But we'd blunder along a path, then suddenly find fresh grizzly crap, look at the map again, and say, *Oh, my God, we're on the wrong trail*. We'd hike twenty miles a day, half of it in the wrong direction. Still it was a great experience, even though we didn't even know what we didn't know.

I graduated from Rockford East in 1977. I'd applied to nearly all the colleges in Illinois, Wisconsin, Indiana. Not willing to ask my parents for money, I took upon myself the challenge of paying my way through college. I planned to take out loans, apply for grants, and get work-study jobs on campus. Despite my urge to get away from the tension that hung over the dining room table, I thought maybe I'd stay close to home. Most of my older friends who'd gone to college had stayed close. My sister, Velta, had gone to a couple of local community colleges. It seemed like a scary prospect to pack up and head far away.

Then one day, as I was riding home from swimming practice in the back seat of a car driven by the mother of one of my friends, she mentioned that her older son had just graduated from the University of Washington, in Seattle. In that moment, I made up my mind that that's where I'd go to college. Seattle—there were lots of mountaineers there, I knew, and there was

Mount Rainier. When I got home, I told my dad. He said, "Great, I'll drive you there."

Because I had good grades, I got into all the colleges to which I'd applied. But I didn't hesitate in choosing the University of Washington. And sure enough, Dad and Mom and Velta drove me to Seattle. We took three or four days, stopping at places like Mount Rushmore and the Badlands. Except for Glacier National Park, I'd never been west before. My parents and my sister spent a little time in Seattle, then got into the car to drive back to Illinois. I watched them go from my dorm window. I felt as though I didn't have a friend in the world and I'd just made a huge leap into the unknown.

At U.W., I was a walk-on on the swim team. In high school, I'd been a top-notch swimmer at the state level, but I wasn't sure I could reach the next echelon. Basically, I wasn't tall enough. Nearly all the Olympic-caliber swimmers are at least six foot two. Arms up to the ceiling, great reach and torque. I was five-ten.

I majored in zoology, taking classes in anatomy, physiology, and organic chemistry. I liked science, and I'd already decided to become a vet. It wasn't just that I loved animals; I felt it was my duty to help them. Even as a kid, if I found a bird with a broken wing, I'd take it home. Once I found a baby rabbit with a broken leg. I took it home, we splinted its leg, and I nursed it through the winter. Saving that rabbit's life was a big thing for me.

I knew I didn't want to be a doctor. I thought that as a doctor, you ended up being more of a psychologist, because so many people who aren't really sick think they're sick, or want to be sick. Animals don't fake it. When something's wrong, they really need your assistance.

When I eventually became a vet, I realized that some of the pet owners needed more help than their pets. At one clinic where I worked, the vet in charge had a practice of drawing a peanut at the top of certain charts. That meant that the owner was a bit of a loony-tune, a nutcase. They'd come in once a week. This week it would be "Fifi's itching her bottom." Next week: "Fifi didn't like her turkey pâté. There's got to be something wrong." There was nothing we could do but run a battery of tests to prove that Fifi was fine. But once you'd figured out the owner, you'd accept that she'd be coming in once a week. We'd mollify her: "Come back next week and we'll take Fifi's temperature." Meanwhile, Fifi would come in covered with lipstick because the owner had kissed her to death all the way to the clinic.

The first year at U.W., since I was from out of state, my tuition was something like $3,000 a year. By my second year, after I'd established Washington residency, my tuition dropped to $600 a year. Yet even $600 seemed like a colossal sum to me then. So besides taking out loans, I had to do all these work-study jobs, helping professors with their research. One job was with a psychologist who was slicing mice brains—I had to measure the surface area of certain parts of the brain that he had dyed. Another job was dealing with radioactive vials of animal tissue. I was supposed to empty the vials, pour out the fluid, and use tweezers to extract the tissue. I had to wear a respirator and keep a Geiger counter on the tabletop next to me. Once I heard the gizmo go *beep-beep-beep* like crazy. I stopped immediately. Pulling off the respirator, I said to the prof, "You're paying me four dollars an hour to risk my life? See ya." It's the one job I quit after only a few minutes.

Summers I'd work in sweltering heat scraping tar off the roofs of buildings, or painting the insides of apartments. I'd scrub down the crumbly floors and cupboards, wearing a mask and a protective suit, then spray-paint the insides of these crappy old apartments. Often I'd be so tired riding the bus home that I'd fall asleep and miss my stop. I looked so filthy, people were afraid to wake me up.

Not having an athletic scholarship, I had to quit swimming after just a few practices my freshman year. I couldn't study, work, and swim at the same time.

The first two years at U.W. I lived in a dorm on campus. The bonus was that I could see Mount Rainier out the window. That was my beacon: I'd quit studying and just gaze out the window at Rainier in the distance. The second two years, I lived with a bunch of guys in off-campus houses. One time there were eight of us in a single house. To save rent, I shared a room with another guy, so we each paid $75 a month instead of $150. We slept in bunk beds.

I tried to be really frugal. I'd go to the grocery store, pick up a jar of peanut butter, then realize, Nope—can't afford it this week. So I'd buy Top Ramen instead; you could get six packages for a dollar.

Although I couldn't fit swimming into my hectic life, I figured I could make time for climbing by setting my own schedule. I'd study voraciously all week, so that Friday night I'd be out of there and could climb all weekend. I started running to train for climbing—stadium stairs, courses around the university on bike trails and ship canal towpaths. Each day after classes, I'd try to run forty-five minutes to an hour, five to seven miles. Eventually, with two or three friends, I started running around Lake Union, a good seven-to-eight-mile course. After running, I'd study until quite late. Then I'd go to the nearly deserted gym to lift weights. I devised my own workout regimens, focusing on what I thought would build strength and endurance for climbing.

There was a North Face store near campus, and a cool little climbing shop called the Swallow's Nest. They had message boards on which you could post an ad looking for climbing partners. Most of the ads were from people like me—new to the area, lacking regular partners, but avid to climb.

I remember one day finding Jon Krakauer's name on a message board. He was living in Seattle then, doing carpentry for a living—this was long before he wrote *Into the Wild* or *Into Thin Air*. But he'd started to publish articles in *Outside* magazine. To me, he was a famous climber: I knew he'd done a new route solo on Devils Thumb, for instance. I didn't dare call him. I knew he'd never want to climb with me. I assumed he wouldn't even want to *talk* to me. We're good friends today, and when I told him about my trepidation back then, he got a kick out of it.

From the message boards, I slowly put together a list of people to call. I had two criteria: I was looking for people who had experience in the mountains, and they had to have a car, so we could get to the peaks.

My number one guy became Curt Mobley, who worked on campus for NOAA. He was about ten years older than I was. Very conservative in the mountains, very experienced, and he had an orange VW bug. He loved climbing, and he was single, so he had his freedom. Every Wednesday night, I'd call him: "Curt, can we go climbing this weekend?"

We plunged right into the Cascades. The first real mountain I climbed was Mount Saint Helens, in 1977—just three years before the top of it blew off. It was 9,677 feet tall, this beautiful cylindrical volcano. Even though it was just a walk-up, we were on glaciers, roped up, using crampons and ice axes. On the summit, I knew: *This is it*. This was what I was looking for. This was the greatest thing in the world.

As a teenager, I'd read about mountaineering in *Annapurna*. But you never know whether the real thing will be much harder than you thought— too hard, in fact, to keep striving for. On the summit of Mount Saint Helens, however, the real thing perfectly matched my expectations. It was hard, no question, but the challenge and reward made for sheer enjoyment.

From the start, I wanted an alpine experience. I wasn't interested in driving up to some crag, getting 'out of the car, and doing a rock climb. I wanted multiday trips on mixed snow and rock, camping out, the whole experience. I knew this was what I needed to do to get to the Himalaya.

But my first major goal was Mount Rainier I was well aware that the peak was hopelessly crowded in summer, so I resolved that my first climb of Rainier would be a winter ascent.

Meanwhile, Curt and I cruised all over the Cascades, as many weekends as possible. If Curt couldn't go, I had a couple of other guys on my list. Sometimes they'd say, "Ed, it's going to rain this weekend." I'd answer, "That doesn't matter—we gotta go anyway." And if I couldn't get anybody else to go, I'd hitchhike. Believe it or not, I was happy camping alone in the rain. Anything, just to get out.

My gear was a hodgepodge of used and discarded stuff. In the basement of the old REI store in Seattle, there was a collection of used and broken gear, stuff nobody wanted. I'd root through the bins, looking for the very cheapest bargains. I got a funky pair of old ski goggles. Army-surplus wool pants and sweaters. My rain jacket was a yellow plastic bicycle poncho. In the wind, it would flap up and cover my head, and I'd have to keep beating it down. My footwear was a used pair of Habeler leather boots, rigid old clompers. To save money, I thought I could get away without a sleeping pad, just lay my sleeping bag on the ground, but one autumn night I learned that you just can't economize like that—it's too cold. I made some of my own gear, and I patched the holes in the seat and knees of my pants with fabric from other cast-off clothes.

The Mountaineers was the huge organization that presided over climbing in the Northwest, but I never joined. I'm just not a clubby guy. I'd quit the Boy Scouts, after all. I just wanted to go out and do something, not sit around talking about it.

At the same time, I was galvanized by the lectures certain famous Euro climbers gave on their visits to Seattle. Kane Hall at U.W. would be packed to the rafters for Chris Bonington or Kurt Diemberger. All of us in the audience were in awe. These guys had done all these great climbs, but they were so casual, sitting on stage and chatting about their deeds. I went to a party where Georges Bettembourg was in the crowd, a French master who'd done a new route on Kangchenjunga. I was too much in awe to dare to speak to him.

I did some rock climbing, at places like the Peshastin Pinnacles and Index Town Wall, especially in summer and when we could only take one day off. I got good enough to lead 5.10, maybe 5.11 on my best days—not all that far below what the top rock jocks were doing at the time. But I was never interested in big-wall rock climbing; I never went to Yosemite. I was too preoccupied with alpine mountaineering.

Curt and I did some steep, semitechnical routes on big mountains in the Cascades, including the north face of Mount Baker and the north face of Mount Shuksan. And we tried Rainier in December 1977 and again in January 1978, getting blown off both times. Finally we climbed the peak successfully in March 1978, still in my freshman year in college. We wore snowshoes up to Camp Muir at 10,000 feet, carrying really heavy packs—ropes, snow pickets, willow wands, the works. Rainier in winter's a full-on mini-expedition, with a very low success rate.

Living in Seattle, I was very much aware of Rainier Mountaineering,

Inc., then the only guiding concession on the mountain. RMI was run by Gerry Lynch and Lou Whittaker, the twin brother of Jim Whittaker, the first American to climb Everest. Lou himself was a veteran of K2 and Everest expeditions, though he hadn't reached the summit of either. Gerry was the RMI operations manager, Lou the chief guide. Among the guide corps were guys only six or eight years older than I, but who'd been on real expeditions; they were guiding Denali as well as Rainier. Guys like Eric Simonson and George Dunn and Phil Ershler—Phil had been a Rainier guide since the age of sixteen! Just a couple of years later, in 1982, Simonson, Dunn, and Ershler would go to Everest on an expedition led by Lou Whittaker; and in 1984, Ershler would be the only member of another team led by Lou to reach the summit of Everest, via a new route on the north face.

I thought of these guys as the "super-senior guides." And though the salary of a Rainier guide was minimal and the job was for the summer season only, I couldn't help thinking that it would be the ideal job and the ideal place to work. What I wouldn't give to be in the company of guides like Simonson, Dunn, and Ershler!

In May of my junior year at U.W., in 1980, I tried out for RMI. All of us aspirants assembled at Paradise, the trailhead at 5,400 feet on Rainier. We were all quite nervous, because there were twenty or thirty of us competing for maybe one slot. A senior guide such as Eric Simonson would go up to each of us candidates and say, "Demonstrate for me, and teach me, how to self-arrest." Or "Talk about pressure breathing." Or "Tie me in with a bowline, and talk my way through it." They wanted to see that we not only knew a technique but could teach it to clients.

The tryout was on May 18—it's impossible to forget the date, because at eighty-thirty A.M., before we'd even started, we watched Mount Saint Helens explode. The tryout was canceled. Only an hour after the eruption, a cloud of falling ash engulfed us and it became almost pitch-dark. I'd borrowed a car from a roommate to get to Rainier. Now I drove home slowly with headlights on and windshield wipers cranked to the max. On the radio, broadcasters were advising against driving at all, because the ash could get in through the air filter, chew up the cylinders, and destroy your engine.

But I had no choice. Once I got back to Seattle, I vacuumed and cleaned the car and got every trace of ash removed. My roommate was never the wiser.

Thanks to that colossal eruption, Rainier itself was covered with ash and the mountain became dangerously icy; so RMI's 1980 summer season was pretty much a wash. They didn't hire any new guides that year; I spent the summer scraping tar and painting apartments.

I went to the tryout again in 1981, at the end of my senior year in college. The same routine, twenty or thirty of us sizing one another up, competing for maybe one or at most two new positions. They don't tell you then and there if you've made it; they send you home with a vague promise: "We'll be in touch."

That summer, after the tryout, Gerry Lynch called me. "We may need a few new guys," he said, "but we don't know when. We might bring you on." All summer I worked painting houses, taking whatever jobs I could scrounge up. I didn't want to get too committed to any one job, because if Gerry called back, I was going to drop everything. But it was really frustrating, just hanging in limbo all summer. I knew I'd done well in the tryout, because Gerry had called me. I knew I was on the cusp. But in the end, it never came to pass.

Meanwhile, all during my senior year, I lived in a veterinary clinic called Northeast Veterinary Hospital, north of the university. They gave me a small apartment, rent-free, and a small monthly salary. Each night from six o'clock until seven the next morning, I was on duty to answer the emergency phone. If a dog was hit by a car or a cat was choking on something, I had to decide whether the pet should come in right away or if it could wait till the morning.

I still had only my bike for transportation, and I was studying hard at U.W. Typically that year I'd be up most of the night at the clinic, sleep through my alarm, jump on my bike and pedal like crazy (usually in the rain, in winter) eight or ten miles to school, and get there just in time for a morning exam.

Each night, a different vet was on call. If the pet came in, I'd perform a preliminary exam, then phone the vet to discuss the case. He'd decide what treatment to apply. Often I'd perform the treatment—there were certain things I could do, certain other things I couldn't. As I got more experienced, they trusted me to do more and more.

It was great pragmatic, hands-on training. But to my dismay, when I applied to Washington State—one of the best veterinary grad schools in the country—I was rejected. They said I didn't have enough experience. I actually got rejected twice. Only later did I find out that an odd hyperprofessionalism dictated the rejections; it was almost like a kind of hazing. They wanted to make sure you were dedicated enough to stick with the program.

After graduating from U.W. in the spring of 1981, not having been accepted to vet school, I was at loose ends. That autumn, I signed up for a few extra classes at the university. I got a job out in Fall City, east of Seattle, near the foothills of the Cascades, at a farm owned by a family I'd befriended. I learned to drive a tractor and plowed fields all day. I chopped wood, pulled weeds, cut the grass, and built shelves. On the property, they had huge piles of stuff—timbers, pieces of metal, and the like. I'd use a front loader to move a pile from here to there, piece by piece. A few days later, they'd decide to move the pile somewhere else.

The family also operated a meat plant. Some days I'd work there, pushing carcasses into the freezer after they'd been "processed" on the cutting floor. Some days they would cut faster than I could push, and I'd be overwhelmed by freshly butchered sides of beef dangling all around me. All this work was just to make ends meet.

That was a scary and depressing year for me. Despite my good grades, despite having lived and worked in a clinic, I didn't know whether I'd ever get accepted to veterinary school at Washington State. And for all the summer climbing I was doing, I wasn't getting any closer to my dream of the Himalaya.

In May 1982, I went to the RMI tryout again. By now they knew me well, and I had the tryout wired. Gerry Lynch actually told me, "Ed, you're pretty much a shoo-in by now." Yet they'd strung me along all the previous summer. Nothing seemed like a sure bet.

At the end of the tryout, Gerry took me aside. "Ed," he said, "you can pretty much count on working here this summer." Yet until I got the official letter in the mail, I didn't dare to really exhale.

It turned out I was the only new guide hired by RMI that summer. As the designated "peon" (as rookies were called), I got all the shitty jobs, like sweeping the floor and cleaning the toilets after the clients had left the buildings. At RMI, I'd have to work my way up the ladder, starting on the bottom rung.

It didn't matter that the pay was a less-than-princely $500 a month. At age twenty-three, I'd joined an elite company of thirty, the only professional guides on Rainier, and among the only such pros in the country. I couldn't imagine a better way to spend the summer, and that June, as I started work, I couldn't have been happier or more proud of myself.

The Long Road to Everest

Although I'd landed my summer job as a Rainier guide, my professional goal was still to be a veterinarian. In those days, there were no sponsored climbers in America. Making a living as a mountaineer seemed inconceivable—the only guys doing it were people like Yvon Chouinard, who'd founded Patagonia, and Doug Tompkins, who'd started The North Face. But those were successful clothing and gear businesses, so you couldn't really call either Chouinard or Tompkins a professional climber. ▲ My fellow Rainier guides had other jobs in the off-season. A number of them were teachers or ski patrolmen. A few were still in college or graduate school. ▲ By that autumn of 1982, however, I'd been rejected twice by Washington State's vet school and was in the process of applying a third time. The guiding season proper ended around the beginning of September, but a few of us lingered on, leading special five-day seminars. After that, I worked on the trail crew for the National Park Service as long as I could.

That year I was renting a room in the house of Steve Swaim, a vet I'd worked with at Northeast Veterinary Hospital, where we'd become good friends. By late winter, I was hovering in an agony of expectation, waiting for the letter of acceptance or rejection. Every day I'd come home late from my job out at the Fall City farm, often to find Steve and his girlfriend hanging out on the front stoop. "Any mail?" I'd ask.

"Nah, nothing."

It was really getting to me. Then one day, after Steve said, "No mail today," I walked up to the front door to find a letter taped to it.

"You fuckers," I burst out, "you opened my mail!"

They'd known at once it was an acceptance letter, because the envelope was so fat. All three of us went out that night, drinking and carousing.

The only trouble with Washington State was that it was located in Pullman, way to the east, on the plains beyond the mountains, almost on the Idaho border. I was enrolled in the full four-year program leading to a doctorate in veterinary medicine. I wanted desperately to be in vet school, but I sure didn't want to be in Pullman. For four years, I just suffered through the landscape while I learned my métier.

During those four years, from 1983 through 1987, I went to vet school in the winter and guided in the summer. Some Septembers I'd get started at Washington State, then skip out for a week to work in a little more guiding during the shoulder season. To cover my absences, I'd have a friend in my classes take notes for me.

But before all that, in the summer of 1982, as the peon at RMI, I spent quite a few days doing the job called "shop" on the master schedule posted on the wall. In the guides' headquarters at Paradise—the "shop"—I'd sign out rental gear to the clients: boots, crampons, ice axes, backpacks, and the like. Once everybody had left for the day, I'd spend hours water-sealing the leather boots that had come back in the day before. I'd sweep the floors and take out the trash. At the end of the day, as the climbers returned from the mountain, I'd sign the rental equipment back in.

Other days I'd be scheduled to work down in Ashford, the town nearest to Rainier, where the guides bunked up in three or four houses owned by RMI. I'd mow the grass and take out the trash and clean the bathrooms. This was the least glamorous of the RMI tasks, but being on the daily schedule meant that you had steady work.

Some days, however, I'd be assigned to "school"—the one-day climbing school, in which we taught the basics of roped glacier travel, self-arrest, even simple hiking techniques. Clients didn't sign up beforehand; they'd just walk in the door, and we'd take out anybody who came along. "School" was the prerequisite for the actual climb of Rainier. You had to pass the one-day course before you could try to climb the mountain. We used that trial to evaluate the clients for fitness, and to see if they might turn into liabilities on the climb. On the mountain, we'd be roped to our clients, so those basic skills were critical for the safety of the whole team.

What I loved more than anything, though, was to guide on the two-day climb. The first day we'd take a group up from Paradise, at 5,400 feet, to Camp Muir, at 10,000. We'd leave the next morning at one or two A.M., go to the summit, then all the way back down to Paradise. That was the RMI formula: get 'em up, get 'em down, as efficiently as possible. It's pretty rough—nine miles each way, almost 9,000 feet of altitude gained and lost. The second day was very trying for a lot of clients. They'd get partway down, then wail, "I can't go any farther. I've got blisters and I'm exhausted." We'd just have to keep them moving, herd them down to Paradise. The motto I uttered to spur the stragglers along was "Pain is temporary; glory is forever."

The two-day climbs could be hard on us guides, too, especially if you had a "back-to-back," two trips to the summit without a single day's break between them. On the rare occasion, if there was an abundance of clients, we'd do three back-to-backs.

RMI's system was very conservative. If a client couldn't go any farther on the summit day and we didn't have the manpower to take him down right away, we'd park him in a very safe place. Put him in a sleeping bag on top of a pad, but without a tent (we didn't carry tents on summit day, so we'd do this only if the weather was good). The client would have to wait as long as five or six hours before we could pick him up on the way down. On occasion, we'd get a client who'd say, "No way I'm staying here. I'll go down by myself." Well, of course we couldn't let a client go down on his own. So if we thought the guy might "run rabbit" on us, we'd take one of his boots with us. In essence, we hobbled him.

RMI had a good success ratio—about 80 percent of the clients on our two-day climbs made the summit. The independents, as we called them—climbers trying Rainier without guides—had only a 50 percent success rate. Typically they'd head out too fast, too soon and blow a gasket. In contrast, we guides kept a constant, steady pace.

RMI also had a really good safety record. In the ten years I guided for the company, we had no fatalities, not even a serious accident. There was a teaching motto handed down to us by the senior guides. When the clients were still in the shop, checking out gear, we'd drum that motto home: "Safety is first; fun is second; success is third."

All of us guides kept track of the number of ascents of Rainier we'd made. By now, I've climbed the mountain 194 times. That's not even close to the record, which is held by George Dunn, with something like 450. Phil Ershler is close to 400.

People often ask me whether it isn't monotonous to climb the same mountain over and over again, by the same route. I didn't think so; I really liked guiding. In those days, I thought, Where would I rather be? Not working in some office somewhere. It was the clients who made it interesting. Just seeing the joy on their faces when they reached the summit, or helping somebody who had it physically but maybe needed a little mental boost. On the summit, a lot of clients would break down and cry, or say, "This is the greatest experience of my life."

We guides were all friends. It was like summer camp. Down in Ashford, we'd have volleyball games and barbecues at night. Sure, at the end of the season, you'd feel a little burned out. Then Lou Whittaker would give us a pep talk. He'd gather all the guides together and say, "Listen, you guys, we're all working our butts off, and it's the end of the season, but we have customers. We need to give them the same service we gave at the beginning of the year."

Yes, the pay was only $500 a month to start, but you'd get free room and board in Ashford. Climbers were clamoring to snag the job. Year by year, you'd slowly get raises—by the end, I was making about $1,200 a month. The first season, you were being constantly evaluated: it was, in effect, a probationary period. If you weren't up to snuff or you didn't have the right personality, you wouldn't get rehired. I quickly learned to keep my mouth shut, to do my job, and to absorb every lesson I could from the senior guides. Once you got through two or three seasons, you pretty much had the job as long as you wanted it.

Another young guide, Andy Politz, and I invented what we called the "load wars." From our bunkhouse in Ashford to "shop" at Paradise was eighteen miles along a road, with an elevation gain of more than 4,000 feet. Andy and I would often ride our bikes up to Paradise before a summit climb, just to get an additional workout. Then, at Paradise, we'd find a big pile of groceries laid out on the floor of the shop. The system was that the "cabin girls," who did the cooking for us at Muir in five-day shifts, bought all the groceries, but we guides had to carry them up to Camp Muir. The food wasn't lightweight freeze-dried dinners and powdered soups—the girls would buy fresh steaks and chickens, blocks of cheese, bread, cold cuts, fresh vegetables.

Usually, a group of six guides would head up to Camp Muir with our clients. The guide officially leading the climb could be forgiven for not taking more than a loaf of bread, since he was busy organizing the logistics of the ascent. The bulk of the groceries would be divvied up among the other five guides. But Andy and I wanted to get another workout, so we'd cram as many groceries as we could into our packs, leaving very little for the other three guides to carry. We had monstrous loads, sometimes as much as eighty to ninety pounds, the pack straps nearly ripping out. When we got to Muir five hours later, we'd each dump our groceries on the floor. Then the other guides would judge who had the bigger pile, who had won that day's load war.

Another little trick that all the guides practiced had to do with the climb from Muir to the summit. You'd load up your pack the night before—it would be fairly heavy, since we each carried a medical kit, an emergency sleeping bag, snow pickets, an ice hammer, and other rescue gear. In the night, while the packs were sitting outside the huts, a guide would grab a bowling-ball-sized rock and slip it into the bottom of some other guide's pack.

You'd break the news to the poor guy on the summit. Or you'd wait till after you got back to Camp Muir, or even all the way down to Ashford. The victim would unload his pack, only to find that rock in the bottom. You had to keep a watchful eye on your own pack, since the guides all had a great knack for getting even. But it was really just good-natured horseplay. What's another ten pounds when you're in great shape?

Later on, I came up with an even more strenuous workout challenge, which I called the "bike and climb." A guide named Jimmy Hamilton and I would bike the eighteen miles from Ashford to Paradise. We'd time our arrival for late in the day, down a quick beer in the Glacier Lounge, then head up Rainier in the night—not with clients, just the two of us. Climbing conditions were actually best at night. With headlamps, we'd bomb to the summit, then get back to Paradise well before dawn. The last leg was the eighteen-mile ride down to the park entrance, going as fast as we could, drafting off each other like Tour de France competitors. We covered the round-trip—including 12,000 feet of altitude gained and lost—in eleven hours. To this day, nobody else has equaled our time.

Then we'd celebrate with breakfast at the Gateway Inn. Rail thin, Jimmy usually ordered French toast. Once the waitress asked, "Two slices?" "No," answered Jimmy, "I'll take the whole loaf."

At Camp Muir my first summer, since I was the peon, I was in charge of what we called the water system. Outside the huts, a dozen yards up the slope, stood two huge barrels. It was my job to fill them with snow, then fire up the burners. A hose siphoned the meltwater to two other barrels on the roof of the cook shack, from which yet another hose led inside the building, with a faucet to turn it on and off. That was the water supply for all our cooking, and to fill the water bottles that guides and clients carried to the summit.

Taking care of the water system was a never-ending task, assigned to the peon or the lowest-ranking guide. The minute you arrived at Muir, having come up from Paradise, you were expected to get on it. The minute you got back to Muir from the summit, you got on it.

One day I'd gotten the burners going, and the siphon was working fine, so I took a break and entered the cook shack. That was a kind of privilege, because the senior guides hung out there; they were the only ones who got to sleep in comfort inside the cook shack. A peon virtually needed permission to cross the threshold. That day Phil Ershler was there. He said to me casually, "So, Ed, you been working on the water system?"

"Yeah," I answered, "everything's under control."

"Have you looked out the window?"

I looked, and saw a cascade—virtually a waterfall—pouring off the roof. I'd let the system run so long, the barrel was overflowing.

"You might want to go out and check on it," said Phil, deadpan. I bolted, red-faced, out the door.

As I mentioned, during my ten years with RMI, we never had a serious accident. But sometimes we were caught up in rescues of independent climbers who got in trouble on the mountain. Since we were on Rainier every day, we were usually in position to help. The worst such episode came in 1991, my last year guiding for RMI full-time.

A week earlier, a heavy rain had fallen on Rainier. Then it got cold and clear. That turned the upper mountain into a sheet of ice. We'd still go out with clients, but each time we had to turn back around 12,000 feet. It was too treacherous to push on with inexperienced climbers. Yet we kept heading out every day, hoping the conditions had improved.

One night at Camp Muir, we got news over the radio that two independent climbers had not returned from their summit attempt. We agreed to keep an eye out for them when we went up the next morning. This particular climb was being led by Robert Link, with four other guides, including me. So the next day, we climbed with our clients up to Disappointment Cleaver, at 12,300 feet. There, once again, we saw that the summit dome was still too icy and dangerous for us to push on.

All at once, we heard a shout from above. When we could make out the words, we heard, "I'm here! My partner's dead! I've got a broken leg! I need help!" We spotted a lone figure about 400 feet above us. The two overdue climbers, it turned out, had had an accident up around 13,000 feet. They'd gotten off route coming down the evening before. There was slack in the rope. One guy slipped and fell, and when the rope came tight, he pulled his partner off. They both went over a fifty-foot cliff. The more seriously injured of the pair had died from his injuries in the night.

In such a situation, we became the first responders. We parked the clients with one guide in a safe spot on top of the Cleaver, while the other four of us went on up to see what we could do to help the survivor.

In the middle of this rescue, a guy came storming up toward me from below. He was climbing solo, so he ought to have had a special permit (it turned out later that he hadn't gotten one, telling the rangers instead that he would find someone at Camp Muir to pair up with). He had brand-new crampons on, all the highest-tech gear. As he surged past me, I said, "Listen, man, it's a sheet of ice up there. Be careful."

He just blew me off: "Oh, it's only Mount Rainier."

He climbed on up, crested a hump, and disappeared. Only five minutes later, I heard a noise. I looked up. There was the guy, flying down toward us, rocketing over the hump. He shot past me, missing me by only three feet—if I hadn't ducked to the side, he probably would have taken me out.

As he went by, he was sitting upright on his butt, his feet pointed downhill, his hands on the surface. He was holding his ice ax, but it was just clattering along loose. His eyes were like saucers, his mouth wide open. He didn't look like he was even trying to roll over onto his stomach and get into the self-arrest position.

All four of us guides screamed, "Arrest! Arrest! Arrest!" The guy hit a little bulge in the slope and slowed down. We thought, *Now's your chance! Arrest!* But he just sat there. Slowly he slid over another bulge, then hurtled a thousand feet down the Emmons Glacier.

The four of us split up. Robert and another guide continued up toward the climber with the broken leg, while Dave Hahn and I headed down to look for the soloist. All the way down, we could follow his trail by splotches of blood on the ice. We found his ax, which had happened to stick in the ice, probably after he had lost control of it. The trail finally ended in a crevasse. We could see where the guy had shot into the crevasse and hit the lower wall, and we could see his body lying there. I belayed Dave down into the crevasse, but we knew at once the man was dead.

Okay, we said, there's nothing we can do for him. So we climbed the thousand feet back up to help Robert and the other guide. Then we splinted the guy with the broken leg. Meanwhile, a big Chinook helicopter was coming in. It was a really steep slope, a dicey place for a pickup. The pilot had to hover with only one tire resting on the slope, while the front rotor blades spun just inches from the cliff face above us. We were ducking under the blades as we got the survivor on board. Then, with no time to spare, we jammed the dead body of his friend into the chopper. It was a horrible struggle— the guy's climbing harness kept snagging on the door. At last the Chinook took off. The pilot had pulled off an amazing rescue and body retrieval.

The soloist's last words to me stayed with me for a long time: "It's only Mount Rainier." It doesn't matter how good you are—in the mountains, just when you think you're in control, you aren't.

Lou Whittaker has a saying: "Just because you love the mountains doesn't mean the mountains love you."

One winter in the early 1980s, Andy Politz and I decided to try Rainier by the Gibraltar Ledges route, not acting as guides, just climbing on our own. Winter ascents were few and far between, but we were intrigued by the challenge and delighted to have the mountain all to ourselves. We got up to Camp Muir, only that night the winds came up and the weather got really gnarly. We convinced each other to make an attempt anyway—it'll be good training. We put on all our down gear and charged out into the storm. But after a few hours, we agreed that it was far too windy, and we made our way back down to Muir. Andy had already gotten minor frostnip on his windward cheek.

I thought we should spend the night in the guides' hut, sit out the storm, and go down the next day, but Andy said, "I have a date tonight. If we get down early enough, I can still go out with her."

So, against my better judgment, we started to battle our way down in high winds and complete whiteout. Since we had carried our skis all the way up, Andy insisted on trying to ski down the 4,000 feet of the Muir Snowfield, a scheme I tried to veto. On skis, without being able hold compass bearings on each other, it took us only ten minutes to get completely disoriented. I put my foot down and said, "Okay, Andy, let's walk from here on." For a while, we'd leapfrog, one of us going ahead while the other tried to hold a compass bearing on him. It took us eight hours to descend what normally took two or three. The slopes were steep, loaded with new snow. We needed to be careful.

Eventually, right at dusk, we got down to tree line, but we were still not "out of the woods." All at once Andy became determined to head down a really steep slope. I balked. He said, "I'll just check it out."

Suddenly he disappeared into the void. He'd set off a small slough of an avalanche and ridden it down. I yelled, "Andy! Andy!"

After a moment, I heard his distant answer: "Don't come down!"

I said to myself, I'm not going another step until I can see a lot better. I yelled, "Andy, I'm staying here!"

He ended up staggering down to Paradise in the night without a headlamp, then sleeping on the floor of the public bathroom. Meanwhile, I dug myself a snow cave. I didn't have a shovel, so I used a pot lid. No sleeping bag or pad, either, since we had counted on the bags and pads that were permanently stashed at Camp Muir. All I had was a batch of bamboo willow wands, which I laid out as a mattress. Inside the cave, it was about twenty-five degrees Fahrenheit. I spent a sleepless night, but it wasn't a life-or-death ordeal. All I had for food was a single Snickers bar. I kept staring at it. I wanted to scarf it down right away, but I thought that if the storm continued, I might have to bivouac another night, or even two. Should I just take a small bite, I debated, to make it last?

In the morning, with the sun out, I could orient. I got down to Paradise in an hour. My night out became infamous in RMI circles as the "bamboo bivouac."

Andy's frostnip had begun to fester; by the morning it was oozing some kind of vile pus. As soon as we were reunited, the first thing he said was "I missed my date last night, but I can probably go out with her tonight."

I answered, "Yeah, you look really attractive with that oozing cheek. Maybe she can dip her chips into it instead of salsa."

▲
▲
▲

Meanwhile, from 1983 through 1987, I was spending the off-season in Pullman, working my way toward my DVM at Washington State. As hard as I studied, I found everything about becoming a vet both fascinating and challenging. Because animals can't talk to you, you have to be something of a detective. Getting an accurate history of a pet's symptoms, then running a series of tests that can lead by a process of elimination to a diagnosis presents many of the same difficulties as does pediatrics, since children, too, are not always reliable reporters of what's wrong.

In intensive anatomy courses, I learned every single muscle, bone, organ, nerve, and artery of not only the dog and the cat but the horse, the pig, the cow, and the chicken. I studied the basics of radiology, surgery, pharmacology, and pathology. We were in classes all day, then studied nights and weekends. We'd take dozens of pages of notes each day, then try to absorb it all each evening. At times I felt overwhelmed by the volume and complexity of the material we were being force-fed.

During those school years, I had no time to climb—my only climbing was in the summer guiding for RMI. My compensation was to run mile after mile on the county roads that wound through the rolling hills around

Pullman. Still, the lack of freedom felt oppressive. I kept telling myself, *Once I'm out of school and get a job, I'll be free to do whatever I want.*

Wrong! After I graduated in 1987, I took a job with my friend Carl Anderson, who ran a clinic in Seattle. I had met him and Steve Swaim at Northeast Veterinary Hospital. They had both promised me jobs after I graduated. But now I discovered that work was, if anything, more intense than school. Carl would say, "Ed, you're on today. I'm not even going to show up."

Whoa...suddenly I'm in charge of everything, I'm making life-and-death decisions. I guess I was a bit hyperresponsible, but I was always aware that the animals needed me, and that people were paying good money to rely on me. For them, a pet was a member of the family.

On any given day, I'd be vaccinating a puppy in one room while another dog was dying of something or other in the back room. I'd be waiting for lab results on one pet and scheduling surgery on another. And there'd be three or four phone messages I hadn't answered. It was all interesting work, but I'd go home every night completely wiped out. I'd have three dogs in the clinic that I'd treated that day. At home, I'd get out my textbooks and read up to make sure I'd done the right thing. Sometimes I'd drive back to the clinic at night just to check that the dogs were still alive, that their IVs were still dripping on schedule.

I never had any true disasters, but there were some pretty freaky cases. One time, while I was working at Steve Swaim's clinic in Reston, he scheduled surgery for a big rottweiler, a well-known breeder whose puppies sold for high prices. The owner had decided to have the dog spayed. It's a fairly routine procedure: you make a small incision in the abdomen and remove the uterus and the ovaries. Since it was going to be his day off, Steve turned the job over to me.

So I gave the dog a sedative, hooked up an IV drip, then injected a general anesthetic. Once the dog was intubated, I had to lay her on her back, shave her belly, scrub and rescrub her, scrub myself, get gowned and masked, then surgically drape the site of the incision. There was a tech assistant monitoring the anesthesia, adding a little more or cutting it to a little less. You can lose an animal under anesthesia.

I made the small incision. Then I took a special hook, which you're supposed to run inside the body wall to catch the uterus and bring it into view. I dug in and dug in—nothing. Where is it? I thought. I made a larger incision. All of a sudden, I realized the dog was pregnant. There were maybe sixteen puppies in there, not full-term, but just the same.... The uterus looked like two big sausages pressed together. Because of the pregnancy, the dog's uterine blood vessels were swollen to the size of my thumb. The uterus was huge—five times its normal size. The hook had been way too small to catch this oversized organ.

Under my surgical cap, I was sweating bullets. I thought, Oh, my God, I hope I don't screw this one up. In the middle of the operation, I had to call the owner to make sure she didn't want the puppies. She didn't. I carefully tied off and cut the throbbing uterine blood vessels, hoping they wouldn't explode. Then I had to remove everything inside the dog's womb.

That rottweiler went home with a ten-inch, rather than a two-inch, incision in her belly. But I'd done the procedure all right. And this was after only a year of veterinary experience. In school, they don't teach you all the stuff you're going to need in the operating room. Sometimes you just have to think on your feet.

▲
▲
▲

My life's plan was to work as a vet so I could support my passion for climbing. But even by the early 1980s, I was starting to wonder if those two pursuits were incompatible. I went on my first expedition in the summer of 1983, after my first year of vet school. RMI had already started its program of guiding clients on Denali (Mount McKinley), at 20,320 feet the highest peak in North America. That year, Phil Ershler had Dick Bass and Frank Wells as clients, in the middle of their campaign to be the first climbers to bag the Seven Summits. Ershler invited Andy Politz and me as assistant guides.

Bass was a Texas oilman, Wells a Hollywood executive. Both men had come to climbing relatively late in life—Bass was fifty-three that summer, Wells fifty-one—and they were, strictly speaking, amateurs, since they needed guides to get up such mountains as Denali, the Vinson Massif in Antarctica, and Aconcagua in Argentina. Bass would complete the Seven Summits in 1985 when he climbed Everest, guided by David Breashears.

Bass was a character. Loud, boisterous—he brought along a big hard-back copy of Robert Service's poems, and every night he'd either read them out loud or recite them from memory. He was our evening's entertainment. For someone who'd started climbing late in life, he was actually quite good; he'd just plod steadily along. And he had considerable nerve. On the summit ridge of Everest with Breashears in '85, he climbed the final slopes without the aid of fixed ropes—a feat almost never performed nowadays by clients. On Denali, Wells was a little more of a stumbler, left-footed on both sides, so we had to keep an eye on him.

We climbed the West Buttress route, which had become the standard itinerary after Bradford Washburn had pioneered it in 1951. With relative ease, we reached the plateau at 14,000 feet, then got slammed by a five-day storm. After that, we made it to high camp at 17,000 feet, only to sit out another four-day storm. We started to run out of food. Bass and Wells were hell-bent to knock off Denali, however: they had a tight schedule for their Seven Summits. In the middle of the storm, Bass said, "We may just have to go all the way back down to base camp, resupply, and come back up here."

Then it cleared. Bass and Wells had hired cameraman and climber Steve Marts to make a film of their quest. It was Andy's and my job to take turns carrying the heavy tripod. One of us would run ahead with Steve and set up the tripod, so he could film the heroes climbing past; then we'd pack up the tripod, dash ahead, and set it up again. This kind of leapfrogging was hard work, but I thoroughly enjoyed the whole thing. Other than lugging the tripod, the summit climb was almost routine. It wasn't that cold on top, not like it often gets on Denali, thirty below with a wind. The successful climb only whetted my appetite to go higher, to see how I'd perform at Himalayan altitudes.

We didn't get paid to go to Denali, just a free trip to Alaska, so Andy and I actually took a financial hit by going on the expedition. Two years later, Eric Simonson invited me on a more ambitious project, a traverse of Denali—up the West Buttress and down the Muldrow route, fording the McKinley River, and hiking across the tundra all the way out to the Denali Highway. There were eight clients, with just Eric and me as guides.

It's a lot harder descending a route you haven't seen before than climbing up it, and the Muldrow, even though it was the first ascent route way back in 1913, is considerably more difficult than the West Buttress. And traversing the mountain meant that we'd have to carry all our gear up and over, rather than leaving much of it in stocked camps. Our loads were so heavy that we dragged them in sleds. There were huge crevasse fields on the Muldrow Glacier that we had to negotiate our way through. But we pulled that trip off, too, without a hitch, completing the traverse in nineteen days.

Coming out across the tundra, we were in grizzly bear country. Eric carried a .357—a real Clint Eastwood *Magnum Force* handgun—all the way up and over. I remember him in the tent one night taking out the gun to polish it. "Ed," he said, waving the .357 in front of me, with a glint in his eye, "there's six bullets in this thing. If you see a bear, use five bullets on the bear, and save one for yourself."

Besides the fact that both of my Denali expeditions were great adventures in their own right, by going along I got in good with senior guides such as Simonson and Ershler. I knew that if I performed well on Denali, they might think, Hey, Ed's the kind of guide we'd take along somewhere else. My motto was "Keep your mouth shut and work hard."

Sure enough, in 1987 Eric invited me to go to Mount Everest. He'd been to the mountain in 1982, on an expedition led by Lou Whittaker that had attempted the Great Couloir route on the mountain's north face. On that trip, Eric had climbed as high as the Yellow Band, just above 27,000 feet. But no one had summited. The expedition had turned tragic when Marty Hoey, one of the leading American women climbers and the only woman on the expedition, fell to her death. In the middle of what should have been a completely routine procedure, while she was clipped into a fixed rope, she leaned back to let a teammate pass. Somehow her waist harness came undone and she plunged out of control, thousands of feet down the couloir. It was later surmised that Hoey had made the simple mistake of not back-buckling her harness. Without that double insurance, the webbing of the waist loop can actually slide through the buckle under tension. It's now common practice, even among the best climbers, not only to double-check your own harness but to check your partner's as well.

In 1987, a rich fellow from Arkansas named Jack Allsup hired Eric to lead another expedition to the Great Couloir. Allsup's wife and two others, all four from Arkansas, made up the clientele. (We officially called ourselves the Arkansas Everest Expedition.) Eric invited four other RMI guides: George Dunn, Greg Wilson, Craig Van Hoy, and me. It was a strong party— this would be George's third try at Everest, Greg and Eric's second. And we had five Sherpas and a cook. Allsup paid for the whole thing, although in those days an Everest permit cost only $3,000.

The trip was a bit of a boondoggle for us, since the Arkansans thought they had enough experience to climb the mountain themselves. Our job was to carry loads, including the Arkansans' oxygen bottles; to fix ropes; and to establish the camps, but not to guide the clients on their attempt. We were free to make our own summit bid first; once the way was paved, they'd go up on their own.

I was thrilled to be invited. I was twenty-seven, and the dream I'd cherished since I'd first read *Annapurna* in high school was on the verge of coming true. Thanks to Rainier and RMI, I'd worked my way into position to go on a Himalayan expedition.

Yet in another sense, the invitation couldn't have come at a more awkward time. The spring of 1987 was my last semester in grad school at Washington State. How could I just skip out for two months or more and still graduate with my doctorate in veterinary medicine? School got out on June 1, but we were scheduled to leave for Tibet on March 1.

Fortunately, the system of the school broke the senior year into ten "blocks" from August through May—one-month periods of intensive study in surgery, advanced radiology, and other disciplines. Of the ten blocks, two were designated as vacation blocks, and we always had June and July off. Another block was called "externship," during which you worked at a clinic instead of taking classes.

In the summer of '86, I guided for RMI in June and July and started my blocks at Washington State in August. The system was flexible enough that I could trade blocks with other students, arranging them to fit my needs. I managed to schedule March for my externship block, then talked the vet at the clinic where I was supposed to work into postponing my commitment to him until I got back from Everest. And I kept April and May free as my vacation blocks. That alone allowed me to accept Eric's invitation. I missed graduation, but I was awarded my doctorate while I was on Everest. To my surprise and delight, I was also granted the honor of being chosen as the best surgeon in my class.

In the end, the Arkansas group never got above 25,000 feet. The climbing proved too hard for them. Meanwhile, we guides fixed ropes up the steep, exposed route. Near the top of the endless couloir, there are two obstacles, bands of rock that sweep across your path. The Yellow Band is at 27,000 feet, the Gray Band even higher. Greg Wilson and George Dunn had managed to fix ropes through the difficult Yellow Band on their bid for the summit. Having used up precious time and energy on this effort, which was crucial to our getting higher on the mountain, they were unable to push on to the top.

Three days later, Eric, Craig Van Hoy, and I jumared up the ropes in the couloir to our highest camp, at 26,800 feet. There, the three of us jammed ourselves like sardines into a small two-man tent pitched on a very steep slope.

On May 20, after a sleepless, claustrophobic night, the three of us set out for the summit. Eric got moving first; I was a few minutes behind him. Craig simply peered out the tent door, decided he didn't like the looks of the top of the Great Couloir, and chose to go down.

From that very first Himalayan expedition on, I was determined to climb without supplemental oxygen. On both Denali trips, I had felt stronger than the other guides. We'd get back to camp after a rough day, and they'd be exhausted. I'd feel tired but not wiped out. I'd actually feel pretty good. Of course, 20,320 feet (the height of the summit of Denali) is a far cry from 29,035 (the top of Everest).

I'd also been deeply impressed by the achievement of Reinhold Messner and Peter Habeler in 1978, when they defied the doomsayers and climbed Everest without bottled oxygen, and then by Messner's amazing solo, oxygenless climb in 1980 of the very Great Couloir we were now attempting. I'd never worn an oxygen mask, but I had a notion that to put one over your face was to isolate yourself from the mountain. I wanted instead to stick my nose in the reality of 29,000 feet. Besides, a mask, a regulator, and a set of bottles seemed cumbersome, and the whole thing amounted to a system that could fail, and when it failed, you failed. To me, the mechanical apparatus of supplemental oxygen complicated the climb, whereas I wanted only to simplify it as much as possible. I thought, If you're going to go to a 29,000-foot mountain, then climb a 29,000-foot mountain—don't artificially reduce it to a 26,000-foot mountain.

So we set off that morning, Eric with oxygen, me without. We still had to fix ropes up the Gray Band, to safeguard our retreat. I remember Eric saying, "Ed, I've got three oxygen bottles—you think you can carry the five-hundred-foot coil of rope?" I groaned inwardly, but I carried the rope and some other gear.

As we climbed slowly, with Eric in the lead, a Swedish climber from another expedition came zooming up the couloir toward us. It was unbelievable how quickly he was gaining on us. He'd left his own camp, which was two hours below ours, and now he had his oxygen cranked up to the max. He climbed through the Yellow Band with us, right to the foot of the Gray Band, then suddenly ran out of oxygen and literally stopped in his tracks. Having shot his wad, he turned around and descended. Now it was down to Eric and me.

We fixed our last bit of rope up a steep snow gully through the Gray Band, running out of line fifty feet short of the top of the gully, so we had to climb the last sixty-degree section unroped. Finally we reached the summit pyramid. The slope above was too exposed, the snow too dry and dangerous to head straight up, so we traversed right toward the West Ridge, the route that Willi Unsoeld and Tom Hornbein had pioneered in 1963 in the course of their brilliant traverse of Everest. High on the West Ridge, they had climbed technical terrain they knew they couldn't get back down, making an irreversible decision—up and over or die.

Aided by the gas he was breathing, Eric stayed a few hundred yards ahead of me all day. We got to the West Ridge. I was tooling along as a thought dawned on me: *My God, we're going to make it to the summit!*

But by now it was after one P.M. The sky was starting to get cloudy. Up ahead, I could see Eric scooting around on the West Ridge, trying to find a route through the technical rocks. And then he was turned around, coming back toward me. "Ed," he said, when we stood together, "we can probably get up this thing, but there's no way we can get down without a rope."

I took a hard look of my own. We were only 300 vertical feet below the summit, but that could take us a couple of hours. And the weather was worsening, a light snow beginning to fall. Eric was right: we could probably get to the top, but coming down would be epic at best, suicidal at worst. I said, "All right. I agree."

The disappointment was huge. But it wasn't an "ah, shit!" kind of thing—it was a completely logical decision. Yet all the way back to camp, and then down the Great Couloir, I kept thinking, Damn it, now I have to go all the way home, then come all the way back here, just to climb those last three hundred feet. When I start a project, I don't like to leave it unfinished. I can't let it go. And even though we'd been really close to the top, I had no guarantee that I could climb those last 300 feet without oxygen. At 29,000 feet, the difficulties increase exponentially. There was still a mystery: would I be strong enough to finish that final bit of the mountain?

I thought about those last 300 feet every day for the next three years.

With Andy Politz, I went back to Everest in the autumn of 1988. By then, I'd graduated from Washington State and was working in Steve

Swaim's clinic. The freedom to do whatever I wanted that I'd thought would come after grad school hadn't materialized; my job as a real vet was more demanding than school had been.

When I asked Steve about taking time off to go to Everest, he was nice enough. "Yeah, you'll still have your job when you get back," he said. "But this isn't going to happen again, is it?"

Andy and I had been invited to try the east, or Kangshung, face of Everest. The rest of our team was a group of five guys from Georgia—they were more rock climbers than mountaineers, but they had some alpine experience in the Andes. They'd hired Andy for his Himalayan experience, and Andy had invited me. The Georgia guys had raised the money.

The Kangshung is the most dangerous of Everest's three major faces, and it was the last to be climbed, by a very strong American team in 1983. Two years earlier, on the first attempt on the face, John Roskelley, who at the time was probably our country's finest Himalayan mountaineer, took one look at the face, declared it unjustifiably dangerous, and promptly left the expedition.

In the spring of 1988, just four months before we went to the east face, a four-man team worked out a new route far to the left of the 1983 line. That new route had one aesthetic drawback, in that it led not straight to the summit but to the South Col, so that the last 3,000 feet of climbing repeated what by then was becoming the "trade route" on Everest, the line pioneered by Tenzing and Hillary. Even so, the climbing was so difficult lower down that it took a stern toll on the party. Only one member, the gutsy Brit Stephen Venables, eventually made the summit. On his way toward the top, Ed Webster, a fine American climber, made the mistake of taking off his gloves for a few brief moments to shoot a picture, incurring frostbite that later cost him several fingers—and cost him the summit, as well.

Andy and I chose to try the Venables-Webster route, but it was something of a mistake to go in the autumn, postmonsoon season. There was more snow on the mountain than in the spring; the avalanche conditions were atrocious. The face was also exposed to huge ice cliffs dangling above, which could calve loose big seracs at any moment. For this reason, the Kang-shung Face was regarded as dangerous in all seasons.

One camp at the foot of the wall lay in the hollow of a bowl surrounded by avalanche slopes on three sides. We pitched our tents there as far away as we could from these slopes, but even so, our camp got pummeled by the windblasts from gigantic avalanches coming from all three directions. On one occasion, when the camp was unoccupied, a formidable blast destroyed half our tents. In our absence, the goraks—giant Himalayan ravens, famous for eating the bodies of dead climbers—scarfed down all the food the windblast had exposed.

To minimize the risk, we chose to climb at night, when the temperatures dropped, making the slopes above relatively stable. One such night, wearing headlamps, Andy and I were climbing on the lower but fairly severe first pitches of the face. We heard something big come rumbling down from out of sight above. We just hung on, a fixed rope in one hand, an ice tool in the other, as we got blasted—whether by spindrift or by the edge of a real avalanche, I was never sure. All that I could see was the chaos of moving snow spotlighted in the narrow beam of my headlamp. I said to Andy, "This is not fun. This is scary. In fact, it's ridiculous."

Back at camp, I told the others, "This route is nuts. I'm not going back up. If you want to, I'll support you guys from below." Pretty soon the others agreed: "Yeah, you're right. This is not smart." We reached an altitude of only 19,000 feet—a full 10,000 feet short of the summit. In a sense, the expedition was a complete fiasco. But at least we backed off before anybody got hurt or killed.

That setback only fueled my Himalayan addiction. When Lou Whittaker organized an expedition to 28,209-foot Kangchenjunga, the world's third-highest mountain, for the spring of 1989 and invited me along, there was no way I could say no.

But by now it was time for me to take a long, hard look at the juggling act I was trying to pull off: a career as a veterinarian somehow folded into my burgeoning ambitions as a Himalayan mountaineer (not to mention spending summers on Rainier as an RMI guide). I decided something had to give. Sadly, it was my practice as a vet.

It had been hard enough to take off two months in the fall of 1988 to go to the Kangshung Face. By then, I was working two days a week each at two clinics, run by Steve Swaim and Carl Anderson. No sooner had I gotten back from Everest than I was invited on an expedition to Aconcagua, the highest peak in South America. It would take place in the winter months, when it was summer in the Southern Hemisphere. And Kangchenjunga was already looming for the spring of '89.

The writing was on the wall. I had to tell Steve, "Yeah, it *is* going to happen again." Both he and Carl said to me, "Ed, this just isn't working out for us. But it's totally okay. You can't turn down an invitation to go to Kangchenjunga. You need to do what you need to do."

So, with regret, I resigned from my jobs at both clinics. At the time, I thought that maybe I'd just take a two- or three-year sabbatical from being a vet. Had I known I would never return to the profession I'd worked so hard to attain, I might have been even more regretful—if not completely freaked out.

The Kangchenjunga team was a very competent one: the nucleus was RMI guides with previous Himalayan experience, including George Dunn, Phil Ershler, Larry Nielson, and Greg Wilson. Eric Simonson was our ground man, in charge of getting the gear, which we had shipped months earlier to Calcutta, through India and across the border to us in Nepal.

Our cadre of climbers was reinforced by the addition of John Roskelley and another top-notch Washington State climber, Jim Wickwire. I was slightly intimidated by the prospect of these two legendary mountaineers joining our team. If you're into basketball, climbing with Roskelley or Wickwire might be likened to shooting hoops with Michael Jordan. As a kid in Rockford, Illinois, I'd put a poster of Wickwire up on my wall. And Roskelley seemed to me the finest American alpinist of his generation. He was never afraid to speak his mind, no matter whose feelings he bruised. He lived by his own rules, one of which was never to jumar up a fixed rope he hadn't placed himself. His refusal to be swayed by others' opinions seemed to me a valuable attribute in risky places.

John and Jim planned to arrive at our base camp later than the rest of us, fresh off an expedition to a spectacular unclimbed 23,559-foot peak called Menlungtse, on the Nepal-Tibet border.

Kangchenjunga is a huge, sprawling mountain with lots of possible lines on it. We chose an approach from the north, leading to a new route on the west face sandwiched between a pair of lines originally put up by the famous mountaineers Doug Scott and Reinhold Messner. At first the expedition was jeopardized by the late arrival of most of our gear at base camp, a delay caused by political friction between India and Nepal. The timing could not have been worse. Our cargo truck was stuck in a massive jam of vehicles trickling across the border between India and Nepal. It was only thanks to Eric, who negotiated brilliantly and greased palms with a bribe or two, that we got our truck to the head of the line. Meanwhile, we'd done what climbing we could, managing to establish two camps on the lower slopes of the mountain.

Eventually about three-quarters of our gear arrived via helicopter, allowing us to work our way higher up the mountain. The crux of our route was the 3,000-foot west face leading to the north ridge. Here there was a lot of steep rock and ice—terrain at angles of up to fifty degrees—and fixing ropes up these pitches took us a full two weeks. Roskelley and Nielson performed most of the leads on the face; in 1983, Larry had become the first American to climb Everest without supplemental oxygen.

I was often teamed with Roskelley and Wickwire, and I belayed John on many of his spectacular leads. Still comparatively green at high-altitude technical climbing, I learned a lot by watching a master perform his craft. Usually, Jim would follow us, carrying the rope we'd need to fix on that day's climbing. But now he was moving uncharacteristically slowly—something didn't seem right with him.

Eventually, a doctor would diagnose Jim with pneumonia. To everybody's regret, he decided to head home. About this time, John and I reached the top of the north ridge. The most difficult part of the climb was behind us, but the ridge above looked like no cakewalk. As we sat there, John told me he was going to head home with Jim. I was blown away. This was John's second attempt on Kangchenjunga, and now he was in a perfect position to reach the summit. But he alluded vaguely to "personal reasons," while admitting that something to do with our team dynamics didn't sit well with him. He also wanted to accompany his good friend Wickwire on the trek out.

After Jim and John's departure, we hunkered down through a spell of bad weather. But by May 17, three of us were established in Camp V, at 24,000 feet. The next day, under perfect skies, in eight and a half hours of climbing, Phil Ershler, Craig Van Hoy, and I got to the summit, Craig and I without supplemental oxygen. We climbed roped, with Craig in the middle. When Phil was out in front, it was all Craig and I could do to keep up with his pace, abetted as it was by bottled oxygen. When I led, I found it tremendously tiring to kick steps, but at least I could set the pace. Other than a stretch of snow with an annoying crust we had to kick our boots through, the conditions were excellent.

At one P.M. on May 18, the three of us reached the top. After forty-three days on the mountain, at last I'd climbed an 8,000-meter peak. Three days later, another trio of teammates made it to the top. All in all, it was a wonderfully successful expedition.

Before the first ascent of Kangchenjunga, by the British in 1955, the team leader, Charles Evans, had been told that the people of Sikkim, the Indian state that borders the great mountain on the east, were dead set against its being climbed. To the Sikkimese, *Kangchenjunga* means "the Five Treasures of the Snow"; the mountain was a god and a protector. In an audience with the maharaja of Sikkim before the expedition got started, Evans won permission for the ascent only by promising that his team would not set foot on the very summit. Accordingly, on May 25, 1955, George Band and Joe Brown stopped twenty feet short of the summit, with only an easy snow slope ahead. No other mountaineers, however, have ever quibbled with their claim of the first ascent.

And on May 18, 1989, Phil, Craig, and I, out of a kindred respect for the mountain gods, stopped just short of the true summit, which was only a few seconds' stroll away. Instead, we spent an hour on that high ridge, in calm, sunny weather, taking in the views and feeling the kind of profound satisfaction that climbing one of the world's highest peaks can bring. Eighty miles to the east, I could see the clear outline of Everest, beckoning me to return.

The moment I got back to base camp, Lou Whittaker told me that his brother, Jim—the first American ever to reach the highest point on earth, back in 1963—was planning a big multinational expedition to Everest for the spring of 1990, and that Jim wanted me along. Once again, there was no way I could say no.

After his ascent of Everest in '63, Jim had entertained certain political ambitions, as he made friends with top figures in the Democratic establishment of the day. In 1965, he led the first ascent of an unclimbed 13,904-foot peak in the Yukon. Among the party was Senator Robert Kennedy, who had never climbed a real mountain in his life. The team named the virgin peak Mount Kennedy, after Bobby's brother, assassinated just two years before.

Mount Kennedy has some truly imposing faces and ridges, on which later mountaineers have put up cutting-edge routes. But the route of the first ascent was little more than a snow slog. The scuttlebutt had it that Bobby Kennedy was all but dragged up the peak, prodded onward by Jim Whittaker and the other climbers, who saw the political value for themselves—as well as for Bobby's eventual campaign for the presidency—in his reaching the summit. In any event, Bobby was a good athlete in reasonable shape, thirty-nine years old at the time, and he got to the top.

The naming and first ascent of Mount Kennedy were decried by many mountaineers as a publicity stunt, but the deed did work its predicted political magic.

By the late 1980s, Jim had befriended other figures in important government positions. It was the height of the Cold War, and Jim and two of his political cronies were discussing how to make a statement for world peace. Out of their confab came the idea for what Jim would call the Everest International Peace Climb. The concept was to bring together mountaineers from the three mutually antagonistic superpowers—China, the Soviet Union, and the United States—for a joint campaign on the north ridge of Mount Everest, the route of the first attempts on the mountain in the 1920s, where Mallory and Irvine had disappeared near the summit in 1924. As Jim would write in the 1991 *American Alpine Journal:*

Our goal was to place three climbers, one from each country, on the top of the world. They would demonstrate that through friendship and cooperation high goals can be reached. We chose our enemies to climb with—the Soviets and the Chinese. This was before glasnost, *before* perestroika, *before the Reagan-Gorbachev summit, before Gorbachev went to Beijing. We would hold the summit of all summit meetings, enemies becoming friends.*

The expedition was also to be a cleanup campaign, as the members removed trash from camps and empty oxygen bottles from the north ridge. In Jim's pithy phrase, we would try to "clean the world off from the top down."

For me, the invitation to go on the Peace Climb meant another crack at Everest. The sting of stopping only 300 feet below the summit in 1987 had diminished almost not at all over the succeeding three years.

And for once on a Himalayan expedition, everything seemed to go like clockwork. In the end, the Chinese sent only Tibetan climbers to Everest; either they regarded Tibetans as true Chinese, because they had occupied that country since 1950, or the principal climbers from China proper simply weren't strong enough. I thought it a cruel irony that the Chinese government would choose their Everest representatives from among a people they had oppressed for decades.

By early May, after eight weeks of work, we were in position for the first summit attempt. Jim had asked me to be on that team, but now he was insisting that every climber on the first assault use bottled oxygen, to maximize the chances of success. Even before the expedition, as I'd accepted his invitation, I'd told Jim, "I know how you want to plan this climb, but I'm not going up with oxygen." But Jim's a stubborn guy. So am I. A day or two before the first summit team set out, he pleaded with me to be one of the two Americans in that six-man party. He later told a journalist, "I picked Ed because he was so strong, but also because of all his experience as a guide on Rainier, watching out for other people."

I had to repeat my demurral: "Sorry, Jim, I'm not climbing it with oxygen. It's fine with me if you put somebody else on the first attempt."

He said, "Go to bed and sleep on it."

"Jim—I'm not going to change my mind."

On May 7, two Soviets, two Tibetans, and the Americans Robert Link and Steve Gall made it to the top. The pressure was now off—the Peace Climb had succeeded in its stated goal. As Jim himself later wrote in the *American Alpine Journal,* "After placing the two from each country on top together, we were free to try for the summit in any style we wished." The next day, May 8, two Soviets and I set out from our high camp at 27,000 feet.

The last section of the northeast ridge is actually the most technical part of the entire route. It's made of downsloping slabs of rock, like roofing tiles, covered with loose powder snow, with thousands of feet of exposure below your boots. The two chief obstacles are the notorious First and Second Steps, both of which present blank thirty-foot-high vertical rock faces. Each was equipped with a short fixed rope, and the Second Step is now made much easier by an aluminum ladder that, quite amazingly, the Chinese carried up and bolted to the cliff in 1975. Otherwise, however, there were no fixed ropes in place in 1990.

As my crampons scraped and skittered for purchase on the slick, angled rock, I moved with the utmost caution. Any slip here would mean a fatal fall. One of the Soviets was using bottled oxygen, so he quickly got far ahead of me. Yet his partner, Andrei Tselinshchev, was so strong that even without oxygen he kept up with his buddy. Climbing solo behind them, I still felt confident of my abilities.

Once I'd surmounted the Second Step, I found myself again only 300 feet below the summit, just as Eric and I had been in 1987. First I had to traverse a slope that was smothered in deep, unconsolidated powder snow. Plowing through these drifts was both physically and mentally taxing. I had to take fifteen breaths for each step, and after some steps I slid back, losing half the progress I'd gained with my last stride. I looked ahead for land-marks. A small outcrop of rock or plume of snow became my immediate goal; once I reached it, I'd pick another landmark. The summit still seemed inconceivably far away. I felt sluggish and lethargic, ready to doze off midstep—whether from hypoxia, boredom with my snail's pace, or simple lack of sleep over the previous several days, I couldn't say.

Near the end of that traverse, I met the two Soviets coming down from their successful summit push. We clapped each other on the back and hugged briefly but exchanged few words, since they spoke very little English and I spoke no Russian. Then I pushed on, as they descended be-hind me.

Finally I reached the summit block of rock. The vigilance required to climb it snapped me out of my daze, back to full attention. A steep snow gully led to the summit ridge. As I climbed the last few feet to the top, I was overwhelmed with a sense of incredulity—here, at last, was the goal toward which I had been striving since I'd dared to dream about it as a teenager. I stepped onto the very summit, tears freezing to my cheeks.

At that moment, alone both physically and emotionally, I was the highest person in the world. I felt that there was little chance I'd ever return to the top of Everest, so I wanted the memory to last. I shot several self-portraits with my camera, then took in the panoramic view of ridge upon ridge of lower mountains receding from me likes waves on the sea. After less than an hour on the summit, I turned to start my descent. As I always would on every 8,000-meter peak, I reminded myself that the climb was only half over. An inordinate number of even the most experienced climbers have come to grief on the way down from a successful summit bid.

Thanks to good weather and impeccable logistics, the Peace Climb be-came the most successful Everest expedition in history; we got twenty climbers to the summit without a single serious accident. In spite of certain conflicts within the team, Jim Whittaker's leadership was the glue that held our expedition together. I was the only American to top out without sup-plemental oxygen, though four of the Soviets also pulled off the feat.

After three years, I had solved my Everest bugaboo. And I'd climbed the mountain in the style I had determined to practice on all my climbs of the highest peaks.

In the years since I first stood on top of Everest, the question I get asked more than any other is "Why? Why do you do it? Why is climbing so great?"

It's the eternal question every mountaineer has grappled with, and to which few have given coherent replies. I have a short answer and a long answer. The short answer is "If you have to ask, you'll never know."

In my long answer, I try to be a little less flippant. Because, after all, it's a reasonable question: the nonmountaineer watching my slide show sees mostly suffering, cold, risk, and even loss of life. So I try to explain that simply by nature, I'm extremely goal-oriented and personally motivated. I have a lot of drive and like to push myself. I like things that aren't too easy, that don't come too quickly.

And the mountains are a beautiful arena in which to face such challenges. On top of that, you face them with a few carefully chosen friends who have similar goals, aspirations, and work ethics. A great climb is a wonderful mixture of difficulty and intimacy. The challenge is both physical (that's where my fanatic training comes in) and mental. If your body is willing, your mind can push it to do amazing things.

Finally, big-range mountaineering is itself addictive. When I come down from a peak, come home from Nepal or Pakistan, it doesn't take long before I'm craving more of the same. I need that fix once more.

Immediately upon my return from Nepal, I went back to Rainier for my ninth straight summer of guiding for RMI. But that fall, instead of working as a vet, I was building houses for twenty dollars an hour, just because it was the kind of job you could drop at a moment's notice to go off on another expedition.

I was working for a friend of mine named Dan Hiatt. I already possessed basic carpentry skills, but Dan taught me the finer tricks of the trade. And he was perfectly understanding about my absences—basically, he said, "Ed, you can come and go as you please." Even so, it was a scary plunge to leave my veterinary career on indefinite hold while I tried to make ends meet by pounding nails and guiding for RMI.

The winter of 1990–91 was frightfully cold and wet, even by Seattle standards. To get a house built in the Pacific Northwest, you have to work come rain or come shine. That winter, Dan and I were building the house that he would move into with his family, once it was finished—a big three-story structure in West Seattle on a bluff overlooking Puget Sound. The house was perched on a hill some twenty feet above the street that led to it. Every week, a delivery truck deposited a huge pile of raw lumber. We had to carry it piece by piece—roof beams, plywood panels, and countless two-by-sixes—up to the site. Then we hand-nailed every stick in place.

Dan had a crotchet about not building any stairs until the house was almost completed. Stairs would have made our lives a lot easier, but since I didn't yet know how to build them, I was at Dan's mercy. Instead, for months on end, we climbed like monkeys up a series of ladders, carrying our precious lumber as we built higher and higher on the house. It was a hell of a workout.

We'd keep working even during steady downpours or in freezing temperatures. Finally, though, we established our "three-shock rule." On a rainy day, if we got three shocks as we operated our power tools, we could call it quits and go out for coffee. On the bad days, our cries would echo through the house. *Zap!* "One!" Dan would yell from the living room. "Two!" I would call out from upstairs. "Three!"—upon which, we dropped our gear and fled to Starbucks.

For me, time was money. On days when Dan had other commitments, I'd work on my own to keep the twenty-dollar-an-hour pipeline flowing. One day when Dan was out of town, I had to wrestle four-by-eight-foot sheets of plywood up to the steeply-angled roof, thirty-five feet off the ground. The forecast was for freezing rain in the afternoon, but I was determined to work till the last minute. Using the nylon webbing of my climbing slings, I rigged a handle on each sheet. Then I climbed the ladder to the roof beams. To the peak of the house, I'd tied a climbing rope from which dangled my waist harness. With this static belay as a safeguard, I could climb the final roof slope, hauling on the rope with one hand while I towed the plywood sheet with the other. Once I'd fought the panel into place, I nailed it down. Eventually the rain came in. By the time I quit, I was tempting fate as I slipped and slid on my forty-five-degree wooden skating rink.

Steve Swaim had sold the house in which I'd rented a room the year before, so I needed a new place to live. A friend named Dave Magee, who rented a house north of the university, invited me to live in his basement. The place was such a dismal dungeon, he claimed he'd never entered it. But he knew how broke I was, so he said, "Come over and take a look."

The basement was grim. No windows, and it was full of cobwebs and mouse shit. "Looks fine to me," I said without hesitation. Startled, Dave rejoined, "How about fifty dollars a month?" "Deal," I answered.

I scrubbed the place down, swept away the mouse and spider debris, painted the walls, and threw down a scrap of carpet remnant. Because of the absence of windows, sometimes I didn't know whether it was day or night. I lived for almost two years in that dungeon.

At the end of each exhausting day of working on Dan's house, I'd go home to my basement. By then, it was usually dark and cold. I knew that if I sat down, I wouldn't be able to get up for hours, so instead I'd go running. Dan learned about my evening workouts. "I can't believe you're going running now," he'd say as we quit after another eight-hour day of construction. But I thought I had to keep up my training. Carpentry was hard work, but climbing Himalayan peaks was harder.

▲
▲
▲

Through Phil Ershler, I'd met a fellow in his late forties named Hall Wendel. He was the CEO of Polaris, the snowmobile company, and was quite successful. He'd gotten the climbing bug late in life, and now he hired Phil to guide him on Everest in the spring of 1991. Phil invited Robert Link and me as assistant guides. It would be my fourth expedition to Everest, but it loomed as another free Himalayan outing, with a small salary to boot. And the team would try the South Col route, a side of the mountain I'd never been on.

Then, sometime in the winter before the trip, Hall and Phil had a falling out. Robert and I agreed to take over as co-leaders. The only clients were Hall and his daughter Amy, who, at about age twenty-five, was a Rainier guide but had never before been to the Himalaya.

That was the first time I ever used bottled oxygen on an 8,000er. I'd already climbed Everest, so I was there not for my own goals but to take care of my clients. In that situation, I felt that using oxygen myself added a safety factor in case somebody got in trouble. As it turned out, Amy got sick at Camp III on the Lhotse Face and couldn't go higher. Hall got to the South Col, at 26,000 feet, but just barely, climbing very slowly and struggling all the way. He'd actually performed quite well for a first go at an 8,000-meter peak, but the toil had worn him down. Part of that debilitation is due to the uncertainty of not knowing what to expect on a mountain like Everest. Often it takes two or three attempts to figure out how to prepare and how to endure. Although it really hurt to do so, the next day I had to tell Hall, "This is as high as I think you should go."

By the time we got settled in our tents at the South Col, it was ten P.M. and I felt exhausted. I was so hammered from all the work of guiding and establishing camps, I felt the only way I could get to the summit was by using bottled oxygen the rest of the way.

In the morning, nobody else wanted to go for the top, not even Robert Link. This was not surprising: after eight weeks of carrying loads, fixing ropes, and stocking camps, most climbers are physically wiped out, as well as mentally drained and homesick. If you catch a cold at high altitude, it can last for weeks. You develop a hacking cough that won't go away. A small cut on your finger never heals. It's all your body can do to function at a minimal level. Faced with the last 3,000 feet to the summit, you all too easily decide to throw in the towel.

Still, I felt that going on was more rewarding than quitting, and the snow conditions and weather were good. In the Himalaya, there's an old and honored tradition of the whole team working together just to get two climbers in position to go to the summit. I felt that if I could get to the top, it would be a minor victory for our whole crew.

At one A.M. on May 15, I set out from the South Col. I was using bottled oxygen, but shortly thereafter the whole system went kaput. I just chucked the mask and tanks and kept going without oxygen—after all, I'd pulled it off the year before.

That day, as I trudged slowly upward into the clouds, I reveled in the thought that I was following in the footsteps of my heroes, Edmund Hillary and Tenzing Norgay. Although I'd climbed Everest from the north, every step of the way here was new terrain for me.

Twelve hours after leaving camp, as I approached the summit, I saw this guy standing on top, looking down, taking pictures of me. He said later that he was trying to figure out who I might be. Before the expedition, Hall Wendel had wanted to outfit us all in matching down suits. Robert Link placed the order, but the only fabric available was called "magenta" in the catalog. The real suits looked pretty damned pink to us! Still, a free down suit was a free down suit.

So as I climbed closer to the top, wearing this garish pink outfit, the guy on the summit was thinking, Hmm, climber with no oxygen, solo, pink suit—he must be French.

I could see him waiting above as I struggled up the last few yards. I was irritated that this fellow had somehow ruined my wilderness experience. Even more irritating was that he kept taking pictures of me, while I wanted to be left alone during that final struggle—not the potential subject of a spread in some magazine. When I got to the top, I confronted the climber. Eventually he took off his oxygen mask, and I got a good look at his face.

"Andy?!" I blurted out.

"Ed?!"

It was Andy Politz, my old friend from the RMI load wars and the Kangshung Face, who'd come up the north ridge as part of an expedition led by Eric Simonson. An hour earlier, Eric himself, as well as George Dunn, had topped out, too—the first Everest success for both of them. Andy and I just happened to summit within minutes of each other. We were both simply dumbfounded by the coincidence.

Andy wanted to linger there and shoot the shit, but I'd seen that the weather was starting to turn, and I wanted to get down quickly. I said, "I'll give you a call when I get home—we can chat then." After only a few minutes on top, we hugged, then started down our separate ways. "See ya later," we each called back.

By the winter of 1991–92, I was busy planning for K2 with Scott Fischer. Climbing the 8,000ers had really gotten into my blood, although I still hadn't formulated the dream of going for all fourteen.

At the same time, that winter was one of the most anxious periods of my life. Scott and I were desperately scrounging just to raise the cash to buy our way onto a Russian permit for K2. From my school years, I was about $25,000 in debt. I was settling my loans with the absolute minimum monthly payments.

That year, in weak moments, I was thrust face-to-face with the sorry reality of my professional life. I'd worked my ass off for nine years to get through college and vet school. I'd earned my doctorate in veterinary medicine, then landed a couple of solid jobs, only to give up the whole thing because it was incompatible with my climbing career. At the moment, on the verge of turning thirty-three, I was pounding nails and guiding to make ends meet. Would that be what I did for the rest of my life? Many a climber had chosen just such a course to feed his habit. Just a decade before, living a few miles from me in Seattle, Jon Krakauer had been working construction jobs so he could toss down his tool belt and head off for the Devils Thumb or Cerro Torre on a moment's notice. It wasn't until 1981, after some five or six years of pounding nails and working on Alaskan fishing boats, that Jon had gotten up the nerve to try to make a living as a writer.

In the spring of 1992, as Scott and I planned for K2, I was full of excitement about the upcoming challenge. But as for ever making a decent living out of anything to do with mountaineering—well, the chances seemed close to zero.

*Twofers
and True Love*

I will never be able to look back on our 1992 K2 expedition without mixed feelings. No matter what Charley Mace or Scott Fischer thought about our decision to push on to the summit as the storm rose and engulfed us, I'm still convinced that it was the one big mistake of my climbing career. And to this day, Scott's and my ride in the avalanche before I was able to self-arrest and stop us both remains the kind of close call I hope I never have again. ▲ At the same time, I came back from Pakistan that August feeling a great deal of pride in our accomplishment—not only for our roles in rescuing Gary Ball and Chantal Mauduit, but for persevering so long on the mountain, through so many setbacks, so that we could finally have a shot at the summit. And I was proud to have become the first American to have topped out on the Big Three—Everest, K2, and Kangchenjunga, all without bottled oxygen.

So I was completely unprepared for what happened within a few weeks of my return to Seattle. Sometime that fall, I called up Lou Whittaker to talk about guiding in 1993. I fully expected to put in a full summer at RMI the next year.

Lou said, "Well, Ed, you know, you've been gone for a season. I don't think we can bring you back at the same salary level. We need to bring you down a notch."

I was completely blown away. I'd been guiding at RMI for ten years. I'd gone from being the peon to a relatively senior guide. My salary had risen from $500 a month to $1,200 a month. And now, hearing Lou's pronouncement, I thought, *What? You're going to cut my pay? Just for being gone while I was on K2?* I hung up without making my decision.

Before I'd headed off to Pakistan that June, I'd told Gerry Lynch, the co-owner of RMI, "Listen, I'm not sure how long I'll be gone. But don't count on me for this summer." Meanwhile, on Rainier, all my RMI guide friends were saying to each other, "Hey, Ed's off on K2. Isn't that cool?"

I just couldn't understand Lou's thinking. If I owned a guide service, and one of my guides was just back from climbing Everest or K2, I'd think the clients would just eat that up. Wouldn't I love to be able to say, Look how many RMI guides have climbed Everest? It would be like a billboard advertising our experience and accomplishments.

I stewed over the phone call for a while, but I knew I'd made up my mind. I said to myself, *I'm not going to grovel. I won't beg to get back on Rainier. That's it. That's the end of it. I'll find another job.* I wrote Lou a letter, politely declining his offer at the lower salary—thanks, but no thanks. As it turned out, I would never again guide full-time.

What seemed so inexplicable was that Lou had led three Himalayan expeditions himself: to Everest in 1982 and 1984, and to Kangchenjunga in 1989. On Kangchenjunga, we'd gotten along fine. He was the expedition leader, while I was voted the climbing leader by my peers. Lou had raised all the money for the trip and selected the team, but he'd had no summit ambitions himself. In the end, he never got higher than Camp II. But he considered the expedition a rousing success, because six of his RMI guides had reached the summit.

The difference, apparently, was that all three of those Himalayan expeditions had taken place in the spring, between March and May. Thus they hadn't conflicted with the RMI summer guiding season on Rainier. In Nepal, for climbers the summer is almost always a complete wash—virtually no expeditions go into the field then, because the monsoon, with its endless snowfall, smothers the Himalaya from June through August. But in Pakistan, the monsoon has negligible impact, so expeditions to K2 and the other high peaks in the Karakoram usually occupy the summer months. By going to K2, I'd necessarily missed the RMI season for '92. But I never dreamed I'd be cutting my throat by doing so.

By that summer, Lou was sixty-three years old. When he was younger, he'd been in the thick of the climbing scene. He'd even gone to K2 himself, in 1975, on an American expedition that was rife with interpersonal conflict and never got very high on the mountain. (Galen Rowell, a member of that team, later wrote a tell-all account of the trip, called *In the Throne Room of the Mountain Gods*.)

So Lou had been to Everest, K2, and Kangchenjunga, but he'd never gotten near the summit of any of those three highest peaks. Yet because he was an identical twin with his brother Jim, Lou was always being mistaken for the first American to get to the top of Everest. People meeting him for the first time would say, "Oh, you've climbed Everest." He'd have to answer, "No, that was my brother." Those denials must have grown stale after a while.

Meanwhile, Lou was making something of a name for himself. He had started and was now running one of the most successful guide services in the country. For many years, he had been involved with JanSport; as the firm's primary mountaineering spokesman, he'd brought the company to a new level. He was a great raconteur and after-dinner speaker—still is. The legend that he'd created was a masterwork of self-promotion. I admired him for making a living as a climber, and also because he was a gifted teacher.

After that phone call in the fall of '92, whenever I saw Lou, I'd be cordial. I never brought up the impasse between us; I felt that the ball was in his court. But if we showed up at functions together, he'd never quite look me in the eye.

When they returned to Rainier in the summer of '93, all my RMI buddies said to each other, "Where's Ed? What's happened?" The rumors were flying thick and fast: he was fired, he and Lou had a falling out.... When I'd meet one of my guide friends and he'd ask, "Ed, what happened?," I'd tell him. They all said, "What?!" They couldn't believe Lou's "bringing me down a notch," either. Eventually the whole guide service knew about our falling out, but no one really talked about it.

A few years ago, at the Outdoor Retailer trade show in Salt Lake City, Lou came up to me and said, "Ed, I feel really bad about what happened. I hope we're still friends." He didn't admit in so many words that he'd made a mistake, but I took the gesture as an apology all the same. I think it was a matter of his growing older, and finally realizing that it was okay to be the teacher whose student surpasses you.

When we attend functions together today, Lou goes out of his way to laud my achievements. I've always believed that I learned a lot of my mountaineering skills not only from Lou but from other guides he'd also taught. The air has cleared between us, and now I can say that Lou is a great friend.

▲
▲
▲

During the winter of 1992–93, I was still making a living as a carpenter. It had been three years since I'd last practiced as a veterinarian. The "sabbatical" that I once thought I might be taking from my profession was beginning to look like a permanent leave.

Yet in retrospect, the demise of my summer career as an RMI guide may have been a blessing. It freed me up to do as much real climbing as I could finagle the money and partners for. In 1993, I went on three separate Himalayan expeditions, two more than I'd ever before been able to pull off in a single year.

Hall Wendel, the client whom I'd guided to the South Col on Everest in 1991, had become a great friend in the interim. He's always had a voracious appetite for adventure, and he loved to take off on the spur of the moment. He'd call me up and say, "Eddo"—Hall always called me "Eddo"—"what are you doing the day after tomorrow? Let's go to Mexico. I've only got six days, and I want to climb Popo and Orizaba. I'll FedEx you the tickets."

I'd warn him about the chance of getting acute mountain sickness going from sea level to 18,700 feet in a couple of days, but to no avail. As a precaution, I convinced him to start taking Diamox, a drug that helps you cope with altitude. On that trip, we flew from Seattle to Mexico City and drove to the hut at 14,000 feet on Popocatepetl the first day, then reached the 17,887-foot summit the next morning. Down to a village for beer and steaks, the next day to the Orizaba hut, then the day after to the summit. One more day back to Mexico City; then we flew home. In six days round-trip from Seattle, we'd climbed two of the three highest volcanoes in Latin America.

I've literally traveled around the world with Hall. We've sailed and dived in the Caribbean, climbed in Ecuador and New Zealand, and flown aerobatics in biplanes in New Zealand. Hall suffers from an intense claustrophobia, but just to confront his fears, we also went caving in New Zealand. Hall had graduated from the U.S. Naval Academy in Annapolis, where, of all things, he'd done tours of duty inside submarines!

In New Zealand, we hired a wiry, slightly built professional caver to guide us. Rigged with acetylene head torches and harnesses, we did a warm-up trip into a moderately difficult grotto. A few days later, we hoped to tackle a far more serious cave called Howard's Hall, which began with a 600-foot free rappel straight into the abyss. The only way out was to keep descending to the exit, which required some really tight squeezes through narrow passages.

Hall would have gone for Howard's right off the bat had I not talked him into warming up in the "practice" cave. There, several hundred yards in,

Hall couldn't handle the confinement, so he headed back out. I went a little farther, but after watching our diminutive guide squeeze through a tight, underwater tunnel, I said, "No way, man!" Practice cave indeed!

The crazy thing is that despite freaking out in our warm-up cavern, Hall still wanted to try Howard's the next day. I nixed the plan.

At first, the deal with Hall was always that he hired me for these trips as a guide, but after a while, I had to tell him, "Hall, we're too good friends for me to charge you anymore." He always picked up the tab for our trips, however.

In 1993, undaunted by his struggles on Everest two years earlier, Hall hired me to guide him on Pumori, a beautiful 23,488-foot peak that flanks the southern approaches to Everest. Of all my expeditions to the Himalaya and Karakoram, Pumori was the only one I ever undertook to a peak lower than 8,000 meters. There were just four of us on the expedition—Hall and me and two Sherpas. I did all the leading and all the fixing of ropes. In the end, we couldn't go to the top because we ran into dangerous seracs on our summit day, but all in all, it was a very congenial expedition. From high on Pumori, where we had the mountain to ourselves, we could see the mobs at Everest base camp below, on the Khumbu Glacier. At night, to amuse ourselves, we'd signal climbers on Everest with our headlamps, and they'd signal back.

Without even returning to the States, I went straight from Pumori to Tibet to join an expedition led by Eric Simonson. He was running a commercial attempt on Shishapangma—at 26,286 feet the lowest of the fourteen 8,000ers, but the last to be climbed, by the Chinese in 1964. Eric hired me not to guide his clients one-on-one so much as simply to add strength to the party. It was an ideal arrangement for me.

As it turned out, only one client got to Camp IV, at 24,400 feet, and he could go no higher. That left another guide and me free to make the expedition's only summit push. Not far out of camp, however, he stopped and said, "Ed, I'm not going any farther. My head's just not into it."

I couldn't believe it. I said, "Well, I'll go on by myself, then. I'm not ready to turn around." I'd already gone to the summit of Everest alone in

1990 and 1991, so I was confident I could do the same on Shishapangma. And everything seemed to go fine—there were no crevasses to worry about, and the climbing was well within my limits.

By eight A.M.—wonderfully early for an 8,000-meter peak—I stood on the central summit of Shishapangma. But then, all at once, I saw the problem. The true summit lay only a hundred yards away and less than twenty feet higher, but the ridge between the two was horrendously threatened by avalanches. I told myself, I can't do that alone. It's too risky.

It was agonizing to turn back so close to the top—much closer than the 300 vertical feet that had loomed between Eric and me and the top of Everest back in 1987. Had the conditions been different, I could have crossed that hundred-yard ridge in less than an hour. Persistent rumors have it that other climbers going for all fourteen 8,000ers have fudged ascents such as the one I almost made on Shishapangma, counting a subsidiary summit as the real thing. But I would never do so, and even if I were tempted, Elizabeth Hawley would never let me get away with it.

Living in Kathmandu since 1960, a former journalist for *Time* and *Life*, Liz Hawley—eternally "Miss Hawley" to all but the few friends who have known her longest and best—has installed herself as the scrupulous chronicler and fierce arbiter of Himalayan mountaineering. Every spring and fall, she waylays the members of each expedition in their Kathmandu hotel rooms on the way to and from their various objectives. Even at the moment you're checking in, after thirty hours of flying to Nepal, Miss Hawley knows you've arrived. The phone at the front desk rings, and you have no choice but to schedule a briefing.

Miss Hawley grills the climbers like a demon district attorney as to what they've actually accomplished. Her more than four decades' worth of records (available only recently from the American Alpine Club on a CD) amounts to an irreplaceable archive of mountaineering history. Yet in person, Miss Hawley, who's never married but is reputed to have had affairs with a number of glamorous and exotic suitors, is a formidable grande dame. On my way home from Tibet in 1993, after Miss Hawley had cross-examined me, she peered over her eyeglasses and said sternly, "You realize, don't you, Ed, that you haven't climbed Shishapangma? You're going to have to come back and do it right."

Both Hall and Eric had paid me small stipends to guide on Pumori and Shishapangma, and they'd covered my expenses. But that money, and the feeble amounts I'd been able to save up from a winter of carpentry work, amounted to my only income for 1992–93. And that had become a big problem, because the project I had my heart set on was going to cost a lot of money.

I'd decided that in the fall of '93, after the monsoon season, I wanted to return to Everest's Great Couloir and try to climb it solo, unsupported even by Sherpas. It would be the most audacious thing I'd ever tried in the mountains—even more "out there" in some ways than K2. The model was Reinhold Messner's astounding 1980 three-day solo of the Great Couloir and north ridge without oxygen—a deed that had long represented to me a kind of ultimate performance in the Himalaya.

My other source of motivation derived from my K2 experience. After all the difficulties we'd had there working with such an ill-assorted team, with many members performing backbreaking chores just to help out others, I wanted to focus my energies on a mountain that I had to myself. The psychological challenge of being alone in a dangerous place for weeks intrigued me, too.

So all through the winter, even while I worked construction, I tried to raise money for my Everest solo project. Scott Fischer and I had first learned the drill before K2, when we'd finally raised a minuscule pile of dough by selling T-shirts supplied by JanSport. The key to pulling off a trip like Everest on my own, I knew, was to attract sponsors. But in those days, in the United States, a sponsored climber was an almost unheard-of creature. The climbing-equipment companies, such as Black Diamond, would tell me, "Ed, we can give you a bunch of free carabiners, but we just don't have any budget to give you cash." Free gear wouldn't help me pay for a permit and airfare.

Basically, I spent the winter of 1992–93 begging. I'd pick up the phone and cold-call some big company like Coca-Cola. This was before the Internet was very accessible, so I couldn't even look up the name of Coca-

Cola's head of marketing. I'd end up getting passed from one assistant to another. Companies like that have "blockers"—people whose job it is to *keep* you from getting through to the head of marketing or the true boss. They might say, "I'll give him your message and he'll call you back." Then, of course, he'd never call.

If I actually did get through to a marketing type, I'd deliver my spiel: "Here's what I want from you. Here's what I can offer in return. I'll wear your logo on my clothing. I'll endorse your product. I'll give a free slide show and talk to your employees when I get back."

I'm not good at selling myself like this, and I absolutely hated the process. That winter I spent more on phone bills than I earned from potential sponsors!

I slowly realized that cold calls wouldn't do the trick. I needed to make face-to-face contact with people who knew people who knew people. . . . I went to all the cocktail parties I could. I schmoozed shamelessly.

My first breakthrough came from one such chance meeting. On Jim Whittaker's Everest International Peace Climb in 1990, he'd raised some money by offering slots on a "support trek." Clients would pay pretty good money just to hike with our team to base camp and hang out with the climbers. One of the trekkers that year was a New Yorker named Jodie Eastman. She was married to John Eastman, an attorney who had represented the Beatles—he was, in fact, Linda McCartney's brother. So the Eastmans had all kinds of contacts in high places. Jodie and I had stayed in touch over the years. She'd call me or write, asking, "Ed, what's your next plan?"

When I told her about my Everest solo project and all the difficulties I was having raising money, Jodie said, "I'll keep my ears open." One day, out of the blue, I got a call from a fellow in Los Angeles named Gil Friesen. He'd recently retired as head of A & M Records, after working his way up from the mail room. He was a supremely savvy and accomplished fellow, and for some reason he was intrigued by people like me. Now he said, "I'm going to try to help you." I was floored by this generosity coming from a total stranger. Just to get the ball rolling, Gil paid the Chinese for my Everest permit.

Shortly thereafter, Gil had lunch with a buddy, Tom Freston, who was the president of MTV. Gil must have had a silver tongue, for all of a sudden some executives from MTV let me know they were ready to be my first sponsor. They'd offer me a substantial amount of money, in exchange for which they hoped to make a documentary film of my climb to run on the MTV channel, in which viewers would see the company flag planted on the summit.

Meanwhile, Jodie had been talking to someone at Polo Ralph Lauren. That company was launching a line of outdoor clothing called Polo Sport. Just like that, I landed my second sponsor. Polo had never made a down jacket or a climbing mitten before, but I sent the designers my old gear and they copied it. I helped them design some of their new line as well. And on Everest, everything I wore would have the company logo on it. I like to say today that in the fall of '93, I was the best-dressed climber on Everest—ever.

Yet I had the bad luck to choose one of the worst fall seasons in recent memory in the Himalaya. Basically, the monsoon never went away that year. I ended up making five attempts to climb the Great Couloir, every one defeated by bad weather and atrocious avalanche conditions. It was up and down, up and down, up and down.

At base camp, I was supported by a small staff consisting of a Sherpa and my friend Carolyn Gunn, an American woman who doubled as cook and doctor. On each attempt, they'd wish me well as I set off toward my Camp I at 21,500 feet, right at the bottom of the north face. I'd pitched my tent in the middle of a field of crevasses, hoping that these chasms would swallow most of the avalanches sweeping down from above. In my tiny tent, some nights I'd hear the thunder of those slides. I was ready to run at a moment's notice, but how could I judge the real threat? Sometimes I'd crank my Walkman to full volume just to escape the noise. But then a new storm would roll in, and I'd flee back to base camp to bask in the camaraderie and comfort my friends lavished on me. After a short break, though, I'd psych myself up for another attempt.

My plan was to climb alpine-style from Camp I, carrying everything with me on what I hoped would be a three-day ascent to the summit. On my fifth try, my pack weighed forty pounds. At one A.M. it was cold and clear, and I thought I could take advantage of the freezing that ought to stabilize the snow in the couloir. But after a few hours, I had to angle up a steep slope to the right. Here the conditions were only marginal, and by now thousands of feet of exposure yawned below my boots. I took a few tentative steps. All of a sudden, the whole slope settled with a loud *Whompf!* I nearly shat my pants: that kind of settling meant that the whole slope was on the verge of cutting loose in a massive avalanche. I backed down as carefully as I could, collected the rest of my gear, and turned my back on the north face for good. In five attempts, I'd gotten no higher than 23,500 feet.

At first, I thought only of abandoning the expedition. But part of me protested, *Damn it, I'm not ready to go home.* I decided to hike over to the North Col and try the northeast ridge route, the one I'd already climbed in 1990. But when I got there it was too late in the season. That fall, a handful of climbers summited on Everest in early October, by the two "standard" routes—the South Col and the northeast ridge—but nobody topped out after October 10. By the time I got in position, it was almost November. I made two attempts, but it was much too windy and too cold. On the northeast ridge, I got to 25,000 feet—only a bit higher than the altitude I'd reached in the Great Couloir.

Seven attempts stretched over two months, and nothing to show for it but failure. I hadn't even come close to getting up Everest. MTV never got its documentary film. And because their sponsorship, as well as Polo Ralph Lauren's, was a one-shot deal, when I got back to the United States in November 1993, I was going to have to start all over again at square one, begging money from strangers.

That late autumn was one of the most depressing times in my life. I would just sit there in my basement apartment, staring at the phone, wondering, What the hell am I doing? I seriously considered going back to being a vet. When I glanced up, I could see my framed diploma from Washington State, staring down at me from the wall. It was not only depressing— it was a truly scary time. I was thirty-four years old, I'd abandoned my profession, and for all the expeditions I'd gone on, I could see no way in the future to make my living from mountaineering.

One day I was sitting there with my head literally in my hands when the phone rang. It was John Cumming, a fellow Rainier guide. John's father, Ian Cumming, was a wealthy entrepreneur who was connected to a small group of designers and other employees who worked for the venerable outdoor equipment company Sierra Designs. That fall, six of them had tried to buy the company, and when their bid had failed, they'd walked out. Now they wanted to start their own company. It would be called Mountain Hardwear.

Ian Cumming had put up the money to launch the start-up. Both Ian and John would be members of the board. Now, over the phone, John, who knew about my expeditions and also about my financial doldrums, explained the situation, then said, "We want you to be part of Mountain Hardwear. We want you to be our key sponsored climber."

Holy Jesus! I thought. *This is the Messiah!*

That phone call would be one of the true turning points in my life. By November 1993, for all the work I'd put into big-range mountaineering, I had little to show for it. Suddenly, along come John Cumming and Mountain Hardwear. Here was somebody willing to recognize what I was trying to do.

At first the company could afford to pay me a salary of only about $15,000 a year. For me, though, that was a gold mine. In exchange for sponsorship, I'd not only wear the Mountain Hardwear logo everywhere, I'd help the company design their gear.

Thirteen years later, I count John Cumming, Gil Friesen, and Jodie Eastman among my enduring friends. And I'm still sponsored by Mountain Hardwear. The company and I came of age together. My association with this group of wonderful people, born in that moment of dark despair in the basement, has been the happiest and most fruitful business arrangement of my career. It made everything that followed possible.

Almost at once, I started planning for the spring of 1994. The previous year, Rob Hall had lost his inseparable partner, Gary Ball, on Dhaulagiri, when he collapsed and died of pulmonary edema. Despite his grief, Rob was determined to keep Adventure Consultants going. He already had a permit to guide Everest by the South Col for '94. Now he invited me along as his second-in-command.

By the time we reached base camp in mid-March, we were a team of seventeen: six clients, six climbing Sherpas, two base-camp cooks, Rob, his wife, Jan Arnold, and me. I was really pleased that Hall Wendel was back as one of the clients. We were a pretty eclectic bunch, with two clients from Germany and one from Norway, but we functioned well as a team. The Norwegian, Erling Kagge, had reached both the North and the South Poles. He had no real climbing experience, but he was as tough as nails. On Everest, Erling hoped to become the first person to reach all three of the earth's "poles."

I also had a new idea to try out on Rob. I'd seen hundreds of photos of the south side of the Everest "horseshoe"—the gigantic cirque formed at the head of the Khumbu Glacier by Everest and its neighboring peak, Lhotse—at 27,890 feet the fourth-highest mountain in the world. And, of course, when I'd climbed Everest from the south in 1991, I'd spent a lot of time staring at Lhotse over my shoulder. I was well aware that the route up Lhotse shared exactly the same path as the route on Everest for 60 percent of the way. Only on the last two days of climbing does the Lhotse route diverge from the Everest itinerary, cutting off to the right at about 25,000 feet. On Lhotse, you follow a steep and very direct snow-and-ice couloir straight to the summit.

My thought was that we'd already be there, guiding on Everest. There'd be other people going for Lhotse at the same time. To save money, maybe we could buy places on their permit. Then, if everything went well on Everest, and we had the time and energy left, Rob and I could try to make a lightning-fast ascent of Lhotse without clients. We'd already be acclimatized, and we could go at our own pace. It would be a fun style of climbing, without all the tedium of load carrying and establishing camps. We'd just put pedal to the metal and go as fast as we could, alpine-style, hoping to reach the summit in three days. Part of my rationale was that despite the windfall of my Mountain Hardwear sponsorship, I still couldn't quite afford to organize two separate expeditions, one to Everest, one to Lhotse, in the same year.

Rob was intrigued. He said, "Okay, but we're here for the clients. Our first commitment is to them. If things work out right, yeah, maybe we could take a crack at Lhotse."

That spring, things indeed worked out. Without incident, we got all six of our clients and three Sherpas to the summit of Everest. After having failed on Everest before and on Pumori, Hall Wendel was overjoyed to make it to the top of the world. The experience he'd gained on those previous expeditions made Hall unstoppable in 1994. He was the first of our clients to stand on top. Following my personal rule of thumb for guiding on Everest, I used bottled oxygen, as did Rob. And since we summitted so early, on May 9, we had plenty of time left before the monsoon arrived. Rob and I got our clients safely down to base camp and rested for two days. Then, with packs weighing only forty-four pounds apiece, we headed back up the route, aiming for Lhotse.

I hadn't invented this tactic. Like so many others, this great precedent had been set by the visionary Reinhold Messner, in 1984, when he and his longtime partner, Hans Kammerlander, had made a continuous, alpine-style traverse of Gasherbrum I and Gasherbrum II, an adjoining pair of 8,000ers in the Karakoram. But since then, very few comparable feats had been accomplished.

The problem is that after succeeding on any 8,000er, a climber is usually so depleted that all he wants to do is go home. So as we geared up for our 1994 campaign, I kept reminding myself that Everest was only half the plan. I prepared mentally to save myself for the second half.

Rob and I were in such great shape, and so well acclimatized, that we just flew up Lhotse. He used bottled oxygen; I didn't. Other teams were already coming down, cleaning off the mountain, so we couldn't even use their fixed ropes. We climbed Lhotse alpine-style in only four days round-trip from base camp. We got to the top on May 16, just a week after summiting on Everest. Going up the mountain, as we'd passed Camp II, we'd found it still thronged with climbers. Only two days later, we descended all the way from the top to Camp II in one push, only to find it completely deserted. We pitched our little tent there. It was so cool. We were all alone in this beautiful place. We had the whole of the Western Cwm to ourselves.

Jocularly, we nicknamed our double triumph a "twofer," as in "two for the price of one." It was a tactic I would employ to great advantage in the coming years. When it worked to perfection, it almost felt like cheating, it was so smooth. Eventually, my friend Neal Beidleman coined another nickname for the gambit. We'd pick off the second peak so quickly and effortlessly, it seemed appropriate to call it a "drive-by."

During the summer of 1994, fresh off Everest and Lhotse, I was working once more for my friend Dan Hiatt, the carpenter who'd taught me the tricks of the trade. We managed to build two houses from the bottom up. I loved the work. It was physical, I was outside, and every day we'd walk away from our project with a new visual reward.

By now, I was living in the basement of Dan's mother-in-law's house, on a quiet private lane. I'd escaped Dave Magee's dungeon, and though I was still living in a basement, this one had windows and a porch that opened onto a panoramic view of Puget Sound. I had a million-dollar vista at a rock-bottom price. Dan lived across the street, with his wife and two sons, in the three-story house we'd constructed two years before. That June we were working on a semiunderground garage, pouring concrete, which involved moving a lot of plywood forms and steel rebar. It was heavy, hard labor, and we'd finish the day just wiped out. Yet every day after work, I'd still do my training run. Dan would gasp, "I can't believe you're going running now."

Dan was a hockey player. He and his hockey buddies threw a lot of parties. On July 3—it's not hard to remember the date, in view of what happened that day—he invited me to one of these shindigs. I thought, Oh, no, not another dudes' party. I almost didn't go. But Dan said we'd be outdoors, drinking beer, barbecuing burgers, playing Ping-Pong. So I went—in part because it happened to be a beautiful sunny Sunday.

Since all these guys were jocks, we naturally turned the Ping-Pong into a round-robin tournament. You'd put your beer cup on the table, and if the other guy landed the ball in it, he got an extra point.

While I was playing Ping-Pong, I took a look over at the barbecue area. "Whoa," I said to myself, "she's cute!" She was about five foot four, with blond hair swept over one eye. She was wearing an orangish-yellow skirt, a jean jacket, and clogs. I noticed right away that she had great legs. After that, I had a little trouble focusing on my Ping-Pong game.

When my match was finished, I got up the nerve to walk over and chat. Her name was Paula Barton. She'd just moved to Seattle from Portland. She was hanging out at the party with her best friend and roommate, Janine Duncan, a tall blonde who was nicknamed J.D. J.D.'s boyfriend, another hockey player, was hosting the party. It turned out that Paula also had almost not come to the barbecue, feeling like a bit of a third wheel among all these strangers. Up close, I noticed that she had striking blue eyes and a great smile.

Paula later admitted that she was checking me out at the same time. She noticed that I was really tan, with muscular calves. But she was a little unnerved by the glances I kept stealing. "Who is that guy who keeps gawking at me with those big brown eyes?" she asked J.D.

"That's Ed Viesturs. He's a mountain climber. He's just back from climbing Everest."

Paula hesitated, then said, "Umm...where exactly *is* Everest?"

We made small talk for a while. I was trying to act casual, so I didn't ask Paula for her phone number. I knew I could get it from J.D.'s boyfriend. Later during the party I waylaid the guy. "So what's the deal with Paula?" I asked.

"Oh, she's single."

"Great. Can I get her phone number?"

Meanwhile, Dan and I were going to host a Fourth of July blast the next day, on the deck of Dan's house. While we were still making small talk, I'd invited Paula and J.D., but they had plans they couldn't break. Still, they seemed genuinely disappointed that they couldn't come, which gave me additional hope. The talk shifted to mountain climbing. Somebody said, "You know, I've been up to Camp Muir on Rainier." Out of that remark, we made a vague plan for the whole group of us to take a day hike up to Camp Muir sometime that summer. It wasn't like I actually asked Paula out on a date.

Now I had Paula's phone number. But a few days later I still hadn't gotten up the gumption to call her. One day I was out running on Alki Beach, and after I finished my workout I decided to lie down on the grass. It turned out that the condo Paula and J.D. lived in was on Alki Beach. They'd fast-walk along the beach for exercise. Paula saw me sprawled on the grass and said to J.D., "That looks like Ed, the guy we met at the party the other day." By now, J.D.'s boyfriend had told her, "Hey, Ed's been asking for your phone number." They came up to talk.

I said, "We're going to the Red Door tomorrow night. Why don't you meet us there?" The Red Door was a pub in Fremont, one of the hipper Seattle neighborhoods.

Paula had an evening class the next night, but it happened to be in Fremont, just a block away from the pub. She said, "I'll meet you at the Red Door after my class."

By the time Paula got there, Dan and J.D. and I had already had a few beers. Now there was a long line of patrons outside waiting to get in. Paula went straight to the head of the line, where she somehow talked her way inside.

We chatted for hours, half-shouting over the music and the hubbub. Finally Dan said, "Ed, I've gotta go." We'd come to the Red Door together in my car. I looked at Paula. Without hesitating, she said, "I'll drive you home." I gave Dan my keys.

We knew by now that we lived less than two miles away from each other, so her errand wasn't some outrageous detour. We got into her old convertible VW bug. She drove me to my house, then accepted my invitation to have a nightcap on the porch, overlooking Puget Sound. We talked for hours, drinking wine as the candles melted to stubs. From then on, it was full-on. We never really dated. We just knew each other right away.

Paula was twenty-seven that summer; I was thirty-five. We had a great time getting to know each other during the next few months. We'd work all day at our jobs, then eat pizza and drink beer in front of David Letterman in her apartment. On weekends we'd go hiking and running, or take in yet another of a seemingly endless succession of barbecues. I took Paula to the engagement party in Ashford for my fellow guide Robert Link. It was there that she met all my RMI friends.

Earlier that day, at work, I'd been dismantling a porch structure, hammering away from beneath at a particularly recalcitrant floorboard. I had the thing almost loose when I took an extra-strong swing, missed the board altogether, and slammed the hammer straight into my forehead. I saw stars and almost passed out. In the bathroom mirror, I could see a perfect impression of the hammer's waffle pattern printed square in the middle of my forehead. By the evening it was oozing blood. Paula just laughed over my mishap. One of my RMI buddies snickered, "Nice third eye."

Over the years, I'd had a number of girlfriends, several of them moderately serious, though I'd never lived with any of them. For the most part, they weren't climbers, but initially my adventurous lifestyle would intrigue them.

But then I'd be gone on trips, or I'd be talking climbing. And the intrigue would wear off.

If I was headed off on an expedition, some would get depressed and sad. I got so that I was afraid even to bring up climbing in a conversation. Finally I'd have to say, "This is what I do. I'm not going to quit climbing. Perhaps our relationship's not going to work out." Sometimes she'd pull the plug before I did, sometimes the agreement was mutual.

Sometimes over the years I'd hook up with somebody really attractive in an exotic foreign place—like Chantal on K2. But then it would become obvious that it couldn't lead to anything serious.

When I went off to Everest and Lhotse in the spring of 1994, I'd been in a relationship, but it was with a girlfriend who couldn't stand that I was away so much. When I came home, I broke it off. I finally realized that I didn't need a girlfriend to feel good about myself.

And that June, I felt very good about myself. I'd just climbed two 8,000ers on one expedition. I was sponsored by Mountain Hardwear. I had a career that gave me adventures all over the world. Already I was planning to go to Cho Oyu with Rob Hall in the fall.

Paradoxically, feeling good about myself and realizing that I didn't need a girlfriend gave me the freedom to open up. That's when I met Paula. That July, I wasn't even looking for a girlfriend.

At the time that we met, Paula had two jobs—one at Nordstrom, the big clothing store, the other at a local pizzeria, Pegasus Pizzas. Having recently moved to Seattle from Portland, she'd taken these interim jobs until she could find more meaningful work, perhaps in management or social work. Paula had gone to college at the University of Oregon and Portland State, where she'd majored in sociology. The main reasons she'd moved were to escape a relationship that was going nowhere and to expand her personal horizons. J.D., whom Paula had known since childhood, had just rented a condo and needed a roommate. Despite being eight years younger than I, Paula had had several serious relationships and had lived with one boyfriend, though none of these men had shaped up as a potential husband.

She told me later that on the face of it, I wasn't her type. She'd never before dated anyone as athletic as I was, preferring instead what she thought of as "artistic" guys. But at the moment, Paula was starting to get into her own athleticism. With J.D., she'd recently completed the Portland-to-Seattle bicycle race. It was a two-hundred-mile jaunt that the two of them accomplished on old clunker bikes, taking two days to finish the course, laughing and joking all the way. The hard-core leaders finished the race on the first day.

From the start, I really loved Paula's personality. She was happy, confident, assertive, interesting, and willing to seek out new adventures. I liked the way she dressed—feminine yet fun. She was a natural beauty. She didn't bother with makeup or nail polish. I had no patience for women who took an hour in the morning to "put their face on." I always needed just to get up and go do something.

Slowly, I introduced Paula to my world. That summer, with J.D., we hiked up to Camp Muir. Paula had a great time, enjoying the novel physical challenge of hiking in the snow. Eventually we climbed Mount Baker together, and after a year or two, Rainier. On the summit, it was miserably cold with a stiff wind, but Paula laughed as she gnawed on a frozen bagel.

On those hikes and easy climbs, I was showing Paula what I saw in my mountain domain. She liked the athletic part of it, but she didn't know much about serious climbing. At first, she didn't realize how dangerous it was; she didn't know enough about it to be freaked out by it.

So when I told her I was going to Cho Oyu in the fall with Rob Hall, she just said, "Okay." She had her own ambitions for the fall: she was hoping to get a job in social work at a place called Childhaven, a day-treatment center for abused, neglected, and drug-affected children. Paula was a true born-to-volunteer kind of person, and if it had anything to do with kids, she was all over it.

We fell in love pretty quickly. We just connected—everything clicked. Paula was the first girlfriend I had been with who didn't pull the "Oh, my God, you're leaving again?" stuff. For me, this was hugely important. Paula accepted what I did; she had no need to try to change it. I needed someone who would let me be me, and in turn I vowed to let her be her.

I also knew that Rob would be taking a satellite phone on Cho Oyu. It was the size of a suitcase, so we wouldn't be carrying it above base camp, and it was really expensive to use—something like twenty dollars a minute. But I told Paula, "I'll probably be able to call you about once a week from the expedition." She said, "Great."

It was after Rob and I got to the top of Lhotse the previous spring that I first started thinking seriously about trying to climb all fourteen 8,000ers. I had the four highest under my belt by now, and I sort of privately counted Shishapangma, despite having stopped a hundred yards short of the true summit. It was an 8,000er with an asterisk attached. Having the backing of a committed sponsor, in Mountain Hardwear, gave me the confidence that I could realize my dream.

That year I finally got up the nerve to talk publicly about trying for all fourteen. And though I hadn't realized the effect it would have, that very announcement became a promotional tool. I had set myself a goal that would stretch over a number of years, supplying Mountain Hardwear with a venture around which to design a long-term marketing campaign. I gave my quest what I thought was a catchy title: Endeavor 8000. Mountain Hardwear took it and ran with it.

By 1994, I still wasn't anything like a famous mountaineer. After I'd climbed K2, becoming the first American to bag the Big Three, *Outside* magazine ran a small article about me. Significantly, it was titled "Ed Who?"

Only twenty miles northwest of Everest, Cho Oyu, at 26,905 feet, is the world's sixth-highest mountain. First climbed in 1954 by an Austrian team, it had since acquired the reputation of being probably the easiest of the 8,000ers to get up. Rob was interested in going there because he hadn't yet climbed it, but also to see whether he could add it to the roster of Adventure Consultants' guided trips on a regular basis. I wanted to go, obviously, because Cho Oyu would be yet another 8,000er on my résumé.

We were a modest team: only two clients, a few Sherpas, Rob, me, and Rob's wife, Jan Arnold. Once more, I was getting paid a small stipend to go to the Himalaya. I would also be able to field-test and showcase a few of Mountain Hardwear's newest products.

On the long flight to Kathmandu, frustrated because I couldn't get the audio program to work, I took out my diary and wrote an initial entry:

It's been an unbelievably fantastic summer. But it went by so fast. The best part without a doubt was Paula. Wow, zowie, hot, hot, hot! She is the most wonderful woman I've ever met. I love her madly and think of her constantly. My heart is Velcroed to her. I've had so much fun with her, and I know there's more to come.

On Cho Oyu, unfortunately, our clients fizzled out early. But that left Rob, Jan, and me free to go for the summit at our own pace. We climbed all the way from Camp II, at 23,300 feet, to the summit in one day. Without clients, we were strong enough to bypass the normal high camp at 24,500 feet. I got to the summit without bottled oxygen, while Rob and Jan both used it.

The top of Cho Oyu is an immense plateau, three or four football fields long. From the top of the normal route, you have to cross most of this plateau, taking nearly thirty minutes to get to the tiny nipple of a summit, which is festooned with wands, prayer flags, and other mementos of previous ascents. If you've climbed Cho Oyu, on your way out of Nepal, as you stop in Kathmandu, Elizabeth Hawley ambushes you with a trick question: "What did you see from the top?" If you don't answer, "Everest, Lhotse, and Nuptse," she knows you didn't go to the true summit.

We reached the top on October 6. A week before, from base camp, I'd called Paula on the sat phone. It was great to catch up with her. Just before I'd left Seattle, she had applied to Childhaven. Now, over the sat phone, she excitedly announced, "I got the job!" As it would turn out, with Childhaven Paula finally found work that inspired and fulfilled her. As for me, I could hardly wait to get back home once the expedition was over.

▲
▲
▲

Rob and I felt so heady after our '94 success that we planned to climb four 8,000-meter peaks in 1995, doing two twofers in a single year. First, we'd guide Everest, then hike only partway out, to a village where we could arrange for a helicopter to pick us up and ferry us over to Makalu. The world's fifth-highest peak, at 27,824 feet, Makalu stands even closer to Everest than does Cho Oyu, though on the opposite side, to the southeast. It was first climbed in 1955 by a very strong French team spearheaded by the Annapurna veterans Lionel Terray and Jean Couzy.

We'd come home for a little while, only to fly to Pakistan, still during the summer months, where we'd try to link Gasherbrum II and Gasherbrum I. If all went well, I could add three new peaks to my Endeavor 8000 roster, which would give me eight total—or nine, with the asterisked Shisha-pangma. I'd be more than halfway home to my goal of all fourteen.

Jan Arnold would be coming along as base-camp manager for Everest and Makalu, so I thought it would be neat to invite Paula. She accepted at once, even though she'd never before traveled to any part of the Third World.

For Everest, Rob had lined up a number of clients, including Doug Hansen, a postal worker from Renton, Washington. Doug was so keen to go to Everest, he'd moonlighted by taking the night shift at the post office and working construction by day just to raise the dough to buy a place on the Adventure Consultants team. Another nominal client was Chantal Mauduit, who'd bought her place just so she could try to fulfill her ambition to be the first woman to climb Everest without bottled oxygen.

As luck would have it, that was the year the snow conditions were really bad on the upper ridges of the South Col route. Rob, fellow Kiwi guide Guy Cotter, and I got five clients to the South Summit, less than 350 verti-cal feet short of the top, but we knew it would be too dangerous to push on. That was the expedition on which Chantal collapsed on the South Summit and had to be dragged down to the South Col.

Doug Hansen was an extremely likable guy, and Rob was so disap-pointed that he hadn't been able to get the postal worker to the top that he offered him a big discount if he came back in 1996; he virtually promised Doug he'd get him up the mountain then. It was a vow that was to have profound consequences.

Meanwhile, acting as Jan Arnold's assistant base-camp manager, Paula was actually frustrated that she didn't have more responsibilities. She'd rev-eled in the ten-day hike in, through the increasingly high and remote vil-lages of the Khumbu Valley. She wasn't at all squeamish about primitive lodges or less than sanitary conditions. It impressed the others to see this woman casually pick a dead spider out of her bowl of rice, say "Yuck," and then continue eating. But by now, she had too much downtime. She knew she didn't have enough experience to go above base camp, but aside from monitoring the radio, there weren't many highlights to each day. Over the radio, we may have minimized, say, the drama of getting Chantal down to the South Col. As was to be expected, Paula worried about our safety, but she trusted my ability and judgment. For one thing, I'd emphasized again and again how cautious I'd be up high.

But Everest is never easy, and it's always dangerous. I've found through the years that whenever I give a slide show or a talk, in the question-and-answer period people are curious about the most basic things. What do you wear on summit day? What do you eat and drink? How do you go to the bathroom?

Perhaps, then, a longish digression is in order here, to lay out the nuts-and-bolts answers to such questions, to explain what it's really like, day by day, minute by minute, to climb an 8,000-meter peak.

First of all, what do you wear on a typical climbing day above 24,000 feet? On your feet, double boots—a plastic outer shell and an insulated insert made out of Alveolite, a kind of noncompressable foam. Inside the boots, I wear two pairs of heavy socks, made of a blend of wool and spandex. The old leather boots that climbers favored for more than a century are vastly inferior to plastic, because leather absorbs moisture, which then freezes. It's a natural recipe for frostbite. Lachenal and Herzog lost their toes to frostbite on Annapurna in 1950 because they were wearing leather boots. (It's not as though they had any choice, since plastic boots would not get invented for another thirty years.) In spite of the recent advances in boot technology, however, climbers still get frostbite on Himalayan expeditions and lose toes as a result.

On top of your boots, you wear insulated overboots made of foam covered by a layer of Gore-Tex. I favor overboots that have insulation under the sole as well as covering the upper part of the boot. You don't need the Vibram rubber cleats of the boot sole to grip the rock, as you would doing alpine climbing at lower altitudes, because in the high Himalaya you wear your crampons all the time, even when climbing rock. The crampon has ten points under the sole to bite into snow and ice, as well as two front fangs for kicking steps in steep terrain. For years, I favored strap-on crampons, which are harder to put on than the more recent clip-on style, because I thought a good set of straps affixed the crampon more securely to the boot. A crampon that twists off in the middle of a technical slope can lead to disaster. Another thing that all good climbers learn is not to snag a front point on the trousers of the opposite leg as you take a step, which can make you fall flat on your face—not a good idea in steep places.

One of the problems with crampons is that on certain kinds of relatively wet snow, a clump of snow tends to stick to the instep with each stride. These balls of snow underfoot can make you slip. The only remedy on such terrain is to bang the side of your crampon with the shaft of your ice ax, knocking loose the clump. It's a tedious, even vexing process.

Another thing: you can't put your crampons on inside the tent. If you did, you'd soon be riddling the nylon floor with puncture holes. So you have to be able to put the crampons on outside, without removing your gloves. That's why nearly all climbers today favor clip-ons. When I still used straps, I had to make sure they had the simplest possible system of buckles.

On your torso, you wear long johns, top and bottom. Synthetic fabric is preferable to wool—wool tends to be itchy. You don't want cotton, because it soaks up your sweat and does not retain heat as well as wet synthetics do. Over the long johns, a one-piece sleeveless fleece suit. You don't want an upper fleece vest that you have to tuck into fleece pants; with a harness and a waist belt from your pack girdling your midsection, there's already too much going on.

If it's really cold, I'll wear a separate fleece jacket on top of the fleece suit. Then a one-piece down suit on top of everything, with a hood attached that draws down to a small tunnel in front of your eyes, nose, and mouth. Over the years Mountain Hardwear has favored red or yellow for my down suits—those colors show up better in photographs.

Protecting your hands is absolutely critical. On the summit push, even the thickest gloves don't cut it—you need mittens. I favor a double-fleece inner mitt, with an outer made of leather on the palm side (leather is better for grasping things) and down-filled nylon on the back of the hand. And the elastic sleeve gauntlet should slide all the way up to the middle of your forearm. A lot of us use "keeper strings" that attach your mittens to your wrists—not unlike the cords mothers tie to their tykes' mittens in winter to keep them from losing them. To hark back to Annapurna again, on the way down from the summit in 1950, Herzog took off his mittens and laid them on the snow so he could fetch something out of his pack. Then he watched, helpless, in a daze, as the gloves slid away down the precipice. Because of that simple error, he would later have all his fingers amputated.

Under my down hood, I wear a heavy wool knitted cap. Also a face-and-neck garter—a kind of wool-blend sleeve that you slide over your head, which then covers your face from your neck all the way up to just below your eyes. I cut a hole in this sleeve over my mouth, to allow me to breathe, but the sleeve covers my nose. Finally, goggles. If it's not too cold, I can get away with sunglasses, but in extreme weather I need super-dark wraparound ski-type goggles. The air is so thin at these altitudes, and the ultraviolet radiation so fierce, that even on a cloudy day, if you take off your goggles or sunglasses to see better, you run a serious risk of going snow-blind, just as Chantal did coming down from the summit of K2.

You can imagine that with all this clothing on, you look something like the Pillsbury Doughboy. And it's hard not to feel clumsy. You can have up to five layers on your feet, three on your hands. If you're also wearing an oxygen mask, you might as well be trapped inside a space suit. Despite being puffed up like a balloon, you need to be able to see your feet at all times. The whole business takes some getting used to, and you can imagine how long it takes to get dressed. At one A.M., with two guys in a tiny tent struggling to suit up, it's almost like playing a tortured, breathless game of Twister.

On an 8,000er, I carry a single-lens reflex camera with a plastic body. I'm starting to use digital equipment, but for years I shot slide film. Changing a roll is one of the trickiest of all tasks at altitude. You have to gauge very carefully whether you can take off your mittens just long enough to perform the job. You have to get out of the wind, or at least turn your back to it. And it's easy to drop the little cartridge—there it goes, thirty-six images from your last day or two of climbing, irreplaceable pictures that you went to great pains to take. On a few occasions when I've dropped a roll,

I've actually carried out a brief debate with myself about whether it's worth risking my life to chase the skittering cartridge down the slope. With film, I'll shoot two frames of every picture, so I'll have an in-camera duplicate to give to my partner later.

The waist harness is also critical. You put it on inside the tent, and you make sure it's good and snug. If you're roping up, you tie in to the waist harness with either a figure-eight knot or a bowline. On the side loops of your harness, you clip in a minimum of hardware. I'll take one or two ice screws, a knifeblade piton, two or three nylon slings, and only four carabiners, two of them with locking gates. The hardware is for the odd little technical bit you have to solve—it's not nearly enough gear to climb a serious pitch, like the ones we faced low on the Kangshung Face of Everest in 1988.

You also need a metal figure-eight descender for rappels, whether you're going down fixed ropes or setting up a rappel with the climbing rope. And you need a pair of jumars or ascenders, devices that grip the rope tight for a downward pull but slide easily upward. You use these to ensure your safety as you climb fixed ropes. To pass each anchor, you clip the upper ascender to the next rope above before unclipping the lower one—that way, you're always attached. All of this gear also becomes vital in the event that you have to pull a teammate out of a crevasse.

I carry an ice ax, fifty-five centimeters (less than two feet) long, with an adze for chopping snow or ice on one end of the head and a radically drooped pick on the other for stabbing into steep ice. This tool is a far cry from the classic ice ax favored by nearly a century of mountaineers, an ash- or hickory-shafted device at least three feet long—long enough to serve as a walking stick on glaciers, which ended up being its principal function. As late as the 1960s, these stylish but less than efficient axes were the going tool for mountaineers worldwide.

My ice ax is my most treasured tool in the mountains. With it I can stop a fall on snow or ice, securely climb steep terrain, use it for balance on precarious slopes, and chop a ledge in the snow or ice for my tent platform. On moderate terrain, I'll also use a ski pole for balance.

I also usually carry a bundle of willow wands to mark the route. These are the three-foot-long green stakes sold to tomato growers. I add a piece of red flagging tape to one end of each stake. Before an expedition, I'll go to a local garden store and buy a couple hundred. The guy will say, "Boy, you're planting a lot of tomatoes this year."

On the mountain, I carry the willow wands slotted into my pack like arrows in a quiver. It flabbergasts me that some mountaineers don't think of bringing wands. They're cheap insurance—they've saved our butts numerous times. You can't assume that the weather will be as good on the way down as it was on the way up.

So, everybody wants to know, with that virtual space suit on, how do you go to the bathroom, especially if you have to take a crap? It can be a real pain in the ass, so to speak. I'm lucky—I'm pretty regular, so I can usually go just before leaving camp in the morning. But often at altitude, climbers develop diarrhea. It can be truly messy.

As a result, three layers—long johns, fleece undersuit, and down over-suit—come equipped with what we call "moon zips"—trapdoors so you can take a dump without having to pull your pants down. Usually you have to unbuckle the leg loops of your harness as well, so it's crucial to have a harness with that feature.

You try to go a bit away from the climbing route, preferably just off the ridge, above a steep face. Or you try to dig a little hole if you can. Yet a place like the South Col on Everest is just covered with human feces. People will lay a rock over their dump, but at that altitude, nothing decays. The toilet paper, however, just blows away.

In the night in the tent, if you have to pee, it's best to get up and go out. But we all keep a pee bottle as well, for nights when it's too stormy or you feel too lethargic to go out. You draw a skull and crossbones on the pee bottle, so you won't confuse it with your water bottle. (More than one climber has made that mistake in the dark.) By morning, the urine has turned to vile yellow slush that you try to dump somewhere outside the tent. Some guys master the art of using the pee bottle lying down, but I've never been able to do it reliably.

The tent has to be strong enough to withstand gale-force winds yet relatively small, both to save weight (five pounds for a two-man tent is typical) and to trap as much body heat as possible. No sound is more familiar to the Himalayan climber than the ceaseless flapping of the tent walls in the wind. I'd call it too loud to let you get to sleep, except that the night before a summit push you don't sleep anyway—partly because you're consumed by anxiety but also because you're going to try to get moving by one or two A.M.

The tent fabric has to be breathable, but another annoying aspect of high-altitude camping is that all the breath you exhale during the night condenses as frost on the roof and walls. If it's windy, the frost trickles down on your face all night. If it's not, when you get out of your sleeping bag in the morning, it's impossible not to brush up against the coating that's accumulated. Moving around as you get ready to go, it's as though you've set loose a small snowstorm inside the tent.

You'd think you'd need the warmest possible sleeping bag at 26,000 feet, but I carry one rated good only down to zero degrees Fahrenheit. It weighs a mere four and a half pounds. I can get away with this because I wear all my clothes, except my boots, to bed. My down suit is like a second, inner sleeping bag. Often when a partner and I are going really light, we carry only one sleeping bag between us, which we unzip and lay on top of us like a blanket, "spooning" as we lie together, back to front. For a sleeping pad, I prefer a three-quarter-inch-thick closed-cell foam mattress, full-length, head to toe.

When you turn in for the night, anything you need to keep warm goes into the sleeping bag with you. Boot liners, mittens, water bottles, camera, batteries, extra socks, and even the next morning's fuel canister for the stove.

What about eating and drinking? By far the most important thing at altitude is to hydrate the night before a climb. Easier said than done. We use stoves that burn canisters of a propane-butane mixture. Before getting inside the tent, one of us will fill a big garbage bag with ice that we've chopped, then park it just outside the door. When ice isn't available, we have to fill the bag with dry snow. That's our water supply. You fill pot after pot, but if you're forced to use dry snow, the stuff can be so airy that a full pot may yield as little as one-eighth of a pot of water. The boiling point is so low at these altitudes that the water barely gets warmer than tepid. It can easily take three or four hours in the evening to get minimally rehydrated for the next day.

Melting ice or snow, drinking, and filling water bottles is a tedious yet utterly necessary procedure. Typically, if I do the melting at dinner, my partner will take the job at breakfast the next morning. The stories are legion among high-altitude mountaineers of serious interpersonal tension arising because one guy doesn't do his share of melting and cooking.

We'll drink tea with sugar and milk. Or instant soup—I'm fond of split pea. And we'll fill our water bottles for the summit day, then sleep with them so they won't freeze. The higher you go, the worse your appetite. Both intense exercise and extreme altitude act as appetite suppressants. We'll try to eat dinner, sometimes splitting a freeze-dried meal such as rice and beans or chili mac. We'll spoon the meal right out of the foil pack it comes in. I prefer spicy dinners, both for the flavor and for the tiny warming effect the seasonings provide.

Other times, you don't have the energy or patience to cook, so you try to snack instead. Cashews, cheese and crackers, salami with mustard, beef jerky, dried fruit. But you can never eat enough to supply the calories you need—that's why almost everybody who climbs an 8,000er loses quite a few pounds in the process.

Breakfast is minimal: if you can boil water, then maybe some coffee—our one little luxury—with tubes of condensed milk. Cookies or Pop-Tarts. For some reason, Pop-Tarts have become a favorite Himalayan food. Something like oatmeal would just make you want to vomit. Ultimately, whatever you can choke down serves to supply you with calories, no matter how bad the stuff may be for you at sea level.

On the summit day, it's important to go as light as possible. Lunch, which you eat almost anytime during the day, can be as little as a candy bar or two—Snickers, Twix, and hard semisweet chocolate bars are my favorites. A typical energy bar would freeze like a rock; you'd need your ax to knock chunks off it. I've come to favor energy gels—tubes of high-calorie slime that come in a variety of flavors. You squirt the gel into your mouth and swallow it like a raw oyster. I like to point out, only half-jokingly, that with a gel you don't even have to waste calories on chewing.

You can't carry more than two liters of water; often, I'll carry only one liter for an eighteen-hour day. Sometimes I won't even carry a pack—I'll just stick lunch and a single water bottle in my pockets. It's often so hard to stop that it's almost too much effort to pause for a drink or a bite of candy bar. Without bottled oxygen, you start to get cold in minutes. It's a question of metabolism: the extra oxygen helps you break down food, supplying warmth and energy to the rest of your body. In the rarefied air above 26,000 feet, without that artifical boost, you metabolize poorly. I often think that I'm blessed with an unusual physiology that allows me to go hours or even days on end without eating much at all, yet suffer no ill effects.

If there are no crevasses or stretches steep enough to belay, sometimes we won't even take a rope on the summit day. And, of course, when I went from the South Col to the top of Everest solo in 1991, a rope wouldn't have done me much good.

What else do I carry? A headlamp, because you start in the dark, and for safety if you get caught out the next night on the descent from the summit. Backup batteries. An extra pair of mittens (losing a mitten can cost you your life, not just your fingers). A minimal first-aid kit—Band-Aids, gauze, Diamox for altitude acclimatization, dexamethasone, which is a steroidal anti-inflammatory in case of cerebral edema. A little vial of anesthetic eye-drops. I carry some kind of speed, such as Dexedrine, as a last resort in case I need to keep someone else moving; so far, I've never used it.

Even going light, especially without supplemental oxygen, your pace is reduced to an interminable crawl. Fifteen breaths to each step, as I had to take in the deep snow above the Second Step on Everest in 1990, is not at all unheard of. If you look up at the summit and say to yourself, "I've got four thousand vertical feet to go over the next twelve hours," that's psychologically overwhelming. You probably won't make it. What I do is break it down into the smallest possible units. That rock forty feet away becomes my first target. I tell myself I won't stop till I get to that rock. Once I'm there,

I pick another nearby goal. Each stretch between a pair of mini-targets becomes its own private struggle. It's only by nibbling away at these immense distances that you can achieve the whole.

Even so, I've always found that the summit day is five to ten times harder than any of the load-carrying days earlier during the expedition. After weeks of hard work on the mountain, you're physically drained and emotionally tattered. You need tremendous focus and desire to keep it all together on the final push to the top.

All this may make climbing an 8,000-meter peak sound like one of the most miserable occupations known to humankind. Indeed, such climbs bring with them inordinate doses of sheer misery, discomfort, tedium, and frustration. Not to mention fear, if things start to go wrong.

Yet there's an immense pleasure in getting all this business down to a science, in carrying out the climb of an 8,000er as efficiently and safely as humanly possible. And there is nothing else in life like getting to the summit. What's more, I've always felt that the greater the challenge, the greater the reward.

▲
▲
▲

While Rob and I had been guiding clients on Everest, Veikka Gustafsson was climbing Lhotse, the neighboring 8,000er that is the world's fourth-highest mountain. Most of the way, we shared the same route, so we saw each other often that April and May. In the spring of 1993, Veikka had been Rob and Gary Ball's client on Everest. When he reached the summit, he became the first Finn ever to do so. In the autumn of '93, on Dhaulagiri, Veikka was no longer a client but Rob and Gary's full-fledged partner. After Gary died, Veikka stormed up the mountain solo, reaching the summit in honor of Gary.

I'd met Veikka briefly in Kathmandu in the spring of '93, at a café called Mike's Breakfast, where Rob introduced us. I liked the guy immediately, but I had no inkling at the time that Veikka would become my favorite partner of all on the 8,000-meter peaks. Eventually, he and I would share no fewer than thirteen expeditions to the world's highest mountains.

Now, in May 1995, after we'd finished our respective climbs, Veikka met us at the joint Everest-Lhotse base camp. We hiked three days down the valley to the hill town of Lukla, where, by prearrangement, a helicopter picked us up and flew us directly to base camp on Makalu. There were six of us: Rob, Veikka, and me, with Jan Arnold, Paula, and a Sherpa cook. Since we were planning to try Makalu alpine-style, we didn't need a lot of gear and food. We got everything shuttled to base camp in one flight.

As we packed up for our rapid ascent, I set up the new Trango 3 tent that I was testing for Mountain Hardwear. I wanted to convince Rob and Veikka that this was the shelter we should use on the climb. It was a windy day, so instead of staking out the tent, I threw a few rocks inside it to keep it from blowing away. Veikka and Rob immediately approved the tent, so I packed it up. Veikka grabbed it to carry as part of his load.

We knew that just a few weeks earlier there had been an Australian expedition on Makalu. One of their members had fallen to his death on the descent, so the team had evacuated the mountain in haste. They told us they had left a tent at each campsite, and that we were welcome to use them. You can't assume the tents will still be there, though, so we carried my Trango 3 as a backup.

The idea behind a twofer was that you used the first mountain to get acclimatized so that you could be really fast on the second mountain. And that spring, it worked to perfection. Rob, Veikka, and I climbed to the summit of Makalu from base camp in only four days. We reached the top only ten days after leaving Everest. On the summit push, Veikka and I climbed without oxygen, while Rob used it.

All the way up, we found a battered Australian tent at each campsite. We dug each one out of the snowdrifts, fixed a broken pole or two, and used these as shelters. Even a battered tent already pitched requires a lot less effort than setting one up from scratch. As a result, Veikka carried the Trango 3 all the way to high camp and back down without our once using it.

Jan was a physician who had often served as the team doctor on Adventure Consultants trips. She was also an excellent mountaineer, having climbed Everest and Cho Oyu. But that spring, she was content to hang out around base camp with Paula. There wasn't much for them to manage, since we got up and down the peak so quickly; instead, they went on hikes as high as 21,000 feet, and they reveled in the beauty of their surroundings, so different from the crowded squalor of Everest base camp.

From the fact that we got everyone down Everest safely that spring, then knocked off Makalu with such apparent ease, Paula may have formed a slightly skewed idea of what Himalayan climbing was all about. Certainly she never got the slightest bit freaked out about any risks I might be taking on Everest or Makalu. Summit day on Makalu was quite windy and cold. From far below, Jan and Paula saw the streaming clouds racing over the top and concluded that our chances were nil. Yet just as we gained the summit ridge, the wind died. From the top we radioed down, catching Jan and Paula completely by surprise. From the summit, we could actually see the tiny dots of our base-camp tents, 10,000 feet below.

That spring, Paula wasn't waiting at base camp on pins and needles, but rather enjoying the novelty of it all. Unfortunately, this would soon change.

I guessed that I couldn't count that Everest-Makalu duo as a true twofer, since we hadn't gotten to the summit of Everest, but it was as close as you could come without completing the task. And with Makalu, I now had six 8,000ers to my credit. I'd begun to realize that I couldn't really number Shishapangma among my 8,000ers until I obeyed Miss Hawley's injunction to go back and do it right—to cross that final hundred-yard ridge to the true summit.

We got back to base in one day, then used Rob's monster sat phone to call Kathmandu for the helicopter to pick us up. And then for five mornings in a row, we repeated the same routine: pack up everything by six A.M., observe the bad weather down-valley, and slowly realize the chopper wasn't coming that day. Our food supply dwindled down to a bag of tortilla chips and some M&M's. Veikka used a spoon to excavate the last crumbs and the salt from the bottom of the chips bag. We spent each day playing cards and dreaming of salads and pizza.

Finally, on the sixth morning, the helicopter retrieved us. As soon as we could, we flew home, Rob and Jan to New Zealand, Paula and I to Seattle. Rob and I had agreed to meet two weeks later in Islamabad, where we'd go after Gasherbrum I and II. If you have to go from Nepal to Pakistan, you might as well go home, do your laundry, eat some pizza, and drink some beer in between.

By late June, Rob and I were hiking up the Baltoro Glacier toward the Gasherbrum base camp. We were on a permit with two Poles and a Mexican climber. One of the Poles, Krzysztof Wielicki, and the Mexican, Carlos Carsolio, were well on their own ways to climbing the fourteen 8,000ers.

At base camp, I finally set up the Trango 3 tent that Veikka had carried all the way to high camp on Makalu and back. As soon as I got it pitched, I discovered a softball-sized rock inside it. It was one of the stones I'd tossed in to anchor the tent at Makalu base as I demonstrated its virtues to Veikka and Rob. Wrapped up inside the tent, the rock had traveled up and down Makalu on Veikka's back, all the way home to Seattle, back to Pakistan, and up the Baltoro to our Gasherbrum base. Unable to control my laughter, I gently removed the rock and placed it among the rubble in its new home. A little later, Rob and I used the sat phone to call Veikka back in Finland and tell him the news.

I felt that the fitness and acclimatization we'd gained on Everest and Makalu should tide us over on our efforts in the Karakoram. And for me, it worked. Rob and I got to Camp III on Gasherbrum II, at 23,900 feet, in only three days. The next morning, we set out for the summit, but we hadn't gone far when Rob stopped and said, "Ed, I'm going back. I just don't feel strong enough today." I was very disappointed, but I decided to push on alone. I climbed with more caution than usual up the final ridge. I hadn't brought willow wands this time, so I left a ski pole sticking out of the snow to mark the crucial turn on my descent route, in case the wind should drift over my footsteps.

I stood on the summit on the morning of July 4. I could visualize all the fireworks and partying that I knew must be going on back home, all across the United States, but I didn't want to be anywhere on earth except here. I thought, God, this is great, to be so fit, to feel so good, to climb another 8,000er in only four days.

Rob and I descended to base camp and regrouped. He was still not feeling right, and after a day or two, he made his decision. "Ed," he told me, with a hangdog look on his face, "I just don't have what it takes anymore this year. I'm going to hike out and go home."

It was a terrible shame to lose the companionship of the guy with whom I'd now been on six expeditions to 8,000-meter peaks, but I had the good fortune to join up with the Poles and Carlos Carsolio, who also had their eyes on Gasherbrum I. In the end, we were feeling so strong that we climbed all the way from base camp to the summit of Gasherbrum I in only thirty hours. In some sense, it was my strongest performance yet on an 8,000er.

Coming down off the summit, I stopped to radio Rob, who was hiking out down the Baltoro. "Rob," I announced, "we got to the top today. I'm so sorry you weren't with us. But do me a favor, okay? When you get to Islamabad, will you please phone Paula and tell her that we're safe and sound? We're on our way home." At that very moment, back in Seattle, Paula was moving into my apartment.

On my own hike out, I kept thinking what a fantastic campaign I'd had that spring and summer. A pair of twofers, with only two weeks at home to separate them. Three new 8,000ers on my roster. And even though the South Summit of Everest is actually higher than Makalu and the Gasherbrums, I couldn't say that I'd climbed four 8,000ers in one year. I'd climbed three, and 99 percent of the fourth.

▲
▲
▲

One evening that fall, Paula and I were lying in bed together in our apartment. That day we had traded in her convertible VW bug and bought a used Nissan Pathfinder together, and by now we were living together. As we chatted in bed, the subject of the future of our relationship came up. Paula asked, "With all that we're doing together, where is this heading?"

At once I answered, "I'm ready for the next step." There was a short silence.

"What do you mean?" Paula asked.

"Would you marry me?"

"Wait a minute," she said. "What did you just ask me? Let me turn on the light so that I can see your face."

I asked again. Paula said yes.

In retrospect, it's a bit embarrassing that it was she who had directed our conversation to something as serious as marriage. When I met Paula, I was finally ready to get married—but not before. In 1994 and '95, there were plenty of occasions when I might have, should have, could have proposed. I knew she was the one with whom I wanted to spend the rest of my life. From the moment we met, I felt that I had known her for a long time. I began to love her almost immediately. We had a comfort level that was perfect in my eyes. But asking someone to marry me was unfamiliar terrain for me, and finding the right moment and summoning up my nerve were not easy. My lack of confidence around women, I guess.

Anyway, as soon as she accepted, I got out of bed, went to the fridge, and pulled out the lone beer, which we shared as we toasted our future. It was a sweet and exciting moment.

So now we were engaged, but already I'd planned an Everest expedition for the spring of '96. I had two options. One was to guide again with Rob. The other project was far more intriguing but not yet fully funded; it was thus a real gamble to commit to it. I explained my dilemma to Rob. He promised that if the other project fell through, he'd still welcome me as his second-in-command on Everest.

So the big question now was, when can we fit a wedding into our schedules? Paula was pretty busy with Childhaven, and I was on the road quite frequently, doing slide shows and talks for Mountain Hardwear. We looked at our schedules and settled on one week in February. It would be just two weeks before we headed off to Everest. In '96, Paula was going to serve as the full-fledged base-camp manager for our new project, not as someone else's assistant.

We both wanted to get married on a beach somewhere, in an intimate wedding with friends, not a lavish production in a church. It didn't take us long to choose Puerto Vallarta, on Mexico's Pacific coast. We rented out a small villa with four bedrooms, planning to share it with three other couples. Then we invited friends and family to join the festivities.

I'd already met Paula's mom and dad and three sisters in Bend, Oregon. That first visit was a bit of an eye-opener for me, since her family's style was so different from mine. Paula and I slept on a mattress on the floor in the house of the boyfriend of one of her sisters. During that three-day visit, I was shocked at first to witness a kind of ritualized catfighting among the four sisters. They'd be literally yelling and screaming at each other, dredging up old history from their childhoods. Then, a moment later: "Hey, what's for dinner?" They could yell at each other and hug and make up within five minutes. Nothing could have been further from the endless, silent tension that had hung over the dinner table in Rockford when Velta and I were teenagers.

But I liked Paula's family immensely, and apparently they liked and approved of me. The same thing with Paula and my family.

We told our friends and family, "Come down to Puerto Vallarta and make a week's vacation out of it, with a wedding in the middle." This excursion would be a bit more expensive and complicated than the usual wedding, so we had no idea how many people would show up. As it turned out, forty guests made the trip, including all our parents and siblings. There were even a few folks from Mountain Hardwear.

Since Paula and I weren't religious, we paid the airfare for a lay minister from Seattle, named Gib Curry, to come down to Mexico and perform the service. Gib's since become a very good friend. Scott Fischer, who had ambitions as a professional photographer, came down to shoot our wedding pictures. He was so ruggedly handsome, all of Paula's girlfriends swooned, asking, "Who *is* that guy?" Scott milked the attention for all it was worth.

The wedding happened on Wednesday, just as the sun set. Dan Hiatt was my best man, and J.D. was Paula's bridesmaid of honor. The ceremony took place on the third-floor patio of our villa, overlooking the beach, the ocean, and the sunset. Everybody wore shorts. We drank margaritas and ate from a catered buffet while a mariachi band played. Later, lots of our friends said that it was the best wedding they'd ever been to.

We didn't have time for a honeymoon before Everest, so we just treated the week in Puerto Vallarta as a "built-in" honeymoon. By early March, we were on our way to Nepal, looking forward to another great shared adventure. Ordinarily, I wouldn't have been keen to go on yet another Everest expedition: I'd been on seven previous ones and had reached the summit three times. But our semisecret project loomed as an incredible challenge. If we could pull it off, it would be a radical first in high-altitude mountaineering annals.

I was always aware that on any expedition to an 8,000-meter peak, things could go wrong. After all, on K2 in 1992, the Mexican who'd ripped loose his ski-pole rappel anchor had died, and we'd been lucky not to lose four or five other climbers—including Scott Fischer and me, in the avalanche on the shoulder of the Abruzzi Ridge.

Yet as we hiked up the Khumbu Valley in the spring of '96, not even in my most pessimistic fantasies would I have imagined that we were about to plunge into the midst of the worst disaster in Everest history.

Time to Say Good-bye

At base camp on the south side of Everest in 1995, I'd bumped into David Breashears. I'd first met him briefly in 1987, when we shared a Chinese truck on the way into base camp on the north (Tibetan) side of the mountain. In 1990, we overlapped again on the north side of Everest, where we were on separate expeditions. That was when I was a member of Jim Whittaker's Everest International Peace Climb and David was making a film for the BBC, using the actor Brian Blessed to re-create Mallory's 1924 attempt and disappearance on the northeast ridge. But after that I hadn't seen David for another five years. ▲ In 1995, David had no intention of going for the summit of Everest, which he'd already climbed twice. Instead, he was just fooling around near base camp, conducting a trial run for the semisecret project that would unfold in the spring of '96.

David had been approached by MacGillivray Freeman Films, the company that had produced a number of groundbreaking IMAX movies, with a wild idea: to make a big-screen documentary of an ascent of Everest. Greg MacGillivray had come to David because he was something of a legend as a documentary filmmaker in difficult places—including Mount Everest. He figured if anybody could do the job, it would be Breashears.

At first, the idea seemed impossible to David. The IMAX camera of the day weighed 110 pounds, in large part because it had to incorporate a giant flywheel to stabilize the camera, much as a gyroscope would. With images projected on a fifty-foot-high screen, the slightest camera wobble would make everybody in the audience seasick.

Yet David was intrigued, and for much of a year he worked with the engineers of the IMAX corporation as they radically redesigned the camera. Eventually they came up with a model that hit the scales at only forty-two pounds (including battery, lens, and a loaded film magazine). That's still a tough load to carry up the South Col route, and such problems as positioning a super-stable tripod in the wind or changing the giant magazines could prove insurmountable.

I got pretty intrigued myself, and when David asked if I could take a day off and go climb a few seracs in the Khumbu Icefall so he could shoot some trial footage, I said, "Sure." In his 1999 autobiography, *High Exposure,* David later wrote a flattering paragraph about watching me go to the summit without oxygen on the Peace Climb in 1990:

> *I remember sitting at Advance Base Camp all morning, with a 1,000 mm telescope trained on Ed....[He] was affable, good-natured, and quiet. But that low-key exterior cloaked a thoroughly focused, highly motivated Himalayan climber. Watching him through the telescope, I was thrilled to see Ed make it to the top. This was his third try at Everest and I knew how hard he'd trained for the climb.*

After I clambered around on the Khumbu seracs while David shot what would in effect be a kind of promotional trailer for the upcoming film, it didn't take him long to say, "If this all works out, Ed, I'd like you to be involved next spring." Nor did I hesitate to accept. I thought, David's got a stellar reputation, and making the film could be fun and interesting, and it would be a whole new challenge. I asked myself, How could you make Everest harder? This is how. Get the damned camera to the summit, when everybody was saying it would be impossible.

Right from the start, David told me I'd be the climbing leader of his team. He said, "I'm going to be so involved in filming and directing, I don't want to have to think about the logistics of getting up the mountain. I just want the camps to be ready when I get there. I need somebody else to run the expedition. That's you." It was also understood that up high, the cinematic story of the climb would in part be focused on me. David wanted to build the film around someone topping out without bottled oxygen.

Going to Everest in 1996 to make the IMAX film, of course, might mean putting my Endeavor 8000 quest on hold. Nonetheless, I planned, if there was time before the monsoon, to go straight to Manaslu after Everest for another twofer, with Rob Hall, Scott Fischer, and Veikka Gustafsson. Chantal Mauduit, who would be on Lhotse while we were on Everest, had plans to come along as well. We would be sharing our permit with Carlos Carsolio, the very strong Mexican climber I'd gone to the summit of Gasherbrum I with the summer before. If Carlos got up Manaslu, he'd have climbed all fourteen 8,000ers, becoming only the sixth person to do so.

But I was never in any hurry to bag all fourteen 8,000ers. I didn't set my timeline year by year. I just thought, This is too good to miss out on. I got Mountain Hardwear involved right away. The film, I figured, could be huge for a fledgling company like theirs. Think of how big a logo looks on a fifty-foot screen!

At the same time, a lot of pressure came with my accepting David's invitation. Privately, I thought, I'm thirty-seven years old now—can I still get up Everest without oxygen? It had been five years since I'd last pulled off the trick. I knew that millions of dollars would be invested in the project—far more than for any of my previous expeditions. In the back of my mind was a caveat: *If I forget one critical detail, and we fail on the mountain because of it, well, I will have let a lot of people down.*

David chose the team, and he did so with a shrewd eye for the marketing possibilities of the film. Jamling Norgay, the son of the famous Tenzing, had always wanted to climb Everest as a tribute to his father's first ascent in 1953. If he could make it to the top, that story line alone might carry the film. The Austrian Robert Schauer was not only a talented filmmaker in his own right, he was an absolutely first-rate high-altitude mountaineer, with such climbs to his credit as a pathbreaking ascent of the huge and highly technical west face of Gasherbrum IV, only 71 meters (233 feet) short of the magical 8,000-meter altitude. Schauer's route is still considered to be one of the greatest and most difficult climbs ever done anywhere in the world. On the mountain, Robert would not only be David's one-man backup unit behind the lens, he would be in charge of much of the complicated logistics of getting the film and camera up and down the hill. He also took on the arduous and thankless task of preloading all the film magazines each night, so they'd be ready for the next day's filming.

Araceli Segarra was a strong, twenty-six-year-old Spanish climber David had met at Everest base camp in 1995. During her team's unsuccessful attempt that spring, one of her ropemates was killed in an avalanche. David went over to the Spanish base camp to offer his condolences and ended up in a long conversation with Araceli. As he wrote in *High Exposure,*

As she and I talked, an entire world of emotions flickered across her face, from disbelief to grief, and finally resignation. I'd never seen such an honest but hauntingly open display of human feelings. No actor could have summoned them—or shown them—so easily and with so much grace.

Araceli would help bring to the film not only the European market but an interest among women worldwide. It didn't hurt that she was beautiful enough to earn part of her living as a model back home in Barcelona.

Finally, David rounded out the team with another woman, Sumiyo Tsuzuki, whom he'd met on the north side of Everest in 1990. The Japanese appetite for IMAX films was already a lively one, and Sumiyo and Jamling together represented a major Asian presence in a film that, after all, would be shot in Asia.

To my delight, on meeting Paula at base camp in 1995, David decided at once that she would make a perfect base-camp manager for the IMAX expedition the next year. And Paula was thrilled to accept. In '96, she would no longer be someone else's assistant, with too much free time on her hands, but a full-fledged organizer with all the responsibilities she could ask for. And we thought that Everest might serve as a second honeymoon, only weeks after our "built-in" honeymoon around our wedding in Puerto Vallarta.

Of our team, David later wrote in his autobiography, "There wasn't a prima donna in the bunch. None of us harbored any illusions about who the real diva was. Everest would take center stage."

The winter of 1995–96 came close to overwhelming me. Not only was I still traveling frequently on behalf of Mountain Hardwear, even while Paula and I were planning our wedding, but on top of that, I had the task of organizing equipment and food for the entire IMAX expedition.

Figuring out the equipment needs, then ordering and buying all the stuff was relatively routine. Much of this chore took only simple math: a certain number of tents for base camp, four three-person tents for Camp I, six two-person tents and a large dining tent for Camp II, this many feet of fixed rope and that number of ice screws for the Lhotse Face, and so on. I also had to supply the camps with stoves, pots, fuel canisters, sleeping pads, tent cords, tent anchors, shovels, lighters, and radios. David and I calculated how much oxygen we would require, then added a certain extra percentage for unforeseen contingencies. We ordered the bottles from a Russian company called Poisk, hoping that they would arrive in time in Nepal.

The food was a much trickier task. How could I guess what foods

twenty different people would want, and how much of each they would con-
sume during a three-month expedition? Creating menus for such an under-
taking was not my forte. Paula was a tremendous help. We sent a
questionnaire to everyone on the team to find out what their preferences
were. Then we made up a master menu that was long on variety. I figured
we'd just get all the food to base camp, then let the members sort it out before we sent it up to the higher camps. David was a proponent of having
fairly luxurious foods at base camp, since that's where you recover from your
forays on the mountain. On an expedition, I can get by with local foods like
rice, potatoes, chicken, and eggs. But now we ordered smoked meats, canned
bacon, exotic sauces and spices, and even a few bottles of good wine.

Paula and I did virtually all the shopping in Seattle, loading up my little red truck on trip after trip to REI, Costco, and various grocery, hardware,
and specialty shops. I had rented a small garage where I could store and pack
everything. All the food and gear went into waxed cardboard boxes, each capable of holding sixty-five pounds, a normal porter's load. I numbered each
box and listed its contents, making sure not to put our only two of any given
item into a single box.

At the end of our shopping marathon, we had ninety boxes loaded and
stacked in our rented garage. Almost three tons of supplies. That did not
even include all the additional film equipment, film, batteries, and other
technical camera gear that David would bring. In previous years, we would
have shipped all our baggage ahead of us; but now it seemed safer, quicker,
and no more costly to take everything with us as excess baggage.

I rented a panel truck, which Dan Hiatt and I stuffed to the rafters;
then he drove Paula and me to the airport. I had called the airlines a week
before to warn them of our impending onslaught of baggage, but when we
got to the airport, they were nonplussed. Needless to say, the cost of all the
excess freight far exceeded the price of our tickets, so the airlines graciously
upgraded Paula and me to first class. We flew to Nepal sipping chardonnay
while our tons of expedition supplies sat beneath us, in the belly of the 747.

On the ten-day approach march up the Khumbu Valley, as it turned
out, David would often suddenly request a certain item. My system allowed

me to figure out very quickly just where that item was. Sometimes the box would still be one or two villages behind us, since our porters tended to straggle. It then became my job to get the box up to us in time for David to use whatever he needed. I sweated bullets during the hike in, trying to keep all our gear corralled and accounted for. Only once we got all of the wayward boxes to base camp was I able to relax.

▲
▲
▲

That spring, there were more climbers on the south side of Everest than ever before in history. There was a Taiwanese team of five; a South African team of twenty-one (including Sherpas and base-camp personnel); a nine-man assemblage of British, Danish, and Finnish climbers; a small American team of six; and a maverick Swede named Göran Kropp, who hoped to make history by bicycling to and from Everest all the way from Sweden and climbing the mountain solo, without so much aid from other climbers as a single spoonful of shared breakfast. Rounding out the throng were two large expeditions of guided clients led by my good friends and erstwhile Himalayan partners Scott Fischer and Rob Hall. Scott's Mountain Madness team numbered twenty-three; Rob's Adventure Consultants entourage, twenty-six.

Among Rob's clients was Jon Krakauer, on assignment for *Outside* magazine. In 1987, *Outside* had sent Jon to Denali to report on the absurdities that had started to crop up annually on the mountain's wildly popular West Buttress route. The piece Jon wrote, called "Club Denali" (reprinted in his collection *Eiger Dreams*), was a deft comic narrative centering around the exploits of a zany madman nicknamed Adrian the Romanian. Nearly a decade later, *Outside* hoped to elicit from the follies that were beginning to bedevil the equally thronged South Col route on Everest another such wry and hilarious article from Krakauer.

Jon and Scott knew each other from Seattle, and for quite a while both of them had assumed that he would go to Everest as a nominal client on the Mountain Madness team. But by 1996, a place on either Scott's or Rob's teams was selling for $65,000—far more than *Outside* was willing to pay. At the last minute, the magazine's publisher worked out a deal with Rob Hall, involving a fee of only $10,000, the remainder to be made up in free advertising in the pages of *Outside*. On learning what had happened, Scott was crushed, for the publicity he was counting on that would issue from an article in the leading outdoor magazine in the world could have made a lasting difference for his business. As Jon later wrote, when Scott got the bad news, in January 1996, he was "apoplectic. He called me from Colorado, as upset as I'd ever heard him, to insist that he wasn't about to concede victory to Hall." In the end, though, Scott couldn't match Rob's deal with *Outside,* and Jon came to Everest as an official Adventure Consultants client.

I'd never met Jon Krakauer before Everest, having quailed a few years earlier at contacting him after finding his notice on the message board of a Seattle climbing store, when Jon was looking for partners. I'd read everything he wrote for *Outside,* and by now I'd read his best seller *Into the Wild.* To me, he seemed not only a highly respected writer but a very talented climber as well. At base camp, Jon turned out to be a plain nice guy, unassuming, with a ready smile. It's a pleasure for me to meet someone I think of as famous who, in person, is friendly and unpretentious.

And at base camp, it was great for me to catch up with Scott again, and especially to hang out with Rob. I had fond memories of guiding Everest with Rob in '94 and '95, as well as of our climbs together on Cho Oyu, Lhotse, Makalu, and Gasherbrum II. But I was happy for once not to be guiding the "Big E." This year, Jan Arnold had stayed home in New Zealand, for she was pregnant with the couple's first child.

Veikka Gustafsson was there, too, as part of the British-Danish-Finnish team. He was going to try to make his second ascent of Everest, this time without supplemental oxygen. Chantal was there as well, hoping to climb Lhotse. It was as though all my closest Himalayan buddies had gathered for a reunion.

At the same time, all of us on the IMAX team were seriously concerned about the mob of Everest aspirants that had gathered at base camp. Aesthetically, it posed a problem for the making of our film—we didn't want viewers to see footage of dozens of climbers straggling along in the background and wonder, *Who the hell are those folks?* But it also posed a real safety dilemma. The most exposed and dangerous part of the whole South Col route comes up high, on the final ridge, at tricky spots such as the Hillary Step, only 250 feet below the summit. Too many climbers strung out along that ridge can create a bottleneck, even a true traffic jam, with the slowest-moving clients dictating the pace for everybody else.

To sort out the convoluted logistics of this multipronged assault on the mountain, we held weekly meetings of the team leaders at base camp. One team had already taken on the job of fixing ropes through the chaos of the Khumbu Icefall (in many ways the most dangerous part of the mountain), and the rest of us paid them a fee for the effort. Higher on the mountain, ropes fixed by various teams would be used by all the climbers, so we tried to divvy up the necessary chores. Though there was occasional friction between different teams, the general mood was one of cooperation.

Rob had fixed May 10 in his mind as the day to go to the summit. That date had been lucky for him in the past. There's a window each spring, a stretch of calm, mostly clear days that occurs as the monsoon, moving up from India, dislodges the air ahead of it and pushes the jet stream away from Everest. Some years that window comes in early May, other years not until late May. In Rob's experience, May 10 was right around the most likely middle of that window. But in retrospect, maybe he fixed his sights a little too rigidly on an arbitrary calendar date.

Rob and Scott were friends, but they were also rivals. So once Rob decided on May 10, Scott also opted for the same date. In fact, they decided to join forces for their summit attempt. Meanwhile, unbeknownst to Rob and Scott, the Taiwanese team chose to tag along, too. This meant that on May 10, there would be an unholy throng—forty or more climbers—going for the summit from the South Col. Both Rob's and Scott's teams each had three guides, eight clients, and seven climbing Sherpas.

So during one of those meetings of team leaders at base camp, it was agreed that our IMAX team would try to get out a single day ahead of the throng. If all went well, we'd go to the summit on May 9—that day we'd have the upper mountain to ourselves, which would be ideal for David's filming.

All through April, we were putting together IMAX footage lower on the mountain. The logistics of even the simplest setup were mind-boggling. The tripod itself weighed thirty-seven pounds—it needed to be that heavy just to ensure the stability of the camera mounted on top of it. And a mechanism called the tilt head and metal pan, which connected the unwieldy camera to the tripod, weighed another ungodly forty-seven pounds. Each loaded film magazine weighed ten pounds. Yet because the 65-millimeter film we were exposing raced through the camera at 5.6 feet per second, that meant that a single roll—five hundred feet of film—was good for only ninety seconds of footage.

The hardest job of all was loading and threading the film. As David would later write,

> *I needed to feel the film and the camera mechanism with my bare hands. With the film flying through the camera at 5.6 feet per second, a malfunction could have damaged the camera, ending our filming for the day or for weeks. If an image was going to be unusable, I wanted it to be because of a mistake in executing a shot, not because my gloved hands performed clumsily or left "hairs" in the camera.*

Nothing could be shot spontaneously, the way David so often had before, with handheld video cameras. Even the most mundane scenes had to be laboriously set up. And the film stock was so heavy and expensive—an hour's worth of 65-millimeter film cost $20,000—that we couldn't afford to shoot much footage that would end up on the cutting-room floor. Filmmakers ordinarily count on at least a twenty-to-one ratio of footage shot to footage that makes it into the final film. Up high on Everest, we would have to use pretty much every precious second of action that David and Robert would be able to expose.

David is nothing if not a perfectionist, however, and he managed not only to wrestle the cumbersome equipment into some pretty hairy places but to film some startling sequences. One of the most impressive bits in the film—audiences always gasp in unison when they see it—follows Araceli crossing a huge crevasse in the Khumbu Icefall on a metal ladder. Wearing crampons, roped up, with hand lines for added safety, she nevertheless moves agonizingly slowly and uncertainly. Suddenly, David pans and tilts the camera down, revealing the depth of the crevasse in all its hideous glory.

Throughout the expedition, I was in awe of the hard work that David and Robert put into making our film. They were always up before anyone else in the morning, and they went to sleep long after the rest of us in the evening. People who see the IMAX film often assume that we had a camera crew and "talent," plus a whole separate team to carry loads and establish camps. In fact, we did everything ourselves: carry loads, fix ropes, establish camps, as well as fit filming and acting into our daily schedules.

At last it was time to make our attempt. By the evening of May 7, we were ensconced in Camp III on the Lhotse Face, at 24,000 feet. The plan was to go up to the South Col and Camp IV the next day, then to the summit on May 9. The horde of other climbers—mainly Scott's and Rob's teams—would follow us only a day later, so we had no wriggle room in our schedule. While we were at Camp III, they were digging in at Camp II, in the Western Cwm, only 2,800 feet below us.

That evening, we were very excited. A year of planning and hard work would be coming to fruition in the next two days.

Yet during the previous week, I'd been keeping a close eye on the weather. Every afternoon, the clouds would roll in up high. And it was far too windy along the summit ridge. That magical window of calm, clear days wasn't yet upon us.

On the morning of May 8, as we roused ourselves at Camp III, it just didn't feel right to me. I discussed it with David and Robert. All three of us were of the same mind. The conditions were okay, but not great. If we were going to make the summit, we needed the best possible weather we could get. We'd have only one shot.

David and I agreed: we had plenty of gear and food cached back at Camp II. There were still at least two weeks, maybe three, before the monsoon would roll in. We'd be idiots to force it and go now, in unsettled weather. The decision was unanimous: we'd go back down to Camp II and wait there.

So on May 8, instead of pushing up to the South Col, we descended the fixed ropes. Before long, we ran into Scott's and Rob's teams heading up. Both trip leaders asked me, "What are you guys doing?" I answered, "Going down. It just doesn't feel right."

Of course, their surprised reactions made us start to question ourselves. Were we missing our one good shot for the top? Yet I'd seen summit fever before. If eight climbers head up, they pull ten more with them. The mood is "So-and-so's going today? Shit, we should be going too." But on Everest, or on any mountain, you've got to make your own decisions.

There on the Lhotse Face, as we crossed paths on the fixed ropes, I shook hands with Rob and Scott, gave them each a big hug, and said, "Have a great trip. Be safe."

After hugging me, Rob said, "I'll see you on the bottom, mate."

I answered, "I'll buy you a beer when we both get down."

▲
▲
▲

Because of the immense popularity of Krakauer's *Into Thin Air,* it seems that nearly everybody is familiar with at least the broad outlines of what unfolded on Everest on May 10, 1996—how the traffic jam indeed seized the upper part of the mountain, paralyzing climbers in their steps; how the storm suddenly moved in, turning a snafu into a disaster; how only the heroics of certain key players kept the death toll from being worse. Characters in that drama, such as Sandy Pittman, Anatoli Boukreev, and Beck Weathers, have entered the folklore of adventure.

Into Thin Air was not only an instant and a lasting best seller, it remains one of the finest mountaineering books ever written. Jon managed to sort through the details and find a hauntingly vivid dramatic arc for a very messy story. Yet for all of his assiduous reporting, there will always be mysteries about exactly what happened on May 10. For one thing, the drama involved so many different climbers from a number of autonomous expeditions (Jon had to preface his text with a six-page "Dramatis Personae" just to keep the players straight) that no single point of view can possibly encompass the definitive story. Ten years after the disaster, armchair mountaineers who've never been near Everest still argue fiercely over whether Anatoli did the wrong thing by dashing ahead down to the South Col to brew up tea for the stragglers, whether Sandy was in fact "short-roped" by Lopsang Jangbu.

There's little point, then, in going over all that ground again in step-by-step detail here. Of necessity, though, in *Into Thin Air* Jon dealt only glancingly with the IMAX team's role in the debacle of '96. Because he himself was in the eye of the storm, caught up in a pivotal role in the chaos, Jon had no need in his book to capture our experience of the disaster. Yet our perspective may, in the long run, add something to explaining just how things went wrong on the mountain that spring.

The debacle of May 10 actually had a "prequel" the day before, in an accident that would have been farcical had it not had such grave consequences. On the morning of May 9, a Taiwanese climber named Chen Yu-Nan crawled out of his tent at Camp III to relieve himself. He didn't bother either to clip in to the fixed ropes or to put on his boots. In smooth-soled inner boots, he slipped and slid down the face some seventy feet, before catching up in a small crevasse.

Two of his teammates descended, lowered a rope, and pulled Chen out of the crevasse. At first the man seemed to be more embarrassed than hurt. He assured his teammates that he was all right, but they insisted that he rest in the tent that day, rather than head up to the South Col.

The next thing we knew, Chen was headed down the fixed ropes toward our Camp II, escorted by one of his team's Sherpas. Suddenly Chen collapsed in his tracks. Meanwhile, one of our own Sherpas, Jangbu, was headed up the fixed ropes. When he reached Chen, he ascertained that the Taiwanese had no pulse and was not breathing. "He's dead," Jangbu radioed down to us. Internal injuries suffered in the fall had apparently been the cause of death.

On Everest, Sherpas perform all kinds of incredibly difficult and dangerous tasks—efforts that go largely unsung in the articles and books Western climbers write about their own deeds. But they have a profound horror of dead bodies on the mountain. Normally, for a Sherpa, merely to see a dead person on the mountain is very bad luck—handling one is out of the question. So Jangbu and the Taiwanese team's Sherpa left Chen dangling from the fixed rope and continued their descent.

Thus it fell to Robert, David, and me to retrieve Chen's body. It was a brutal job, as his crampons and one arm kept snagging on protuberances in the ice when we tried to lower him. At last, several of Chen's Taiwanese teammates met us, put the body in a sleeping bag, and helped us lug it back to Camp II. There, ghoulishly enough, nobody (especially not the Sherpas) wanted to share a tent with a corpse, or even have one in camp. Instead, we lugged Chen out onto the ice, reasoning that a frozen body would be easier to wrestle down through the Khumbu Icefall.

As David would later write in *High Exposure,*

I felt terrible about this man's death. He had died, staring into the eyes of strangers with whom he shared no language, unable to say goodbye to the people he loved.... As his pallbearer I felt acutely aware of the loneliness of his last minutes.

The next morning, May 10, we knew that Rob's and Scott's teams would have set out from the South Col around midnight to go to the summit. That day dawned perfect, so there was no reason for them not to go. We had a telescope in camp with us, to monitor the climbers' progress. Though we weren't in direct radio contact with the teams up high, we could talk to Paula at base camp and get their reports secondhand.

It got to be one P.M. Then, around two, through the telescope we could make out climbers scattered along the high ridge—they appeared just as little specks of red and yellow, lined up, waiting their turns to climb the Hillary Step. It was alarming how much of the time those specks were standing still, not moving. The traffic jam had indeed started to work its mischief.

A few folks had reached the summit by then (Jon got there at about one-ten, just a few minutes after Anatoli, who was guiding for Scott's team without bottled oxygen), but the vast majority were still heading up. Staring through the telescope, I muttered out loud, as if those anonymous specks could hear me, "Guys—you left at midnight. It's two o'clock! It's going to be three or four before you get to the summit." Then, as I watched the all but immobile procession, my mood darkened. "Dudes, what are you doing? Wake up! Guys, turn around, turn around," I urged. It was as if I were trying to send them a telepathic message. And of course it never got there.

Then the big storm rolled in. The summit disappeared, the clouds lowered, swallowing up more and more of the upper mountain, until finally our visibility was cut off even below the South Col. All the while, things were falling apart up high. Radio batteries started to die. There was little word as to just what was going on.

At Camp II, we just sat in our tents, waiting and waiting, all of us growing more somber by the minute. It wasn't until ten P.M. that we got any news. At that hour, Paula radioed up to us. She said, "Only half the people who left the South Col this morning have made it back."

We cursed out loud. I tried to imagine the nightmare that must be unfolding up there. It's windy, it's dark, it's freezing cold, and we knew that everybody must be out of bottled oxygen by now.

At Camp II, Rob's team had set up a command station with a radio in a tent. Veikka Gustafsson, who was camped near our IMAX tents, now moved into Rob's tent, to sleep beside his radio. We lay in our own tents, with our little handheld radios on, waiting for further news, but none of us slept a wink that night.

We got up and made coffee around three or four in the morning, still hoping for the best. And then, around five A.M., we heard the first transmission from up high. It was from Rob. By now, we'd all crowded into the radio tent with Veikka, so we could hear the play-by-play. And what Rob said was both deeply troubling and utterly puzzling. In a tired, weak voice, he said, "I'm all fucked up. I'm on the South Summit. I sat out all night. Doug is gone."

Doug Hansen, the postal worker from Renton, was the client Rob had taken such a liking to the year before, and when Doug had had to turn around at the South Summit, Rob's disappointment had been as keen as Doug's. Doug had pushed himself so close to the limit in '95 that it was all I could do to get him down to the South Col, shouting at him with my laryngitic voice to keep him moving. But after that expedition, Rob had offered Doug a big discount on the client fee if he came back in '96, and had all but guaranteed him the summit on his second try.

We later pieced things together from broadcasts Rob had made to his base-camp manager, Helen Wilton. On May 10, Rob had gone up the mountain near the tail end of his own Adventure Consultants team. He reached the summit himself well after three P.M., where he waited for Doug, who was once again giving it all he had—too much, in the face of the worsening weather. As Doug came into sight, Rob descended to him, then helped him the last bit of the way to the top. I can imagine Rob putting his arm around Doug's shoulder, then walking him to the top. But it was not until four P.M. that the exhausted Hansen topped out. That was at least two hours beyond the turn-around time Rob had otherwise so firmly insisted on. His passion to get Doug to the top, sadly, had clouded his usually impeccable judgment.

Rob had broadcast to base camp from the summit to report his and Doug's success. Then, only half an hour later, he had come on the radio again to say that the two were in trouble and needed oxygen. Mike Groom, an Adventure Consultants guide, overheard Rob's broadcast from lower on the ridge, as he shepherded another fast-failing client down toward the South Col. Groom knew that there were two full oxygen bottles cached on the South Summit. But he was having transmission problems of his own, and it took a while before he could get through to Rob with that news.

Meanwhile, Doug Hansen had collapsed at the top of the Hillary Step. Unable to lower his client down the forty-foot cliff, Rob stayed with him, apparently willing to risk an overnight bivouac well above 28,000 feet.

Guy Cotter, who had been our fellow guide on the South Col route the year before, was leading a Pumori expedition. At base camp, overhearing Rob's increasingly sketchy broadcasts, Guy got on the radio himself, pleading with his old friend to leave Hansen and get down to the South Summit, if only to retrieve the oxygen bottles so he could start breathing gas and gain the strength to aid his client. Rob radioed back that he could get down to the South Summit himself, but that Doug couldn't. Forty minutes later, he had not moved a step.

At this point—just before six P.M. on May 10—Guy urged Rob to perform a desperate triage: to leave Doug behind so he could save himself. As Guy later told Krakauer, "I know I sound like the bastard for telling Rob to abandon his client, but by then it was obvious that leaving Doug was his only choice."

Yet it was not advice Rob was willing to heed. At two forty-five A.M., Guy heard a few words of broken transmission over a background of howling wind. Guy suspected that Rob wasn't even trying to broadcast, but that his clip-on mike on the shoulder strap of his pack was getting bumped and keying on in interrupted bursts. What Guy heard was Rob yelling, something like "Keep moving! Keep going!" Evidently he was trying to push Doug down to the South Summit in the middle of the night, in all-out storm, by sheer force of will.

Of all this drama through the night of May 10–11, we at Camp II were unaware—until, at five in the morning, we heard Rob's despairing radio call, beginning with the terrible pronouncement, "I'm all fucked up."

By that morning, Rob had gotten down some 350 vertical feet to a spot just short of the South Summit. Somehow he'd survived the night, without even a bivouac sack for protection. But *Doug was gone.* We would never learn what that three-word formula really meant. Did Doug die on the way down, from hypothermia and exhaustion? Had he broken through a cornice and plunged down the Kangshung Face? Or had he frozen to death bivouacking there beside Rob, only to be buried by snow? To this day, Doug's body has never been found.

Now Rob's voice over the radio was badly slurred. "I'm stuck here," he said. "My hands are fucked. When is somebody coming up to help me?" Listening in the tent at Camp II, Veikka was in tears.

It was then that David exhorted me, "Ed, you get on the radio. You know Rob best. Talk to him. See if you can get him to move."

By now, we knew from relayed reports from the South Col that people were missing all over the south ridge. Scott Fischer himself had not made it back to the col. The plan was for whatever Sherpas had the strength to try to go up on the morning of May 11—all the way up to the South Summit, if possible—to try to bring down Rob, Scott, and the other missing guides and clients. But that was asking a lot of Sherpas who had gone to the top only the day before. And the storm was still raging.

This was the hope, however, that I had to hold out to Rob. We knew that he was about twenty feet below the South Summit, in a little saddle on the far side. He'd actually have to climb up those twenty feet to start down. I got on the radio. "Rob," I pleaded, "crawl if you have to. Get to the South Summit. If you can start moving that part of the way down, the Sherpas will meet you somewhere below. You can shorten their day getting to you."

When there was no answer, I tried to joke with Rob, anything to rally him to action. "When this is over," I radioed, "we'll go to Thailand, and I'll get to see your skinny white legs on the beach for the first time." Rob never wore shorts, even in the hottest weather, so in fact I'd never seen his bare legs.

He actually laughed and said, "Thanks for that." I'd gotten Rob to laugh! That gave me new hope that we could rescue him. "We'll get you off the hill," I radioed. My mantra was *Don't say anything negative.* "But Rob, you've *gotta* move!"

At this point, Paula radioed us. Others at base camp, especially Guy Cotter and Helen Wilton, had also been trying to rouse Rob. Now Paula said, "Ed, everybody's being too nice. You've got to yell at Rob. Get mad at him."

She was right. Even though it belied my true feelings to express anger, now I broadcast, "Rob, come on, man! You can't just sit there!"

To support our IMAX ascent, we'd already ferried gear up to the South Col ourselves. Inside our Trango 3 tent on the col, there were fifty bottles of oxygen and fresh radio batteries. The tent was closed, however, with a cheap lock fixed to the zipper pulls, because, sadly enough, there'd already been instances of some teams stealing other teams' gear. We hated locking our tent, especially in such a wild place as the South Col, but our Sherpas had insisted. Now David didn't hesitate, although he knew the sacrifice could spell the end of any hope of our getting to the top. Jon Krakauer, we knew, was at the South Col. David wanted to radio him and tell him, "Jon, tear into that fucking tent and take what you need!"

But Jon's own radio was dead. When David broadcast, he reached the leader of the South African team, which was perched on the South Col. He asked the man to lend the radio to Jon. Incredibly, the South African refused! Eventually, however, the message got through.

Meanwhile, we were encouraged to hear from Rob that he'd found the two full oxygen bottles on the South Summit. It had taken him four hours to deice his mask, but by nine A.M., he was breathing gas once more. Over the radio, all of us were exhorting him to get moving down the ridge. From base camp, Helen Wilton commanded, "Rob, you think about that little baby of yours." In New Zealand, Jan Arnold was now seven months pregnant. "You're going to see its face in a couple of months, so keep on going."

For hours, I cajoled Rob myself. Sometimes I'd joke, sometimes I'd yell, sometimes I'd promise that the Sherpas were coming to help him. I told him, "Don't talk much. Just get ready, start moving." Broadcasting uses up battery power far more quickly than listening does. All this while, we assumed that Rob had started down. Meanwhile, Ang Dorje and Lhakpa Chhiri had started up from the South Col in a truly heroic rescue attempt. The skies had cleared somewhat, but a fierce wind still swept the upper mountain. The uncertainty was killing me. After four or five hours, I had to ask. "Rob," I pleaded over the radio, "how's it going?"

"I haven't moved," he said.

All of us listening to the radio were totally shocked and demoralized by this news. We knew now that the only hope for Rob was if the two Sherpas could get to him and help him down.

At this point we got mobilized ourselves. We weren't sure what we could do to help, but David, Robert, Araceli, Veikka, and I decided to head up the fixed ropes on the Lhotse Face toward Camp III. I made one last broadcast. "Rob," I said, "I'm leaving now. I'm heading up the hill. I'll see you tomorrow. We'll talk again as soon as we can."

A couple of hours later, I was about fifty feet above David, jumaring on the fixed ropes, when I heard him yell, "Ed, stop! I've got some news, and it's not good." David was carrying our only handheld radio, and he'd just gotten word from base camp. "Ang Dorje and Lhakpa are back at the South Col," David reported. "They simply couldn't climb up in these conditions."

David took a deep breath, then said to me, "I think it's time to say good-bye to Rob."

That's when I lost it. I just hung on my jumars, sobbing. David was weeping, too.

Amazingly, despite having been out for some thirty-six hours, most of it without bottled oxygen and above 28,000 feet, Rob was still alive and coherent by nightfall on May 11. By then, we were settled into Camp III, preparing to do whatever we could to help the following day. At six-twenty P.M., Guy Cotter managed to patch through Jan Arnold via satellite phone from New Zealand. Rob's and Jan's farewell exchange has become part of the Everest legend.

Before Rob could gather up the nerve to talk to his wife, he begged for a minute so he could eat some snow and moisten his mouth. Then he spoke: "Hi, my sweetheart. I hope you're tucked in a nice warm bed. How are you doing?"

"I can't tell you how much I'm thinking about you!" Jan answered. "You sound so much better than I expected.... Are you warm, my darling?"

"I'm reasonably comfortable."

"How are your feet?"

"I haven't taken my boots off to check, but I think I may have a bit of frostbite."

Jan knew there was little hope—she'd been on top of Everest herself. And Rob must have known, too. But in their parting words, they kept up the poignant fiction of a coming reunion. "I'm looking forward to making you completely better when you come home," Jan promised. "I just know that you're going to be rescued. Don't feel that you're alone. I'm sending all my positive energy your way!"

Rob closed with "I love you. Sleep well, my sweetheart. Please don't worry too much."

Those were the last words Rob ever spoke—or if he said anything more, there was no one there to hear it.

▲

▲

▲

We'd been so focused on Rob's plight that it scarcely registered with us that we had no idea what was going on with Scott Fischer. Part of the problem was that Scott had no functioning radio, so none of us could communicate directly with him. We didn't even know whether he was alive or dead. At some point it dawned on me that Scott was probably suffering the same fate as Rob. Later, Jon Krakauer and others reconstructed Scott's movements on May 10 and 11.

Scott reached the summit at three-forty P.M.—also well after his own prescribed turn-around time. The Mountain Madness sirdar (or head Sherpa), Lopsang Jangbu, one of the strongest climbers on the mountain, was waiting for him there. According to Lopsang (interviewed later by Jon), Scott lingered on the summit for fifteen or twenty minutes, during which he complained about his condition. In Lopsang's paraphrase, what he said was "I am too tired. I am sick, also, need medicine for stomach." Alarmed, Lopsang urged, "Scott, please, we go fast down."

As they started the descent, Rob was still on the summit, waiting for Doug Hansen. Scott was so out of it that he couldn't handle the short, normally easy rappels over the rock steps high on the ridge. To circumvent one series of steps, he glissaded, sitting on his rear end, down a snow slope parallel to them—but then he had to perform a 330-foot traverse through knee-deep snow to regain the route.

At six P.M., just above a broad shoulder called the Balcony, at 27,600 feet, Lopsang, who had stayed behind to aid others in trouble, caught up with Scott. Seeing that Scott had taken off his mask, Lopsang put it back over his face and made sure he was breathing oxygen. But the words Scott uttered were further proof of his deterioration. According to Lopsang, "He says, 'I am very sick, too sick to go down. I am going to jump.' He is saying many times, acting like crazy man, so I tie him on rope, quickly, otherwise he is jumping down into Tibet."

Short-roping Scott, Lopsang got him some 300 feet farther down the ridge before he collapsed, unable to walk. In an act of extraordinary loyalty, Lopsang hunkered beside his team leader on a small, snow-covered ledge, preparing to spend the night with him. As Lopsang later reported to Krakauer, "He tell me, 'Lopsang, you go down, you go down.' I tell him, 'No, I stay together here with you.' "

At eight P.M., another refugee appeared out of the darkness. It was Makalu Gau, the leader of the Taiwanese expedition, accompanied by two of his team's Sherpas. Equally played out, Makalu settled onto the same ledge, freeing his Sherpas to head down to the South Col.

For another hour, Lopsang shared the vigil with the two stricken climbers, even while he got so cold that he doubted his own chances of survival. But Scott once more urged him: " 'You go down, send up Anatoli.' So I say, 'O.K., I go down, I send quick Sherpa up and Anatoli.' "

Anatoli Boukreev, the brilliant Russian climber who was guiding for Mountain Madness, was the strongest man on either Rob's or Scott's team. Climbing without bottled oxygen, he had still been the first person to reach the summit on May 10, a few minutes ahead of Jon (who was using oxygen). In the aftermath of the tragedy, there were many, including Jon, who questioned Anatoli's decisions and actions that day. Should he have used bottled oxygen so that he would have had a reserve of strength and energy in case his clients got in trouble? It's not my habit to second-guess others, but I myself had always resorted to bottled oxygen when guiding Everest for just that reason.

Anatoli was later criticized even more vehemently for dashing to the summit and back down to the South Col, rather than helping his faltering clients. To his most severe detractors, this was the act of a selfish mountaineer out for personal triumphs, ignoring the clients. Yet Anatoli insisted that he did exactly what Scott ordered—that Scott had asked him to go down to the South Col to prepare tea and to gather up oxygen bottles to carry up to those who were in trouble above. This may well be true, but, to me, it doesn't make sense. You stay with the group to prevent a disaster; you don't leave the group to prepare for a disaster.

In any event, Anatoli's decision to climb without supplemental oxygen may itself have dictated his rapid ascent and descent. Without gas, you simply get too cold to sit around and wait for others.

There are several different lines of reasoning about why Anatoli did what he did that May on Everest. Jon's critical account in *Into Thin Air* is only one of them. In a book called *The Climb,* cowritten with journalist Weston DeWalt, Anatoli offered his rebuttal of Jon, explaining his actions and, in turn (through the mouthpiece of DeWalt), attacking Krakauer for his own doings, or lack thereof, during the catastrophe. A better version, I think, appears in *Above the Clouds,* a narrative based on Anatoli's journals and edited by his girlfriend, Linda Wylie. I recommend that anyone interested in Everest '96 read this book before passing judgment on Anatoli. Sadly, *Above the Clouds* was published after Anatoli's death, which occurred on Christmas Day 1997, when he disappeared in an avalanche while making a typically bold attempt on Annapurna in winter. Those posthumously published journals now represent Anatoli's only chance to defend himself—and, in my opinion, they best represent his phenomenal character.

At the moment in the night that Lopsang started down, Anatoli was looping out in the storm from the camp at the South Col in search of a large band of exhausted climbers who had lost their way, missed the camp altogether, and were now huddled in the darkness on a plateau dangerously close to the edge of the Kangshung Face. In finding those stragglers and leading them back to camp, Anatoli performed a genuinely heroic mission. There is no doubt that he saved several lives that night.

The next morning, two Sherpas from Scott's team, Tashi Tshering and Ngawang Sya Kya (the latter Lopsang's father), headed back up the ridge to try to rescue Scott. Despite the pummeling wind, they forced their way up to the bivouac ledge. There they found Scott barely breathing, his eyes fixed in a vacant stare; they tried to administer oxygen, but it seemed to do no good. Scott was only a little more than a thousand vertical feet above the safety of the South Col, but he might as well have been on the far side of the moon. Makalu Gau was in almost as bad shape as Scott, but he was able to drink some tea and breathe from the bottles the Sherpas had brought up.

In another heroic rescue effort, Tashi and Ngawang put Makalu on a short rope and got him down to the South Col.

Having failed to rouse Scott and get him moving downward, the Sherpas had, in effect, given him up for dead. But Anatoli could not bear to accept that verdict. Though near exhaustion himself, he set out at five P.M.—only a little more than an hour before dark—to make one last effort to save Scott. It was not till seven-thirty or eight that he reached the bivouac ledge. There, in the beam of his headlamp, he saw that it was too late. As Anatoli later told Jon, "His oxygen mask is around face, but bottle is empty. He is not wearing mittens; hands completely bare. Down suit is unzipped, pulled off his shoulder, one arm is outside clothing. There is nothing I can do. Scott is dead." Anatoli covered Scott's face with his own backpack, then descended to the South Col.

What most of us believe today is that Scott was in the grips of cerebral edema. The hallucination that he could jump back to camp is a typical manifestation of that ailment. Yet because he was the expedition leader, there was no one else in a position to recognize Scott's condition and send him down. The very edema probably prevented Scott from recognizing what a predicament he was in. He simply thought he was tired, feeling ill, just having a bad day. There was no reason for him to go to the summit, but it would have been unthinkable for him to let the clients go up without him. In a sense, too, Scott had probably come to underestimate Everest. He was known to joke about how easy the South Col route was, referring to it as the Yellow Brick Road to the summit. In the same way, after our successful '94 expedition, Rob had advertised a "100 percent success rate" for Adventure Consultants' clients on Everest.

Yet timing was everything. Without the onset of that sudden and violent storm late on May 10, both Rob and Scott might have gotten away with it—even with their late arrival times on the summit. In '95, for instance, in decent weather, we had gotten utterly spent clients such as Doug Hansen down safely, as well as one climber—Chantal—who had totally collapsed in the very place where Rob would die in '96.

By May 12, five climbers from the two teams were dead: not only both leaders, but Rob's guide Andy Harris, his client Yasuko Namba, and, of course, his client and friend Doug Hansen. By the end of the deadly spring season of 1996, Everest would take the lives of twelve of its aspirants.

On May 11, we got up to Camp III on the Lhotse Face, where we spent the night. By the next morning, up on the South Col, the surviving guides were trying to organize an evacuation. They were greatly aided by Todd Burleson and Pete Athans, the leaders of yet another American expedition, who had interrupted their own campaign to go up to help the day before. Experienced climbers and veteran guides (by now Pete has reached the top of Everest seven times, more than any other American), Burleson and Athans acted, in effect, like air-traffic controllers on the col.

It was David's idea to set up a kind of way station at Camp III. As the exhausted climbers and clients slid down the fixed ropes on the Lhotse Face, they could stop briefly at our camp, drink some hot tea or soup, and crawl into our tents to get warm. But it was essential to keep them moving down the mountain.

We met the first group of refugees as they came to Camp III, led by Neal Beidleman, Scott's third guide, who'd been part of our team on K2 in 1992. As David later told Jon Krakauer, "When I saw those guys, I was astounded. They looked like they'd been through a five-month war."

Yet I was astounded for an altogether different reason. One or two of Scott's clients, on seeing us for the first time, blurted out, "I made the summit! I'm so happy!" I just stared at them, speechless, thinking, "Do you have any idea what's going on here?"

By now, we had heard the news about the miraculous survival of Beck Weathers. Given up for dead on the South Col plateau near the Kangshung Face, Beck had somehow gathered the willpower to rouse himself late on the afternoon of May 11 and stagger into Camp IV. To the rescuers on the col, Beck's arrival presented an unworldly apparition. As Jon would later write, "The person's bare right hand, naked to the frigid wind and grotesquely frostbitten, was outstretched in a kind of odd, frozen salute.

Whoever it was reminded Athans of a mummy in a low-budget horror film."

Realizing that it would take a coordinated effort to get Beck off the mountain, Robert Schauer and I decided to head up toward the col on May 12, leaving Araceli, Veikka, and David to maintain our way station. A little above a broad cliff that crosses the Lhotse Face at 25,000 feet, we met Todd and Pete, who were shepherding Beck down. The job was so arduous that they were wiped out. Robert and I took over for them. At the top of the Yellow Band, I tied Beck in to a short rope and lowered him from above, while Robert rappelled right next to him, both clipped in to the fixed ropes. Beck was snowblind and his hands were useless, so we had to refix his figure-eight device at each anchor, but at least he could stand and walk.

We got Beck down to Camp III. Recognizing how near death the man still was, David joined our team to get Beck all the way down to the next camp. Now David and Robert literally placed his feet in each step, while I followed a little behind him, one arm wrapped around the fixed rope, the other holding the back of Beck's waist harness.

Beck's frame of mind was amazing. Despite his suffering, he blurted out, "Man, I'm with the superstars of climbing!" He was telling jokes, he was singing.

At one point I said, "Beck, you've got the best attitude of anybody I've ever rescued in the mountains."

He replied, "Ed, once you're dead, everything else is gravy!"

Slowly but steadily, we got Beck down to Camp II. There, Ken Kamler, the doctor on the Athans-Burleson expedition, started to treat his frostbite, thawing his fingers.

Meanwhile, at base camp, Guy Cotter had been doing everything he could to mobilize a helicopter rescue—an extremely dicey proposition at these altitudes. We got instructions from base camp to collect Beck and push down to Camp I, just above the upper lip of the Khumbu Icefall, at 19,000 feet. Once there, aided by Jon Krakauer, we scouted out a landing platform near the upper edge of the icefall, which David marked in the snow with a big X painted in Kool-Aid. I tied a large bandanna to a ski pole to use as a wind sock. Just as we heard the distant *thwock-thwock* of the chopper's rotors, Makalu Gau arrived with severely frostbitten hands and feet, having been sledded like a corpse down the mountain by half a dozen Sherpas.

One of the truly unsung heroes of Everest '96 was Lieutenant Colonel Madan Khatri Chhetri of the Nepalese army. In a B2 Squirrel helicopter, he had flown to base camp, then stripped the craft of every unnecessary piece of gear, even removing the doors. We heard a rumor later that Madan had drained his fuel tanks down to a few gallons to lighten the chopper further. Then he'd headed up to our landing site.

Only once before had a helicopter landed in the Western Cwm: in 1973, an Italian expedition had used one to ferry gear. That chopper had eventually crashed in the icefall, ending the Italian experiment. No one had tried the feat in the past twenty-three years, and we all knew that dumping a load of gear was not the same thing as taking off with the added burden of an invalid. Colonel Madan came in, then made a gingerly touchdown and test takeoff. He was ready to attempt the evacuation.

The helicopter had been sent specifically to rescue Beck. But when Gau unexpectedly appeared on the scene, David, Jon, and Pete Athans decided that the Taiwanese climber should be evacuated first, because his horribly frostbitten feet made it impossible for him to walk or even stand, and the flying conditions were deteriorating rapidly. Beck would have to wait for a second flight, if one was possible.

In this moment, Beck's magnanimity was sterling. A doctor himself, he agreed with the decision: "Makalu's in worse shape than I am. He should go out on the first flight."

Jon, David, and I loaded the Taiwanese on board, then watched with our breath held as Colonel Madan strained the rotors, barely getting airborne. Next he peeled over the edge of the icefall and flew out of sight. We listened to the receding thunder of the rotors, praying for the chopper not to crash.

The whole time, I was thinking, *Oh, my God, what if there isn't a second flight?* Somehow we'd have to get Beck down through the perilous labyrinth of the Khumbu Icefall. With enough manpower, we could pull it off—it had been done before—but it wasn't a job any of us would have relished.

But then Colonel Madan returned and took off with Beck. Within an hour, he was in a Kathmandu hospital, getting treated alongside Makalu Gau. We gathered up our gear and, realizing how exhausted we were ourselves, stumbled down to base camp that day.

At base camp, we held a memorial service for the dead. On a stone altar, we built a small fire of juniper boughs to perform a *puja*, the traditional Sherpa ceremony to propitiate the gods—usually carried out before an expedition, not at the end of one. By turns, people stood up and spoke a few words about our friends who had died. Their hair was all disheveled, the faces and noses of some of them purple with frostnip patches, partially covered with Band-Aids. There were many things I wanted to say about the close friends we had lost, but I wasn't able to speak. I knew that if I stood up and tried to, I wouldn't be able to get two words out without choking up.

Paula was in something like a state of shell shock. The year before, at base camp on Everest and Makalu, she had lingered in a kind of blissful innocence, never worrying unduly about what I was doing up higher on the mountain. She'd come to believe that if I climbed as safely as I claimed I could, very little could go wrong. She'd never known anyone who'd died in the mountains.

Now she'd seen the treachery of mountaineering in the Death Zone at its very worst. Rob and Scott had become close friends of hers, and she'd had to keep vigil by the radio as they slowly froze to death. She'd seen all the survivors come limping down the Khumbu. The sense of catastrophe that hung over base camp deeply affected her.

Yet that wasn't the worst of it. In the middle of the various teams' retreat down the mountain, she'd overheard David on the radio, broadcasting to someone on our IMAX team at base camp. David said, "When this is all over, we'll regroup and go back up."

Paula was stunned. As any normal person would, she'd assumed that after such a disaster, we would at least discuss what to do next. The prospect of having to wait weeks more at base camp while our team—and I, in particular—surged back up the very mountain that had killed some of the best climbers in the world seemed unbearable. And she felt outraged that the decision was presented as a fait accompli. As she later recalled her feelings at the moment she heard David's transmission, she wanted to shout, "Hey, aren't we a team? Aren't we going to discuss this? Aren't we even going to have a meeting?"

Though she stayed for the memorial service, Paula felt that she had to get out of base camp. Guy Cotter's team was packing up to go home, taking the survivors from Rob's team with him, so she decided to join them and hike down the valley for a few days. As she put it to me, "I need to get out of here. I need to see some green grass, some trees, some rhododendrons. I need a few days to clear my head."

I could sympathize with her feeling of helplessness during the previous days. While the rest of us higher on the mountain were caught up in rescues and evacuations, she could only listen over the radio, then run from one team's base camp to another's to relay information. Her role was invaluable, but it frustrated her profoundly not to be able to deliver hands-on help herself.

So, a couple of days after the memorial service, Paula hiked with Guy's team down to the village of Dingboche, one of the loveliest spots in the whole Khumbu Valley. But by the time we were ready to head back up the hill, she had returned to base camp. Mentally restored, she now fully supported our decision to go back up the mountain.

Two decisions that David made during the '96 disaster struck me as wholly admirable—and Jon, too, singled them out for praise in *Into Thin Air*. The first was to offer the parties in trouble, without a qualm or the slightest hesitation, our vital oxygen bottles, batteries, and other gear cached in the Trango 3 tent on the South Col. The oxygen, in particular, proved a godsend for the more debilitated clients and almost certainly saved lives. The second was David's refusal to film any of the dramatic episodes unfolding in front of us as the survivors straggled down the Lhotse Face. In box-office terms, such footage would have been pure gold, but David was dead set against exploiting the tragedy for IMAX purposes.

During the crisis, David had been in touch with the MacGillivray Freeman folks back in Laguna Beach, California. They, too, were admirably altruistic and sympathetic. They'd sunk $5.5 million into our project, but they never put any pressure on us to complete the climb. Instead, they told David, "It's up to you guys to decide. We understand what you've been through. Your friends have died. If you want to come home, that's okay. We'll go back next year." David, in turn, left the decision up to the rest of us. If we wanted to go home, he was fully prepared to return the following year with a smaller team.

As for me, even as we got caught up in the rescue, I was pondering what I hoped to do after the smoke cleared. I realized early on that I wanted to go back up. Part of it was just my old compulsion to see a project through to completion, to hammer the last nail into the deck. I can't stand quitting with the end in sight, after putting so much effort into a project—like turning around on Everest in 1987 only 300 feet below the top. And by now, I'd put eight solid months into our IMAX venture.

I had a second reason for wanting to go back up the mountain. I wanted our film to send the message that you can climb Everest and live to talk about it. I'd already done just that three times. I wanted people to learn that you can walk away from Everest without frostbite. The urge to climb it is not a death wish. And, finally, I didn't want to flee the mountain while a pall of death hung over it. I wanted to turn the end of the season into something positive.

People ask me, though, how I could go back up the mountain only days after losing two of my best friends and dearest companions. I suppose I rationalized. The disaster wasn't our fault. Our team hadn't gotten in trouble—so far, we'd done everything right. What Scott and Rob did on May 10, I wouldn't have done. I wouldn't have gone to the summit at four P.M.

Long before 1996, I'd developed a formula that was my cardinal rule in the big mountains. By now, I've repeated that formula so often in the talks and slide shows I give, it's sort of stuck to me like a tattoo.

The formula: *Getting to the top is optional. Getting down is mandatory.*

That rule derives, I think, from my training as an RMI guide. But it's my deepest article of faith. When people ask me if I think Mallory got to the top of Everest in 1924, I answer, only half-jokingly, that the question is moot. He didn't make it back down.

Even while I'm going up an 8,000er, everything in my planning is calculated toward getting back down. You can't arrive on a summit and then make a plan for getting down. By then it may be too late.

In a sense, I plan my climbs backward. The time that I want to arrive back in my high camp dictates when I need to reach the summit, which in turn dictates the hour I need to leave high camp on the way up. I always know that if I'm not near a summit by two P.M., I need to turn around and go down. If I allow myself twelve hours for the final ascent, then I need to leave high camp no later than two A.M. Usually I leave even earlier. All this is predicated on my choice not to use supplemental oxygen.

If, on the other hand, you're using bottled oxygen, then you're constrained by the number of hours' worth of gas you can carry. Thus on May 10, for the climbers going with oxygen, the two P.M. turn-around deadline was irrelevant. They all left that morning around midnight. Each of them had about an eighteen-hour supply, not only to reach the top but to have enough left over to get back to the South Col. Pushing on to the summit after twelve or thirteen hours meant that one would inevitably run out of oxygen on the descent.

This is why—not only in '96 but recurringly on Everest—climbers get into trouble on the way down. If you leave the South Col at midnight, breathing bottled oxygen, two P.M.—not to mention four P.M.—is far too late to be still moving upward. Besides, a sixteen-hour day with or without gas utterly debilitates most people. Too many climbers put all they've got into getting to the top, leaving no reserves to get down. If you've been breathing oxygen and suddenly you run out, it's like pulling a plug. You simply shut down and stop moving.

That may seem a harsh judgment to lay on Rob Hall and Scott Fischer, but they lost their lives in part, I believe, because they didn't subscribe seriously enough to the second half of the formula: *Getting down is mandatory.*

Paula says that in the mountains, I compartmentalize my feelings.

That's probably true. In a way, you have to in climbing, because if you fully opened your heart to the anguish of losing a best friend, it would paralyze you.

At any rate, even before we got down to base camp, I knew I wanted to go back up. All of us did—David, Robert, Araceli, Jamling, and Sumiyo. There was still time to make an IMAX film on Everest.

Yet I knew that if we got to the top, on the summit day I'd have to climb right past the bodies of Rob and Scott. And I knew how hard that would be.

By now, we'd given away so much of our supplies, we needed to restock our higher camps. Guy Cotter offered us oxygen bottles, and we received some from the survivors on Rob's team. Even so, it took us a week to get all our stuff back up to Camp IV, on the South Col, in preparation for our summit bid. Everybody on the team was gung-ho to go by now, but at the same time we agreed with David's assessment: "We're going to make one safe, very conservative attempt. If it doesn't work, then we're out of here."

We did a bit of filming on our way back up the Lhotse Face, but we knew that the crucial footage would have to come on the summit day. David's a very demanding leader. If you're not up to snuff, you're going to hear about it. He has something of a reputation, in fact, for sternly reprimanding people who he feels aren't doing their jobs. That's fine with me: if you're hired or expected to do a task, then do it. And, in fact, David's never reprimanded me. I always made sure I did my job. And David's acknowledged that, saying things like, "Ed, with you, I know that I won't have to worry whether the tents are up at Camp III. I know you'll have them there."

David himself works harder than anyone. And he always leads from the front. That's my definition of a good leader. I don't think there's anybody else in the world who could have pulled off what David did with the IMAX film.

And Robert Schauer worked his ass off, too. He was always by David's side, handing him film, setting up the tripod, and so on. And every night in his tent, he had to reach inside a black bag and blindly reload the film magazines.

By the evening of May 22, we were established on the South Col, ready to go for the top in the morning. Sadly, at this point David had to tell Sumiyo that she wasn't going to be part of our summit team. She was having severe problems adjusting to the altitude, wracked with coughing fits that strained her diaphragm even at 24,000 feet. David had already shot plenty of footage of Sumiyo lower on the mountain, but he was afraid that her weakness could jeopardize our summit effort. In "parking" her at the South Col, David was, as he later wrote, not "thinking as a filmmaker [but] thinking as a mountaineer."

The plan was for me to leave camp at ten P.M., everybody else at eleven. Climbing without oxygen and breaking trail, I'd probably be slower than the others, all of whom would be breathing from their bottles, so I needed a head start. Ideally, they'd catch up with me somewhere around the Balcony, at 27,600 feet, where we could start filming at first light.

By now Paula had been in base camp since we'd started back up the mountain. I called her on the radio the evening of May 22. Even though she later admitted she was deeply afraid, over the radio, she told me, "Climb the mountain like you've never climbed it before."

All I could answer was "Roger." Paula misconstrued our exchange. Later she said, " 'Roger'? That's all you could say?" She thought I was compartmentalizing again.

But the truth is that her pledge was so moving to me, I got completely choked up. All I could get out was that clipped, radio-speak "Roger"—while what I really wanted to say was "My God, that's so beautiful. Thank you."

Her words stayed with me all the next day. Her spontaneous imperative had many different meanings. On my eighth expedition to Everest, I would be climbing the mountain for a reason entirely different from that of any of my previous attempts. I'd be climbing the mountain as I never had before. And I'd be climbing it as hard as I could. I desperately wanted to finish the project in which I'd invested eight months of my life.

I didn't even try to sleep before heading up the mountain. Nor did

David or Robert, who had to stay up getting the camera and the film gear ready. I got off as planned at ten P.M. It was a clear, moonless night, with the temperature at 35 degrees below Fahrenheit. After you cross the broad expanse of the South Col, you need to find the proper gully on the slope above, but I knew the way from '91, '94, and '95, and even in the darkness, navigating by headlamp, I had a good intuition for the right line.

As I climbed, eventually I saw the distant beams from the headlamps of the others below; I was puzzled when they didn't seem to be gaining on me. Just below the Balcony, where I was still somewhat sheltered from the wind, I dug a seat in the snow and waited for almost an hour. But I started to get too cold, so I had to get moving again.

Already, a few hundred feet below the Balcony, I had come across an object on the rocky ledges that intersect the route. I knew it was Scott's body. He was lying in the position in which he had died, with his backpack covering his upper torso, just as Anatoli had left him on May 11. I couldn't see Scott's face. I'm not sure I wanted to—I preferred to remember him as he was when he was alive. I wanted to spend some time with Scott, and some time with Rob up above, but I'd resolved that on the way up, I had to keep going. I didn't want anything to slow me down, or jeopardize the success of our expedition. I'd stop and spend time with Scott and Rob on the way down.

For hours, as I climbed on, the headlamps below got no closer. David later told a writer for *Men's Journal* that as soon as he'd gotten out of his tent, he'd looked up and muttered to himself, "My God, that headlamp's a lot higher than I thought it would be." Apparently, without oxygen and breaking trail, I was able to move as fast as or faster than the others breathing gas and following my footsteps. Anticipating how difficult this climb was going to be, I'd trained really hard for it. And now I was focusing and visualizing as intensely as I could. Plowing through the deep snow was hard, but it was a spectacular day, and I felt that nothing could stop me. Even David had underestimated the pace at which I could move. As he told the *Men's Journal* writer, "I got off-line and had to break trail for a hundred feet, and I was exhausted."

David was also plagued by a mix-up in the Sherpas' loads. He'd assumed that the heaviest and most crucial piece of equipment—the unloaded camera itself, which weighed twenty-five pounds—would be carried by Jangbu, our strongest Sherpa. Instead, it was given to one of the weaker Sherpas. As the main group started up the ridge, the camera lagged farther and farther behind. Eventually Jangbu dropped his own load and went back to retrieve the camera from the slow-moving Sherpa, but it took hours to sort out the problem.

Meanwhile dawn came, and the others were no closer to catching up with me. I made several more stops to wait, but each time cold drove me onward. The problem was, this meant that David wouldn't be able to get the footage he was counting on of me leading the climb without bottled oxygen.

He made a quick decision to set up a shot of Araceli and Jamling moving along the ridge in the early morning light. In the cold, it was incredibly difficult to mount the camera on the tripod and position the shot. In the finished film, that sequence is perhaps the most dramatic footage of all, but David came very close to not getting even a second's worth of it. He describes the snafu in *High Exposure:*

> With a gesture from Robert, Jamling and Araceli plodded up the Southeast Ridge. Ten seconds into the shot, I noticed that they had strayed off the ridgeline. Viewed through the lens, it looked strange, as if they were descending. The shot wasn't working. Robert continued counting off the seconds. I gave them another ten seconds, fifty-six feet of film, to straighten their ascent and then shut down the camera. I was incredulous, twenty seconds of precious film wasted, and the shot was unusable. Furious, I stood up, ripped off my oxygen mask, and demanded they go back down and climb toward me again, in a more direct line.

Araceli and Jamling backed down the ridge and retraced their steps toward David as he refilmed them. This piece of footage is now known as "the highest take two in the world."

Oblivious to David's filmmaking tribulations below, I kept marching upward. Although I stopped as often as I could, it wasn't until I got to the South Summit, at 28,700 feet, less than 350 feet below the top, that David finally caught up with me. But the camera itself was still far below. David said, "Ed, keep going. There's no way you can wait for the camera to get here."

In the end, it took me twelve hours to go from the South Col to the summit. Without my stops to wait for the others, I might have been able to do the climb in nine to ten hours. For the third time, I had effectively soloed Everest. I felt that May 23, 1996, was my strongest day ever in the mountains. My body and mind were in perfect alignment, and despite how hard I pushed myself, I still felt well within my limits.

On top, I was able to radio down to Paula. "I can't go any farther," I said. "I've reached the summit. Yahoo!"

Our plan for the film had backfired slightly, in that David got no footage of me going for the top. Personally, I felt no disappointment about that. I was just so happy to get to the summit, and to know I'd done my job. For the first time in months, it seemed, I could begin to relax. In spite of all the obstacles created by the tragedy of May 10, we had stayed focused and completed our mission. Starting the expedition as relative strangers to one another, we had used our setbacks to catalyze a close-knit, virtually unstoppable team of selfless climbers and filmmakers.

I spent about an hour on top before starting down. Only David joined me there, still without the camera. On the way down, I passed Araceli, Robert, Jamling, and our six Sherpas. We all hugged, because we knew everybody would make it safely to the summit. And on the sturdy back of Jangbu, the camera itself would arrive on the summit, where David captured Araceli and Jamling embracing, then Jamling placing his offerings in the snow—a toy elephant for his daughter, several prayer flags, and photos not only of the Dalai Lama but of his mother and his famous father.

The film MacGillivray Freeman eventually put on the big screen, titled simply *Everest*, remains to this day the highest-grossing IMAX movie ever made. That's gratifying, of course, but more important to me is the testimony of individual viewers who come up to me and tell me how the film affected them. Recently I met a guy who has a five-year-old daughter, with whom, he said, he'd watched the movie every day for two or three years. Others tell me, "What a wonderful thing you did"—and they mean not just making a movie but how we behaved and performed on the mountain in the midst of its worst disaster ever. Lots of people have simply said, "Thank you for giving us this film."

On the way down, just short of the South Summit, I stopped to spend some time with Rob. Before that day, May 23, nobody had been by this spot since Rob had died on May 12. Now he was lying on his side. His upper body was drifted over with snow, covering his head. One arm and a leg were visible. His glove was off, and his hand looked like a big blue swollen claw. There were oxygen bottles piled around him, as if he'd tried to improvise some kind of wind shelter.

Strangely enough, there were three or four ice axes planted in the snow near Rob. I took a photo of them, and later we determined that one of them had belonged to Rob's guide Andy Harris. What happened to Andy remains as much of a mystery as what happened to Doug Hansen. Neither man's body has been found. Perhaps they both simply stepped off the ridge and fell down the gigantic Kangshung Face. But then why were the axes there? You don't let go of your ax, no matter what.

During the ten days since the disaster, word had trickled up the mountain that Jan Arnold, in New Zealand, and Scott's wife, Jean, in Seattle, wanted us to try to retrieve a single keepsake from each of the bodies. Jan wanted Rob's old Rolex watch, which he wore everywhere. And Jean knew that Scott always wore his wedding ring on a leather cord over his neck, tucked inside his shirt.

But when I got to Rob's body, I couldn't do it. I couldn't make myself roll him over, dig for the watch, and take it off his wrist. I just didn't want to disturb him.

Instead, I simply sat next to Rob, taking in the scene, trying to figure out how things had played out during the storm. This wasn't just a dead body next to me—it was someone I had known really well, with whom I had shared many expeditions. Those moments sitting there were like a funeral, with me the sole mourner. I told myself, Okay, this is the last time I'll ever see Rob. This was not a place where I could hang out very long—I needed to keep moving. So I said good-bye to Rob and headed on down.

During the previous ten days, I'd thought a lot about how composed Rob had remained throughout his ordeal. It was hard for me to imagine what it must have been like to sit stranded at the South Summit and face your last hours alive. Rob was smart enough and experienced enough to know that during his second night there, he would fall asleep and not wake up. Yet over the radio, he assured Jan that all would be well. That was not denial; it was, instead, I think, an act that sprang from a magnificent strength of character.

Two hours later, I sat down again, next to Scott's body. He was lying mostly on his back, with one leg flexed, the knee sticking up. His upper torso and head were covered by the backpack, encircled with rope that Anatoli had strung to fix it there.

Once again, I couldn't bring myself to disturb him, to rummage through his clothing to retrieve the wedding ring on the cord around his neck. If it had been someone I didn't know, perhaps I could have done it. As I sat there it struck me forcibly that while Rob had been in communication till his last hours, talking to Jan and others, who could in turn talk to him, Scott had died the loneliest of deaths. His last hours had been full of nothingness.

I glanced around, then looked again at the body of my friend, frozen into the slope. I spoke out loud. "Hey, Scott," I said, "how you doing?" Only the sound of the wind answered me.

"What happened, man?"

Closing In

It took us two more days to get down the mountain. Then—talk about perfectionism!—when we were a hundred yards short of base camp, David made us stop so he could film our arrival. There was Paula, just a hundred yards away—I couldn't wait to hold her and kiss her. But David said, "You guys just sit here until Robert and I get set up. I'll tell you when to go." It had to be real; David wouldn't settle for a reenactment. I mouthed to Paula, like a little kid on the verge of tears, "I can't come yet!" ▲ At last David said, "Action!" and we could trudge those last hundred yards. I hugged Paula as tight as I could. We all hugged, in fact, in every possible permutation, as David filmed the reunion. ▲ We all wanted to leave base camp immediately, but we still needed a couple of days to pack up the remainder of our equipment. Finally we left, heading down the valley, toward thicker air. After a very long day we reached Dingboche, where we were surrounded by the green grass and rhododendrons that had restored Paula's spirits. Nothing could have felt more satisfying than the realization that we were finally *done.*

I have a photo of David, Araceli, Paula, and me on the stone steps of the lodge in Dingboche, drinking beer. We look shell-shocked: happy, sad, and exhausted, all at the same time. Relieved to be off the mountain, but still in a state of disbelief about what had happened around us.

During the last few days of our trek out, I reflected long and hard on what we had been through and what we had accomplished. The emotional and physical toll that both the tragedy and the filmmaking had taken on us seemed almost unfathomable. I had never been involved with a project so all-consuming as this one.

I didn't go through any lasting depression after the Everest disaster. And my resolve to climb the 8,000-meter peaks never wavered. The therapeutic part of it was that we talked and talked about what had happened— not only Paula and I, and not only on the hike out, but for years afterward, whenever I'd meet up with David or Araceli or Robert again. And every time I give a lecture or a slide show, I talk about Everest '96. Ten years later, at certain points in the story I still get choked up, and it's hard to go on.

Rob, Scott, Veikka Gustafsson, and I had bought places on the Manaslu permit, since we'd originally hoped we'd have time for a twofer in the spring of '96. Now, since we'd used up virtually all of May going through the tragedy, then getting the IMAX team to the summit of Everest, Manaslu was obviously out of the question, even if we'd had the stomach for another climb. After losing Rob and Scott, all that Veikka and I wanted to do was go home.

That summer, Jan Arnold gave birth to a girl, whom she named Sarah. Three years later, Paula and I visited them in Queenstown, New Zealand. Sarah was the spitting image of Rob. At three years old, she was talking a blue streak. I was more than a bit surprised when she called me "Dad." I might even have been freaked out about it, except that Jan made it clear that Sarah was just playing around. She had apparently called a few other men

"Dad." In a way, I took it as a compliment that Sarah felt comfortable enough with me to use that word. Eventually, Jan remarried and had a second child with her new husband.

Rob and I had planned to guide on Cho Oyu together in the fall of 1996. When he died, in fact, he already had clients signed up for the autumn trip. Guy Cotter, who had been working for Rob, now took over the reins of Adventure Consultants. We decided that to keep the company afloat, we needed to run the programs that had already been advertised and sold. Since I had already been planning to guide on Cho Oyu that autumn, I decided to go ahead and lead the trip for Adventure Consultants. It was an uneventful expedition—thank God. I managed to get two clients to the summit. Since Cho Oyu is more than two thousand feet lower than Everest, I felt well within my limits guiding it without bottled oxygen. On summit day, the three of us climbed roped together, so the clients' safety was completely ensured.

The next February, Paula and I returned to Puerto Vallarta around the first anniversary of our wedding. The trip also coincided with her thirtieth birthday. One day, as we were tossing a Frisbee on the beach, I saw that Paula couldn't stop looking at another tourist, a pregnant woman playing with her two-year-old son. On the plane back to Seattle, she said, "I'm ready to have children."

Startled, I answered, "Okay, let's do it." We'd already agreed that we wanted to have children. Paula used to say that she'd known she wanted kids since she was old enough to hold her first doll. I wanted kids, too, but I just wasn't sure when. And I wasn't sure how becoming a father would mesh with Endeavor 8000. But now the timing seemed right.

Gilbert Edmund Viesturs was born on October 29, 1997. We named him after three Gils who had been important friends to us: Gil Friesen, the entrepreneur who had befriended me sight unseen and helped line up my first sponsors; Gil ("Gib") Curry, the lay minister who had married us at Puerto Vallarta in a ceremony that combined spiritual grace with an easygoing ambience; and Paula's grandfather Gilbert Bremicker, also a minister.

It was not the easiest delivery. We knew Gil was going to be a breach birth, and we'd been warned that when Paula's water broke, there was a chance that the umbilical cord could prolapse, or start to slip out before the baby. This could compromise the blood flow to him in the moments before delivery. We were advised that during the drive to the hospital, Paula should stay in a variant of the yoga position called "downward-facing dog"—i.e., head down, butt in the air.

Paula's water broke at around one A.M. We quickly got into our small SUV, the back seats already laid flat, and she assumed the position. With almost no traffic in the middle of the night, I drove slightly faster than the speed limit from West Seattle to the downtown hospital, slowing for but running red lights. The only other car on the road, naturally, was a police cruiser. The cop pulled alongside me, lights flashing, and signaled, "What's up, buddy?"

I pointed my thumb toward the back of the car. The cop saw Paula in her "downward-facing dog" position, smiled, and waved me on. We arrived safely at the hospital, and Gil's untraumatic birth followed shortly thereafter.

▲
▲
▲

By now, I was starting to become somewhat well known, not only in climbing circles but to the general public. And when the blockbuster IMAX film came out, my recognition factor jumped another notch. David turned Paula's and my "second honeymoon" on Everest into a minor story element. There's footage of us bicycling in Utah together before the expedition, as I trained for it. And at base camp, Paula appears on camera to say, "I wasn't ready for Ed to go back up the mountain. I just summoned up my courage and told him to go for it. It was the hardest thing I've ever done."

The corporate world took note of the film as well. The phone started ringing, and soon both David and I were in demand as speakers at company retreats and seminars. Though I'd felt nervous and awkward when I'd first given slide shows about my expeditions, I soon grew comfortable speaking in front of large crowds. I did my best to entertain and inspire, while hoping I never went overboard by impersonating a showman. I was just a climber telling a tale—nothing more, nothing less.

By 1997, I'd also started attracting other sponsors in addition to Mountain Hardwear. I needed the financial help of companies to do what I wanted in the mountains. Free gear was not going to buy plane tickets, permits, or pay my bills back home. I became more aggressive about asking companies for money as well as equipment. In essence, I was proposing that companies pay me to use their products and to help market them. Of course, I knew I needed to be able to offer the companies something in return. What could I give them of value? Credibility, above all. If a top mountaineer endorses a company's product and that endorsement comes across as sincere, any number of "weekend warriors" will be eager to buy it.

As those relationships developed over the years, though, I was able to give my sponsors other benefits besides credibility. I gave them design feedback by field-testing prototypes of new gear in the most demanding conditions. Sometimes I came up with my own ideas for new products, and the sponsors marketed them with my name attached. And, depending on the level of the company's investment, I would agree to a certain number of "work days" each year, when I'd appear in stores to give slide shows, sign posters, and schmooze with customers. At the annual Outdoor Retailer convention in Salt Lake City, I'd participate in the company's sales meeting.

As I got more experienced at the whole game, I drove a harder bargain. I wanted multiyear contracts rather than one-shot, single-year deals. Though the company was getting my credibility in return for its investment, I made it clear that I would make all the decisions regarding what and how I climbed. I would drive the ship and they could come along as passengers. As soon as a company tried to pressure me into doing something in the mountains that sprang from their agenda rather than my own, I cut the cord and sought out someone else.

In the outdoor industry, companies do not have huge budgets for sponsoring athletes. But I pushed a number of companies financially by proving to them that it was worth their while to support me. As a result, instead of having only one major sponsor, Mountain Hardwear, I eventually had nearly a dozen smaller ones. This diverse portfolio allowed me a certain freedom and flexibility. If I lost a sponsor or two, I could get by with the ones I had left. I always felt the financial hit of losing of a sponsor, but it wasn't the end of the world.

Some of the relationships that I developed in this way worked as smoothly as a good marriage. A few, however, were as uncomfortable as blind dates. Sometimes, at the end of a year's contract, the relationship felt so awkward that I thought it was better to just call it quits. Often a terminated sponsorship came about because of change in management or in the direction of marketing within the company—factors, obviously, that I had no control over.

For example, one sponsor's new head of marketing called me in for a two-hour meeting in 2002. It was shortly after I'd failed on two attempts on 8,000-meter peaks I hadn't yet climbed. In effect, she asked, when was I going to get my act together and perform better in the mountains? She didn't have a clue about big-range climbing; she didn't realize that failure was part of the game. At the conclusion of the meeting, she said she'd call me in a week. I never heard from her again, despite my leaving her a bunch of messages. In the end, I wrote the relationship off as no great loss.

Since my early guiding days on Rainier, I had known one of the heads of JanSport, Skip Yowell. He had always provided me with packs on an informal basis. Lou Whittaker was JanSport's key sponsored athlete, and I certainly didn't want to step on my boss's toes. But as Lou edged toward retirement, I thought it was high time to try to formalize my relationship with JanSport. By the late 1990s, I was helping with the design of the company's new packs.

Another firm with which I had a long-standing informal relationship was Seattle-based Outdoor Research, a maker of technical gloves, mittens, gaiters, and overboots. The products were superbly made—which is one of the reasons I still have all of my fingers and toes. After the IMAX expedition, I entered into a formal arrangement with Outdoor Research, which now markets a line of "Ed's Choice" products, each of which I had a hand in designing.

Some relationships I sought out personally because I already used the products that the company made. But in several cases, the product filled such

A family photo, Easter 1960: Velta, Dad, Mom, and me at ten months.

On the summit of Magic Peak in 1980, one of my early ascents in the North Cascades.

Leading a group of clients up Mount Rainier in 1993. *Preston Spencer*

With Lou Whittaker
(right) on the summit
of Rainier, circa 1990.

At base camp on K2 in 1992, I'm brewing up morning coffee with
Charley Mace (center) and Chantal Mauduit. *Scott Fischer*

Just after sunrise, I'm negotiating a very dangerous traverse ▶
high on K2 on the day we reached the summit. Scott Fischer
waits behind me. *Charley Mace*

Back at base camp after our success on K2. Left to right: me,
Charley Mace, Scott Fischer.

With Rob Hall (left) on the summit of Everest in 1994.

A difficult pitch near the summit of Lhotse in 1994. Everest is in the background, with its characteristic windblown plume of snow. *Rob Hall*

From left: me, Paula, Rob Hall, and Jan Arnold, riding the helicopter from Everest base camp to Makalu base camp in 1995.

I'm straddling the summit ridge *à cheval* on Shishapangma in 2001, finally traversing the last stretch below the summit, which had stopped me cold eight years before. *Veikka Gustafsson*

With David Breashears (right) below Annapurna in 2005, just days before I completed my Endeavor 8000 quest. *Veikka Gustafsson*

Annapurna base camp, 2002. From left: J.-C. Lafaille, Veikka Gustafsson, me.

At home on Bainbridge Island with Paula.

The kids—Ella, Gil, Anabel.

Family portrait. From left: Gil, Ella, Paula, me, and Anabel. *Elisha Rain*

a specialized niche that giving me financial support didn't make sense for the company. An example is the kind of wool hat I've worn on all my Himalayan climbs. It's made by a small family-run company called Wapiti Woolies, out of Greenwater, Washington. Even though Mountain Hardwear and Outdoor Research make hats, they understand that I'll be wearing Woolies on the mountain. It's a hat I've grown to love, and I don't want to change it.

By this time, I'd become a lot better at networking than during those dreary days when I'd made cold calls to companies from my windowless basement; now I found it relatively easy to snag introductions to the right people. The turning point had come with Jodie Eastman's help with Polo Ralph Lauren and Gil Friesen's with MTV.

One day in the spring of 1994, I was returning from a speaking engagement with Ian Cumming, one of the founders of Mountain Hardwear and the father of my fellow RMI guide. Out of the blue, he asked what my dream sponsor would be.

"Rolex," I answered. I always thought that that company was the crème de la crème. In the mountains, I was always a fanatical clock-watcher, so it would have seemed really cool to wear the best watch in the world on my wrist. Ian immediately arranged a meeting for me with the president of Rolex. In a few months' time, I was scheduled to go to the Rolex office in New York City to give a slide presentation of what I had so far accomplished on the 8,000-meter peaks and what I was still attempting to do. Shortly before that meeting, Ian and Mountain Hardwear gave me a beautiful new Rolex Explorer II. They thought it would make a better impression if I was wearing that watch on my wrist for the New York meeting rather than my twenty-dollar Casio.

At the corporate headquarters on Fifth Avenue, I was brought into the boardroom, where I gave my slide show to Roland Puton, the debonair and distinguished president of the U.S. branch of the Swiss company. Afterward, we had an elegant lunch at a French restaurant. Puton was intrigued with my endeavor but could promise nothing at that point. He told me to stay in touch.

For the next year and a half, I corresponded with Puton, and I sent him postcards from the base camps of my various expeditions. To my great surprise, I received a letter in December 1995 stating that I had been invited to join Rolex as an ambassador. I was in heady company, with the likes of Sir Edmund Hillary, racing legend Sir Jackie Stewart, Arnold Palmer, and Chuck Yeager. With Rolex's recognition, I felt that I had arrived. Ian Cumming had paved the way for my association with one of the most prestigious companies in the world.

Thanks to years of hard work selling myself, hundreds of phone calls, networking like crazy, and, of course, doing what I was doing in the mountains, I gradually accumulated enough financial support so that by 1996 I could finally say that I was a self-sufficient professional climber. It had taken me sixteen years, since I had first tried out as an RMI guide, to get there.

That summer, Paula and I bought our first house. Handing over the largest check I had ever written as a down payment to the escrow company, I felt overwhelmed. Years of working shit jobs, scrimping on expenses, and saving every spare dollar had gone into the signing of that piece of paper. That night I needed several cocktails to calm my nerves. But as Paula and I moved into our West Seattle bungalow with a peekaboo view of Puget Sound, I felt that I was finally living my dreams.

▲
▲
▲

In the next four years, from the spring of 1997 through the summer of 2001, I would go on eight expeditions to 8,000-meter peaks. Yet I was still in no hurry to finish the fourteen. It wasn't a race, and knowing that another American mountaineer, Carlos Buhler, had six of the big ones under his belt by 1997 didn't nudge me in the slightest to try to beat him to the so-called finish line. It had never been my goal to put up a signboard as the First American to Climb All of the 8,000-Meter Peaks; it was a campaign I pursued strictly for personal reasons. As evidence of my willingness to put Endeavor 8000 on hold, I went back to Everest in the spring of 1997 to help make another film.

This time it would be a documentary for NOVA, the highly regarded

PBS series hosted by station WGBH, out of Boston. Liesl Clark, a very talented director, was interested in making a film that for the first time seriously explored the physiology of high altitude. Liesl had become David
Breashears's girlfriend, so they were committed to codirecting the documentary.

For the story line of the film, I needed to have a role on the mountain,
so the premise was that I was working as a guide for Guy Cotter. A former
fellow RMI guide, my friend Dave Carter, was to be my on-camera "client."
Dave was competent enough not to be guided, since he'd guided Rainier numerous times, as well as Denali, and in 1991 he'd worked for me when we'd
guided Hall Wendel on Everest. Since Dave had failed to reach the summit
on that expedition, he was eager to sign up as a client on Guy's trip so that
he could give Everest another shot. For the sake of the documentary, he was
the perfect choice. Dave would be studied by the physiologists as the client,
while I would be studied as the guide. David Breashears would also take part
in the testing. The a priori assumption was that Himalyan veterans like
Breashears and myself ought to do better at altitude than a client such as
Carter.

Veikka Gustafsson would also be on our team, though not on camera.
He joined so that he could make an attempt to climb Everest without bottled oxygen. When he'd reached the summit in 1993 as a client of Rob
Hall's, he'd been breathing gas. This would be my fifth time climbing Everest, but it would be a new experience to play a guide on film.

Despite the tragedy of the previous spring, the South Col route was
once more thronged with climbers. Once again, we managed to elude the
traffic jam on the summit day—though just barely. This spring, everyone on
the mountain got stalled for weeks by bad weather. The result was that all
the climbers planned to go for the top on the first perfect day. On the
evening of May 22, as the skies cleared and the wind dropped, we were surrounded by dozens of others climbers camped on the South Col. We actually
contemplated not going up the next day because of the crowd. A repeat of
the previous year's disaster seemed to be staring us in the face.

Was there any way to go on the morrow and still escape the traffic jam?

We knew that most of the other teams would leave no earlier than midnight, and perhaps even as late as two A.M. So David and I came up with the plan of sneaking out of camp at ten P.M. that night. A bottleneck would still almost certainly develop at the Hillary Step, with us trying to get down the forty-foot cliff as the throngs waited their turns to climb it. So we carried an extra rope to fix on the Step—a "down staircase" for our descent while the hordes used the line already fixed in place as their "up staircase."

As it turned out, we reached the summit by seven A.M. in pristine conditions. It was a year to the day after our IMAX team had summitted in '96. And because of the good weather, this spring no disaster unfolded on Everest.

On the ascent, I saw Scott Fischer's body again, still lying on the rocky ledge where he had died the previous year. The climbers' beaten path now took a line farther away from his resting place. Only because I knew the place so well could I see where he lay, the upper half of his torso still covered with his backpack, roped in place. As I had in '96, I once more visited briefly with Scott, again saving that vigil until I was on my way down.

Higher on the mountain, at the South Summit, there'd been no sign of Rob Hall. He had perhaps been slowly pushed by the pressure of the snowdrift his body had created, until he was nudged off the ridge and plunged down the Kangshung Face. Not seeing Rob was both a relief and a disappointment. We'd planned to investigate the scene this year, in hopes of casting further light on the disappearance of Andy Harris and Doug Hansen. At the same time, I was glad to learn that Rob's corpse no longer lay there, where every climber going to the summit would have to step around his frozen form.

Higher still, at the Hillary Step, we'd found the last victim of the '96 tragedy: the South African climber Bruce Herrod. His party had been the last to reach the summit the previous year, two days after our IMAX team. Though he was the deputy leader of his team, he had lagged far beyond the others, yet been unwilling to turn around. Climbing alone, he reached the summit only at five P.M.—a full seven hours after his teammates, who had already regained the South Col. He broadcast the news of his reaching the top to his team, then was never heard from again.

Herrod was the most likable and friendly member of the South African team. I remembered patting his shoulder in '96 and wishing him well as I passed him on my way down. The mystery of his disappearance was solved only now, in '97, when we found his body at the Hillary Step. He was hanging upside down among the fixed ropes, one foot ensnared in a tangle of old lines. We speculated that as he had rappelled down a new fixed rope, his crampon had snagged on one of the old ones, flipping him so that his upper body dangled below his feet. Exhausted, unable to perform a vertical sit-up, he must have hung there upside down until he died.

We retrieved Herrod's camera so we could later send it to his family. (The film, once processed, included a self-portrait on the summit.) Then we did the only thing that seemed to offer the man a modicum of dignity: we cut his body loose and let it fall down the southwest face.

At such extreme altitudes, in such precarious places, there is really nothing one can do to bring back a body. Cutting Herrod loose to plunge to a snowy grave where, in all likelihood, he would never be seen again may seem like a heartless act. But it was better than leaving him strung upside down from the fixed ropes, a ghastly memento mori for every subsequent climber going to the top of Everest.

It's a very rare occasion when climbers can bring down a dead body from an altitude above 24,000 feet. In 1997, our Sherpas were offered a handsome sum by the husband of Yasuko Namba, Rob's Japanese client who had died in the storm on the South Col, to bring her body down from its resting place at 26,000 feet. Despite their sense of taboo about dead bodies, the Sherpas managed the job, but it was a difficult and dangerous operation, despite the fact that Yasuko weighed less than a hundred pounds.

People sometimes assume that Everest is littered with bodies, as in a war zone, but it's not true. Perhaps half the climbers who die on the mountain simply disappear, falling off one face or another or getting covered with snow. The few bodies that remain in sight are not particularly conspicuous.

Yet those corpses are essentially freeze-dried—dehydrated by the extremely dry air and frozen solid, in a form of natural mummification. In 1999, on an expedition led by Eric Simonson, Conrad Anker discovered the body of George Mallory on the north face of Everest, where it had lain unobserved for seventy-five years. His corpse was so well preserved that his alabaster skin and the strong muscles of his back and legs retained an eerily human aspect, and his fingers still clawed at the scree in the position in which he had died, evidently trying to stop his fall with his bare hands.

In 1997, however, our ascent was nearly marred by death once more. As we climbed to the summit, Dave Carter began having difficulty breathing. He had developed a cough earlier on, a quite normal occurrence on Himalayan expeditions, but his airways seemed to be constricting more and more as he went higher. By the time we had all arrived back at the South Col, after a fifteen-hour day, Dave was in dire straits. No amount of bottled oxygen could assuage his anguished panting. We knew we had to get him farther down the mountain that same day or he would die.

Having just returned from the top of Everest, we agreed that the last thing anyone wanted to do was climb farther down right then. But I volunteered to escort Dave down the Lhotse Face. I had hopes of getting him all the way down to Camp II, at 21,000 feet.

Unfortunately, we descended at a snail's pace. Even with his oxygen set flowing at maximum output, Dave could manage only a half dozen steps before he would collapse, coughing and choking on the mucus obstruction that was accumulating in his throat. After several minutes I would prod him to go on. The process repeated itself over and over: a few downward steps, then Dave would collapse in a fit of racking coughs. He was fully aware of his predicament, but he just could not suck enough air into his lungs through his constricted air passages.

By nightfall we had only reached Camp III—just two thousand feet below the South Col. We were both exhausted. We crawled into one of the empty tents. Even though I was in radio contact with our expedition doctor, Howard Donner, at base camp, who gave me invaluable play-by-play advice, I felt as isolated as a man on the moon. As tired as we were after having been on the move for almost twenty-four hours, we knew we would get no sleep. I spent the night hovering over Dave to make sure he was still breathing. I was also trying to keep him relaxed, because as soon as he got anxious about choking to death, his panic would cause him to go into another bout of gagging and coughing.

The mucus plug seemed to be getting bigger by the hour. Following Donner's advice over the radio, when Dave felt he could take it no longer I would perform the Heimlich maneuver on him. With all my might, I would jerk my fist into his chest by giving him a massive bear hug from behind, hoping to get something dislodged. After several painful squeezes from me, Dave could only cough out a tiny portion of the plug, but it was enough to give him relief for another hour or so, and my vigorous efforts caused him to lose bladder control.

We finally came up with a system. Dave would point to his throat, indicating it was time for some more Heimlich action, but first he would urinate out the tent door. Despite my best efforts, we could hardly get anything to come out of his throat. The mucus plug grew larger and Dave more anxious. Fearing that he would pass out and die, I was ready to perform an emergency tracheotomy. I'd learned the technique in veterinary school. As a last resort, I would slice his throat and cut into his trachea below the obstruction, creating a new air passage. Once I made this hole, Donner advised me, I could keep it open by putting the plastic barrel of a syringe into it. I sat there all night, knife in hand, ready to perform the surgery.

At dawn, before we could start heading down, I gave Dave's chest one final Herculean series of Heimlich thrusts. After several violent squeezes, Dave suddenly chucked up a half-dollar-sized plug of slimy green, bloody mucus. We were elated: it felt as though we had jointly given birth to a child. The bane of our existence during the last twelve hours lay there in the snow just outside the tent door. It was so disgusting that we nearly puked just looking at it, but Dave felt an incredible relief.

Guy Cotter arrived soon thereafter from the South Col, and the three of us began the descent to Camp II. Dave's recovery through the rest of the expedition was complete. A few weeks later, back in Seattle, Dave's fiancée came from Ohio to visit him. At the final meeting to discuss the results of our high-altitude testing, I was introduced to her. Her name, believe it or not, was Marta Heimlich!

⏶
⏶
⏶

The film that Liesl and David put together, *Everest: The Death Zone,* was less commercially splashy than the IMAX movie, but it had a lot of good science in it, and it garnered much critical acclaim. I found working with David and Liesl a real pleasure—though she's a fairly demanding director herself, she has a personal charm and sensitivity that took some of the edge off David's perfectionism. Also, because this was a documentary rather than a scripted film, we had a more relaxed regimen up high. We shot events as they happened, not by following a screenplay, as we had in '96.

Instead of the heavy IMAX camera, in '97 David shot (as he often had before) with a much smaller video camera. The only real difficulty of the ascent had to do with the drudgery of taking physiological and mental tests at every camp, as well as on the summit. Dave Carter, David Breashears, and I were the test subjects. We'd be handed a plastic card on which the words *red, green, blue,* and *black* were printed, but each in a different color—not the color the words signified. For instance *red* would be written in green letters. Against a time limit, we had to flip through as many of these cards as possible, identifying the color of the printed word, not the color the word defined.

Or we'd be read a long, convoluted sentence over the radio and then asked to repeat it from memory. An example: "On Monday, John went to his cousin Frank's red house and together they bought three blue leather jackets at Joe's store, which had mostly pants for sale, but Joe was able to order the stuff that John and Frank wanted for delivery on Wednesday." As you can imagine, this exercise got more hilarious the higher we got on the mountain.

As expected, David and I performed a bit better than Dave, since Breashears and I were far more accustomed to operating at high altitudes. Ever the perfectionist, and a pretty competitive guy to boot, David was determined to score well on every test. As we climbed higher, we all naturally started to falter a bit. But David blamed his poor performances on "test anxiety," and many times he asked if he could start over again. We just laughed at him, saying, "No way, dude, that's it." Perhaps the most tedious of our chores called for us to sit on the summit reading these stupid plastic-coated test cards for the last time, as we radioed our answers to base camp.

The previous year, in conjunction with a magazine profile about me, I was put through a battery of tests by Brownie Schoene and Tom Hornbein at the University of Washington Medical Center. Both men were doctors who specialized in high-altitude physiology, and ever since I was a kid, Hornbein had been one of my heroes, enshrined forever as the pioneer, with Willi Unsoeld, of the epochal 1963 ascent of Everest's West Ridge and the first traverse of the mountain.

Brownie and Tom hooked electrodes to every part of my body and made me breathe into a tube, then they ran me to exhaustion on a treadmill that started slowly, then got faster and faster as they sadistically raised the angle of ascent. Only when I lay on the mat gasping and nearly vomiting did the two mad scientists read their results from a computer printout.

Even with my training as a veterinarian, the printouts looked like Greek to me, but Brownie summed them up succinctly. Probably the best indicator of one's ability to perform in thin air is called VO_2 max. It's a ratio of milliliters of oxygen inhaled to body weight in kilograms, per minute. In simpler terms, VO_2 max is basically a measure of how much oxygen you can take in and effectively use. The normal score for test subjects is 40 milliliters per kilogram per minute. I came out with 66—way up in the 98th or 99th percentile. The other measure they tested me for was anaerobic threshold. This indicates at what percentage of VO_2 max you start functioning in an anaerobic (that is, an oxygenless) state. Average is 55 percent; I tested at 88 percent. In a nutshell, this meant that at a point when normal folks are bonking from lack of oxygen, I can still cruise along.

These two parameters are especially interesting because they're not completely subject to training. Where you'll top out with VO_2 max and anaerobic threshold is limited by your own physiology. They're inborn, genetic capacities. As Brownie told me, "You picked your parents well."

Another key to the puzzle was that Tom and Brownie measured my lungs as larger than normal. My lung capacity turns out to be seven liters, versus an average of five. I had always thought that I tended to perform better than others at altitude because I trained so hard. But here was another reason: I was lucky enough to have good genes.

▲
▲
▲

What happens to the human body at high altitude is still far from completely understood. Much of the pioneering work in this esoteric field was done by Dr. Charles Houston, one of the preeminent American mountaineers of his generation, who co-led the 1938 and 1953 K2 expeditions. In 1946, trying to solve the question of how high humans could go without supplemental oxygen, Houston concocted his Operation Everest. He put his subjects inside decompression chambers, then slowly decreased the oxygen supply, simulating the effects of going to altitude, as he carefully monitored the vital functions of his guinea pigs (including himself).

In more recent years, experts such as Brownie Schoene and Tom Hornbein, as well as Dr. Peter Hackett, who was chief adviser to the NOVA film, have increased our knowledge of all the things that can go wrong with your body up high, and what to do about them.

Basically, above an altitude of about 17,000 feet, the human body inevitably starts to deteriorate. Centuries, perhaps millennia before science would demonstrate this threshold, native peoples learned it the hard way, through generational trial and error. Today, there are no permanent villages anywhere in the world above 17,000 feet, though certain mines in the Andes have been operated at altitudes up to 20,000. (There's a famous story about the executives of one such mine offering to move the workers' village higher, to save them the daily climb to and descent from work. The villagers politely declined.) Johan Reinhard, the pioneering "alpine archaeologist," has discovered temporary shelters in the Andes as high as 22,000 feet that apparently supported pre-Columbian rituals during which Inca rulers sacrificed native victims on the summits of high volcanoes. But no ruins of permanent-looking towns above 17,000 feet have ever been found, either in the Andes or elsewhere.

Working with his decompression chamber, Charlie Houston came to the startling conclusion that if you transported even the fittest, healthiest climber from sea level, at a rate of 800 to 1,000 feet an hour, to 25,000 feet, at that altitude he would remain conscious for only one to two minutes, and he would die within less than an hour. Research such as this, combined with the experience of pioneer climbers on Everest, led to the widespread conviction that humans would never reach the highest point on earth without bottled oxygen—an axiom disproved not by science (though its overthrow was predicted by Houston) but by Peter Habeler and Reinhold Messner's breakthrough oxygenless ascent in 1978.

It was also Houston who first systematically analyzed most of the serious or potentially fatal conditions that attack the body at altitude, including acute mountain sickness (AMS) as well as high-altitude pulmonary edema (HAPE) and high-altitude cerebral edema (HACE). All of these conditions are caused by hypoxia, the deprivation inflicted on the body in thin air as it takes in less oxygen than it needs to function normally. At 29,000 feet, on the summit of Everest, the atmosphere contains only one-third as much oxygen as it does at sea level.

Most climbers have been afflicted by AMS at some point in their lives. The typical symptoms are headache, fatigue, shortness of breath, trouble sleeping, and sometimes nausea and vomiting. After a few days, however, those symptoms usually go away. As Houston puts it in his pathbreaking book *Going Higher: The Story of Man and Altitude,* "AMS is much like a bad hangover and like a hangover usually subsides in a day or two." Yet AMS can also progress to more serious conditions, including HAPE and HACE.

The symptoms of HAPE are shortness of breath, a severe cough, terrible fatigue and lassitude, and a frothy, bloody sputum in the lungs that can be heard if you put your ear to the victim's chest. HAPE is caused when hypoxia increases both blood pressure and arterial flow in the lungs to the point that fluid starts leaking from the capillaries. The sequence of physiological changes is very complicated; climbers sometimes simplify the explanation by saying that the victim essentially drowns in his own pulmonary fluids.

Brownie Schoene and Peter Hackett, operating a research station on Denali at 14,000 feet over a number of years, discovered that Diamox and dexamethasone can temporarily alleviate HAPE (as well as HACE), but the only real cure is to get the victim down to lower altitude—as fast as possible. However, an invention crafted in the mid-1980s by Igor Gamow, a brilliant Colorado scientist, has also proved efficacious. The Gamow bag is a coffinlike nylon tube in which the victim is placed; then the bag is zipped tight. Using a foot pedal, teammates increase the air pressure inside the bag, effecting an artificial descent of as much as 8,000 feet. Four to six hours inside the bag can allow an otherwise moribund climber to regain the strength to hike down the mountain with assistance. Gamow bags have already saved dozens of lives up to altitudes as high as Camp II on Everest (21,000 feet), but the devices are too cumbersome to carry up to, say, the South Col, at 26,000 feet, and too demanding to operate there. The Gamow bag, finally, is not a cure—it offers only a temporary remission.

HACE, which we presume killed Scott Fischer on Everest in 1996, is like HAPE, except that the leakage occurs in the space around the brain instead of in the lungs. As the fluid leaks out, because it is confined within the rigid superstructure of the skull, it creates pressure against the soft cranial tissue, with devastating results. Since brain cells are affected, the symptoms that crop up include hallucinations (Scott thought he could jump down to camp) and extreme mental confusion. Again, the only cure is to get the victim low, fast.

HAPE and HACE are not confined to Himalayan altitudes. Both ailments have been well documented in climbers, hikers, and skiers at altitudes as low as 9,000 feet. The usual culprit in the onset of either condition is a sudden ascent from a relatively low altitude. A peak like Kilimanjaro, in Tanzania, is a perfect breeding ground for HAPE and HACE, as hundreds of trekkers each month go from 3,000 feet to 19,000 in a matter of days. Yet, maddeningly for the scientists, it is not simply the unfit or the inexperienced who come down with edema. Nor has anyone yet figured out who's potentially more susceptible, or who's relatively immune. And, apparently, getting HAPE or HACE once doesn't mean you're any more likely to get it again.

Given what Charlie Houston discovered with his decompression chamber, it's amazing that humans can climb Everest at all. The mitigating factor is the mysterious process called acclimatization. At extreme altitudes, the atmosphere still contains the same ratio of oxygen to nitrogen, but the oxygen molecules are spread farther apart. Thus each breath a climber takes brings in less oxygen. To compensate, the heart pumps faster, trying to carry an adequate blood flow to the oxygen-starved tissues. This works for a while, but once the heart reaches maximum rate, the body can absorb no more oxygen; the climber shuts down, incapable of further exertion.

The body also produces extra red blood cells in an effort to carry the increasingly scarce oxygen molecules. This, too, works up to a point; but if the climber's blood gets too thick, it can form clots, often in one's legs as he lies immobilized in a tent. This is precisely what happened to Art Gilkey during the 1953 K2 expedition on which Charlie Houston was the doctor. Houston diagnosed thrombophlebitis and recognized the danger that the clot in Gilkey's leg could break loose, travel through his bloodstream, and lodge in his lungs, causing sudden death. In a desperate attempt to lower the immobilized Gilkey from high on the Abruzzi Ridge, one man slipped, causing pairs of ropes to snag and yank other climbers off their feet. Six men slid out of control toward the fatal precipice, saved only by Pete Schoening's legendary "miracle belay." Later that terrible day, Gilkey, wrapped in a sleeping bag and dangling from the slope, was swept away by an avalanche—an act of fate that, his teammates reluctantly agreed, may have saved their own lives.

On our NOVA ascent in '97, along with radioing down to base camp our fumbling answers to the fiendish mental tests, we tried to measure pulse and blood oxygen saturation at every camp and even on the summit. The latter is a simple calibration of how much oxygen is in the blood, compared to its theoretical capacity. You measure with a gadget called an oxymeter, a little clip that you clamp to your finger or thumb.

At sea level, a fit climber such as David Breashears had 100 percent blood saturation and a pulse around 60 beats a minute. But at Camp I, he measured a resting pulse of 78 and a saturation level of only 80 percent. The higher you go, the more the pulse goes up and the saturation percentage down. At his worst, near death on the descent, before we got him breathing bottled oxygen at four liters per minute, Dave Carter's saturation level dropped to a potentially lethal level.

As Peter Hackett, who supervised our tests, explains, above 17,000 feet the body is steadily deteriorating, while acclimatization fights to compensate. But above 26,000 feet, acclimatization is, in Hackett's phrase, "essentially impossible." That's one definition of the Death Zone. And that's where the Himalayan climber's motto "Climb high, sleep low" comes from. You can stave off the deterioration for only so long. That's the reason we always come back from an 8,000er having lost a lot of weight. I typically lose eight to twelve pounds on an expedition, but I've lost as much as twenty. And the loss is not just fat. Once the fat is gone, the body starts chewing up its own muscles. I've returned not only skinny but withered, my muscle mass having shrunk to that of my middle-school days.

Even well below 26,000 feet, the body steadily deteriorates. There is simply not enough oxygen for your tissues to regenerate. Your fingernails stop growing, wounds take forever to heal, and you need weeks to get over a cold, rather than the few days that would be normal at sea level. Most climbers develop persistent, dry, racking coughs. It's not uncommon for climbers on Himalayan expeditions to cough so hard they break their own ribs.

And as our mental tests in '97 vividly demonstrated, everything becomes harder to do or think about at altitude. It takes a huge mental effort to perform such simple tasks as cooking, putting your boots on, or shoveling snow off a tent. Motivation quickly atrophies. Those who go high need to summon up extraordinary reserves of motivation to go higher. The summit day is always the hardest. That's why so many climbers throw in the towel and give up.

Yet the whole business of what happens to the body at altitude remains in many ways a mystery, one that scientists such as Hackett and Schoene are chipping away at year by year. As Charlie Houston eloquently writes in *Going Higher*:

> *Acclimatization to altitude is a wondrously complex process where many interlocking changes enable survival under extreme conditions. When we look at sea level man and observe how within seconds he becomes unconscious when deprived of oxygen, the wonder grows that he is able to get anywhere near the harsh and hostile summit of Everest. We wonder even more that whales can dive without breathing for an hour, that turtles can hibernate for months underwater, that the lungfish can go for years without breathing. The adjustments of such animals go far beyond us.*

▲
▲
▲

Coming off Everest in '97, Veikka and I planned another twofer. After only ten days at home, we met up again in Islamabad, with our eyes set on Broad Peak, at 26,401 feet the twelfth-highest of the fourteen 8,000ers. Broad Peak's first ascent, by a quartet of Austrians in 1957, had included the legendary Hermann Buhl. Buhl, in fact, reached the summit only eighteen days before he would die on a neighboring peak, Chogolisa.

This year, the twofer principle worked like a charm. In fantastic shape after Everest, Veikka and I stormed most of the way up Broad Peak in a mere three days in early July. There was only one problem: on the third day, we topped out on a prominent point that's sometimes called the foresummit. A lot of climbers stop there, crediting themselves with bagging Broad Peak. But from the foresummit, the ridge leading to the true summit is an interminably long haul with only a minimal altitude gain. It took us a few more hours to traverse it. Then, only a hundred yards short of the top, we were stopped in our tracks. The last bit of ridge was corniced on one side, ready to avalanche on the other. There was no way to judge where the narrow, invisible middle path between those suicidally risky alternatives might lie. We agreed: roped up or not, there was no way we could proceed.

It was like Shishapangma all over again—stopped only a hundred yards short of the summit, not by fatigue or weather but by treacherous snow conditions. Another 8,000er with an asterisk attached. We were only slightly mollified to discover a set of footprints that stopped exactly where Veikka and I did. They had been left by Anatoli Boukreev, climbing solo the day before. If a climber as strong as Anatoli had turned back here, we didn't feel quite so bad about making a U-turn ourselves. Since we were climbing alone that day, we could always have fibbed by telling others that we'd climbed Broad Peak, but neither of us could have lived with that untruth.

With Rob, Veikka and I had climbed Makalu in '95. And during the '96 rescue effort on Everest, he and I had spent a lot of time together. But '97 really marked the beginning of the most perfect partnership I would ever find among the 8,000ers, a bond that would last through the next eight years, on ten more expeditions after Broad Peak.

Veikka's an inch or two taller than I am—about five-eleven or six feet—and ten years younger. He's got classic Finnish good looks: short-cropped blond hair, blue eyes. He's never married, but he always has a girlfriend. Veikka's very outgoing and friendly; he works hard and he plays hard, and he loves to party. I've seen him, at the end of a celebration, just collapse in the nearest tent, without knowing whose it was. But when we're climbing, he's totally focused and dedicated.

Veikka's English was a little sketchy at first, but it's gotten much better over the years. My Finnish, needless to say, is nonexistent. Sometimes, though, I can have Veikka in stitches by uttering long mumbo-jumbo monologues in what I pretend is Finnish.

Thanks to becoming the first Finn to climb Everest, in 1993, Veikka's a superstar in his own country. He's got major sponsors, and there's even an action figure modeled after him, sold in toy stores. Couples in Finland name their newborn sons Veikka.

For some reason, we're on exactly the same wavelength. Many times when I say something to Veikka, he chuckles and answers, "I was just thinking of that." We have a kind of telepathy, silently making the same decision—to go right or go left, to stop and camp or push on. We've never had a serious conflict.

Veikka's really good at routefinding. If you have to go through a difficult icefall, say, he's like a coonhound on a leash. He has this canny ability to find the right way. And coming down a mountain, unlike some of my partners, he's sharp at recognizing features we passed on the way up. "Do you remember this hummock?" I'll ask. "Yeah, yeah," he'll answer, pointing with his ice ax, "we've gotta go this way."

We have complete trust in each other's abilities and judgment. You have to, if you're going to tackle steep terrain roped up, with no anchors in. I have to trust that Veikka won't slip and fall, and he has to trust that I won't. In a tight situation—a storm, or pushing through the night—it's reassuring to see that Veikka never freaks out; he stays calm and logical.

If there's any difference between us, it's that I'm the detail guy. I do more of the organizing, getting the permit, telling him what equipment to bring. At first, of course, I had a lot more high-altitude experience than he did, but Veikka's a quick study. He's always willing to go for something, yet he also knows when to turn back—as we did facing those last hundred yards of summit ridge on Broad Peak.

For several years, Veikka couldn't quite keep up with my pace. Normally breaking trail, you swap leads every hour or half hour. I noticed that when I offered to take over, he'd say, "No, no, I'll go a little farther." I finally asked him why he wouldn't let me lead. "You go too fast!" he exclaimed.

By now, however, we're equally strong on the 8,000ers. And that makes him as strong as any partner I've ever gone with. Like me, Veikka's committed to climbing the highest peaks in the best style, without bottled oxygen.

In the spring of 1998, Veikka and I joined Guy Cotter to try Dhaulagiri, the world's seventh-highest mountain, at 26,795 feet. That was the season when Chantal Mauduit died in her tent at Camp II, with her Sherpa partner Ang Tshering—either by suffocation or, as the French inquest concluded, of a broken neck (presumably the result of being struck by a falling ice block as she lay in her sleeping bag).

Dhaulagiri and Annapurna form a striking pair of 8,000ers some 250 miles west of Everest—the westernmost 8,000ers in Nepal. On the famous 1950 expedition led by Maurice Herzog, the French team initially planned to climb Dhaulagiri. With wildly inaccurate maps, they spent fruitless weeks trying to find a way through the outer defenses of Dhaulagiri before giving up. It was only then, on the improbably late date of May 14, that they turned their attention to Annapurna. That they solved a complex and dangerous approach route and climbed the mountain on their first try, only a little more than two weeks before the monsoon swept in, makes their achievement all the more extraordinary.

Dhaulagiri was finally climbed on the sixth attempt on the mountain, by a Swiss-Austrian team led by Max Eiselin in 1960. By then, the peak was one of only two unclimbed 8,000ers left, the other being the remote and little-reconnoitered Shishapangma, in Tibet. Eiselin's team bypassed many of the difficulties of getting to the mountain by using a Pilatus PC-6 aircraft (flown by a very bold pilot) to land tons of gear and personnel on a glacier at 18,700 feet, beneath the northeast ridge. Those landings remain today the highest ever performed by a fixed-wing aircraft anywhere in the world. The Pilatus eventually crashed on one of the load-hauling forays. Fortunately, no one was seriously hurt. The wreckage of the plane is still visible on the lower approaches to the mountain.

Veikka had already climbed Dhaulagiri in the autumn of 1993, after Gary Ball's death by pulmonary edema lower on the mountain. But a successful summit bid would have given me my tenth of the fourteen 8,000ers—or my twelfth, if I was willing to count the asterisked Broad Peak and Shishapangma (which in the long run I wouldn't). But the spring of 1998 was not a good time to be on Dhaulagiri. Veikka and I got only within 1,500 vertical feet of the top via the northeast ridge, the route of the first ascent. We turned back in the face of fiendish slab avalanche conditions that seemed to have formed all over the upper slopes of the mountain.

A strange and vexing thing happened during that expedition. On our first attempt, we left a depot of gear at our high camp, a bunch of food and equipment wrapped up in a tent. The next time we got up to the camp, ready to spend the night there and make our summit bid the next day, we were shocked to discover the depot completely gone. We had to retreat all the way to base camp to resupply. Down low, we ran into some members of the Spanish expedition trying the same route. "Hey, you guys," we asked, "did you see our stuff at Camp III?" No, they insisted, they hadn't seen a trace of our gear.

Yet the Spaniards were the only other party that had been up to or above Camp III, and in fact they'd made a summit bid just before we climbed up to find our gear missing. Years later, one of their members ran into Veikka and confessed, in tears. The Spaniards had been turned back by the same slab avalanche conditions that had thwarted us. Out of sheer disgust, they had kicked at this wrapped-up bundle of stuff in camp—kicked it, in fact, right off the mountain. I've heard plenty of stories of teams stealing each other's gear, but nothing quite like this!

When I left for Dhaulagiri in March 1998, Gil was less than five months old. In 1995, Paula had had a good time as our assistant base-camp manager on Everest and Makalu. The next year, though traumatized by the tragedy, she had been from start to finish a vital member of our IMAX team. And her support when I finally went for the summit on May 23 had been incredibly valuable to me—just as it was thrilling to embrace her back at base camp and to share the hike out with her.

After we had Gil, though, Paula would never again come to base camp on one of my 8,000-meter expeditions. We'd always have a sat phone at base camp, and eventually got one light enough to carry up the mountain. It's important to both of us that I be able to call her from the mountain. Paula usually prefers that I make the call only when I've gotten back to high camp after reaching the top. Calling from the summit is a tremendous rush, but it leaves a lingering uncertainty in its wake. Paula always knows that on the summit, the climb is only half over. *Getting down is mandatory:* too many mountaineers have declared victory on the summit, never to return to sea level.

Paula is an extremely devoted mother. In my absence, she's always had a lot of friends in Seattle for moral support. She seldom hired anyone to help her—she always said she'd rather be there for the kids herself.

While I was gone in the Himalaya or Karakoram, Paula would immerse herself into being the sole provider. Unlike me, she's comfortable with chaos all around her—toys scattered everywhere, spilled food, tots crawling every which way. As she would tell me, when I was gone and she knew she had to take care of everything, she felt more useful than when both of us were home. And in some ways, it was hard for her when I came back. In her words, it meant that she had to relinquish a certain power she'd spent months building up.

I was sorry not to be able to have Paula at base camp after we had children. But there's something to her recurrent complaint that on the mountain I compartmentalize my feelings. I'd seen relationships with someone waiting at base camp undercut other climbers' resolve. If I have work to do on an 8,000er, I need to conserve all my energy for myself. If I'm worrying about whether Paula is happy or busy at base camp, that can distract me from the business of climbing. You've got to be 100 percent there. If you're only slightly not there on a big mountain, it can cause you to fail or to get in trouble.

At the same time, I like to think I'm a good father. In the spring of 1998, it was very hard to leave Gil behind in Seattle. At five months, he was a beautiful towheaded boy, already developing the character that he manifests today—gregarious, intelligent, a comic actor.

Later, as Gil got older, my leaving became really hard for him. Paula told me that sometimes, just as I was getting ready to go off on an expedition, Gil would come to her with a stricken look on his face. "Mommy, why does Daddy have to go?" he'd bleat.

Bedtime was the hardest. "This is what Daddy does," she'd explain. "You have friends whose daddies go to work every day from eight to five. They're off at the office every day. At least when Daddy comes home, he stays." But the stricken look would not go away. For Gil at that age, my absences were incomprehensible. How could anything possibly take that long to do?

Other climbers I know have radically curtailed their ambitions after having kids, or even quit climbing altogether. And I've seen certain others become truly absentee fathers: they may climb as well as ever, but you get the feeling that an expedition looms for them as a handy excuse to get away from home. I love my family, and I also love what I do. I've always tried my very best to be a devoted father, even while I tried to climb to the best of my abilities. I will admit, though, that once I had children, I did less climbing each year than I had when I was single; but I made the most of the expeditions that I did go on.

During the eight years after Gil was born, I struggled to keep up a delicate juggling act. I wanted to be there for my kids when I was home. It was more than duty—I truly love them and love spending time with them, watching them grow. Yet at the same time, I needed to keep going back to the Himalaya and the Karakoram. In interviews, I would often tell people that it would be fine with me if I didn't finish all fourteen 8,000ers if the risks got too great. I'd insist that I'd be happy to quit with only twelve or thirteen. But I'd put too much effort into Endeavor 8000 to let go of it. It was my old thing about finishing a project, hammering the last nail into the deck.

In 1999, Veikka and I pulled off what I consider today our most nearly perfect twofer. We went initially to Manaslu, the world's eighth-highest mountain, at 26,781 feet, first climbed by the Japanese in 1956. Manaslu stands by itself, some sixty miles east of Annapurna, in a part of the Nepal Himalaya I'd never before explored. We were an expedition of only three: Veikka, myself, and Dorje, a Sherpa who doubled as our cook and sirdar.

There's far less traffic in this part of the Himalaya, compared to the Khumbu Valley or the circuit around Dhaulagiri and Annapurna, thronged by commercially recruited teams of trekkers every spring and fall. As a result, the villagers near Manaslu have not yet become jaded by contact with Westerners. I was constantly surprised by how warmly they received us. On the hike in, Dorje would ask a farmer if we could use his kitchen fire to cook dinner, or we would visit a family inside their house, or sometimes sleep in their barn.

I didn't know the route on Manaslu very well: by 1999, the peak had not been climbed all that often. For all the research that I had conducted, there was not much information to be found. Even though we would be attempting the "normal" route, it would still prove to be an adventure for Veikka and me. There was no dotted line to lead us to the summit. We needed to find the route by seeking the path of least resistance, which Veikka and I figured out as we went. It took us fourteen days and four camps to work our way up the mountain, avoiding an icefall and avalanche slopes, weaving our way through crevasse fields. On the fourteenth day, in perfect weather, we stood on the summit.

Then we hiked out to a nearby village, where we'd arranged for a helicopter to pick us up. We flew straight from there to Dhaulagiri base camp. This "rapid transit" allowed us to take full advantage of the fitness and acclimatization we'd built up on Manaslu. And we knew the route by now on Dhaulagiri's northeast ridge. Climbing alpine-style, going really light, with a custom-made bivvy tent and a down quilt that we shared in lieu of sleeping bags, we stormed up Dhaulagiri in only three days. With the mountain completely to ourselves, I couldn't help imagining the throngs that were undoubtedly swarming all over Everest at the same time.

That was a great season, and Veikka and I performed together like clockwork. Everything that could go right, did. Two climbs back to back and not a major glitch. Yet even when everything is going well, you need to remember that you are still walking the line. You cannot become complacent; you cannot let down your guard. On any 8,000er, inevitably, there are countless things that can go wrong. If you make a trivial mistake, such as losing a mitten or twisting an ankle, it can cost you your life.

On Dhaulagiri, as I climbed out of a very steep gully and crested the final summit ridge, I was reminded of these eternal axioms by a sudden slap in the face. There, several yards in front of me, lay the body of a climber. His clothing indicated that he had lain there for perhaps twenty years. He was resting flat on his back, as if he had just decided to take a nap and had never woken up. He may have exhausted himself on the climb and had no strength left to descend.

Boom! I thought to myself, Dude, one tiny screwup and that could be you lying there. No one can get up here to rescue you. That corpse was an instant reminder of how far Veikka and I had stretched our umbilical cord of safety. On the other hand, to stretch that umbilical cord is to undergo something that not many people ever experience. To be completely reliant on your own abilities and judgment, without any kind of safety net, is quite rare in everyday life—and strangely gratifying for that very reason. Even in such extreme forms of adventure as desert crossings or single-handed sailing jaunts across the oceans, rescue is often feasible. Above 22,000 feet on a Himalayan peak it is, for now, impossible.

▲
▲
▲

Two years later, in the spring of 2001, Veikka and I attempted another twofer. First we went to Shishapangma. I wanted to remove my asterisk, which had nagged away at me for eight years, while Veikka had never been on the mountain. In May, we managed to have the peak all to ourselves. We spent sixteen days establishing only two camps (as opposed to the normal four) and then going for the top. This time conditions were ideal. The upper slopes were composed of crunchy snow into which our crampons bit firmly. When we came to the last hundred yards of the summit ridge, which had been too dangerous for me to attempt solo in 1993, we saw how to traverse it. There was no cornice, but the crest itself was a sharp comb of hard-packed snow. To negotiate it, we practiced a technique called *à cheval,* because it's like riding a horse. You simply straddle the crest, one leg on either side, and scoot along with your hands and your crotch. It may not be the most elegant technique, nor the most comfortable, but it's effective. We felt so secure there, we didn't even rope up. An hour of scooting brought us to the main summit.

From Shishapangma, we traveled home to Finland and the United States, then met a few weeks later in Pakistan to attempt Nanga Parbat. The ninth-highest mountain, at 26,660 feet, it stands in proud isolation 120 miles southwest of the Baltoro chain around K2, where four of the fourteen 8,000ers cluster. Nanga Parbat is a mountain of legends, the principal one being its amazing first ascent in 1953, when, disobeying expedition leader Karl Herrligkoffer's orders, Hermann Buhl went solo to the summit. He spent forty hours alone, climbing nonstop in the Death Zone. On the descent, Buhl endured a standing bivouac and froze his feet, which eventually cost him several toes; but he won enduring fame.

Veikka and I planned to try the Kinshofer route on the Diamir Face, a huge, sprawling precipice festooned with seracs, crevasses, and hanging glaciers. The Diamir, too, is wreathed in legend, for it was here, in 1970, that Reinhold Messner and his brother Günther made a desperate descent, after the pair had reached the summit from the opposite side, the Rupal Face. Near exhaustion, Reinhold pushed ahead of his brother, solved the last intricacies of the great wall, reached the final glacial snout, and sat down to wait for his brother. But Günther never came. Racked with anxiety, Reinhold climbed back up the lower glacier, finding fresh avalanche debris that he was convinced covered the body of his brother. Eventually, exhausted and frostbitten, he descended to the grassy meadows below the glacier, where he collapsed. He was helped by local villagers down to their town, and ultimately was reunited with the rest of his team.

That landmark traverse spawned an enduring controversy that flamed back to life in 2001, when Reinhold Messner attacked his former teammates in a public meeting in Munich. Having kept their silence for three decades, several of those teammates now fired back, accusing Messner not only of making up the story of Günther's death but of abandoning his brother near the summit so that he could win his own Buhl-like fame by traversing the mountain solo, in defiance of the same expedition leader, Herrligkoffer, who had crossed swords with Buhl.

After 1970, Messner kept returning to the Diamir Face to search for Günther's body. Just last year, in July 2005, three Pakistani guides reported the grisly discovery, low on the Diamir Face, of a headless corpse, reduced to jumbled bones, a few tufts of hair, torn pieces of clothing, and a leather boot. Messner rushed to the mountain, declared the remains those of his brother, and then, as if to settle the matter for good, cremated the bones on the spot. He did keep one small portion of bone for DNA analysis in Munich, and the results confirmed statistically that the bone had to have been Günther's. Messner's detractors, however, argued that since the remainder of the body had been cremated, there was no way to double-check the results. For Reinhold, this was the end of an acrimonious chapter in his life; for others, the book remains open.

The charmed luck that had carried Veikka and me up Shishapangma ran out on Nanga Parbat. We quickly got Camp I set up at the bottom of the Diamir Face, and then it began to snow. We retreated to base camp to wait, but it snowed every day for the next two weeks. As the days passed, I realized that conditions were not going to get better. Even if it cleared off, so much new snow would have piled up that the face—prone even in normal conditions to huge avalanches—would be especially dangerous.

As I became extremely anxious about the conditions, I finally decided to go home. Veikka stayed on, joining up with a German team. A few days later, he reached the summit with the Germans.

It would be easy to say that I made the wrong decision in going home. But even if I'd stayed on, I'm not sure I would have continued up the mountain after the weather cleared. I made my own call. I walked away. Veikka later admitted that, despite their success, the climb with the Germans had seemed quite dangerous.

One of the aspects of my mountaineering career that I'm proudest of is that on the 8,000ers, I've never succumbed to summit fever—except perhaps on K2 in 1992. I've backed off a lot of climbs when things didn't feel right. I've lived my motto with a vengeance: *Getting to the top is optional. Getting down is mandatory.*

By the summer of 2001, I was forty-two years old. Gil was three and a half; Ella had just turned one year old. I'd reached the summit of eleven of the fourteen 8,000ers. All that I had left were the asterisk on Broad Peak,

Nanga Parbat, and, ironically, the very peak that had inspired me to become a mountaineer: Annapurna.

When I had first conceived the plan for Endeavor 8000, I never dreamed that Annapurna would prove to be the hardest of all the fourteen high summits for me to reach. Yet just the previous year, in the spring of 2000, I'd been stopped cold at the foot of the north face of Annapurna. Stopped colder than I ever had been on an 8,000er—and intimidated, to boot. It was then that I'd begun to wonder whether I would ever set foot on the 26,503-foot crest of snow first trod by two Frenchmen on June 3, 1950—the triumph that had launched the fourteen-year-long golden age of Himalayan mountaineering, when one after another, all the 8,000ers succumbed to their first ascents. Might it be, I pondered gloomily that spring, that I'd never stand where my heroes Herzog and Lachenal had stood?

Nemesis: Annapurna

After Veikka's and my blithe twofer success on Manaslu and Dhaulagiri in 1999, I thought, What next? Annapurna had long been in my thoughts, and from high on Dhaulagiri, we'd had excellent views of the mountain, only twenty-five miles away. The two great peaks are separated by the deep gorge of the Kali Gandaki, a raging torrent that ultimately flows into the Ganges. It was up that canyon that the French had pushed their reconnaissance in 1950, before switching their objective from Dhaulagiri to Annapurna. ▲ I suggested Annapurna to Veikka for the spring of 2000. He agreed without a moment's hesitation. Neither of us had been on the mountain before, and Veikka had started to launch his own campaign to climb all fourteen 8,000ers. (As of fall 2006, Veikka has eleven of those summits to his credit, lacking only Gasherbrum I, Gasherbrum II—and Broad Peak, on which he and I had stopped a hundred yards from the summit.)

We decided to try Annapurna by the north face, the same side the French had attacked exactly fifty years before. It was partly the chance to reconnect with history that lured me, to tread the same ground my heroes had in the book by Maurice Herzog that had changed my life as a teenager. But if their route proved unreasonable, there were other options on the north, particularly the Dutch Rib, a buttress to the left of the French route, first climbed by a Sherpa and a Netherlander in 1977, as they made only the fourth ascent of Annapurna. To all appearances, because it protruded from the north face, the Dutch Rib looked safer than the long, curving arc the French had pushed up and left across the face, constantly threatened by hanging ice cliffs and avalanches. Somewhat farther away, rising from a different base camp, there was also the Northwest Pillar, a technically difficult line first ascended in 1985 by that formidable duo, Reinhold Messner and Hans Kammerlander—but only after four previous failures by other parties, costing a total of six lives. Messner himself later admitted that this route was quite dangerous.

Contemplating Annapurna, realizing that we would have to establish a long and complicated route up a face with few decent campsites, I felt that the project was too big for Veikka and me alone. I decided it would be good to bring another couple of guys along. Neal Beidleman had been on our K2 team in 1992, but had had to leave the mountain before the rest of us could launch our summit attempt. We had really hit it off, and I thought he had stood a very good chance of reaching the summit. I'd been sorry to see him go. Then in 1996, guiding for Scott, Neal had played a pivotal role in leading the stragglers lost in the storm back to camp on the South Col, then helping the refugees down the Lhotse Face.

Neal is an aerospace engineer by training, a bona fide rocket scientist living in Aspen, where he runs his own design and consulting business. He's not only strong—both very fit and an accomplished technical climber—but a really nice guy as well. Over the years, he'd several times told me, "Ed, if you want to take someone else on one of your expeditions, I'd be excited to go." So now I invited him. And I suggested that he bring a partner of his own, so that we'd have two ropes of two. Neal snooped around and came up with a fellow Aspenite, Michael Kennedy.

The cardinal achievement of Michael's career had been as editor of *Climbing* magazine: he'd taken on a scruffy, homegrown rag for insiders and turned it into a slick journal with an international scope that became perhaps the most-respected publication of its kind in the world. In his late forties, Michael had never been on an 8,000-meter peak, and by 2000 he was in semiretirement from serious mountaineering. But in his tiger days, he'd been a driving force on some of the fiercest routes in the world, such as the Infinite Spur on Mount Foraker in Alaska and a gutsy attempt on Latok I in Pakistan. Jazzed by the idea of Annapurna, Michael whipped himself back into shape that winter.

With the addition of Neal and Michael, I thought we had put together a very strong team. In late March, we began the forty-mile-long hike in from Beni. At the time, Paula was six months pregnant with our second child, who would be born shortly after my return from Nepal. In that sense, the spring of 2000 wasn't the best time for me to be away in the Himalayas. Paula encouraged me to go, however—as she puts it, she's always been my number one cheerleader as I pursued Endeavor 8000. But to mitigate our separation at such an emotional juncture in our lives, I promised I'd call her on our sat phone every few days.

The French got to Annapurna base camp by storming up a deep, V-notched side canyon called the Miristi Khola, formed by an eastern tributary to the Kali Gandaki. By 2000, a slightly better approach had been discovered, but much of it coincided with the French route. The hike in to base camp on the north side of Annapurna is nothing like the stroll up the Khumbu Valley to Everest base camp. It's a serious journey in its own right—not the kind of hike a tour company would sanely market to its trekker clients. You need to traverse grassy slopes so steep that if you slipped and fell, you'd be a goner. At places on these slopes, we had to fix ropes for our porters. (Coming out from Annapurna in 1950, one of the French team's porters fell to his death here. Curiously, Herzog fails to mention the incident in *Annapurna*. We know about the death only from an entry in Lachenal's posthumously published diary.)

As if those traverses weren't grueling enough, as you ascend the Miristi Khola, you go up 4,000 feet to a pass, down 3,000 on the other side, then up another 3,000, then down 2,000. It's exhausting and harrowing, especially for the heavily laden porters. The trek to base camp, which took eight days, gave all four of us an added respect for the French in 1950; they had accomplished that passage in only four days, having to hector their terrified porters across a couple of shaky improvised bridges over the roaring stream.

Preoccupied with the logistics of just getting to base camp, I neglected to call Paula for four days. You can't always get a sat-phone signal in a deep valley, but I think I decided just to wait till we got to base camp to make the call. When I did, she let me know how upset she was. In my diary, I wrote, "I apologized but not sure that did any good. Great to hear her voice & talk & catch up with her. Gil was asleep so I'll call back tonight."

A sat phone can be a blessing, but it's also a pain. Paula and I never had an explicit agreement about how often I should call. But sometimes she expected that I would call more often than I did. When I'm on a mountain, I need to be focused, in the moment. There are times when the last thing I want to think is, *Oh, I've got to make a call back to the States.* Yet once you have a family and kids, the importance of staying connected increases.

Some people might have thought Paula was being unreasonable, but I took full blame for not calling. It's just my nature. When other people get upset, I feel as if it's my fault.

Yet just twenty or thirty years earlier, on expeditions to the remote ranges, calling home was not an option. Climbers went off for two or three months and had no contact with the outside world the whole time. And somehow wives and girlfriends (and the boyfriends and husbands of women climbers) dealt with that prolonged silence, even if they worried every day about whether their loved ones were alive or dead. And you can go back further in history—say, to the British expeditions attempting to sail the Northwest Passage from the 1840s through the 1870s. Often their ships got frozen into the ice, and the crews had to winter over. Some expeditions were gone for as long as three years without being able to send home the slight-est scrap of news. It's hard to imagine how the ones left at home managed to deal with absences of that length—especially knowing that those journeys were at least as dangerous as Himalayan mountaineering.

Anyway, we got to base camp slightly ahead of two other parties try-ing the north face that year—one a Spanish team, the other a group of French military guides. They were both there to honor the fiftieth anniver-sary of the first ascent.

After studying the face intently with binoculars, we started out. Before you even get to the north face proper, you have to do some circuitous climb-ing through the lower glacial slopes that spread out from the mountain like an apron. To avoid a tricky initial icefall, we climbed a rock buttress just to the left of this area, fixing ropes since we'd need to go up and down the but-tress in sometimes icy conditions. It took us a couple of days to establish Camp I, still not on the face proper. From there, however, we could finally see all the features on the mountain. The Dutch Rib protruded way off to the east of us, but how to get there from here? Hovering far above us were all kinds of ice cliffs, crowned by the famous Sickle, the huge, curving ice wall that stands as a barrier between the north face and the relatively low-angle summit snowfield above. Breaking through the Sickle had been the last-ditch key to the French triumph in 1950.

One reason I was pleased to have Neal and Michael along was because they, too, were married men with kids. They'd be as conservative as I would, I thought. But now we all started to feel a little dubious. From Camp I, we watched the face, alarmed at how active it was—small avalanches slid down regularly, and seracs collapsed without warning. The Sickle seemed to hang over the route like a giant sword of Damocles.

Our mixed feelings come across in my diary. As early as April 11, I wrote: "At breakfast we all seemed ambivalent about going up. Outside we looked around, no one made any moves. I suggested a rest day & everyone agreed immediately."

Having studied the face, we thought there was one nook where we could tuck a Camp II beneath several big ice cliffs. Above those cliffs, huge crevasses crisscrossed the slopes. We hoped that any avalanches coming down from higher on the mountain would get swallowed by those crevasses, and that other debris might plunge off the top of the cliffs guarding our camp and shoot right over us.

We got that camp established, spent a single night there, and ventured a little ways above to check out the face. It was so active with slides coming down, we blanched at the thought of traversing it. It would be bad enough to cross a single time, and we knew we'd have to make multiple trips up and down just to get our highest camp in place, somewhere on top of the Sickle. We simply couldn't convince ourselves to do it. As one of us said, "We can't run fast enough!"

So we packed up Camp II and retreated all the way to base camp. We were thinking that maybe there was an alternative route farther to the left. A few days later, we went back up to Camp I to scout our new line, but stuff was still coming down almost continuously between us and the Dutch Rib. Even the traverse we would have to make to reach the Rib was threatened by huge, overhanging seracs several thousand feet above. And Neal noticed a vast crack in the hanging glacier directly above the Rib, which had detached a block of ice the size of a skyscraper that seemed poised to fall at any moment. It was particularly warm that spring, and there wasn't as much snow on the face as usual. In these conditions, the mountain was disintegrating before our eyes.

Looking at our new line, we agreed there wasn't anything there, either. Even as we made a tentative stab toward the bottom of this alternate route, a small avalanche swept over it. At that point we all said, "Let's go home." This wasn't fun, and it wasn't safe. The verdict was unanimous.

Once we'd decided to give up, the tension dissipated like air escaping from a punctured balloon. We told ourselves, Let's just enjoy one last night on the hill, here in Camp I; we're safe here. With that, we felt completely relaxed.

In the middle of the night, I was lying awake in my sleeping bag. Suddenly I heard a huge rumbling sound from above. I zipped open the tent door to look out and saw an explosion of snow, a nuclear bomb of an avalanche coming down the north face. I woke up Veikka. "Look at that!" I exclaimed.

Camp I was a good two miles away from the bottom of the face, so we knew there was no danger of the avalanche reaching us. But a slide that big drives a wind blast ahead of it, full of the finest spindrift. We knew the blast would sweep over our camp. We yelled at Neal and Michael to wake them up. "Get ready!" I shouted. Under a crystal-clear sky with a full moon, the sight of that maelstrom coming toward us was mesmerizing. The distances were so colossal, the avalanche seemed to be moving in slow motion. I watched till the last moment, then zipped the door closed. Veikka and I grabbed the tent poles and hung on.

All of a sudden, the camp was hammered by the wind blast. It felt like a whole gang of people were standing outside our tent, shaking it furiously. Veikka and I stared at each other, wide-eyed, holding on to the poles. Finally the wind ebbed, but a fine dusting of a snowstorm settled over camp, until the lightest particles carried by the wind blast precipitated out.

In the morning, we saw that the nearest ice blocks from the avalanche had come to a stop on the glacier only a couple of hundred yards away. It was the biggest avalanche any of us had ever seen. "Man," one of us burst out, "did we ever make the right decision!" We looked up to survey the devastation on the slope above: it appeared as though a gigantic rake had scraped the mountain clean. All the towering ice structures we had watched over the previous days were gone, wiped out as if a bomb had leveled a city.

You always question turning back on a mountain. You wonder whether with a little more nerve, you might have pushed through to success. But that mother of an avalanche validated our decision once and for all.

▲
▲
▲

That spring, nobody climbed Annapurna from the north. The highest any team got was a paltry 23,100 feet. Our defeat, however, was of a completely different nature from what would happen the next year on Nanga

Parbat. There, the route we hoped to climb on the Diamir Face looked perfectly reasonable to me. It was two weeks of constant snowfall that rendered it, in my judgment, too dangerous to try.

The route on Annapurna, in contrast, had looked intrinsically beyond the pale of safety. Chagrined by our experience, when I got home I reread *Annapurna* for the seventh or eighth time. How had the French done it in 1950? At that time, not one of the team members had any Himalayan experience (World War II and its aftermath had shut down mountaineering in the greater ranges for most of a decade). Was it a case of "ignorance is bliss"? Had the French just been lucky, or had they realized how dangerous their route was? Perhaps the very haste with which they had surged up the face, knowing their days before the monsoon were shortly numbered, had contributed to that luck: the less time spent on dangerous slopes, the less chance of incurring an accident.

There's a long passage in *Annapurna* in which the four principal climbers—Herzog, Lachenal, Terray, and Rébuffat—sit beneath the face, try to trace the right line, and argue about whether it's too hazardous. There's a lot of back-and-forth, but the discussion ends with a decision to forge the route. Herzog's account of the debate closes thus:

> *"Let's get going," Terray kept crying in great excitement. Lachenal, no less excited, came and yelled in my ear:*
> *"A hundred to nothing! That's the odds on our success!"*
> *And even the more cautious Rébuffat admitted that "It's the least difficult proposition and the most reasonable."*

On the descent of the north face in early June, with the temperatures far too warm and the monsoon all but upon them, with the four principals variously crippled by frostbite and snow blindness, the French team indeed played Russian roulette with the avalanches. Climbing down the Sickle, the men knocked loose a big slide that engulfed their Camp IV below, carrying off one tent but miraculously leaving the four Sherpas ensconced there unhurt. Later that day, Herzog and two Sherpas, roped together, set off another avalanche that tumbled them out of control toward a 1,500-foot drop. Only the fluke of the rope snagging on a crest of ice stopped the fall and saved three lives. Yet despite that close call, nowhere in *Annapurna* does Herzog judge his team's route unjustifiably dangerous.

It was only last year that a friend of mine pointed out a very interesting and, in retrospect, prescient passage in Lachenal's diary, *Carnets du Vertige,* published in its full, unexpurgated version only in 1996—forty-one years after Lachenal's death in a crevasse while skiing on the Vallée Blanche above Chamonix. Since I don't read French and *Carnets* has never been translated into English, I was unaware of this passage.

In an appendix to his diary, called "Commentaires," written upon his return to France, Lachenal—whom Herzog consistently portrays as a reckless, impulsive madman in *Annapurna*—writes:

> At the base of Annapurna...we had only a few days left before the arrival of the monsoon to climb and equip the whole of an immense, unknown glaciated wall. This led us right away to choose an extremely dangerous route. Between Camp II and Camp IV this line took on the exact shape of a huge ejection cone [of avalanche debris]. Today I believe that we took unheard-of chances [there]....Face-to-face with Annapurna, we had no choice: it was this route or a complete fiasco....But for the second ascent...I expressly advise against the route that we followed.
>
> In my opinion, one should climb instead on the extreme left of the couloirs leading up to the eastern subsummit.

Twenty-two years before it would be climbed, Lachenal recommended the line that would come to be known as the Dutch Rib. We ourselves would have opted for that alternative, but could find no safe way to traverse to the base of that buttress.

Carnets du Vertige was first published only a few months after Lachenal's death, but it was edited by Herzog's brother Gérard, then heavily censored by Maurice Herzog and his friend and mentor Lucien Devies, the president of the French Alpine Club. Herzog and Devies expunged any comment in

Lachenal's diary critical of Herzog's leadership, or even hinting at dissension within the team. The pair ended up suppressing the whole of Lachenal's trenchant "Commentaires." When the unexpurgated version was finally brought to light in 1996, Herzog—by then the only principal veteran of Annapurna 1950 still alive—sued the publisher, Michel Guérin.

When I'd first read *Annapurna,* at the age of sixteen, I hadn't known enough to judge the danger of the French route. I just thought all the close calls were part of the game. Now, reexamining Herzog's book after I got home from Annapurna in 2000, I could read between the lines. I could see how truly close the team had come to losing several members. I thought, Whoa, they really threaded the needle.

On the one hand, their climb was an astounding deed: to master the difficult approach and climb the mountain in just a bit over two weeks, to succeed in summiting not only on the first 8,000er ever ascended but the only one that would ever be climbed on the first attempt. On the other hand, there may be some truth to the "ignorance is bliss" theory. Those guys were very experienced climbers in the Alps. Terray, Lachenal, and Rébuffat were among the best six or eight climbers in the world at the time. But on Annapurna, the French had no Himalayan experience with which to put their climb in perspective. In 1950, no one really knew what it would take to succeed on an 8,000er. The Himalaya was a whole new arena after the Alps, on a far larger scale.

Someone recently asked me if I thought the 1950 team's triumph was brilliant or recklessly crazy. My answer would have to be "Both."

▲
▲
▲

Perhaps because it was the first 8,000er ever climbed, Annapurna has been seriously underrated ever since. Yet it turns out to be probably the hardest of all the fourteen to climb—or at least the only one without a reasonably safe route on any flank. And Annapurna is also the deadliest 8,000er.

A mountaineering historian has made a careful compilation of the statistics of death rates on the 8,000ers. His analysis, current through 2003, used a simple but stark criterion: the number of climbers who successfully reach the summit compared to the number who die on the mountain. For Everest, the ratio turns out to be seven to one. For K2, which has the reputation of being the hardest and most dangerous of the high peaks, the ratio is a little over three to one. But for Annapurna, it's exactly two to one. For every two climbers who get to the top, one climber dies trying.

Annapurna would haunt my thoughts for the next five years. Perhaps in the spring of 2000, we'd found the mountain in particularly dangerous condition, what with the warmth and lack of snow. But I had no desire to go back to the north face. I couldn't imagine the French route ever being safe enough to fit within my margins of acceptable risk.

For the moment, however, I could put Annapurna on the back burner. I got home from Nepal in late May. Paula gave birth to our second child, a girl we named Ella, on June 25. I managed to stay home during the first eight months of Ella's life, and despite short trips to give slide shows for Mountain Hardwear and other sponsors, I was a full-time dad. As Ella grew, I could see that she was a healthy, sturdy, independent child, with an athletic build. I found her adorable. Because of her strong, confident demeanor, some friends of ours nicknamed her the "Navy Seal." She would turn out to be our earliest walker. She had a knack for soothing herself—she seemed happy to be on her own. Meanwhile, that October Gil turned three. He was developing into quite a chatterbox. His curiosity was insatiable, and he insisted on entertaining anyone who happened to be in the vicinity. Paula and I were delighted to see how gently and sweetly Gil treated his new baby sister.

In the autumn of 2001 we moved from our small West Seattle bungalow to Bainbridge Island, a thirty-five-minute ferry ride across Puget Sound from downtown Seattle. In that original "starter house" for our family, the four of us, along with my trusty old cat, Slick, had increasingly found ourselves stepping on each other's toes. This despite the fact that with the help of my master carpenter friend Dan Hiatt, I'd put in five years' worth of sporadic renovations on the bungalow.

One of those renovations could well have ended my climbing career. To build a curved cedar deck adjoining our kitchen and living room, I was using a circular power saw to cut a severe angle at the end of a wide board. It's a tricky business, because the blade guard tends to catch on the board's edge just as you start the cut, preventing the saw from moving forward. Dan had taught me to jam a pencil into the guard to keep it in the up position. The drawback is that the blade, spinning at hundreds of revolutions per minute, is left dangerously exposed; but by then I'd performed this maneuver countless times.

As I finished the cut and released the trigger, I slowly let the saw swing down at arm's length. Since I'm right-handed, the saw ought to have descended to the outside of my right leg. Somehow oblivious to the fact that my leg was still in the way, I watched as the decelerating blade tore into my jeans and the flesh below, just above my right kneecap. Aghast, I dropped the saw and sat there for a moment, not wanting to assess the damage. I was surprised to feel no pain; nor did I see any outpouring of blood. But all I could think was *Oh, shit, I've done it now!*

Gingerly, I pulled the shredded jeans out of the way and uncovered a six-inch vertical gash in my leg, the ragged edges of my flesh exposing muscle and tissue. As I recognized from my vet training, the crudeness of the rough blade's cut had actually had a hemostatic effect, causing the severed vessels to clamp themselves tightly shut. A sharp incision with a honed blade, as in surgery, would have caused much more profuse bleeding.

My first reaction was that I could sew the wound up myself. I had the right instruments, left over from an expedition, stowed in a sterile pack inside the house. But in the next moment, I realized that I might have damaged nerves or tendons—only an experienced trauma doc could say for sure. Without a word, I limped into the house, taped three Band-Aids across the gash, grabbed the car keys, found Paula, and said, "Would you mind driving me to the hospital?"

There, a resident on his first day in the ER examined the wound, concluded that I had no major nerve or tendon damage, and started to sew me up. But the whole procedure turned into something out of the Keystone Kops. The doctor didn't really know how to hold the forceps or the needle; nor was he sure what was the proper stitch. I had to coach him through the entire operation. It took so long that he had to inject three successive doses of local anesthetic into the edges of the wound as each previous dose wore off. As the last dose was beginning to ebb, he prepared to inject a fourth. I gritted my teeth, ignored the pain, and told him just to keep sewing.

In the end I had a monstrous scar. Now when people see my bare right leg and ask, "Hey, how'd you get the scar?," I nonchalantly answer, "Shark attack." Yet it was sobering to ponder the fact that, having survived umpteen Himalayan expeditions, I'd nearly cut my leg off building the deck of my bungalow!

For our new house, we wanted more living space and a big yard. In 2000, Paula and I had discovered that Bainbridge Island was quite affordable, with first-rate public schools. We wanted our kids to have a growing-up experience similar to our own, in neighborhoods where we'd headed out the door to play in the woods without worrying who might be lurking in the underbrush. After a long search, we found a two-acre plot of land on which a builder had already laid out plans for a spec house. By making a down payment, we could have some say in the choice of finishes, paint colors, flooring options, and cabinetry. The spec house, whose design we already loved, would thus bear lots of personal touches by the time we moved in.

It took a year to build our "modern farmhouse" on the haven of Bainbridge Island—distant enough from Seattle to feel far from the madding crowd, with a little bit of wilderness out the back door, but close enough so that we could stay in touch with the city's cultural scene and with friends who lived there. With thirty-two hundred feet of floor space, the new house was twice as large as our West Seattle bungalow. Now we had two full floors, four bedrooms, three bathrooms, and a detached garage with space above that I turned into a cozy office.

The village of Bainbridge, which centers on a few blocks of quaint downtown shops, has only two traffic lights. Ten minutes away, our pastoral backyard abounds in frogs and salamanders. Thanks to mutual friends with kids and myriad school activities, we quickly felt welcome in this burgeoning community.

Paula and I plunged into making the house our own. With her apparently innate sense of style and knack for interior design, she chose the furniture, drapes, and accessories that made the place comfortable.

We also faced a major landscaping job. After the builders nailed the last board in place, we were left with a plot of raw dirt surrounding the house. A dozen yards beyond that plot, the dense forest of fir, cedar, and alder trees, with an undergrowth of ferns, took over. So we seeded grass and dug beds for flowers and other plants. I felt a keen sense of reward as I watched things grow and fill in year after year.

Whenever I got trapped indoors for too long, lapsing into the funk that Paula calls my "wilted flower" state, she'd send me out to the yard. I found true solace and rejuvenation in chores as mundane yet strenuous as digging holes, moving boulders that some receding glacier had left strewn about our property several million years ago, or chopping firewood. I also reveled in building additions to the cedar deck and in laying cobblestone pathways and patios. Some of my climbing buddies, those who'd seen only the restless vagabond who couldn't wait to go off on his next expedition, would have been shocked to behold the domestic putterer I became on Bainbridge Island.

▲
▲
▲

The spring before we bought the house on Bainbridge Island was when Veikka and I attempted our twofer on Shishapangma and Nanga Parbat. And even while I was climbing those mountains—or waiting out the interminable snowstorms at base camp on Nanga Parbat—I brooded about Annapurna.

As we were coming out from Shishapangma, in a small Tibetan town I ran into a French climber named Christian Trommsdorff. He knew of my failed attempted on the French route, and he'd been on Annapurna himself, though not on the north side. Instead he'd attempted the east ridge, approaching the mountain from the south. The hike in on that side is far easier than the treacherous march up the Miristi Khola—so straightforward, in fact, that the trekkers' route on the popular Annapurna-Dhaulagiri circuit passes under the south side of the mountain.

Christian had failed on the east ridge, but what he told me about it made me sit up and take notice. He said, in effect, that though the ridge was incredibly long, it seemed relatively safe. He recommended enthusiastically that I consider this route. It might, in fact, be the only safe itinerary on Annapurna. And it had been climbed once, in 1984.

When I got home and researched that first ascent of the east ridge, what I learned ought to have given me pause. The exploit was carried out by a pair of Swiss, Erhard Loretan and Norbert Joos. In 1995, Loretan had become just the third person to climb all fourteen 8,000ers. He was renowned for his assaults on the high peaks not by their easiest routes but often by new lines that he himself opened. None was bolder than the east ridge of Annapurna. No less an authority than Reinhold Messner had called Loretan "the most significant high-altitude mountaineer of his generation."

In the fall, postmonsoon season of 1984, Loretan and Joos's Swiss teammates helped the pair establish a Camp III at 22,700 feet, on the south flank of the east ridge. What makes the ridge so "out there" is that the only reasonable line to approach it tops out on the crest fully four miles east of the summit. To go from there to the top, Loretan and Joos had to climb over several subsummits, the whole four-mile gauntlet above 24,000 feet. What's more, the ridge never gentles out, but stays sharp and often corniced throughout.

On their second day on the ridge, having gone up and over three tricky subsummits, the duo ran smack into an unclimbable 330-foot cliff. They had only two rock pitons, which they now sacrificed to make a pair of rappels off the north side. Reaching a climbable snow slope, they pushed on toward the west, and at last stood on top at one-thirty P.M. on October 24.

Their desperate gambit, however, now meant that the two men had no hope of returning via the east ridge: they could not climb up the cliff down which they had rappelled from the crest. Their only chance was to find another way off the mountain. In Loretan's pocket, he carried a postcard of the north face, the pair's only semblance of a route guide. Already close to exhaustion, they plowed down the long summit snowfield, trying to find the top of the Dutch Rib. Another bivouac ensued, during which the two men lost a tent pole and had to hold the roof up with their hands as they brewed tea and soup.

It's infinitely harder to find a route from the top coming down than to launch up it from the bottom. Loretan and Joos did a marvelous job of routefinding, though, and finally located some old fixed ropes protruding from the ice. With only a 165-foot rope five millimeters in diameter (far thinner than any rope climbers usually trust to belay each other) and a single ice screw for hardware, Loretan and Joos half-rappelled and half-downclimbed the Dutch Rib.

That night in their tent, they were struck by an avalanche. Hearing it coming, they were too tired to do anything but pull their sleeping bags over their heads and pray. They survived the slide, then staggered down to the base camp of a Japanese-Czech expedition, whose members nurtured them back to health.

Even in the bare summary of that ascent that I was able to find, the east ridge sounded like an all-out epic. Had I also been able to read a passage from Loretan's own account (written in French), I might have been even further daunted by the prospect of a second ascent of the east ridge. As translated by my French-speaking friend just last year, Loretan's text described the ordeal in these terms: "Throughout the whole descent, which took two and a half days, there were three of us: Norbert, myself, and fear." Of the Dutch Rib as they found it, Loretan added, "Here was a place that ought to be reserved only for those who are tired of life."

Yet I was focused on the notion that a long ridge, even at such extreme altitudes, would surely be safer than a face pouring with avalanches. On a ridge, nothing can fall down on you from above. And if the ridge didn't prove too technical, it ought to be right up my alley, since endurance and perseverance were my forte.

Veikka and I decided to try the east ridge in the spring of 2002. Once again, we thought we needed teammates to make a stronger party, and once more, sharing a permit promised to be more economically feasible than buying one ourselves. To find partners for Annapurna, though, I resorted to a strategy I'd never employed before. I got on the Internet.

It didn't take long to discover that some other world-class climbers were interested in the east ridge of Annapurna. One of the first people I contacted was a French alpinist named Jean-Christophe Lafaille. I'd never met J.-C. (as his friends call him), but I knew him by reputation as one of the most talented mountaineers in Europe, with some of the very hardest routes in the Alps to his credit, many of them pulled off solo.

It's a little strange deciding to go on a serious expedition with someone you've never even shaken hands with. It's a bit like computer dating. As J.-C. and I traded e-mails, we were sort of feeling each other out, trying to judge if we'd be compatible on the mountain. I had almost no qualms about J.-C.—my first thought was, Wow, this guy wants to climb with me?

I think he had a few more reservations. I gave him some references, mutual friends we'd both climbed with. At the time, both of us were working with the boot company Asolo. Our mutual contact there was a fellow named Bruce Franks, who now played intermediary. Like a guy fixing up two friends for a blind date, Bruce extolled the virtues of each of us to the other. Ironically, J.-C. knew what I looked like, because he'd seen the big Hollywood movie *Vertical Limit,* in which I had a cameo role. In his autobiography, *Prisonnier de l'Annapurna,* published in 2003, J.-C. wrote about the process of checking me out:

> *I had only an incomplete image of Ed. . . . I knew that he was very resourceful at getting his projects financed, a conclusion that his Internet site—very professional, very business-oriented—confirmed on my first visit. But I didn't know who he really was. Many climbers vouched for him as a good organizer, at the same time attentive to detail but also humane. A German alpinist even sang Ed's praises as he spoke of "an American who has nothing American about him." These touchstones convinced me.*

Over the Internet, both J.-C. and I were soon in contact with three Basque climbers who also had their eyes on the east ridge. The strongest of the three, Alberto Iñurrategi, was almost unknown in the United States, although Veikka and I had bumped into him on Dhaulagiri in 1998. In relative anonymity, Alberto had become one of the strongest of all Himalayan climbers, and by the spring of 2002 he had reached the summit of thirteen of the fourteen 8,000ers, lacking only Annapurna.

We finally agreed to join forces. I would get the permit. On paper, I was the leader of the expedition; in practice, we would all be equals in the decision-making process. Such de facto democracies have by now become the norm among small teams of experienced Himalayan climbers—in stark contrast to the hierarchically organized national teams of the 1950s and '60s. For J.-C., Veikka, and myself, I'd organize food, gear, and porters. The Basques would work out their own logistics, hiring their own porters and base-camp cook, but they would share our permit. On the mountain, we'd work together to establish camps and take turns putting in the route.

By 2002, the challenge of Annapurna was starting to become part of my personal baggage. But if I thought our defeat on the French route two years before weighed heavy in my soul, it was nothing compared to what Annapurna meant to J.-C.

▲
▲
▲

In the fall of 1992, just a couple of months after I'd climbed K2, Lafaille went on his first Himalayan expedition—to Annapurna. Way back in 1970, a superbly talented British team led by Chris Bonington had made a landmark breakthrough in the Himalaya by climbing the steep, dangerous, 10,000-foot-high south face of Annapurna. The style of the day was the old-fashioned method of fixing ropes, relaying loads, and establishing camps, with a pair of climbers pushing a few new pitches a day while everybody behind them hauled gear and food up to semipermanent tent camps. Over nearly two months, laboriously advancing the route, sometimes gaining only a hundred feet of new terrain in a whole day's effort, the team worked its way up a beautiful icy pillar on the left edge of the south face.

Eventually Bonington's party got six camps pitched on that pillar, often on dizzy ledges carved out of the ice. Among the eight top-notch climbers on the team, a keen rivalry developed, and the politics of who would get to go for the summit spurred some nasty jockeying for position on the route. Finally, on May 27, Dougal Haston and Don Whillans reached the top. They were perhaps the most driven pair on the route, but also the best at playing the position game. A second attempt by two other powerful climbers failed a little way below the summit.

Still, it was a team triumph, and the Brits had put up by far the hardest route done to that date on any 8,000-meter peak. Sadly, just above base camp, as the team prepared its retreat from the mountain, Ian Clough—maybe the nicest guy on the team, and one of the ones who had done the most brute load carrying in support of the leaders—was killed when a serac collapsed on top of him in the icefall on the lower skirts of the mountain.

Twenty-two years later, J.-C. and a single partner, Pierre Béghin, returned to the south face with a wildly ambitious program. With no Sherpa support and only a minimum of ropes fixed low on the mountain, they proposed to attack a line to the right of the British route—an even steeper and more direct itinerary—in a lightweight, alpine-style ascent.

Béghin, at forty-one, was the preeminent French high-altitude climber of his day. Lafaille, at twenty-seven, was his protégé, though he already had many of those solo first ascents in the Alps under his belt, some of them accomplished in winter.

The duo reached 24,000 feet on their new line and prepared to bivouac. Unable to find a decent ledge, they made it through the night hanging from their waist harnesses against a seventy-degree slope. Because of a raging storm, however, they got not a wink of sleep. Nonetheless, the next morning they pushed onward. But as the weather grew even worse, they recognized that they could not continue. Six hundred feet above the site of their bivouac, they turned around.

The wall was too steep to downclimb, so Béghin and Lafaille set up a series of rappels. Because they'd gone so light, they had a minimum of hardware—pitons, cams, ice screws—to use for anchors. They needed to stretch that paltry store of "pieces" across a descent of several thousand feet. Béghin now practiced a frightening parsimony. For one anchor, he was willing to rappel off a single ice screw that he hadn't been able to lodge all the way home to the head. This was too much for Lafaille, who insisted on backing up the screw by sacrificing one of his ice tools, the pick planted in the snow and attached to the screw with a nylon sling.

At the top of their fourth or fifth rappel, Lafaille hammered in a piton, while Béghin slotted a large cam, called a Friend, into a crack. Bégin got on rappel first. Just as he started to slide down the rope, he told his partner, "Take out the piton. My Friend is good."

Béghin crab-walked backward down a snow cone, his crampons biting into the crust. Several meters below, the cliff turned vertical, and Béghin put his full weight on the rope. He looked up, his gaze meeting Lafaille's.

Suddenly Lafaille heard a sharp clattering sound. Before his eyes, the Friend popped loose. Without a word, Béghin vanished into the abyss.

"It was a long time before I could move," Lafaille later told a journalist. "Maybe half an hour. I was petrified with fear and despair."

Lafaille knew that Béghin's pack had contained all the men's ropes and hardware. And the rappel rope was gone with the plummeting body. In his own pack, Lafaille carried a stove, food, sleeping bags, and a bivvy tent—but not a single foot of rope or even one piton or ice screw. What would eventually save his life is that at the last minute before getting on rappel, Béghin had handed his partner his ice ax, to carry down with his load.

Below Lafaille yawned a 700-foot, nearly vertical cliff of mixed rock and ice. On the ascent, the two climbers had belayed each other and placed protection here. Now Lafaille would have to solo down it, with only his crampons and a pair of ice tools—his ax and Béghin's—to keep him attached to the world. "If I hadn't soloed so much in the Alps," he later reported, "I would have died."

Climbing down with infinite care, even as adrenaline and grief coursed through his body, Lafaille at last reached the bottom of the cliff. He carved a ledge out of the snow, erected the bivvy tent, and crawled inside. Once again, he spent a sleepless night.

The next day, with the storm abating somewhat, Lafaille continued his descent. From the bivouac site, he had scavenged a pitiful hank of fixed rope the pair had left on the way up. It was twenty meters long, so Lafaille improvised a series of ten-meter rappels. For anchors, he used tent pegs, and once even a plastic bottle buried in the snow. (Even the best climbers shudder on hearing about these desperate improvisations.)

By midafternoon, Lafaille reached the top of the fixed ropes. He thought that at last he was home free. A warm, windless fog had now swallowed Annapurna. Just as he clipped in to the upper fixed-rope anchor, Lafaille heard a sickening sound. He knew at once that a volley of stones was falling from above. As he jerked his head up, he instinctively raised his right arm to cover it. Only at the last minute did the falling stones emerge from the fog. He shrank tight to the wall, but a stone caught him flush on his upraised arm, breaking it in a compound fracture that exposed the bone.

Even with such a serious injury, Lafaille managed to descend to the tent platform that had served as the pair's highest camp. With only one good arm, he was unable to pitch his bivvy tent. Instead, he just rolled the tent around him. Fortunately, the arm was not bleeding copiously. Lafaille managed to wrap his jacket around it, improvising a kind of splint. Fumbling with his left hand, after forty-five minutes of effort, he also managed to light his stove to melt snow.

Lafaille spent two days on that ledge, never far from utter despair. As he later told the journalist, "It was then that Annapurna started to become not a mountain but a being that wants to kill you. I had the feeling of an animal in front of a hunter. He doesn't want to kill you at once; he wants to torture you first." During those two days of waiting, he felt "completely broken, physically and in my head. I'm thinking, It's finished for me. I am dead."

During the second night, Lafaille roused himself to a last-ditch effort. He decided to go down in the dark, when the face would be frozen, with fewer falling stones. He had nothing to lose. At first he tried to rappel, using his one good hand and his teeth to arrange the rope, but it proved too difficult. Instead, he soloed down once more, using his left arm to swing a single ax.

By morning, he had reached the bottom of the gargantuan face. He staggered toward the base camp of a Slovene expedition he had seen from up high. Remarkably, he had decided against yelling to the Slovenes for help, for fear of dragging strangers into a rescue that could endanger their own lives. Only 300 meters out from the bottom of the face, however, he fell chest-deep into a crevasse. He crawled out, then stumbled on, but it was the last straw. In that moment, he resolved to quit climbing for good.

At last a Sherpa from the Slovene base camp met Lafaille with a pot of tea and a bag of food. The two men embraced, then both burst into tears.

In five days, Lafaille had soloed 8,000 feet down one of the most difficult walls ever attempted in Nepal, the last two and a half days of it with a badly broken arm. His escape from Annapurna is regarded today as the greatest self-rescue ever pulled off in the Himalaya.

Back in France, Lafaille was hailed as a hero, but he sank into a deep depression. Infected down to the bone, his arm underwent several painful operations. It was months before he could take even easy walks around his home town of Gap, in the Dauphiné. Psychologically, he was a mess. Despite seeing several psychotherapists (a rare tactic among hard-core alpinists), Lafaille was overwhelmed with guilt and sorrow over the loss of Béghin, whose body has never been found. "I closed up like an oyster," he told a French interviewer. The turmoil cost him his marriage.

Despite his vow to quit climbing, he started making easy scrambles in the foothills around Gap. A professional guide, he felt that he had lost his true métier. But soon, as he recovered from his ordeal, he was climbing well again, putting up more new routes in the Alps. And during the next few years, he made a solo traverse of Gasherbrum I and II in the Karakoram. He decided to try to become the first Frenchman to climb the fourteen 8,000ers. By 2002, he had seven of them on his résumé.

Yet Annapurna haunted him. In 1995, he'd gone back to the south face, determined to make an unsupported solo attempt on the British team's 1970 line. In a brilliant effort, he reached 24,600 feet—exactly the altitude of his and Béghin's high point three years earlier—before bad weather and snow conditions forced him to retreat. About that expedition, he later told a writer, "That year it was more difficult to rest in the tent than to climb. In the night I had many bad memories."

In 1998, Lafaille went back to the south face with an Italian team to try the Bonington route, but the trip was a washout. He was dismayed at the Italians' decision to climb the route in the old-fashioned style of fixed ropes and stocked camps—by then considered poor form by the best Himalayan climbers. And the whole enterprise folded after a Sherpa was killed in an avalanche.

These further failures only intensified Lafaille's obsession. In several interviews, he repeated a vow: "I would trade ten 8,000ers for ten minutes on top of Annapurna." Our 2002 trip to the east ridge, then, amounted to nothing short of revenge on the mountain that had dealt him the worst blow of his life. I knew that on Annapurna, J.-C. would be pretty darned motivated.

And Alberto Iñurrategi would be motivated in his own right. Not only would Annapurna give him his fourteenth and last 8,000er, but it would serve as a kind of commemorative wreath to lay on the grave of his brother Felix. The two had been inseparable climbing partners, triumphing together on eleven of the 8,000ers. But two years before, in 2000, Felix had died on Gasherbrum II. Alberto's grief was at least as deep as J.-C.'s had been after losing Pierre Béghin.

▲
▲
▲

Veikka and I met J.-C. for the first time in Kathmandu. I confess it came as something of a shock to see that although he was evidently in terrific shape, J.-C. stands only about five foot two. I'd built him up in my imagination as a kind of Superman. Veikka eventually nicknamed J.-C. the Hobbit. And we learned that a running joke back home in Vallorcine—a town just up the Arve Valley from Chamonix, to which he'd moved from Gap—had it that when J.-C. answered the door to strangers or salesmen, they asked if his mother was home.

Since the breakup of his first marriage, J.-C. had met and married Katia, a good-looking, slender blonde who must be five or six inches taller than he is. A talented climber herself, Katia had taken control of J.-C.'s business dealings, and was well on the way to capitalizing on his brilliant climbing feats by running a one-woman publicity machine, converting the shy and private mountaineer into (as the French say) a *médiatique* celebrity.

In *Prisonnier de l'Annapurna,* J.-C. laconically records his first impressions of Veikka and me: "Ed struck me as every bit as engaging and well-balanced as people had told me he was.... Veikka was a solid fellow, a bit taciturn. He was first and foremost an explorer, having carried out a number of long cross-country trips in Finland and the Arctic."

The Basques had arrived in Nepal before us. We caught up with them near the end of our six-day trek to base camp from the hill town of Berithanti. The whole countryside seemed deserted, for we had arrived in the middle of the Maoist terror campaign against the government. And only ten months before, the Nepalese royal family had been massacred—not by Maoists but by the king's son, apparently in a dispute over choosing his bride. The massacre, however, had created a power vacuum that the Maoists took full advantage of. Yet we had heard that the terrorists were not interested in harming tourists, and indeed, the hike in was uneventful.

On April 12, we set up base camp at the relatively low altitude of 13,600 feet on a lateral moraine of the glacier below the south face, not far from J.-C.'s base camp for his 1995 solo attempt on the British route. It was a somber, even a sinister place, with the towering walls of Annapurna and its satellite peaks hemming us in from every side. Every afternoon at about two P.M., the sky clouded over and a strange, damp fog descended upon us. At first, the ground was covered with snow, but after it melted, we could lounge in the green grass of an inviting meadow beside the moraine.

The Basques, with their own cook staff, set up their tents some fifty yards away from ours. Eventually we began to mingle and feel one another out, as we coordinated our plans for climbing the mountain. Because of the language barrier, I didn't get to know Alberto very well at first, though he struck me as gentle, intelligent, and thoughtful. With his low-key personality, this handsome, tall, slightly-built man hardly fit the stereotype of a superstar mountaineer. I was soon to see that he was extremely gifted as a climber, both technically and in terms of his huge reserves of speed and strength.

Meanwhile, Veikka and I shared a number of conversations with J.-C., limited though they were by the fact that the Hobbit spoke very little English and Veikka and I had absolutely no French. One thing that J.-C. and I had in common was that our families were very important to us. He had three children, two by his first marriage and a young son with Katia. We talked about our kids, and about how a family back home supporting us gave us a lot of our motivation on the mountain.

In general, if there was one thing that prevented us from meshing as a tight team, it was the mutual incomprehension of our various languages. Besides the French-English divide between J.-C. and Veikka and me, there was the fact that none of the Basques spoke French at all, nor more than a smattering of English, and J.-C., Veikka, and I were clueless in Spanish (let alone Basque).

In 2003, J.-C. sent me a copy of *Prisonnier de l'Annapurna,* with a warm inscription in his makeshift English. It was not until 2005, however, that a friend visiting me in Seattle translated many of the passages in the book that dealt with our 2002 expedition. And some of those passages came as a real surprise.

I admired J.-C. as a bold, committed mountaineer, and I thought that his passion to get up Annapurna was all-consuming. Yet in *Prisonnier,* he writes of those days at base camp, "I was constantly homesick, and I looked at my watch a hundred times, anticipating the next phone call to Katia." (I'd brought along a sat phone so that we could be in touch with our loved ones back home.) And:

> The heavy humidity floated in the air, just as my doubts floated in my spirit, my fear of the climb to come....The Basques were off in their corner, the Americans in theirs, everyone chattering away in his mother tongue. Worse than simply being alone, I felt isolated. Later, when we got up on the face, the others engaged with me, but at base camp I had the feeling that I was of no interest to anyone else.

This last passage took me aback. At base camp, as is the norm, we each had a personal tent to which we could retreat, reading and listening to music through headphones in privacy. I typically spend a lot of time alone at base camp, since I'm a bit of an introvert and gain strength from solitary time. Veikka, in contrast, spends hours gabbing in the communal dining tent following a meal, long after I've made a quiet exit. J.-C. seemed to blend Veikka's and my penchants, but it struck me that he was quite happy to be alone in his tent.

Up high on the mountain, J.-C. had a tiny bivvy tent in which he slept every night. Veikka and I initially asked if he wanted to share our tent on the ascent, but he always declined. I thought he simply preferred to be by himself. Maybe he in turn thought *we* wanted to be by ourselves! Ultimately, the misunderstanding was probably one more casualty of the language barrier and of the fact that we still did not know each other that well. (It's amusing that in the passage above J.-C. calls Veikka an "American" and implies that English is his mother tongue!)

I did my best to include J.-C. in our doings as often as possible, because I could feel his frustration over his poor command of English. Over the years, I've been in the same situation with many other climbers from other countries. I've learned to speak more slowly and simply in their company, hoping to maximize their grasp of our halting conversations.

Just last year I traded e-mails with J.-C. about this matter, through an intermediary. Perhaps for fear of hurting my feelings, he backed down a bit from his claim in the memoir. Now he wrote, "In fact, at base camp I wasn't really isolated, because I had a lot of exchanges with Ed and Veikka. Very quickly a true sense of teamwork got established among us. My isolation was solely on account of my pitiful command of English." But he went on to say, "The sense of isolation was more onerous for me in the higher camps, because we were separated in three tents and I often felt quite alone." J.-C. admitted that on the mountain, we never discussed this sense of isolation that weighed upon him.

In any case, we started working our way up the glacier, then establishing camps—the first on the broad basin of a hanging glacier, the second one at the top of a very sharp ridgeline. Our route stretched between the east ridge of Annapurna on the left and a peak called Singu Chuli on the right. I couldn't have been more pleased by the work ethic of my teammates, including the three Basques. Normally I'm the one who gets up first each morning, and I often have to push the others to get going. But J.-C. and the Basques were always off by five or six A.M. Usually we'd agree the night before on a starting time for the next morning, but often they'd be moving before that hour. Sometimes Veikka and I felt almost sheepish: "Hey, wait for us!" And not only did J.-C. and the Basques get moving early—they were fast climbers as well.

In my diary, I wrote, "I am amazed at how anti-slackers these guys are. No dilly-dally, no rest.... Great to be with a group like this—extremely competent, confident, & easy-goin' as well."

After thirteen expeditions with Veikka, I will swear to my dying day that he is my ideal partner in the mountains. Normally we click so well together that we operate like a single machine. And normally he always does his full share of the camp chores, the trail breaking, and the routefinding.

Yet on Annapurna in 2002, for the first and only time, there was something not quite right with Veikka. That year he often seemed lethargic, and he sometimes had trouble getting going in the morning. Maybe he hadn't trained hard enough before the expedition. But certain things he did—or failed to do—started to get on my nerves.

With my habitual avoidance of conflict, I never spoke a word of criticism to Veikka. I just took on myself the jobs he didn't get done, or done properly. I'd say to myself, Fuck it—I'll do the cooking. At one camp, I agreed to pitch the tent if he prepared the platform. In the end, he didn't carve out a level shelf, and when I got inside the tent, I found that I was lying with my head downhill. I can never sleep in that position. If I'm going to spend time in a given camp, it's a crotchet of mine to have a flat and level platform under the tent. Veikka hadn't been willing to spend an extra half hour to get the platform truly level. So we had to move the goddamned tent and reshovel the platform.

My diary became the safety valve for my irritation. That day I wrote what I never said out loud to Veikka: "I was a bit steamed—make a decent base!"

Another entry, on May 1:

VG makes no move to get out of his bag—his warm gear is at C II so he needs to stay in bag to stay warm! So I make the move to get the stove going, while Baby Bird stays warm in his bag.... Peeved once again. Hope he gets his shit together soon.

And another: "VG not great @ multi-tasking—i. e., getting dressed while the water is heating."

The worst of these lapses occurred on the day that J.-C. and I set out from Camp II to check out the route above. He and I were off by six-thirty A.M. Veikka was supposed to come with us, but he didn't leave the tent until nine-thirty. In my experience of him, this was a real aberration. That year something must have been wearing him down.

Then one day, as he left camp late to descend to the next one and retrieve some gear, the normally canny route finder got temporarily lost. Climbing above, J.-C. and I witnessed Veikka's late departure. Once again I was puzzled: this wasn't the Veikka I knew. In the end, it took him all day to get back on track, and when he returned to camp, he was on the verge of hypothermia.

Veikka's performance that year was so uncharacteristic that I began to wonder whether something else was wrong with him. A couple of times I went so far as to ask, "Hey, Veikka, what's up?"

"God, I just don't know," he answered.

Though he didn't let on in so many words, Veikka himself suspected that something was wrong. As he'd trained the previous winter, he'd felt constantly fatigued. Driving home from a slide show somewhere in Finland, he'd be so wiped out, he'd have to pull over and take a nap. But by the time he got to Annapurna, he thought he'd just been stretched thin in the preceding months, and maybe hadn't had the time to train properly. He wouldn't get the true answer for another six months.

As the host of a travel show on Finnish television, Veikka crisscrossed the globe, scuba diving in Belize, for instance. In autumn 2001, he'd gone hiking in Papua New Guinea.

Upon his return from Annapurna, Veikka gave a slide show that particularly impressed a general in the Finnish air force, who asked Veikka if he'd like to fly in a fighter jet. "Sure," Veikka answered.

He was required not only to go through training school but to undergo a thorough physical exam. When the blood work came back in September, the doctor told Veikka, "My friend, you've got anemia."

"Not me," Veikka responded. "I'm a mountain climber."

The doctor had discovered that Veikka had hookworm, almost certainly contracted on his New Guinea trip. It's a gruesome-sounding process, as the larvae penetrate the skin and migrate through the lungs to the gastrointestinal tract, where, having hatched as worms, they attach themselves to the intestine and start feeding on the host's blood. Fortunately, hookworm can be quickly treated with a several-day course of drugs.

Within a week, Veikka was feeling like his old self again. He called me up with the news. We had a good laugh about it, but I was mightily relieved to know that Veikka's so-so performance on Annapurna had been due not to faintheartedness or poor training but to a miserable little parasite.

▲
▲
▲

I'm sure that part of my irritation in May 2002 stemmed from the fact that I'd never been on an expedition—not even K2 in 1992—when I felt that I was living under such extreme tension. Day after day, that four-mile-long east ridge hung over us to the north, a high-altitude gauntlet the likes of which almost no mountaineers had ever run in the Himalaya. I knew that once we set out along that ridge on our multiday traverse, we would be entering a true no-man's-land. Annapurna was beginning to loom for me as a personal nemesis.

And I was at least as homesick as I would later learn J.-C. was. There were many times when I just wanted to have the trip over with so I could head home. I never verbalized these feelings to Veikka, but my diary betrays my true state of mind. On May 5:

Really, really *miss Paula, Gil & Ella. I'd love to be home with them right now! Could be 20 more days before I get home—ugh! These days I'm torn when these trips get long—I know I'm here for the duration but I'd love to get home too. Takes energy to be here & thinking of home too! Paula has hands full w/two kids, house, etc. I miss them and love them so much!*

The next day I managed to talk to Paula on the sat phone. "She told me of Ella the fish!" I recorded in my diary. At age two, Ella loved nothing more than swimming around in our hot tub—in fact, that's where she learned to swim. I added, "Gil sleeping with my picture! *Can't wait to get home.*"

In the past, I'd managed to avoid this sort of divided psychic state, even on Everest in 1996. Yet I was still determined to give the east ridge my best shot. In the end, it was J.-C. and I who put in the crucial section of the route up to the crest of the ridge above 23,000 feet. I'd expected the Hobbit to be fast and strong, but on those days, he almost blew me away. "J.-C. unbelievable as point man—go, go, go," I wrote in my diary. "Can't keep up!" This was an experience that I'd never had before on an 8,000er, of actually going slower than a teammate who was also climbing without bottled oxygen.

In early May, the other two Basques, realizing they were in over their heads, threw in the towel. They would support Alberto from the lower camps, but they had no ambition to try the east ridge. We were down to four, two ropes of two: Veikka and I, J.-C. paired with Alberto.

As the most gifted and fastest technical climber among us, J.-C. would usually lead the hardest sections of the route, with Alberto in support. Stronger at load carrying, Veikka and I would haul fixed ropes up to the other pair, or shuttle loads up to camps, sometimes making several carries in a single day. This division of labor seemed the most logical and efficient. J.-C. reveled at being on what climbers call the "sharp end" of the rope—that is, taking the lead on the hardest pitches. On more moderate terrain, we all took turns going first.

Meanwhile, completely unbeknownst to the rest of us, J.-C. was nursing a secret fantasy. I learned of it only in 2005, from a translated passage from his memoir. There, he wrote:

I will admit it: at first, I was not an adherent of this option [the east ridge], which had the drawback of depriving me of returning to the heart of the south face. Without saying a word to anyone, I dreamed that the conditions might allow me, without taking too many risks, to go up solo on my 1992 route. My idea was to form a common cause with the others, to share the same base camp, to acclimatize with the group, to establish the face [leading to the east ridge] with Ed and the Basques, but then . . .

I must admit I was shocked when I learned, three years after our expedition, that J.-C. had toyed with the scenario of abandoning our effort on the east ridge to go back and solo the route that had killed Pierre Béghin and nearly killed him. I suppose that Veikka, Alberto, and I could have pushed on by ourselves, but J.-C. was clearly the driving force. Yet in a way, I couldn't blame the man. For a decade, the wound of the '92 tragedy had festered inside him. What better way to take revenge on Annapurna than to finish that deadly route, and to do it solo?

In the end, J.-C. elected to stick with us. Whether that was because he ultimately judged the conditions unacceptable for an attempt on his 1992 line or because he got caught up in the unique challenge of ascending *and* descending the east ridge (as even Loretan and Joos had not been able to do in 1984), I'm not sure.

By the second week in May, we'd established Camp III at 23,000 feet on the crest of the east ridge, our tents sheltered by a handy vertical wall of ice that partially blocked the wind. Even so, it was still very cold and windy there. An entry from my journal:

Up at 4 AM. Very butt cold outside! Down suits and mittens. Had 2 cups of coffee and a few cookies. Had to take a dump and that always gets your fingers numb—every fucking time! Still gotta get harness on—without gloves! Pack up, crampons on, tie in, butt cold!

We were still four long miles from the summit. After returning to base camp, we set out for good for our attempt on the east ridge. On May 13, we were back at Camp III, ready to go alpine-style the rest of the way. And there, J.-C. got a big surprise. When he radioed base camp, he was shocked to hear Katia's voice answering him. Without telling him her plans, she had flown to Kathmandu, gotten herself to Berithanti, and hiked with porters to our base camp in half the time it had taken us.

As J.-C. later wrote, "Her arrival made me crazy with happiness. After two months of linguistic isolation, I finally had my own little team at base camp." The other huge benefit of Katia's arrival was that she could use our sat phone to call a friend of J.-C.'s in Chamonix and get precise day-by-day weather forecasts. During the past fifteen years, a small corps of specialists—originally hired to support long-distance balloonists and single-handed sailors in remote places—has refined the art of weather prediction to an exquisite degree. Sitting in front of their computers in Europe or the United States, they can forecast the weather on, say, Annapurna far more accurately than any weather service in Nepal. Those transmissions from Chamonix would prove crucial in our attempt on the east ridge.

On May 14, carrying five days' worth of food, we set out along the traverse, going for the top alpine-style. We knew the ascent and descent would take two days minimum, with three or even four a distinct possibility. I'd never tried something so extreme on an 8,000er.

Alberto and J.-C. got off first, with me a little behind them, then Veikka a ways behind me (a very cold call of nature having delayed his start). We moved along unroped.

By seven-thirty A.M., we'd reached a feature called the Roc Noir. It's a triangular pyramid of snow and ice that interrupts the ridge, forming a minor subsummit—very steep on the south side, unclimbable on the north. The only way to get past it was to make a long traverse left across the face of the pyramid to skirt a big crevasse, then head straight up the face to the crest. I stopped at the foot of the Roc Noir to wait for Veikka. J.-C. was already well launched on the traverse, with Alberto about a dozen yards behind. I watched as J.-C., with thousands of feet of exposure below him, carved a trough through deep snow along the traverse.

The only way J.-C. and Alberto could converse was in their limited, broken English. Now the air was calm enough so that I could hear J.-C. call out, his voice tight and urgent, "Be careful! It's bad snow and bad condition!" Alberto paused, then moved forward very slowly, placing each foot deliberately in the steps J.-C. had kicked as he'd led the traverse.

It was obvious to me just how dangerous the Roc Noir was. The loaded slope was poised to avalanche and only needed something to trigger it. By now J.-C. had rounded the crevasse and was heading straight up, but he was plowing through thigh-deep snow, with a layer of rotten rock beneath. The slope was at an angle of at least forty-five degrees, the snow was unconsolidated, and below him yawned 6,000 feet of precipice. J.-C. still had eight or nine hundred feet to climb to reach the crest again.

Eventually, J.-C. waited for Alberto to catch up with him. Then they resorted to a technique J.-C. had learned on big-wall rock climbs. Roped up, he would lead a pitch of 165 feet without a pack, plowing through the snow, place a single anchor to fix the rope, and rappel back down. Then both J.-C. and Alberto would jumar up the rope carrying their packs. All this while a fierce wind from the north lashed their faces.

Confronted by these dangerous snow conditions, and standing there waiting for Veikka, I thought, My God, what do I do? I hated being in this place. I was torn down the middle: my desire was telling me to go on, but my training and my common sense were telling me not to. We had come so far and worked so hard to get to this point.... Having to make really hard decisions like this one is the very worst part of what we do in the mountains.

Even before Veikka caught up to me, I told myself, Okay, give it a go. I started the traverse, got fifty feet out, but with every step I felt worse and worse. My brain was reprimanding me: *This isn't the way to climb. You shouldn't be fearful of every step. This goes against everything you believe.*

I retreated to the safe place where I'd waited, then threw down my pack. Veikka came along a few minutes later. He took in the situation in a glance but then said, "Let's give it a try." I put my pack back on and started traversing once more. But I had the same feeling. *God, this just sucks,* I thought. *I can't make myself do it.* Veikka stood and watched me. I retreated once more. I told him, "This is crazy. This just doesn't feel right." He didn't argue.

We decided to camp right there on the spot. It was a safe place on the ridge to pitch our tent, and we simply decided not to make the decision right then. Maybe, we figured, there'd be better conditions in the morning.

We got the tent erected and ourselves inside it. For hours, we lay there in a gloomy silence. But we could hear the wind picking up, blowing snow that we knew would be loading up the slopes on this lee side of the ridge. Instead of getting better, the conditions were getting worse.

Much later, J.-C. radioed us from the tent he and Alberto had pitched on the far side of the Roc Noir. "I had no intention of minimizing the problems that faced us," J.-C. would later write. Over the two-way radio, he told us about the climb he and Alberto had performed during the last ten hours. In my journal, I wrote down a paraphrase of J.-C.'s report in his minimal English: "The slope even with rope was bad. Then immediately over Roc Noir was steep, hard ice traverse. This was really stretching our safety to do this and then to have to retreat later as well."

It was I who finally made the decision. "I think we're done," I said softly. Veikka murmured his agreement. And the minute we made that choice, a tide of relief swept over me. Five weeks of nonstop anxiety on this, the most anxious expedition of my life, dissolved in an instant.

We descended all the way to base camp the next day. There we found Katia, just arrived two days before from her trek in from Berithanti. We couldn't see J.-C. and Alberto from base camp, but through the next three days, we monitored their progress over the radio. Whenever he could, J.-C. would pause at a stopping point, or in a camp, to broadcast down to Katia. Since her English was a lot better than J.-C.'s, she could instantly translate his messages for us. That vigil by the radio was the most dramatic ascent I've ever lived through vicariously, as opposed to taking part in it myself.

J.-C. said later that Veikka's and my turning back had given him a moment's pause. But then he added, "I had a good feeling that day." It's a phrase, as I'd come to know, that he often employed when he talked about his best climbs. That evening of May 14, he and Alberto had pitched their bivvy tent in a hollow a little way beyond the Roc Noir. Later he would tell a journalist, "After the Roc Noir, I had the feeling of closing a door behind me. I was far from the land of the living. I had never had this feeling on any other mountain."

All the next day, May 15, J.-C. and Alberto wove their way along the interminable ridge, climbing subsidiary bumps only to have to descend to the cols beyond. The ground was not particularly difficult, but a steady wind of thirty to forty miles an hour meant that the men took every step with a guarded caution. They bivouacked again, just short of the east summit, at an altitude of 25,900 feet—only 600 feet lower than the true summit, which, however, still lay at least a mile away.

That evening, Katia was able to relay the weather forecast from Chamonix. The prediction for May 16 was for a perfect, virtually windless day. Even so, that night, J.-C. thought hard about giving up the summit and turning back in the morning. He knew that to push on the next day would necessitate a third bivouac on the wildly exposed ridge.

But in the morning, the two men forged on, leaving their bivvy tent pitched in place. They came to the cliff that Loretan and Joos had rappelled in 1984. Somehow J.-C. found an alternative, downclimbing nearly a thousand feet on the north side of the ridge. Then he angled across on a technically difficult traverse of a very steep cliff of mixed rock and ice. Here, all his training on extreme climbs in the Alps came into play. The two men stayed roped together, but J.-C. led every pitch. Usually he could place no protection except as an anchor at the end of each pitch, from which he would belay Alberto up to him. Later J.-C. confessed, "For me, it was really soloing. If I fell, there was no chance Alberto could have stopped me."

At ten A.M. on May 16, the two men reached the summit. At once, J.-C. radioed the news down to Katia. Sitting there in base camp, she burst into tears of joy. And we could hear from the emotion in J.-C.'s voice that he was crying, too. Alberto had carried his brother Felix's ice ax all the way to the top. Now he held it clutched against his heart. He had climbed his fourteenth and last 8,000er.

In *Prisonnier de l'Annapurna*, there's a powerful account of the half hour the two men spent on the summit:

> *Alberto took several photos while I shouted my overwhelming joy to Katia through the radio. A new wave of emotion surged over me now that we could share this together. My throat was so dry that I could hardly speak, but despite my exhaustion, I could decipher every one of her words and feel the emotion that, four thousand meters below, had seized base camp. The altitude hadn't affected my brain.*
>
> *All around us there was nothing but beauty and immensity. I didn't think, I didn't meditate. I was living an unbelievable moment of my life, a ten-year-old dream that was now being realized: I was on top of Annapurna, and the reality was more beautiful than the most beautiful of my dreams.*
>
> *The crackling of the radio brought me back to the present. Katia's last words were "You be careful. Go slowly. It's not over yet." My gaze turned toward the east; the ribbon of the arête stretching toward the Roc Noir was frighteningly impressive.*
>
> *Liberated from Annapurna?*
>
> *At that moment, I realized how truly isolated we were from the world, still much more prisoners than free men, in a space that had more to do with the cosmos than with the earth.... Katia was right: it wasn't over yet [pas fini]; it seemed to me infinite [infini], when I measured with my eye what lay ahead of us.*

Getting down is mandatory. To regain the tent they had left on the other side of the east summit, Alberto and J.-C. had to retraverse the technical pitches across the steep cliff of mixed rock and ice. Once again, J.-C. led every pitch. Alberto later admitted that at this point he was tempted to bail off the north face, just as Loretan and Joos had. "We had our one map," he later wryly told a journalist, "and some rupees in our pocket"—to buy food from villagers in the lowlands, should they have to hike out to the north.

But J.-C.'s brilliant climbing carried them through. Late in the afternoon, they came in view of their bivouac tent—and the sight was, as J.-C. later wrote, "a vision of horror." The wind had ripped loose three of the four anchors that held the tent in place. Only a single tent peg kept the tent, which was flapping in the breeze like a big flag, affixed to the mountain. J.-C. virtually ran ahead and flung himself on top of the peg, securing the shelter. In his judgment, the peg was only minutes from pulling loose. Had the tent gone, with all their vital gear inside it, they would have been dead men.

They packed up the tent and pushed on, but fatigue and a desperate thirst made every step an ordeal. To save weight, they abandoned their sleeping bags. Finally they chose a site for their third bivouac, where they spent a grim, sleepless night. The pair had run out of fuel for their stove, so they had very little water either for that night or the next day. The normally sanguine J.-C. grew deeply worried.

The next day, to save even more weight, J.-C. threw his telephoto lens into a crevasse. (Katia later scolded him for this expensive loss!) And later, the two men left their tent behind. They knew they could not survive another bivouac, and every ounce less in their packs meant a few more ergs of energy they could summon up.

We monitored the radio all through May 17th. It was a harrowing process. It was like listening to *Apollo 13* limp back to Earth.

Of that fourth day out on the east ridge, J.-C. later reported, "We were exhausted mentally, but not completely physically." Finally they came to the Roc Noir. Both men managed the descent from the crest, backing down the treacherous snow slope facing in, turned the big crevasse, and sidestepped across to safe ground. "At last I had reopened the door I closed behind me four days earlier," J.-C. would put it. "I had once more entered the land of the living." The two men pushed on across easy ground and collapsed in their tent at Camp III.

▲
▲
▲

As Alberto and J.-C. came down from Camp III on May 18, I hiked up the glacier a long way to meet them with food and a thermos of tea. It had started raining, it was miserably cold, and some of the terrain at the bottom of the face was a bit dangerous as well. It seemed the least I could do for those guys. After all, they'd been up high for eight days straight, four of them tiptoeing through the Death Zone. ("The eight finest days of my life as an alpinist," J.-C. would later call them in *Prisonnier*.) I waited for them for quite a while. When they came into sight, I went up and embraced them. Then I carried J.-C.'s pack down to base camp.

J.-C. later acknowledged how much this gesture meant to him. He told a journalist, "After eight days of climbing, we were naturally exhausted, and the weather was now bad.... At a bend in the moraine, there was Ed all alone, waiting for us in the cold rain with a thermos of tea. Silently, we took each other in our arms. What class he showed!"

J.-C. later said that he thought Veikka and I could have made the climb with him and Alberto. And yet he also insisted that the ascent of the east ridge was the hardest thing he'd ever done in his life.

In *Prisonnier*, he expanded on his feelings about Veikka and me turning back:

Sincerely, I was a bit disappointed for Ed. After all, the whole expedition was his project, but the crucial slope seemed too dangerous to him. I know how much that decision cost him. It's often harder to turn back than to go on. I understood his reasons: together we had often talked about our family responsibilities. Those weighed in his decision. For me, there were other givens that tipped the balance of the scale the other way. And for Alberto, yet others. Alpinism is a personal adventure.

As for me, I never for a minute thought we made the wrong decision in turning back. Nor did I think J.-C. and Alberto made the wrong decision in going on. As J.-C. himself admitted, he and I have different levels of acceptable risk.

I believe that what J.-C. and Alberto accomplished was one of the most remarkable ascents of modern times, to this day severely underappreciated. I doubt very much that their climb will soon be repeated. It's not simply a question of danger. On the east ridge that May, two climbers with amazing talent and drive were joined at the right place at the right time to push each other to phenomenal limits. I feel honored and humbled to have had a small part in their success.

At the same time, Annapurna in 2002 remains the only time in my career among the 8,000ers when I've turned back while a partner went on. After K2, I'd vowed, "Your instincts are telling you something. Trust them and listen to them." On the Roc Noir, I'd listened to my instincts.

Other climbers in my position, out of natural envy, might have given only grudging praise to the climb J.-C. and Alberto had pulled off, but I felt an immense admiration. That's easy to say in retrospect, but you don't usually lie to your diary: "What a climb! 4 days in the Death Zone—not many are tough enough to have done what they did. They walked the razor's edge for sure! Awesome achievement!"

In 2005, a writer friend of mine told me that he'd asked his French publisher, Michel Guérin, to name the very best French mountaineers at the moment. Michel, who has a keen grasp of the climbing scene worldwide, immediately answered, "Jean-Christophe Lafaille." Then he paused for long moments and finally shook his head: "There's no one else in his class."

By 2005, after going on two more expeditions with J.-C., I considered him the strongest mountaineer in the world. Up to that point, he had climbed eleven of the 8,000ers. No other living Frenchman had as many. (Benoît Chamoux was attempting his fourteenth 8,000-meter peak when he disappeared high on Kangchenjunga in 1995.)

J.-C. always did the big peaks in outrageous style. In December 2004, for instance, he climbed a new route solo on the south face of Shishapangma in harrowing winter conditions. "Never in my life have I been so cold," he reported on his Web site. J.-C. confided in me that he was saving Everest for last. He planned to end the string of fourteen with a truly extraordinary solo new route on the world's highest mountain—but in the meantime, he was keeping the details a secret.

In December 2005, J.-C. helicoptered in to base camp on Makalu. The world's fifth-highest mountain would be his twelfth 8,000er. He was going to tackle Makalu in an even more extreme style than he had used on Shisha-pangma the year before. He would go solo, alpine-style for the top, with no support above base camp from the three nonclimbing Sherpas who made up his cook staff—his only companions on the mountain. He planned to reach the summit in January, in the very heart of the Himalayan winter. If he succeeded, the ascent would rank as one of the most audacious in history anywhere in the world.

▲
▲
▲

Meanwhile, as for me, turning back on Annapurna in 2002 was a disappointment, to be sure, but not a huge one. I was willing to let it go: it was as if the mountain had made my decision for me. Once Veikka and I were back at base camp, I felt more relief than disappointment.

Yet as we began the hike out, I couldn't help wondering, Where in God's name can I go on this mountain? How am I ever going to get up it? Did I want to go back to the north face after all, despite swearing that I never would?

On his fourth try, J.-C. had finally settled his score with Annapurna. He was no longer its prisoner. But after my second try, I could not escape the conclusion: Annapurna had become my nemesis.

The
Last Step

By 2001, I had my own Web site on the Internet, under the address www.edviesturs.com. In recent years, there's been a vogue of reporting expeditions all over the world "in real time" over the Internet. These range from perfunctory dispatches cobbled together by a techie back in the United States from sat-phone conversations with the expeditioners in the field to really slick operations in which the participants themselves type up their own dispatches on laptops and send digital photos and even video footage. In this way, firsthand accounts of remote adventures can be up and running on the Internet, ready for public consumption, within hours of the events they record. ▲ This has not only changed the way exploring and mountaineering get reported, it's changed the very act of having an adventure. In a sense, it makes the whole business self-

conscious, for even while you're making what could be life-or-death decisions in the field, you're weighing how to recount them in your daily dispatch. And it creates controversies the likes of which traditional explorers
never faced. In 1999, when Eric Simonson's team found Mallory's body on
Everest, there were actually two teams reporting the expedition online from
base camp: Simonson's own Web site, under the auspices of a company called
MountainZone, managed by a publicist in Ashford, Washington, who happened to be Eric's girlfriend, and a PBS team under Liesl Clark, who was
making another NOVA film, this time about the search for the bodies of
Mallory and his partner, Andrew Irvine.

When Liesl broke the news of the discovery of Mallory on the NOVA
Web site before MountainZone had announced it, Eric was furious.

Similarly, in the summer of 2005, when the Slovene climber Tomaž
Humar got stranded in his bivouac at an altitude variously reported as 19,360
or 21,000 feet on the Rupal Face of Nanga Parbat, the whole world could
follow the unfolding drama over the Internet, via dispatches posted by Humar's teammates at base camp after they had talked to him by radio. Humar
would have died but for the incredible nerve and skill of a pair of helicopter
pilots, Lieutenant Colonel Rashid Ulah Baig and Major Khalid Amir Rana,
who pulled off the kind of rescue normally performed in the Alps or
Yosemite, but never before in the Himalaya or Karakoram. He hovered per-
ilously close to the wall, dangled a line weighted with stones to the climber,
then winched him to safety. When Humar neglected to unclip from the ice
screws anchoring him to the face, he came very close to causing the helicopter to crash, for as the chopper strained to pull the climber away from the
ledge, the anchor held both climber and aircraft tethered to the cliff. The
chopper was freed only when the cord attaching Humar to his anchor for-
tuitously broke under the strain, causing him to rocket upward like a bungee
jumper, but saving his life. (Humar's teammates later admitted that they had
deliberately falsified the altitude of the bivouac, citing a lower number in
hopes of luring the chopper into the rescue. The altitude discrepancy may
stem from this irresponsible lie.)

What rubbed a lot of climbers the wrong way about this episode was that, especially in Slovenia, Humar was treated like a hero, rather than a victim of his own mistakes on the mountain, lucky to be saved by a miraculous rescue. The real heroes of the story were Rashid and Khalid, but once he reached Islamabad, Humar was feted by both the president and the prime minister of Pakistan. Back in Slovenia, he was practically coronated.

Imagine if Ernest Shackleton, watching the *Endurance* break up and sink in the Antarctic ice during the southern winter of 1915, had been able to send play-by-play dispatches of the catastrophe to an avid audience in Great Britain! Imagine if Frank Hurley, instead of exposing his magnificent photographs on glass plates that he safeguarded through the rest of the ordeal, including the wintering over on Elephant Island, had been able to snap digital images that the folks in London could download even as the ship disappeared under the ice. As it was, the rest of the world knew nothing of Shackleton's intensely dramatic survival story for another two years, until the leader and two teammates made their harrowing traverse of South Georgia Island and reached the nearest outpost of civilization, the whaling station at Husvik.

In turn, for almost three years Shackleton's men had known nothing of what was going on in the rest of the world. When they had sailed out of Buenos Aires in October 1914, they had learned the latest news about the outbreak of World War I, uniformly predicted to be a relatively bloodless series of skirmishes that would peter out within six months. In 1917, almost the first thing Shackleton asked the station manager at Husvik was, "Tell me, when was the war over?"

"The war is not over," the manager answered. "Millions are being killed. Europe is mad. The world is mad."

It's easy to feel nostalgic for the good old days, when a remote adventure took place in total isolation from the rest of the world. Even the French on Annapurna in 1950 had carried out their first ascent in that kind of sealed-off innocence, for word of their triumph and tribulations reached France only on June 16—almost two weeks after Herzog and Lachenal stood

NO SHORTCUTS TO THE TOP

on the summit—and that soon only thanks to a Sherpa Herzog had dispatched as a runner from base camp to get the news out.

My own first foray into the brave new world of online expedition dispatches came just prior to my 1999 expeditions to Manaslu and Dhaulagiri. A friend and supporter of mine named Peter Potterfield, then editor in chief at MountainZone, had offered to pay me for exclusive progress reports from those mountains. At first I was dubious: the thought of typing away on a laptop inside a frosty tent as I regaled the world with the trivia of my day-to-day doings seemed unappealing. I'd come to realize, however, that, like it or not, we live in a wired age. What tipped the scales for me was the enticing prospect that online technology would allow me to stay in regular touch by sat phone with Paula and Gil while I was on an expedition. In the end, those conversations would prove incredibly important to Paula's sanity and to my emotional stability. And the dispatches posted on MountainZone, and later on my Web site, helped satisfy the curiosity of the increasingly large audience following my journeys as I closed in on my goal of the fourteen 8,000ers.

I agreed to the deal with Peter only under certain conditions. I would carry the smallest sat phone possible—at that time, it was the size of a hand-held mobile home telephone, weighing barely a pound. (I remembered the phone Rob Hall and Gary Ball had had on K2 in 1992. The phone itself was the size of a suitcase, and the antenna dish was as big as a VW Bug! Rob and Gary had needed several porters just to lug the monstrosity to base camp, and a separate tent just to house and protect it.) I did not want to schlep a computer along, as I'd seen other expeditioners do, and feel obligated to type out a report every evening. The process needed to be simple and undistracting. Peter must understand that I was there to climb a mountain, not to play Lowell Thomas checking in from the field. The ascent would take priority; dispatches would be secondary.

At the end of the day, when we were safe in our tents, I would use the sat phone to call Seattle and leave a voice-mail message reporting our progress. It was MountainZone's job to type up the dispatch and post it on the Web. As it turned out, that was a phenomenal season for Veikka and me, as well as for MountainZone, since the company was simultaneously covering not only our climbs of Manaslu and Dhaulagiri but the discovery by Simonson's team of Mallory's body on Everest.

For the next two years, my happy collaboration with Peter and MountainZone continued. But just before I departed for Shishapangma in 2001, Mountainzone.com was purchased by San Francisco–based Quokka.com. I was still under contract to provide the same reports; all that changed was the phone number I called from each camp. In the middle of our expedition, however, as Veikka and I worked our way up Shishapangma, we heard rumors via phone messages that Quokka might be going bankrupt. Absorbed in the task at hand, we brushed off these rumors as idle gossip. Then one evening, as we rested at base camp before making our summit attempt, I called San Francisco to deliver an update. All I got was a busy signal, rather than the usual prompt to leave a message. Thinking I'd misdialed, I called again. Another busy signal. I looked at Veikka. In unison, we blurted out, "No way!" While we were in the wilderness, Quokka had gone under.

With no one there to man the phones, the Quokka Web site had posted a permanent message—something like "Due to circumstances beyond our control, we no longer have information regarding Ed Viesturs." One can only imagine how the scores of thousands of fans following our expedition took this. What had happened to Ed and Veikka? Were they in trouble?

After several more busy signals, we changed course, and shortly thereafter I was redirecting dispatches to my own Web site, www.edviesturs.com.

In 2002, just before my second Annapurna attempt, I signed up with Microsoft to send dispatches from the field. The company could advertise me as a small-business owner sold on its latest product, Office XP, while I could take advantage of some of the most talented Web masters in the world to spiff up my site.

As we climbed on Annapurna, the folks at Microsoft kept track of the numbers of "hits" to my Web site. The figures were staggering. When we made our final push for the summit, the tally went off the chart. On the mountain, I had no idea how many people in the cyberworld were following my progress. Sadly, I could not bring them back a successful ascent.

After Veikka's and my setback on the east ridge of Annapurna, I felt that I owed it to my online audience to explain why we'd turned around at the Roc Noir. "In our own evaluation," I wrote on my Web site, "the level of risk was increasing and the margin of safety was decreasing. There are some risks involved when you climb these mountains, but . . . it's ultra important that you have a very conservative attitude."

That was the credo I had brought to all my mountaineering in the last twenty-five years, since I'd climbed Mount Saint Helens in 1977. But posting my rationale on the Web site only brought the second-guessers out of the woodwork. Some of these guys are like the apoplectic fans who scream curses at their hometown football team on call-in sports-radio shows. On the Web, they even disguise their identities under online aliases. A sample of some of the potshots that appeared on www.edviesturs.com that year:

Is Ed waiting for conditions to be 100% perfect and is that too much like wishful thinking? Has the edge gone out of his climbing?

His fear factor has grown to the point where he backs off where others continue on.

I think it's time for him to go home to Seattle and become a baseball coach.

In my more irritable moods, I wished I could have taken some of these armchair pundits up on the east ridge, handed them my ice tools at the foot of the Roc Noir, and seen what they would have done next. Another commentator organized his own poll on my Web site, asking readers to vote on the likelihood of my ever climbing all fourteen 8,000ers. The tally: 53 percent thought I would, 47 percent thought I wouldn't.

Not exactly a resounding vote of confidence. I was having my own doubts, however, about Annapurna. Just weeks after I got back from Nepal, Greg Child interviewed me for *Rock and Ice*. In an article titled "Unlucky

Thirteen," Greg quoted me as saying, "Annapurna may be a peak I never climb. If I go again and cannot feel safe I may leave it off the list." And: "The bottom line is, you don't want to die in the mountains, no way. I've got a family. If that makes me more conservative and less successful, then that's great." The article closed with a photo I could have used as a Christmas card. All bundled up in fleece, Gil (four years old at the time) and Ella (two) sit on Paula's and my laps. Gil's protectively hugging little Ella, who touches his hand affectionately. All four of us have big smiles on our faces.

Those smiles, however, camouflage one of the few enduring disagreements Paula and I have ever had. Since 1995, when we'd decided to get married, we'd discussed how many kids we wanted to have. Paula had her heart set on four, while I would have been content to stop at two. In retrospect, it seems obvious why we had these disparate visions of our future family. Paula had grown up with her three sisters, I with only Velta as a sibling. The pattern you learn in your own nuclear family comes almost automatically to seem the ideal.

Sometime after Ella was born, Paula started lobbying for a third child. "Eddie," she started one of these discussions (only Paula, my parents, my sister, and certain old high-school friends call me "Eddie"), "I'm not ready to close the door on more kids. I'd love to see what kind of third person we'd create together. It's a beautiful mystery." I agreed.

By now, Paula was willing to compromise—three kids instead of the hoped-for four. But that third was vitally important to her. She has a mothering gene that's just huge. And as she puts it, she likes having a lot of activity around the house.

One time when we were discussing the question, I did little more than hesitate. All of a sudden, Paula was crying. In the end, I decided I could compromise, too. By January 2004, Paula was pregnant. Anabel was born the following October.

Today, I'm incredibly happy to have three children. It never ceases to amaze me that even though all three are being raised by the same parents in the same environment, they are so utterly different from one another. In the old nature-versus-nurture debate, at least vis-à-vis my kids, I lean toward nature: I truly believe that the individual traits that determine personality are set in stone from the moment of conception. As he turns nine, Gil has become this energetic, athletic, gregarious kid who loves to play the clown. At different moments he's said he wants to be a reptile specialist, a diamond hunter, or (his current favorite) a quarterback when he grows up. At six, Ella is busy keeping up with her older brother. She's a quick study in swimming, biking, and reading. She's just as happy being alone in her room playing with dolls as she is catching frogs and digging for worms. And Anabel, though still an infant, seems to be a blend of both Gil and Ella. As Paula says, "She's the loose end that ties the two together—both in terms of her looks and her personality." Outgoing and relatively self-sufficient, Anabel in this respect takes after the extroverted Gil more than the private, solitary Ella.

Paula still teases me, though. Out of the blue, she'll say, "What about one more?" I just keep laughing. But I never underestimate Paula. She's a strong-willed woman who's used to having her way.

One of the few things about me that she says drives her crazy is that we never fight. In ten years of marriage we've never once yelled at each other. When she's wanted to pick a fight, she says, I simply back off.

Last fall Paula told a friend of mine (who then told me), "Eddie's so giving, so considerate, so hardworking, and in many ways he's a perfect soul mate for me. But he has a hard time verbalizing his feelings. It's frustrating trying to read his mind. And he takes on too much responsibility for other people. Sometimes that just sucks the life out of him.

"Eddie has his loner side. He recharges his batteries by being by himself. When he's what I call a 'wilted flower,' he's no fun to be around. He becomes a bit detached from me. He just has to go off and disappear for a while."

Whew. But I can't say I don't recognize myself in that portrait. Paula should know: she's the one who has to live with me, and put up with my going off on expeditions every year.

⚐
⚐
⚐
⚐

Meanwhile, what to do about Annapurna? As I brooded about that mountain, the question of how I was ever going to climb it shifted into speculation about how long could I put it off. Behind my back, some friends of mine kept a running joke alive: that perhaps for years to come, I should keep failing on Annapurna, so that my sponsors would stick around! The summit might be in easy reach, but I'd turn around when I developed a sudden, inexplicable cramp in my leg. The next year, sponsors still aboard, I could return and get a few hundred feet higher before having to retreat again.

There were, however, still two other mountains I needed to confront if I was ever going to complete Endeavor 8000: Nanga Parbat and Broad Peak, with its aggravating little asterisk of the last hundred yards of summit ridge. Since both were in Pakistan, I decided that I could put together a twofer around them in the summer of 2003.

Veikka had already climbed Nanga Parbat with the Germans after I'd gone home in 2001, so he wasn't interested in going back. For 2003, in fact, he had his sights set on Kangchenjunga, the first of all the 8,000ers that I had climbed, way back in 1989. So in 2003, for the first time in nine years, I would not share a mountain with my favorite partner. Instead, I invited J.-C., who was happy to accept. At the very end of our 2002 expedition, in fact, we'd already started talking about tackling future projects together.

There was still the language barrier between us, but on Broad Peak and Nanga Parbat we managed to converse a lot, especially about our respective families. Later J.-C. would write, "Yes, Ed and I became friends on Anna-purna, but especially good friends the year after.... During our time on Nanga Parbat and Broad Peak, I finally discovered the real Ed. We lived the same joys, the same hardships there, the moments of transport up high.... Ed is a profoundly human person."

That year, J.-C. actually climbed Dhaulagiri in the spring before join-ing me in Islamabad. Despite the deep satisfaction of climbing Annapurna on his fourth try, and his lingering sense of having been so far "out there" on the east ridge that for four days he had left the land of the living, in 2003 he set himself the lofty goal of climbing three 8,000ers in a single year.

On Nanga Parbat, we planned to try the same Kinshofer route on the Diamir Face that Veikka and I had aimed at two years before. There was also a strong team of climbers from Kazakhstan on the route, and we shared the hard work with them. The leader of the Kazakh team was Ervand Iljinsky, an old friend of mine who had been a deputy leader of the Soviet contingent on the Everest International Peace Climb in 1990. Now sixty-one years old, Ervand was a wizened veteran of many expeditions, including a landmark 1982 Soviet effort on one of the hardest routes in the Himalaya climbed to that date—a direct line straight up the southwest face of Everest. In a resounding triumph, eleven climbers eventually reached the summit, but Ervand gave up his own bid in order to help his comrades descend from the summit. On Jim Whittaker's Peace Climb, at the age of forty-eight, Ervand had finally stood on the highest point on Earth.

In 2003 on Nanga Parbat, Ervand ran his team in the traditional Soviet fashion, watching their progress through a telescope from base camp and calling the shots via radio. The younger team members complained privately that from below, a leader cannot make sound decisions about which way to go or what to do up high. Our route was visible in its entirety from base camp, a rare occurrence among the 8,000ers, so Ervand could watch his team's every move. To avoid his scrutiny, even on the high mountain the younger climbers hid behind rock outcrops to sneak the occasional cigarette, smoking while climbing being forbidden by their autocratic boss!

In a sense, however, the old Soviet system worked. Stellar individual performances within the framework of the team still get rewarded with spots on future expeditions, paid for by various arms of the government. This year, all the Kazakh climbers pushed one another hard, and as a result a lot of work on the mountain got done quickly and efficiently.

Our own Nanga Parbat permit had been secured by Simone Moro, an Italian who ranked in the very top echelon of Himalayan climbers. In 1997, trying the west face of Annapurna, Simone had been leading on the same slope with Anatoli Boukreev when a cornice broke off up high, starting a massive avalanche. Amazingly, car-sized blocks of ice plummeted to either side of Simone, leaving him unscathed. He shouted a warning to Anatoli and his Kazakh partner Dima Sobolev, but it was of no avail. Both men were carried off by the avalanche and buried under tons of snow and ice blocks.

Undaunted, Simone had gone on to climb difficult mountains all over the globe. I had looked forward to pairing up with this Italian legend, and in person, I found him warm and friendly. At base camp, around the dining table, I was now the linguistic outsider. Simone and his teammates conversed primarily in Italian, while both J.-C. and I listened, uncomprehending. Simone and a few of the other Italians also spoke French, which left me out as well. I began to understand what J.-C. had gone through the previous year on Annapurna. But Simone was a great storyteller and jokester, and after he had spun a story that left his team in stitches, he was kind enough to repeat everything to me in rudimentary English. Although easygoing and considerate, Simone was an extremely talented climber, the driving force behind his team. Unfortunately, as Simone, J.-C., and I approached our high camp on the way to the summit, he contracted pulmonary edema and had to descend to base camp. Sometime later, having recuperated, he made a solo effort, but was halted by high winds at Camp III.

Unlike 2001, this year no two-week snowstorm thwarted our efforts. The Kazakhs and our team made smooth progress up the Diamir Face. The crux of the climb was a 300-foot vertical rock cliff at 19,000 feet, called the Kinshofer Wall. It was a real ass buster, forcing us to grunt and groan as we jumared up the fixed ropes, our heavy loads unbalancing us as the front points of our crampons scratched for purchase on the rock face. Each time I ascended this grueling obstacle I hoped it would be my last. In the end, I jumared up and rappeled down the Kinshofer Wall four times.

It took us about three weeks to get in position for our summit bid. The Kazakhs had reached the top a few days earlier, and they generously offered to leave their tent in place at Camp IV, perched at 24,000 feet. When J.-C. and I arrived there, all we had to do was throw down our gear and prepare ourselves for the final push. At this point, we were totally isolated, since Simone had carried both the radio and our sat phone down with him. We were

2,700 vertical feet below the summit. J.-C. and I bet a couple of beers on how long it would take us to get to the top. I estimated six to seven hours, J.-C. five to six.

On summit day, J.-C. charged off at his usual frenetic pace. We took turns kicking steps in the snow for thirty minutes at a go, sharing the burden and helping each other save energy, just as the leader of the peloton does in a bike race. When J.-C. was in the lead, it was all I could do to keep close to him, but when I went first, he seemed to be breathing down my neck. Hour by hour, though, I maintained the steady pace that I had gotten used to on all my previous Himalayan ascents. On this expedition, I was the "old guy," six years the senior of any of my teammates, surrounded by strong young bucks.

During the first few weeks on the Diamir Face, as we had ferried loads up to the lower camps, several of the younger and less experienced Italians had regularly zoomed past me. I had started to wonder whether I was losing my edge: at forty-four, had age at last caught up with me and slowed me down? My loads felt no heavier than they always had; subjectively, my pace seemed the same as I had always set. Yet these tough young guys were passing me daily.

Then, one by one, the youngsters fell by the wayside. They had their reasons and explanations, but in the end, all the Italians went home without even reaching the higher camps.

I won the beers: our summit push on June 23 (the day after my birthday) took seven hours. The snow above Camp IV was a psychological nightmare, dry as sand, affording hardly any purchase. One step upward—only to slide half the distance back down. We tried all the tricks we knew to get from one tiny rock island, where the footing was more solid, to the next. We really had to spur each other on. In some sense, the mental agony of that push was worse than anything I had experienced on the other 8,000ers.

Suddenly, a few hundred feet below the top, J.-C. hit the wall. Relinquishing the lead to me, he said something like "I follow you now. I see why you keep your steady pace." Perhaps his solo of Dhaulagiri had taken its toll, or maybe it was that he had pushed so hard and fast up to this point. I took the lead for good, with J.-C. "drafting" in my wake, as I worked my way up the final gullies and rock steps to the summit of Nanga Parbat.

What a relief and a joy to have safely climbed this mountain, one of the hardest and most dangerous in the world! (After several devastating tragedies in the 1930s, the Germans had nicknamed Nanga Parbat "the Killer Mountain.") And to sit on the summit, where my heroes Buhl and Messner had stood, with J.-C., now fast becoming one of my closest friends.... Unfortunately, mists had engulfed the summit just as we approached it, so the spectacular view we had anticipated turned into a blur of fathomless white. But with Nanga Parbat, I had released a monkey that had clutched my back for two years. Now only Broad Peak and Annapurna remained.

▲
▲
▲

The next day, with monstrous loads, we descended all the way to base camp. As we approached, we were met by Simone, his girlfriend, and Amin, our helpful sirdar. They had a huge jug of Coke, which we guzzled down; then they carried our packs the rest of the way to base camp. Moments such as these epitomize for me the camaraderie and selflessness possessed by people with the true mountain spirit.

The first thing I did at base camp was call Paula. We talked for half an hour. Though overjoyed by my success and excited to hear her voice, I could not mistake her sudden falter as soon as I mentioned Broad Peak. She knew, of course, every detail of the twofer I had planned, but in that intimate moment over the sat phone, it was hard for her to accept that I still had another 8,000-meter peak on my agenda, perhaps twenty-five more days before I'd be coming home. My absences were worst in the summer months: the kids, out of school, demanded constant attention, and while other families from Bainbridge were planning summer vacations, she was stuck at home as I gallivanted among the mountains, halfway around the globe. For the same reasons, I preferred expeditions in the spring to summer jaunts, but in the Karakoram, summer is when you climb. If I got up Broad Peak, I might never have to go back to Pakistan again.

At the end of the phone call, I felt as if all the wind had gone out of my sails. Avoiding conflict, as is my nature, I'd had nothing to answer to Paula's dispirited comments. Yet shortly thereafter, perhaps picking up on the depression our chat had inflicted on me, she sent me the most wonderful e-mail via Simone's computer. "Hi Baby," she began. "First of all I love you & who you are. I love how committed you are to family, self, friends and climbing. You are my round trip! My mandatory! My natural reaction is to close down a bit—I think I try not to feel so much at least until it is safe to do so. So please don't confuse my somewhat flat disposition with non-support. You have my full and complete backing. Love, Paula."

Rejuvenated by that unwavering love, I now felt completely ready to take on the next challenge.

From Nanga Parbat, we headed straight to Skardu to start the six-day hike up the Baltoro Glacier toward Broad Peak. Katia joined us for that trek. Compared to Annapurna, compared even to Nanga Parbat, Broad Peak proved to be almost a piece of cake. Only a day after arriving at base camp, J.-C. and I began our alpine-style ascent, carrying everything we needed for a four-day round-trip. In typical Gallic style, J.-C. made fun of my voluminous "American" pack. In return, I pointed out that at least I had all of my stuff *inside* my pack, whereas he, like a pot salesman, had to dangle most of his stuff lashed to the outside of his stylishly petite "French" pack.

On Broad Peak, we were joined by some of our Kazakh friends from Nanga Parbat. Now, however, while the others temporized and slept in, J.-C. and I left base camp just after dawn on July 13, in a snow flurry. J.-C.'s Chamonix meteorologist had predicted perfect conditions at 8,000 meters three days hence, so we needed to be in position to take advantage of that window.

Two days later, we set out at midnight for the summit. It was clear, but extremely windy and cold. Taking photos or filming was out of the question, because of the risk of frostbite. We climbed up and over the foresummit, where many climbers stop yet still claim success, and began the long traverse along the final serpentine ridge toward the summit, a good two hours away.

Yet as we traversed this final ridge, J.-C. suddenly said, "Ed, I'm tired. I don't know if I should go on." I was shocked: this wasn't like the super-climber I'd gotten to know on Annapurna and Nanga Parbat.

"J.-C., it's right there," I answered, pointing at the top with my ice ax. "You can do it." Reluctantly, J.-C. trudged on, following me toward the summit. I thought he was just having an off day and needed a little motivation. And this time, the last hundred yards of summit ridge, which had thwarted Veikka and me in '97, was in perfect condition. Still acclimatized from Nanga Parbat, J.-C. and I had made a very rapid three-day ascent. We sat on the summit and gazed north toward K2, another 1,800 feet higher. J.-C. had climbed it in 2001. Now we both mentioned how glad we were not to have K2 still on our list of 8,000ers to knock off.

On the descent, J.-C. lagged farther and farther behind. Back in high camp, he said, "Man, I just can't catch my breath." At first we both thought he was just exhausted from the accumulated wear and tear of three 8,000-meter summits in one season. Late that afternoon, as we sat in the tent, I said, "Let's wait a few minutes and see if you recover."

What was really happening, however, was that J.-C. was in the first stages of pulmonary edema—an ailment he'd never before contracted. (In fact, he'd never before had any kind of mountain sickness.) Now, as we rested, instead of improving, J.-C.'s condition worsened. It finally dawned on both of us what was going on. I knew that we had to go down that very night. It had been a long summit day, but I knew we couldn't risk even a few more hours at 22,800 feet. In 1993 on Dhaulagiri, Gary Ball may have lost his life because his teammates thought it was too dangerous to take an edema-stricken climber down in the night.

Fortunately, that night on Broad Peak was perfect—crystal clear and windless. And when we had left for the summit, our Kazakh friends had ar-rived at high camp. Now one of them, Denis Urubko, gallantly gave up his chances for the top the next day, volunteering to assist me in getting J.-C. down the mountain. I loaded most of J.-C.'s gear into my pack along with my own, then went first, breaking trail by headlamp. Denis tied in with J.-C. and came down the route just behind him—not truly short-roping him, but securing him in case he stumbled or fell. Fortunately J.-C. was able to down-climb the 7,000 feet under his own power, albeit slowly. Having set out at seven P.M., we didn't arrive at base camp until five the next morning. We had been moving now for some twenty-nine hours straight.

But even at base camp, at an altitude of only 15,800 feet, J.-C. didn't seem to be getting better. Katia succeeded in radioing his insurance company back in France, which immediately mobilized a pair of big Pakistani military helicopters, one flying as backup in case the other went down. In tandem they arrived the following afternoon. We knew that each helicopter had a pilot and a copilot in the front seats, with room for two passengers behind. Katia and J.-C. climbed aboard the first helicopter, while the pilots of the second craft encouraged two of us to jump into their empty seats. There was room, so why not? I had already prepared my gear to be shipped out at a later date. Now I faced a choice between a four-day hike down the Baltoro or a one-hour flight to Skardu. Feeling a bit as though I was cheating, I climbed into the helicopter.

In an epilogue to *Prisonnier de l'Annapurna,* as he wrote about that descent from the summit of his third 8,000er in only two months, J.-C. sounded the kind of cautionary note that all the best climbers keep as personal touchstones: "Broad Peak should have been a mere formality. And yet yesterday, I almost died on its flanks. The Himalaya had taught me a new lesson."

Well, now there was no avoiding it. I'd climbed thirteen of the fourteen highest peaks in the world, even cleaned up the hundred-yard asterisks on Shishapangma and Broad Peak. I couldn't keep putting off Annapurna, despite what I'd told Greg Child about maybe stopping after thirteen if, after several attempts, I judged the fourteenth beyond my acceptable margins of risk. But now, having studied Annapurna from every side, and read all the accounts of successful ascents over the years, I resolved—not without feelings of dread—to try the north face again. I would go there in the spring of 2004.

That March, however, would not be an easy time to head off to the most dangerous 8,000er in the Himalaya, with Paula two months pregnant with our third child. She herself felt an anxiety about the upcoming trip that was more bothersome than anything she'd experienced before my other expeditions. Perhaps even more than I did, Paula wanted me to get Annapurna out of my system and be done with the whole perilous business.

I'd actually secured places for Veikka and me on an Annapurna permit when an excuse for putting the trip off a little longer intervened, in the form of yet another invitation from David Breashears that was too good to pass up. Stephen Daldry, the acclaimed British director of such films as *Billy Elliot* and *The Hours,* had become fascinated with the 1996 Everest disaster, even though he'd never climbed a mountain in his life. Daldry wanted to make a film about that debacle—not a documentary but a full-on scripted movie with actors. Even so, it would be hard to shoot the film without actually going to Everest, so one of the first people Daldry got in touch with was Breashears.

Daldry did not intend to base his film on *Into Thin Air,* and in fact he never contacted Jon Krakauer. The question was moot, anyway, for shortly after the 1997 publication of Jon's book, he and his agent had somewhat naively sold the film rights to the first company that made an offer. ABC produced a thoroughly forgettable television film, full of pretty bad acting—to this day, it mortifies Jon to be reminded of it.

Instead, Daldry planned to simplify the extremely complex plot of what happened on Everest in '96 into a drama that interwove only three characters: Rob Hall, Scott Fischer, and Beck Weathers. For the spring of 2004, Daldry wanted David to assemble a team to shoot footage on the real Everest. The acting would come later, shot far closer to sea level, but, thanks to the miracles of digital technology, would eventually be spliced into the authentic Himalayan backdrop.

Besides me, David invited his longtime colleague Robert Schauer, as well as Veikka and several others, including Jimmy Chin, a good climber who was starting to make a living as an outstanding adventure photographer and videographer. On Everest, Jimmy would shoot a video version of "the making of" Daldry's film. Amy Bullard, a Teton guide, rounded out our team.

Even as we accepted, Veikka and I still hoped to go to Annapurna in May, after we'd finished our job on Everest. My plan was that by acclimatizing on Everest, as I had done in the past before both Lhotse and Makalu, we might quickly (and thus more safely) race up the treacherous north face of Annapurna. Yet I had my qualms: as hard and scary as Annapurna had already proved for me, was I being too cavalier to treat it as the second half of a twofer?

Daldry himself came to base camp, where he eventually spent five weeks. Completely out of shape, with a two-pack-a-day habit, he nevertheless got pretty jazzed by the trip. He quit smoking cold turkey and got himself fairly fit. And one day, I roped up with the director and coaxed him up into the first part of the Khumbu Icefall, where he reached 19,000 feet. I thought he might freak out there, but he seemed to dig it. It certainly gave him a vivid feel for what real climbers do to get up the big mountains.

David's main assignment was to shoot scenics. He'd mount a high-resolution film camera—not a monster like the IMAX camera, but fairly unwieldy in its own right—on a tripod, shoot one direction for thirty seconds, then pan or tilt the camera ever so slightly to a different angle and shoot another thirty seconds. He did this repeatedly, until he had "painted" an entire area. As David explained it to me, what he was doing was like painting the inside of a Ping-Pong ball. Back in the studio, with digital technology, the director could blend these film images and create a three-dimensional scene, then shoot an actor placed in front of a blue screen and digitally transport him inside that Ping-Pong ball. An actor filmed indoors, in the comfort of a studio, could look as though he were standing in the center of the Western Cwm or even on the summit itself. I was told that this was how Russell Crowe and his three-masted sailing ships were placed into the center of the Atlantic Ocean for the film *Master and Commander*.

David shot some action shots, but not many. Since we still had no real story line to follow, we had to imagine what kinds of action sequences might be usable, or at least give Daldry, waiting below at base camp, an idea of what a typical climbing scene on the mountain might look like. Thus occasionally David would film two or three of us way off in the distance, unrecognizable (so we could double for the eventual actors) as we trudged across the Western Cwm or climbed the Lhotse Face.

It was great to work with David again, as well as with Robert Schauer. I'd seen David numerous times since the IMAX expedition in 1996, filming with him the next year on Everest for the NOVA film. But in the interim, I hadn't seen Robert at all. After the IMAX campaign, as we parted, he had embraced me with tears in his eyes, murmuring, "Next time let's do something for fun." Now, besides the fact that the pay was good, here was a chance to do something for fun—a third opportunity to combine climbing with innovative filmmaking.

As this would be my tenth trip to Everest, I needed new and challenging reasons to be there. Yet I was also beginning to envision a possible future in filming work, either on high mountains or in other kinds of wilderness. And Daldry had suggested that when the principal filming actually began, he might hire us to teach the actors the rudiments of climbing or advise them as they filmed at lower elevations in some other mountainous region. Both David and I felt that by being involved, perhaps we could help the director avoid the absurdities that had plagued other big-budget Hollywood films about high-altitude climbing. We could help Daldry convey what life is really like in the Death Zone.

We filmed in this fashion all the way up the mountain. It was a smooth ascent: David, Robert, Veikka, Jimmy Chin, Amy Bullard, and I all got to the top—for me, for the sixth time. Our team performed like a well-oiled machine. This year I used bottled oxygen, as I did when I guided, so I could be of maximum use in case anything went wrong—but nothing did. Besides, since I was working for someone else, I had no personal agenda. In the end, the climb was almost a lark: once again, we opted for the strategy of leaving the South Col at ten P.M., and we reached the summit just after dawn.

As it turned out, we spent too much time that spring on Everest to think of trying Annapurna in what was left of the spring season. The filming had allowed me to nudge my nemesis a little further into the future.

Daldry's movie was originally scheduled to come out in 2006. But as we shot our footage on Everest, the director not only hadn't hired any actors, he didn't have a script or even a tentative title. A perfectionist in the stamp of Breashears, he'd been through something like a hundred scripts without finding the one that seemed right. Since then, he's gotten side-tracked by other filmmaking projects, but he assures us that the Everest drama is simply on hold—it will indeed be made.

On his return to England from base camp and his foray into the Khumbu Icefall, Daldry told the press, "It was probably the hardest thing I've ever done in my life."

Since my undergraduate days at the University of Washington, training had always been a vital part of how I prepared for the mountains. By the winter of 2003–04, at forty-four—an age by which most climbers have either quit or tailed off drastically—training seemed all the more important to me to keep my edge on the 8,000ers. Yet that year I would get a startling—but ultimately invaluable—slap in the face, as I learned, almost by chance, what I might have been doing during the past quarter century to maximize my workout program.

There's an old and solid prejudice among mountaineers that the best way to train for climbing is to climb. I won't argue with that. It's entirely possible that during the nearly two decades I'd been pursuing the 8,000ers, the best preparation I could have done would have been to go on numerous outings into the Cascades. But as a hardworking undergrad, then a doctoral candidate in veterinary medicine, and finally a husband and a father, I considered that a luxury for which I couldn't afford the time.

Instead, from my U.W. days onward, I'd always centered my training on running and lifting weights. For years, I've typically run five to seven miles a day five or six times a week, almost always by myself. I've come to love those runs: they give me time to think, to clear my head, and I always have a better outlook on things when I get home. I deliberately incorporate hills into my circuit, to simulate the effort of going up and down a mountain. I push at a moderate yet steady pace, even on the steepest grades. Once we moved to

Bainbridge Island, I found some great quiet, hilly roads that I can lose myself on. To mix up the routine, sometimes I'll go on long bike rides.

In the gym, I've used weight training to work my upper body and torso and to maximize the leg strength I need to climb steep rock or ice, carry a heavy load, dig a tent platform, or just keep moving for twenty hours straight at altitude. No masseuses or hot tubs for me.

Through the years, following my own "Ed-crafted" regimens with both machines and free weights, I'd put in a one- to two-hour gym workout four times a week. I felt that I'd shaped and honed my body to function as well as possible as a high-altitude mountaineer. I focused on becoming strong, though not muscle-bound, on having great endurance, and on being efficient with my climbing technique. Wasting energy through inefficiency, fumbling with your gear, can cost you a summit. All my training is like studying before a big exam. If I fail because of poor preparation, I have only myself to blame. I couldn't live with myself if I squandered all the months prior to a climb by not getting as ready as possible. Suffering through a hard workout is nothing compared to ten weeks of battle in the mountains. Even when I travel, I'll go on a run or ride the creaky rinky-dink stationary bike at the local motel.

By the winter of 2003–04, I thought I had my training regimen perfected. On Bainbridge, the local gym, Island Fitness, was sponsoring me and had given me a free membership. That winter, preparing for the twofer I'd planned for Everest and Annapurna, I was especially diligent, often hitting the gym at six A.M.

As the weeks went by, I noticed one of the trainers at Island Fitness checking me out occasionally, yet he never came up to speak to me. Through Paula, who was taking some fitness classes with the guy, I learned that his name was Ubbe Liljeblad. A handsome Swede, he was a former bodybuilder. One day he finally approached me, introduced himself, and then, without further ado, said, "Ed, I know what you do and you are wasting your time. I can help you."

I was a bit nonplussed by such an aggressive thrust, but I decided to hear Ubbe out. It turned out that I didn't even begin to know what I didn't know about proper training. Soon, Ubbe had me under his watchful eye, as he pushed me to suffer as I had never suffered before.

Ubbe's emphasis was on "functional" training—in essence, simulating motions and movements, with weight resistance, that I would be performing in the mountains. Repeatedly stepping, for instance, onto and then down from a bench carrying two forty-pound dumbells. Balancing on one leg while squatting up and down, then doing curls with weights. Cranking out countless pull-ups with my arms in various positions. Squats, bench presses, lunges, and holding fifty-pound iron plates by my fingertips until they burned. Just when I thought I had done enough sets and repetitions, Ubbe would hector me to do more.

I did a lot of core work as well—exercises that forced me to use my abdominals and back muscles to control all the movements of the rest of my body. Core strength is now known to be critically important for overall fitness. For a mountaineer, in particular, core strength comes into play when you need balance while carrying a load and stepping upward on steep terrain, or hoisting a pack onto your back, or hacking a tent platform out of the ice. During some of the sessions, Ubbe had me stand in balance on a large rubber ball and do squats.

At the end of an hour of one of his merciless sessions, I would be reduced to a quivering lump of flesh and bone. One member of the gym quietly whispered to Ubbe, "Man, you're killing this guy." Ubbe replied, "Yes, but he's paying me to do it."

Then, to top everything off, Ubbe would have me work out on the stair-climbing machine for an hour, carrying an eighty-pound pack. His notion was that we needed to make everything harder in the gym than it would ever actually be in the mountains. After a session with the Swede, I would stagger into the locker room drenched in sweat. Showering, I could barely hold a bar of soap or raise my arms high enough to shave, let alone grip the razor. Driving home, I could hardly grasp the steering wheel. Each night I would collapse into bed and moan to Paula, "What am I doing, training for the Olympics?" But by 2004, I was in the best shape of my life.

▲
▲
▲

Anabel was born on October 25, 2004. Living on an island made us worry a bit about what to do if Paula went into labor when the ferries weren't running (between one and five A.M.). Friends on the island who'd gone through this before told us that the Bainbridge firefighters were some of the best delivery volunteers in the country. Once labor begins, they said, you call 911, and a posse of EMTs show up at you doorstep, ready to assist with the blessed event. I was okay with this, but Paula knew she'd be far less anxious giving birth inside a hospital. Luckily, her water broke in the wee hours of the morning, so the timing was just right for us to catch the first ferry to Seattle. As had been the case with Ella, Anabel's birth was smooth, quick, and uneventful. Paula seemed to be made for having babies.

Sensing that our family was now complete, I found it even harder to go off in the spring of 2005 on yet another Himalayan expedition. But I still had that last nail to hammer into the deck.

In the spring of 2004, the season I'd originally scheduled for Annapurna, two Germans, a Japanese, and our Kazakh friend Denis Urubko had reached the summit by the French route. On hearing this news, my first thought was, Damn, if we'd been there, we could've been done by now! On the other hand, I was encouraged to learn that the conditions on the mountain that year were very different from those in 2000. There was more snow, which covered some of the treacherous rock slabs and ribs, and it was much colder, so the kinds of ice blocks and snowslides that had poured down the north face during our first attempt, in 2000, were frozen in place in 2004. I could only hope that 2005 would repeat the pattern.

Originally I planned to climb with only Veikka. But on Annapurna, an additional team member might give us strength without creating the logistical problems of a foursome. We could carry a single three-man tent and divide the weight of the gear into three loads, not two. And I confess to an ulterior motive in considering a threesome: some of my sponsors had begun clamoring for decent photos of me in action on the 8,000ers, and perhaps video as well. Veikka and I had always done our best to document our climbs, but we had never taken a professional photographer along just for this purpose. I'd always been loath to invite someone on an expedition merely to appease a sponsor or any other third party, but if I got up Annapurna it would be a landmark event for me.

Immediately, I thought of inviting Jimmy Chin. Jimmy was not only an extremely capable climber; he was a rising star in outdoor photography. Living in Jackson, Wyoming, he was strong but easygoing, and on Everest in 2004 his personality had meshed well with Veikka's and mine. Since he'd recently been dubbed one of the country's most eligible young bachelors by *People* magazine, we knew that we'd have plenty of fodder to tease him with on a long trip. In the end, three of my sponsors paid all of Jimmy's expenses, as well as a stipend, in exchange for exclusive rights to his photos and video.

We wanted to climb Annapurna fast, to minimize our time running the Gauntlet, as I'd nicknamed that horrendous leftward traverse up the north face to the Sickle, the shooting gallery for all the debris that came down from above. So it was important that we be well acclimatized before we even got to the mountain. Once again, therefore, I set up the spring of 2005 as a twofer.

Veikka, Jimmy, and I would go first to Cho Oyu, in Tibet. For me, Cho Oyu, which I'd already climbed twice, was strictly a warm-up exercise, but neither Veikka nor Jimmy had climbed the peak. The logistics of this twofer would be a bit tricky. After our climb of Cho Oyu, we would ride a truck out of Tibet, across the Nepal border, and back to Kathmandu. From there, we'd fly to Annapurna base camp, hiring one of the several old Russian Mi-17 helicopters available for charter.

These "flying school buses," as I liked to call them, could carry a tremendous amount of gear and people to remote locations at fairly high altitudes—in our case, Annapurna base camp at 14,000 feet. Instead of repeating the grueling ten-day trek in with porters that we had performed in 2000, we would arrive at base camp less than two hours after taking off from Kathmandu. The Mi-17s were fairly expensive, but when I weighed that cost against the time and money required to deal with hiring dozens of porters, caring for their needs and health during the hazardous approach, the unpredictability of weather and trail conditions, and the simple wear and tear on our bodies, a flying school bus started to look like a bargain.

Wongchu had first served as my sirdar in 1990 on Everest, and he had organized the in-country logistics for our massive 1996 IMAX expedition. A hardworking businessman, he now owned his own trekking agency, called Peak Promotion. For Cho Oyu and Annapurna, I hired Wongchu once more to organize the transportation and cook staff.

As I sat on the airplane, winging toward my twenty-fifth trip to the Himalaya, I gazed into the future, enacting a mental ritual that had become standard for me before each expedition. Ten weeks from now, when I climbed aboard another plane to head home, what would have transpired? Would I have climbed Annapurna and completed Endeavor 8000? Would everyone have survived unscathed? What unforeseeable events would by then have occurred? This exercise serves to put my whole life in perspective.

On the plane, as I riffled through a small pile of magazines and books, my entertainment for the next twenty hours, I discovered two cards that Paula had slipped into my carry-on bag. This act had become Paula's own preexpedition ritual. Preoccupied with the frenetic preparations during the weeks before a trip, I was usually only dimly aware of the undercurrent of stress that my impending departure inflicted on our marriage. Paula's cards were her way of pledging her true love and unwavering support.

The first card contained a quote from a writer named Goemans (first name not indicated): "Dreams are not made to put us to sleep, but to awaken us." The other card bore a maxim from the business writer Clement Mok: "The most exciting breakthroughs of the 21st century will occur not because of technology, but because of an expanding concept of what it means to be human." On the back of this second card, Paula had written:

My dearest Eddie,
You ARE the expanding true concept of what it means to be human.
Be great, Be the stand....Be it!
I love you forever!
Paula

Sitting there on a plane full of strangers flying over the Pacific, I had a tough time holding back my tears. "Be the stand"—that was one of Paula's favorite mottoes, part of a private language between us. Not "take a stand"— *be* the stand. I resolved to carry these cards every step of the way on my journey. On all my climbs, I carry trinkets and mementos of home in my chest pocket. A small fabric bag contains items given to me by the kids and Paula, and talismans that I feel bring me luck: a "power stone" from Gil, a hand-painted paper heart from Ella, a swatch of fabric imprinted with a lipstick kiss and perfume from Paula, Anabel's hospital wrist tag, an energy crystal from my sister, Velta, and a sacred Buddhist mandala—an intricately folded, inscribed prayer from Tibet, given to me by Jodie Eastman fourteen years ago. Whenever I pack to leave on an expedition or set out for the summit, I always make sure to have my "juju" bag with me. I would feel naked without it.

The approach to Cho Oyu, which lies on the Tibet-Nepal border, is quite different in character from the trek up the Khumbu Valley toward the South Col route on Everest. Cho Oyu is not easily accessed from the Nepal side, so we drove trucks from Kathmandu across the border into Chinese Tibet, ultimately reaching the end of the road just above a remote hill town called Tingri. From there, our loads were carried by yaks led by their Tibetan drivers up to base camp at 18,000 feet on the north side of the mountain.

Having Jimmy along reaped unexpected dividends for us. Since his parents were of Chinese descent, he spoke fluent Chinese. His mastery of the tongue helped immensely when we wanted to order food in a restaurant, locate a case of beer in some dusty village, or even converse with our Tibetan yak drivers. We would come flying into town, trailed by a cloud of dust and a pack of yapping dogs; Jimmy would jump out of our jeep, find the local kitchen, ingratiate himself with the cook, and within minutes have a Chinese buffet fit for an emperor spread out before us. With his handsome Asiatic features, he was often taken for either a Tibetan or a Sherpa.

The two-day hike in from the end of the road was teeming with wildlife, and for the first time in all my expeditions I spotted that most elusive of Himalayan animals, the snow leopard.

As we worked our way up the mountain, everything seemed to go routinely. By April 20, we were in high camp at 23,300 feet, ready to go for the summit the next day. So far, we had battled the wind throughout the course of the climb, but that night it got ferocious. We were stalled in high camp for two more days, waiting for the weather to calm down. Whiling away the hours with nothing to do can be tedious at best, and at altitude, even while you lie there and rest, your body is slowly deteriorating. Unbeknownst to us, Jimmy had been fighting a mild case of the flu ever since we'd arrived on Cho Oyu. Not wanting that to stop him, he had kept plugging away during the previous week, all the while feeling that he was slowly recovering. But lying in our tent at 23,300 feet was not doing him any good.

Finally, on April 22, we got off at one-thirty A.M. on what looked like was going to be a perfect day. Then, only fifteen minutes out of camp, Jimmy nearly collapsed. We stopped to see what was wrong with him. His speech was slurred, his strength was gone, and he could not catch his breath. I quickly concluded that he might be suffering from cerebral edema. He insisted, however, that all he needed was a short rest, after which we could continue upward.

I had my doubts: if Jimmy was in this kind of shape now, how could he possibly make it through a ten-hour ascent to a summit some 3,500 feet above us? But at first, Veikka and I indulged him. We let him rest, then started off again, only to have Jimmy nearly collapse once more. In the throes of ataxia (loss of muscle coordination), he stumbled like a drunk, and again his speech was slurred.

"I'm afraid that's it, Jimmy," I said. "You can't go any higher. And we absolutely have to get you down as fast as possible."

Both Veikka and I had lived through too many situations just like this one. After all my years in the mountains, I was not about to lose a climbing partner by ignoring his potentially fatal condition. After a brief discussion, we decided that I would accompany Jimmy down, while Veikka could go for the summit solo. The easiest of the 8,000ers, Cho Oyu ought to be well within his powers, and he could add the peak to his own rapidly growing list. Not wanting to interfere with my chance to get to the top, Jimmy suggested that he stay at high camp while Veikka and I climbed. There was no way, however, that I could have gone on up with a crisis like this on my conscience.

Jimmy and I returned to high camp, where we got inside the tent and warmed up his numb toes while I administered Diamox and dexamethasone to him. Then we headed back down the mountain, following the trail we'd broken during the previous days. As we descended, Jimmy got stronger and stronger, and at base camp he was almost his normal self again.

Veikka reached the summit at eleven A.M. in a stiff wind, then came all the way down the mountain the same day. He arrived at base camp at ten P.M., pretty wiped out but utterly jubilant. Cho Oyu was his ninth successful 8,000er. As I knew well by now, Veikka was as strong as an ox and as motivated as a tiger, especially when it came to getting off a peak. Although I had not reached the summit, I felt that we had made the only rational decision, and I still felt I'd gained enough acclimatization to stand me in good stead for Annapurna.

By April 25 we were back in Kathmandu. Four days later, we helicoptered in to base camp on the north side of Annapurna. Feeling fully recovered, Jimmy badly wanted to try Annapurna with us, but as leader of the expedition, I had to veto that option, even though he pleaded his case eloquently.

During our downtime in Kathmandu, we had discussed the question. In the end, Jimmy had agreed that the decision should be mine. I had agonized over it, but I knew it would not be safe for him to climb high again so soon. Veikka and I thought Jimmy had been stricken by cerebral edema high on Cho Oyu, but when Jimmy later described his symptoms to a doctor back in the States, he concluded that it was pulmonary edema, exacerbated by Jimmy's case of flu and by our extended period of time at 23,300 feet. While he lay inactive in the tent, the edema was not apparent, but as soon as we started to climb to the summit, the exertion caused him to go into an acute hypoxic state. His brain was not getting the oxygen that it needed because his lungs, full of fluid, could not efficiently absorb the oxygen from the atmosphere and send it through the bloodstream. It was the effect on his brain that made us think he was having cerebral problems, but really the lungs were the source of the trouble. In any event, pulmonary edema can be just as deadly as cerebral.

Though my decision was based partly on my determination not to let anything interfere with what I hoped would be my last assault on Annapurna, it was also chiefly for Jimmy's sake. No one knows for sure what the chances are of having either kind of edema recur a few weeks later, but the possibility was not worth the risk. While I admired Jimmy's gumption, I felt he would be asking for trouble if he tried to go to the summit of Annapurna.

Jimmy helicoptered in with us, but on the route he never went higher than Camp II, at 19,000 feet. He did play an invaluable role as our base-camp liaison with the outside world, and he managed to shoot some excellent photos and video. My old friend David Breashears choppered in too—not to attempt the mountain but to shoot some footage of me preparing for my last 8,000er. David wasn't even sure how or when he'd use that footage; he just thought it was an opportunity he didn't want to miss. I welcomed David's joining us, both for his companionship and for the insight and support he could offer as we faced our challenge. For this climb, I needed all of the psychological strength I could get. And there was an appealing symmetry at work here: having first met David on my initial attempt on an 8,000-meter peak (Everest in 1987), I was delighted to have him along on what might be my last, in 2005. Unfortunately, other projects forced David to fly out before Veikka and I really came to grips with the mountain.

As we stepped out of the chopper, we were surprised to find two Italian teams in residence at base camp. One team had arrived shortly before us, but the other had already spent an unthinkable forty-one days on the mountain, fixing ropes up the north face and waiting out endless spells of bad weather.

We had come prepared to fix our own ropes up the face, but now the leader of the long-suffering Italian team, Silvio Mondinelli, walked over to our camp and said, "Please climb with us." I was dumbfounded. It turned out that Silvio was well aware of Veikka's and my history on Annapurna, and he realized that after Cho Oyu, we were sufficiently acclimatized to be ready to go on a moment's notice. I suspect Silvio also thought his own team would be stronger with the addition of Veikka and me, but it was a generous invitation all the same. And it was an unparalleled opportunity for us. Instead of fixing our own ropes up the face, and being exposed for days on the Gauntlet, we could use the Italian fixed ropes already in place up to 23,000 feet. (It would have been absurd, in any case, to fix a whole separate set of ropes of our own right next to the Italian lines, just to prove some kind of autonomy.) What this meant now was that Veikka and I could go up the mountain alpine-style, with only forty-five-pound packs, utilizing the Italian fixed ropes. With luck, we might need to climb the Gauntlet only once up and once down.

During the first week or so, all four of us—David, Jimmy, Veikka, and I—reconnoitered the bottom part of the route and carried some gear up to Camp I, which was situated far from the foot of the face. It was from this camp that we had seen the monstrous avalanche explode down the north face five years before. Meanwhile I watched the mountain, studying it intensely. I listened for the telltate booms of seracs cracking loose way up high. But everything was different from 2000. There was more snow, and it was very cold. The north face seemed relatively stable—as stable, perhaps, as it ever gets.

Yet until the very last minute, the decision to climb teetered in the balance. Veikka and I could have gone either way. If conditions didn't feel right for a safe attempt, we would pack up and go home. I wrestled with this demon for days, as clouds boiled over the mountain and fog enshrouded base camp. We were packed and ready to go up, but each evening we decided to wait another day. I've always believed that you need to listen to the mountain and watch for the signs it's giving you. If you understand what the mountain is telling you, it will let you know what to do. The Italians, who also knew how to listen and watch, were waiting as well. Finally it seemed right.

On May 7, I wrote in my diary, "It's now or never. Feels as good as it's going to." And, in an entry that reveals just how on edge I felt: "If all works could summit on Tues! Too hard to even comprehend at this point. It would be unbelievable. Many feet to climb & miles to go before all of that!! I hope, I hope, I hope, I hope..."

Just as J.-C. had gotten weather reports from Chamonix in 2002, now I was using my sat phone to call an expert named Michael Fagin in Seattle for precision forecasts. On May 7, I got the good news: "Decreasing winds at 8,000 meters and dry weather from the north is on its way."

I also used the sat phone to talk to Paula. I missed her and the kids as badly as ever, but at the same time I was as intensely focused on the mountain as I'd ever been. I agreed to carry the sat phone up the hill and call Paula the moment I reached the summit—if, indeed, I could reach it this year. Usually she prefers that I call not from the summit, only on my return to high camp, but this year reaching the top would be a huge deal, and Paula wanted to know about our success the moment it happened.

By the evening of May 8, after a ten-hour climb from base camp, Veikka and I and three of the Italians were ensconced at Camp II, at 19,000 feet. Silvio and his partner would climb directly from base camp in the morning, join up with us at Camp II, and continue to Camp III on the same day. Theirs would be a phenomenal effort The plan was for all of us to leave Camp II together at four A.M., cross the Gauntlet as quickly as possible, and burrow in at Camp III at 22,500 feet, on a safe shelf at the far end of the Sickle. The next day we'd have a grueling but technically easy climb of 4,000 feet all the way to the summit.

The Italians were carrying nothing, since they'd already been to Camp III and built up a supply depot there. Veikka and I had our forty-five-pound loads. Here was yet another benefit of pairing up with the Italians—going as light as they were, they could break trail much of the way across the face. That night I wrote in my diary, "Thank god for the 5 Italians, fixed ropes, and breaking trail.... Pleeze give us good weather!"

On May 9, it took us eight hours to climb the face, crossing the Gauntlet. There was only one safe place to stop for a rest, halfway through the day. Except for that one short break, we climbed without pause. Though we completed the traverse without the slightest mishap or scare, I had my heart in my throat the whole way. Veikka later told me, "I had to pretend I was not there."

We set up our own tent at Camp III, just seventy-five feet below the Italian camp. The weather was quite cold and windy when we arrived, and it took a major effort to carve a platform out of the steep slope. Though we were relieved at last to crawl inside our tent and relax after an arduous and stressful day, Veikka and I were completely keyed up, ready to go for the top in the morning. We planned a three A.M. start. With 4,000 feet still to climb, we knew it would be a long day.

Gearing up mentally for such a trial always comes fraught with apprehension: Will I be strong enough? Did I train hard enough in the previous months? Can I keep pushing myself hour after hour? Will the weather be good the whole day? We guessed that it might take us eight to ten hours just to reach the summit, perhaps half that time to get back to Camp III. Since it grew dark by seven P.M., even if it took us fourteen hours round-trip, we ought to be back in camp by five P.M., with daylight to spare.

But when we got up at midnight to light the stove and get dressed, a fierce wind was blasting our tent. Veikka estimated it at eighty miles an hour. We called out to the Italians, "There's no way! It's too windy. We'll talk to you again in twenty-four hours." They shouted back their concurrence. Even though our tents were only seventy-five feet apart, there were crevasses between us and them, and the slope was potentially dangerous. So we never visited our allies—we communicated by shouting over the wind.

All day on May 10, we lay under our single sleeping bag, conserving every ounce of energy we could. We couldn't sleep, and we hardly ate anything. We barely spoke—just lay there daydreaming, listening to the angry snapping of the tent walls in the wind. I felt deeply frustrated. Sometime that day, I made a sat-phone call to David Breashears, on his way home from Nepal. His hearty words of encouragement gave our morale a needed boost.

We got up at midnight on the morning of May 11, only to find the conditions unchanged. It was still too windy. Once more, we traded shouted calls with the Italians. We'd have to put off our summit bid yet another day. Twenty-four more hours of miserable waiting. We didn't even have a book to read. That day one of the Italians decided to go down. "I just can't handle the waiting anymore," he said in disgust as he left. It was his first attempt on an 8,000er, so he hadn't yet been forced to learn the stoic, mind-numbing patience that's an integral part of the Himalayan game.

Sleep was impossible, not only because of our excitement and apprehension but thanks to the constant pounding of the wind. We kept our single sleeping bag open and draped over us like a quilt, beneath which we wore our complete down suits. Our five-pound tent—a Mountain Hardwear EV2, partly designed by me—was tight as a drum and solid as a rock. I'll never completely get used to the remarkable fact that a single layer of nylon stretched stiff between aluminum poles can be all that separates you from life and death. Each night as we lay under the sleeping bag, our exhalations would condense and freeze on the inner side of the tent. As the wind buffeted the fabric, our faces would be showered with ice particles. Hiding under the covers was not an option, because then we could not breathe. We prayed for respite from the wind, but it never came.

During those two days of waiting, we'd often hear the distant rumble of a falling serac or avalanche. Each time, we'd sit bolt upright as we tried to figure out where the noise was coming from. We had scrutinized this campsite before pitching our tents here; we knew it was safely placed. But in the middle of the night, your imagination runs riot. In the light of dawn, I'd peek out the door to reassure myself once again that there were no seracs or avalanche slopes lurking above us. I'd also take a quick glance uphill to see if the Italian tents had survived the night's wind blasts. Sometimes we'd see two of the Italians with their heads out the door, smoking cigarettes and smiling.

Surrounded as we were by hidden crevasses, Veikka and I stayed within a yard of the tent even during our infrequent journeys outside to dig away the snowdrifts compressing the tent's uphill side or to take a crap. The latter duty became a precarious and unpleasant procedure. You had to make sure your crampons were on tight, then anchor yourself with an ice ax in one hand and squat quickly to minimize the quantity of wind-blown snow that accumulated inside your pants. Since we could hardly eat anything up there at 22,500 feet, not much came out the other end. At the end of the nasty chore, with hands and butt numb, you'd dive back into the security of the little home our tent had become.

Our diet consisted of some dried fruit, a Pop-Tart, and coffee for break-fast; beef jerky, nuts, and a cookie for lunch; and perhaps cheese and crack-ers with soup for dinner. At this rate our meager food supply would last quite some time. But even though we ate very little, we needed to drink, which meant hour after hour of melting snow. Our limited fuel supply dwindled faster than we liked.

By the middle of that second day, we were down to our last fuel can-ister—good, we hoped, for another thirty-six hours. At some point, Silvio called out, "Do you guys need anything?"

I answered, "If we have to stay longer, we might need a canister and maybe some food."

"We have plenty," he called back. That was reassuring.

The vigil the second day felt especially cruel to me. I kept thinking, If we can just get one good day, I can be done with the whole thing. Psycho-logically, it reminded me of my swimming days, crouched on the starting block, waiting for the gun to go off—except that instead of seconds, the wait stretched over dozens of hours.

I began to think that Annapurna was toying with us, letting us know that she was in control. I've always believed that the mountain tells you whether to go up, stay put, or go down. But now, only one day's effort away from completing my eighteen-year quest, I beseeched Annapurna to have mercy on us and let us climb.

At midnight on the morning of May 12, we decided to go for it. It wasn't an ideal day, but the wind had dropped to about twenty to thirty miles an hour. The last thing I did before leaving camp was pick up the sat phone to give Paula the good news. I turned on the phone: no signal. De-spite having a fully charged battery plus a spare, the damned thing just did not work, even though I had slept with the contraption to keep it warm. Of all the times for the sat phone not to work!

With a curse, I tossed the useless phone into the corner of the tent.

Then we used the two-way radio to call Jimmy Chin at base camp and tell him we were headed up. I asked Jimmy, "Could you please call Paula and let her know?"

A couple of weeks previously, the Italians had fixed one more rope above camp to get us through a small ice cliff. Now, after climbing the ice cliff, we continued fixing ropes on moderate terrain for a few hundred feet, mainly to help us find our way down to camp on the descent. We anchored the uppermost fixed rope with an ice screw driven high into a serac block, where we thought it would be easy to find on the way down. After that, I started placing willow wands.

At first the Italians were in front, but soon Veikka broke out into the lead, with me following. As soon as I had emerged on the broad slope that angles so interminably toward the summit, I realized how cold it was. I had everything on—my ski goggles rather than my sunglasses, my face mask and neck protector, my fleece jacket under my down suit—and I was still none too warm.

Everybody seemed cold; everybody was battling, having a hard time. I watched Silvio stop now and again to swing his legs and try to get the blood flowing to his feet. I don't use that technique myself; instead, all day I kept aggressively wriggling and scrunching my toes with every step. If you stop wriggling, the next thing you know you've lost sensation in your toes, and it can be too late. The other Italians were swinging their legs like Silvio, each locked in his own private struggle against freezing.

That north-facing slope must be one of the coldest places in the Himalaya, especially with a wind. I could viscerally understand now why Herzog and Lachenal, with their primitive 1950 clothing and their leather boots, had felt their feet go numb almost immediately on their own summit bid. Twice that June 3, Lachenal had stopped, taken off his boots, and tried to rub his feet back into feeling, and yet in the end he, like Herzog, had lost all his toes to frostbite.

That day Veikka was in his element—I've never seen him stronger. In the lead, he charged upward hour after hour. The surface was ice and hard névé, into which our crampons bit well, so breaking trail wasn't a problem.

I could keep the distance between me and Veikka even, but I couldn't catch up to him. The Italians were strung out behind us. At one point I saw them huddled together, but there were only three now.

"Where's Silvio?" I called.

"His feet too cold," came the answer. "He turn around."

Poor Silvio! If anybody deserved the summit, it was he. He'd already climbed ten of the 8,000ers. But I admired his judgment. Not only is no summit worth dying for—no summit is worth the loss of your toes or fingers.

The slope was relatively featureless, with only hummocks of ice and an occasional crevasse, but it was steeper than I had at first reckoned. And as we climbed, we couldn't see the summit pyramid, which was discouraging. It seemed that there was no place to sit down; when I paused, I could only crouch. I had a liter water bottle and an energy gel in my pack, but I didn't touch either all day. It just seemed too hard and too cold to stop and take off my pack.

Finally I saw the famous last band of cliffs, through which Herzog and Lachenal had not been sure they could force their way until the last minute. Yet for all my experience, here I badly misjudged the distances. I thought the cliff band was half an hour away when I first saw it. It ended up taking us two full hours to reach it. There was nothing up there to give us a sense of scale.

Veikka just kept going and going. It was too windy to exchange any words. Each of us trudged on, encased in his own little capsule.

We got to the band of cliffs at last and found the gully that offered a way through it. An old fixed rope dangled here. Beyond, the summit ridge stretched in a series of bumps. We climbed over one after another, knowing that the true summit was at the far end.

And then, around two P.M., Veikka and I stood on the summit! We hugged each other hard. I couldn't speak, I was so choked up. But I didn't feel the emotional flood I'd expected. I thought I would break down in tears, but I didn't. Veikka and I sat there for long moments, as I tried to comprehend that my dream of eighteen years had at last come true. I would have liked to linger there for hours...

Finally I got on the radio to give the news to Jimmy at base camp. I'd so looked forward to calling Paula on the sat phone, but now she'd have to learn of my triumph secondhand.

Over the radio, I said, "This is one of the happiest days of my life, and one of the hardest days of my life." In the background I could hear American cheers and Italian "Bravos!"

The sense of elation I reported to Jimmy was genuine. But it was warring with another, darker feeling: my stomach was in knots.

The climb of Annapurna was only half over. Never had getting down been more mandatory.

Other Annapurnas

Veikka and I spent almost an hour on top—longer than I usually do on the summit of an 8,000er, but if I ever wanted to savor the defining moment, it was now. We had both faced the real possibility that, thanks to the inescapable dangers of the mountain, this was a summit we might never reach. And often we had talked about how desperately we wanted to be done with the whole business of Annapurna, while at the same time recognizing that if we could ever get to the top, it promised to be the most magical achievement among all our campaigns on the world's highest peaks. For me, this moment meant not just another 8,000er, not even the resolution of five years of doubt and fear, but the culmination of an eighteen-year quest. ▲ As I gazed from the summit, I was acutely aware that I was taking in the same panorama that Herzog and Lachenal had beheld fifty-five years before. Straddling the ridge crest, I peered down the precipice of the south face, where Bonington's team had made their landmark ascent in 1970, and where J.-C. had fought for his life in 1992.

One by one, the three Italians—Daniele Bernasconi and the two Marios (Mario Merelli and Mario Panzeri; we called them the Mario brothers)—trudged slowly toward the summit themselves. As Veikka and I had traversed the summit ridge, we had checked out every single bump to make sure we had found the highest. Now the Italians were doing the same thing. As one of the Marios said when he joined us, "We must do this right for Miss Hawley." We shook hands and hugged all around.

As we descended, the typical afternoon clouds started rolling in. Before long we were in a whiteout. It wasn't a true storm, such as the one that had made our descent on K2 so treacherous in 1992—it was just the usual afternoon Himalayan sock-in. All the same, a few inches of snow fell, and we realized that down below, any fixed ropes that lay on relatively low-angle ground would probably get covered by snowfall.

It was here that the willow wands I'd placed on the way up, starting above the ice screw that we'd planted in the serac to anchor the highest fixed rope, would prove absolutely critical to our not losing our way on the descent. Daniele, the strongest of the three Italians, came down with Veikka and me, while the Mario brothers lagged farther and farther behind.

At Camp III, I hadn't had an abundant supply of wands left, so I'd had to string them pretty far apart on the way up the relatively featureless summit snowfield. Now the three of us stretched out parallel to one another, like rescuers searching for a lost kid in a forest, as we clumped down the snowfield, looking for each successive wand. In some places, we could still see the crampon marks we'd made in the névé on the way up, and so knew we were on the route, but in other places the wind had scoured our tracks clean, or calf-deep snow blanketed the slope.

Reunited at a given wand, we would then spread out again—about as far apart as we could and still make each other out in the blurring whiteout—and plod downward, searching for the next wand. Needless to say, this was slow, meticulous toil. As the clouds blew in and out, visibility waxed and waned. I wasn't alarmed yet; I still felt pretty confident. I figured we ought to be able to pencil in our dotted line of wands just by being patient and methodical about the process.

As we trudged on down, it was crucial that we not lose sight of the wand we had just left behind. When it had faded almost out of sight, we would stop in our tracks and peer ahead, searching for the next wand. If we could not see it, we would sit and wait—maddening though such a delay was, as we only grew colder—until we got slightly better visibility. If we ever lost track of the wand above without having located the wand below, we could find ourselves genuinely lost, unable to keep a correct heading in the featureless whiteness that had become our world.

This was when Annapurna started to toy with us. Just a few feet above the ice screw in the serac that anchored the top of our highest fixed rope, I'd planted a pair of willow wands in a spot where they could easily be seen from above, as a kind of gateway to the continuous chain of fixed ropes that would guide us effortlessly back to the tents at Camp III. Around six P.M., just as it was starting to get dark, I found those twin wands. The sense of relief was huge. I knew now that all we had to do was turn a little corner, and there would be the ice screw with the fixed rope strung below it—our lifeline back to camp.

We turned the corner. "What the fuck?" I said under my breath. There was no rope, no ice screw—nothing. For a moment I thought it had been covered by new snow, but I quickly realized that was implausible. We had deliberately anchored the rope high off the ground to forestall such a possibility. Had we somehow made the wrong turn in that minuscule distance between my lowest wands and the upper fixed-rope anchor?

We remembered that Silvio had said something about maybe needing to salvage some of the upper fixed lines to safeguard a passage farther down. After he'd turned back that morning, when his feet got too cold to go on, had he done just that—removed the uppermost rope to reuse lower on the route? If so, hadn't he realized how that very act would hang the five of us out to dry?

After the expedition, I corresponded with Silvio. He swore he had not touched the fixed ropes, and I believe him. In the end, the missing rope remains a mystery.

Daniele had been on this part of the mountain before, during his team's many weeks of slowly pushing their camps up to the Sickle and just beyond. Now he said, "I know the way. Follow me." The light was fading fast; within an hour, it would be dark. We turned on our headlamps and followed Daniele. Fortunately, the clouds had dispersed—now there was a clear sky above and no wind but, alas, no moon. Daniele said, "We need to go a ways down here—down this face." But that didn't feel right to Veikka or me. The worst thing we could do would be to plunge down past Camp III without seeing the tents and find ourselves stuck on some unrecognizable slope somewhere on the north face, completely disconnected from our ascent line.

Veikka spoke first. "I don't remember climbing that," he said of Daniele's intended route. "Ed, what we need to do is go up there a bit and traverse to the right." All this time, we had no idea where the Mario brothers were—just somewhere up above, stumbling down the route, following our tracks (we hoped), but already caught by nightfall themselves. A pair of experienced veterans who had climbed many times together, the Mario brothers, we thought, could take care of themselves. By leading the descent and breaking trail, we figured, we were helping them out.

I was really tired. All I wanted to do was find the tent and go to bed. We weren't freaking out. But I trusted Veikka's canny routefinding skills over the unknown quantity of Daniele's hunch. Veikka and I veered off from Daniele's line, climbed up a bit, and started to traverse. Suddenly uncertain, Daniele hesitated, then turned around and followed us. The knots in my stomach tightened. It seemed as though Annapurna just wasn't going to let go of us.

Meanwhile, on Bainbridge Island, Paula was going through the worst ordeal of our married life. From base camp on Annapurna, I had used our sat phone to talk regularly with her. And I'd agreed to take the phone up the mountain, so I could call her as we set out for the top, and again when—and if—we stood on the summit.

There's about a twelve-hour difference between Nepal and the Pacific Northwest. When we'd first arrived at Camp III on May 9, I'd phoned Paula and told her we'd probably take off for the summit at three o'clock the next morning. So by three P.M. the next day, as she was busy with her normal schedule, she was also acutely imagining me getting dressed at 22,500 feet on Annapurna and setting off in the darkness toward the summit. Because this was my last 8,000er and, above all, because it was Annapurna, this by now familiar drill was especially fraught for Paula.

She'd asked me how long I thought it would take to reach the summit. Hard-pressed to come up with an exact figure, I said about eight hours—seriously underestimating the difficulty of that final ascent, which in the end took Veikka and me eleven hours to complete. So, as the afternoon and early evening drifted by back home, Paula pictured me getting closer and closer. Then, around eight P.M., the phone rang—not the right hour for me to be on the summit.

"We didn't go," I had to tell her. "It was way too windy."

"Oh, shit," she answered. "I thought you were on your way."

In retrospect, perhaps I should have called her at midnight Annapurna time, when we'd woken up at Camp III and made the decision not to go. Instead, I'd waited until morning, after we'd caught a few precious hours of half sleep, to deliver the news. Paula wasn't angry—just disappointed.

Then we repeated the whole frustrating scenario the next day, when again the winds were too high for us to go for the top. The prolonged uncertainty was beginning to drive Paula crazy. I was going a little crazy myself, wondering if the weather would ever give us a chance to reach the summit of Annapurna.

Then, on the morning of May 12, when we yelled out to the Italians, "Let's go! Today's the day!," the last thing I did before leaving camp was pick up the sat phone to call Paula. And that's when the machine decided to stop working, to my intense annoyance and dismay.

There was another, fully functional sat phone at base camp, so after we radioed Jimmy to tell him we were setting off, I asked him to call Paula. Jimmy did so, and at last she understood that we were on our way.

It was three P.M. on Bainbridge when Paula got the news. The afternoon wheeled by, the sun set, evening came on. I'd said about eight hours should suffice for us to reach the summit. By ten P.M. she was virtually holding her breath, waiting for the call. Then eleven P.M., then midnight. Jimmy could call her on the sat phone, but she couldn't telephone him at base camp. All she could do was wait.

All the way up to Camp III, I'd carried our sat phone, Veikka our radio. Without even thinking twice, Veikka had stuck the radio into his pack as we set out that morning. As the hours passed, I was intensely aware of what Paula must be going through. It got to be eleven A.M.—eight hours after we'd left Camp III—and we were nowhere near the top.

Part of me realized that we should stop and phone base camp with an update—that way Jimmy could call Paula and reassure her that we were going fine, just a bit behind schedule. But meanwhile, Veikka was charging off in the lead, and though I could stay even with his pace, I couldn't catch up with him. We were so consumed with the climb, it seemed too much of an effort to wave Veikka down to stop for a call. In this once-in-a-lifetime push, all I wanted to do was keep moving upward. Committed to the task at hand, neither Veikka nor I paused to take a single photo on the way up. In the cold and the wind, trying to do so would have been to invite frostbite. It seemed too much of a distraction even to swallow my energy gel or take a drink of water, let alone get out the radio for a call to base camp. Both Veikka and I needed to stay completely focused in the moment. Yet, unable to keep Paula's anxiety out of my mind, I tried to send a thought to her through some kind of telepathy, winging my plea twelve thousand miles around the globe: *Be flexible, babe. You know that eight hours is only a guess. You know it can take longer.*

At base camp, though, Jimmy himself was starting to worry. At some point he called Paula. "They left at three A.M.," Jimmy told her, "but we haven't heard from them since. We don't know where they are."

Paula knew the game on the 8,000ers. We'd always agreed, in principle, "No news is good news." Unless you hear the worst, assume the best. But Jimmy's call hit her hard.

Paula went to bed, but of course she couldn't sleep. Nighttime is the worst time for one's darkest thoughts. She lay there, curled up in a ball, while every possible scenario went through her head. And as the minutes ticked by, her fantasies increasingly dwelled upon the worst case. *Something's gone wrong,* she agonized. *Eddie's not coming home.*

Paula's a survivor. Lying there in the dark, curled up in a ball, she tried to rally herself for a future without me. *I'll be fine,* she rationalized. *I'll sell the house. I'll move closer to my family.*

But, as she told me later, in those wee hours, she modulated from being heartbroken to feeling just plain pissed off at me for choosing this career. The anger came out in a single blazing cry, silently directed at me on the other side of the world: *Screw you! How am I going to tell the kids?*

For hours, Paula rehearsed the formula. She would gather up Gil, Ella, and Anabel in her bed and utter the terrible phrase "Your dad's not coming home." But all she could picture was Gil's wide-eyed stare and incredulous response: "Mom, what are you talking about?"

Around three A.M. came the joyous call from Jimmy, with the news that we had reached the top. But Paula's flood of relief quickly ebbed. She knew the climb was only half over. If it had taken us eleven hours to get to the summit, not the eight I had predicted, what might happen on the way down? Through the rest of her sleepless night, the dark scenarios came fluttering back. And by six A.M., with the morning sun above the horizon over Puget Sound, she knew that night was falling on Annapurna, and that we had not yet gotten back to Camp III.

⸬

Indeed, at that hour, Veikka, Daniele, and I were crisscrossing the slopes, searching by headlamp for the fugitive fixed ropes that might lead us back to our tents. And we still had no idea where the Mario brothers were, no doubt benighted themselves farther up the mountain. Fortunately, the weather continued benign.

As we traversed the slope, following Veikka's hunch, things began to look vaguely familiar. I figured that we had to be in the right general area, and by now we were probably a little bit below where the uppermost rope had been fixed—the one we couldn't find. Thus it occurred to me that the string of fixed ropes winding through the seracs leading back to Camp III probably lay somewhere hereabouts, covered with a thin layer of new snow.

It didn't feel like a life-or-death situation. The weather was fine, we were around 23,000 feet, not 28,000 on Everest, so we could almost certainly have bivouacked. But it would have made for a miserable night. All I wanted was to *be home*—for now, in that cozy tent at Camp III, but ultimately on Bainbridge Island.

As we traversed, I started dragging my crampons with every step. After only a few minutes, my right crampon points snagged on something under the surface. "Veikka!" I called out jubilantly. "I found the ropes!"

We were home free—the fixed ropes, strung end to end, took us directly back to camp. Holding the cords in our hands, we could almost have made our way with our eyes closed. As it was, however, we didn't get to the tents until ten P.M. We'd been going almost without pause (except for that hour on the summit) for nineteen hours straight. Seldom had I been so tired.

As soon as we got inside our tent, I said, "Veikka, give me the radio." I pushed the transmit button, raising Jimmy. "Base camp, base camp," I crowed, "the Eagle has landed!" After their own celebration at base, Jimmy called Paula once more with the news.

I still had strength enough to write in my diary, all in caps: "TODAY WE DID IT! UN-BE-LLEVE-ABLE! DREAM COME TRUE!"

The Mario brothers didn't get in that night. I was concerned about them, but Daniele said, "Don't worry, they're fine."

It turned out that higher on the summit snowfield, stumbling down in the dark, one of the Marios had broken through a snow bridge and fallen into a small crevasse. Unhurt, he said to himself, Hey, this is a pretty good place for a bivouac. The Marios spent the night inside that icy grotto in relative comfort. That bivouac recapitulated the fortuitous turn of events in 1950, when the four lead French climbers, making a desperate descent in a storm, essentially lost on the mountain, were saved by Lachenal's falling into a crevasse, in which the four then spent a wretched but survivable night.

In the morning, as Veikka and I lay under our single sleeping bag, I suddenly smelled cigarette smoke. "The Mario brothers are back," I chuckled. Serious smokers all the way up and down the mountain, these plucky Italians had been unable to resist lighting up once they had arrived safely at Camp III. We were pleased to see that they were none the worse for their night out.

We still weren't down the mountain. I was dreading that last trip through the Gauntlet. After we got into the tent, we brewed up several pots of warm Kool-Aid, hovering over the stove until midnight, though we still ate nothing. Both of us had sore toes, and Veikka's were slightly numb, but we saw no signs of frostbite. For the first time in many days, we actually slept, head to toe under our single sleeping bag.

The next morning dawned perfectly clear, but it was very windy up high. May 12 had offered us the only window of reasonable weather for a summit climb within the last several weeks. Somehow we had threaded the needle. As tired as we felt, we packed up our gear, skipped breakfast, and got off by nine-thirty A.M. We left our tent, stove, fuel, scraps of food, and sleeping pads for Charley Mace, my old friend from the summit climb on K2, who had arrived at Annapurna base camp after us and was planning, with his two partners, a later ascent.

We sped down the Gauntlet across the north face as fast as we could. All the way, I felt as though I were holding my breath through that dangerous passage. Three hours later, having finally escaped the trap of the north face, we trudged as quickly as our tired legs could carry us across the glacial plateau, toward Camp II. We needed to get as far away from the face as possible before we could breathe easily. A vision of the gigantic avalanche we had witnessed in 2000, scouring the upper skirts of this plateau, was imprinted on my memory, as it was on Veikka's.

By one-thirty P.M. we'd reached the relative safety of Camp II. Here we found two liters of water left for us by Charley, which we guzzled down like camels in the desert. I took off my down suit for the first time in five days, only to find my fleece one-piece suit underneath covered with shards and feathers of down that had worked their way through the fabric. The fleece suit hung off me like an oversized sack. Veikka and I laughed out loud at each other's "ninety-eight-pound weakling" bodies.

At Camp II, we picked up some gear we'd left there, roped up, and headed down the final stretch. We had a short, steep crevasse field to negotiate before the terrain eased off. Then there was a long, flat stretch of glacier to cross to regain Camp I. In the middle of that stretch, the afternoon clouds rolled in again, like an evil mist with a mind of its own, determined to torture us with one last trial.

Soon we were in a whiteout comparable to the one on the descent from the summit the day before. To make matters worse, all the wands I'd placed here on the way up had melted out and fallen flat. Now they were invisible under the coating of new-fallen snow. We stopped cold and waited for an hour, for fear of losing the way. Immensely frustrated, we tried to laugh at our situation, but we could just as easily have wept. We knew the general direction of camp, but a minefield of crevasses lay between us and there. I said, under my breath, *"Come on! Give us a break!"* Annapurna did not want to let us go.

At last the clouds cleared. Camp I was just two hundred yards away. We had little or nothing to pick up there: it was simply a critical waypoint on the descent route. From there we knew we had to take a sharp left, then weave our way down through a little icefall.

We were in radio contact with Jimmy. He promised that a whole entourage would hike up to greet us at the bottom of the icefall. I had to keep telling myself not to let up—it wasn't over yet. Only when you step off the mountain and take your boots off for the last time is the climb over.

At last we could see the gang waiting at the bottom of the icefall, and we could hear them yelling and cheering. We downclimbed and rappelled steadily and slowly through the icefall. For the last time, we held our breaths, praying that nothing would collapse while we were in the midst of these last ice towers and crevasses.

And then—boom! We were there. Silvio gave me a tremendous bear hug, picking me off the ground, threatening to suffocate me. The guys had brought up beer and Pringles and our trekking shoes. We changed out of our boots. It was a tremendously joyful reunion with old friends and new. Finally my emotions let go, and the tears streamed from my eyes, hidden by the dark lenses of my sunglasses. I stifled my sobs as I gave in to a wave of overwhelming relief. Veikka and I hugged, without speaking a word. No words, indeed, were needed.

The others carried our packs on down for us. It took us another forty-five minutes to reach base camp. During that time, it started snowing. Nothing could ruin the day now. It felt like Christmas, and I was the happiest man on earth. I'd just been handed the most beautiful present I'd ever received: Annapurna.

▲
▲ ▲
▲

Only five days later, I was home on Bainbridge Island. To my dismay, Paula had not been able to let go of the anguish she had endured through the night of May 11–12. Rationally she knew that it wasn't my fault that the sat phone had broken down, and she understood the reasons why Veikka and I had not had the luxury of stopping in mid-climb to radio updates down to base camp. But in some way she was still angry at me. That searing flash in the night, when, curled up in a ball in our bed, she had silently vented her rage—*Screw you! How am I going to tell the kids?*—had not dissolved.

As Paula had always said, she was my number one cheerleader throughout Endeavor 8000. But during the first few days I was home, I felt as though I were walking on eggshells. In the end, we had to talk it all out, spending several evenings doing so, before we felt reconciled. On May 13, Ron Judd, a reporter from the *Seattle Times* who'd followed my career and become my friend, had written a piece about Paula's vigil through the night. On the front page, the *Times* ran a photo of Paula and the kids. None of them looked happy—not even baby Anabel, holding a washcloth to her mouth. The piece evoked a powerful response of sympathy among the paper's readers. More folks than I'd ever imagined deeply identified with Paula as she'd worried through that sleepless night.

As we'd helicoptered out from base camp on May 14, the spring season on the north face was not over. Waiting to make their own attempt was the second Italian team, as well as Charley Mace with his two partners, one American, the other Australian.

This second Italian team was spearheaded by Abele Blanc, from the town of Aosta, just southeast of Mont Blanc, and Christian Kuntner, technically an Italian but, like Reinhold Messner, a German speaker from the South Tirol. Both men had already climbed thirteen of the fourteen 8,000ers, lacking only Annapurna. As I stood on the summit on May 12, I'd become the twelfth mountaineer worldwide to claim all the 8,000ers, and only the sixth to do so without supplemental oxygen. Just days after my triumph, Abele and Christian hoped to become the thirteenth and fourteenth to finish the round.

During the brief time we'd shared at base camp, I'd found both Abele and Christian quite likable, and I was impressed by their climbing prowess. The two had met in 1999 and become inseparable partners. This was their sixth expedition together. And if J.-C. Lafaille and I had struggled for years with our own nemeses in Annapurna, so had Abele and Christian, who had failed on the mountain on three previous attempts.

Christian's record was particularly exemplary. Forty-three years old that spring, he'd climbed every one of the other thirteen 8,000ers without supplemental oxygen or Sherpa support. And in 2003, he'd tried to attack the formidable south face of Annapurna. Abele had turned back lower on the face, then watched nervously as Christian and several teammates pushed up to 24,500 feet—only 2,000 feet below the top. A self-effacing man who wrote almost nothing for public consumption about his deeds, Christian nonetheless posted a dispatch online about what happened at that juncture:

> It was late, already 12:30, but I wanted to keep on climbing, and get to the top. My friends said no, the descent in the middle of the night would have been too dangerous....
>
> How long will this mountain want to fight me?... This year, for two days, I thought that, at last, Annapurna was holding out its hand to me in

friendship. Just before I started to abseil [rappel], I raised my head and looked at the summit, muttering to myself: I'll come back, and, this time, please let me have you.

A day or two after we'd helicoptered out from base camp, the last wave of climbers set off up the north face. Charley Mace and his two partners climbed as a team on their own, while Abele and Christian's team was joined by Silvio Mondinelli, who'd had to turn around on our summit day with cold feet, and Silvio's less experienced teammate, the one who'd bailed from Camp III because he couldn't stand the waiting.

Above Camp II, there's a gully you have to cross that acts like a funnel for a huge sector of the upper face. You want to enter and exit that gully as fast as possible—I think we did it in about thirty seconds. That day, Charley and his partners had crossed the gully and were working their way up a broken face to the left of it. Abele and Christian were in the gully. Christian paused for just a moment, shooting some footage with his video camera.

Everybody heard the sharp, cracking report from above. Acting on instinct, Charley hung on his jumars, which were attached to the fixed rope, and swung off leftward to the far side of a small snow arête. Just seconds later, he was pummeled by spindrift, the edge of a major avalanche, but he hung on. As soon as the sliding snow had cleared, he heard screaming in Italian from far below.

Caught in the dead center of the gully, Christian and Abele had been slammed by big ice blocks and swept several hundred feet down the face. All the other climbers now zipped down the fixed lines to go to the aid of the stricken pair. They found both Christian and Abele conscious but deeply shaken. Christian complained of a shoulder injury, and he had a deep gash on his forehead. Abele had no visible injuries.

At once the rescuers started to help the two survivors down to Camp II. They had been descending for only twenty minutes when Christian started spitting blood, and when he urinated, a red stream emerged. The others made a sledge for Christian, strapped him to it, then started lowering him down the slope. All the while, they were terrified of the possibility of more debris descending from above. But the team succeeded in getting Christian to Camp II. The whole way down, as he lay in his sledge, he remained lucid and coherent.

Then, perhaps two hours after the accident, he fell asleep. Charley took his pulse and was deeply alarmed to find only a faint throbbing of twelve beats per minute. He performed CPR, but it was too late. Within three hours of the accident, Christian was dead, apparently of hemorrhaging caused by internal injuries.

Abele seemed to go into post-traumatic shock. Moaning and wailing, he acted, as Charley put it, "like an infant. He wanted somebody to hold him."

With their sat phones, the survivors called for a chopper. That same day, Christian's body and Abele were lifted off the mountain from Camp II, at 19,000 feet, and whisked within hours to Kathmandu. Abele spent three days in the hospital, where doctors could find nothing physically wrong with him—except the paroxysms of a life-shattering grief.

That was the end of the spring season on Annapurna. As Charley later put it, "In seconds, we went from the best of worlds to the shittiest."

He added, "There's no good line on that north face, no safe way up. Ed was lucky."

I'd been home for only a day or two when the phone rang. It was Veikka, calling from Kathmandu, where he'd planned to hang out a bit after the expedition. "Hey, bud," I said cheerily, "how's it going?"

"Ed, it's bad news," Veikka answered. "Christian just died this morning on Annapurna."

I almost dropped the phone. So, after all, Annapurna had been unwilling to let her suitors off easily; she had once again taken her toll, the cruelest of any Himalayan peak.

It may seem strange, but the moment I hung up, my overriding thought was, How am I going to tell Paula? What will she think? I was just there, crossing that same gully, and now somebody's just been killed in it. Is she going to think I was an idiot? She might now doubt me forever.

Perhaps that reaction stemmed from my lifelong instinct that if some-one else is upset, it's my fault. And perhaps it was tinged by her lingering anger about my failure to call her on summit day. I actually had to steel my-self later that day to tell Paula the terrible news.

To my vast relief, she took it like a trouper. Her faith in my judgment and safety prevailed. As she put it, "Christian was just in the wrong place at the wrong time. Perhaps he shouldn't have been there at that moment. He hesitated there to film. And the conditions must have been different when you crossed the same gully."

A day or two later, Abele, still in the Kathmandu hospital, remained so traumatized he could not recognize his closest friends, though doctors still detected no serious physical injuries. Eventually, Christian's Web site posted a photo of Christian, juxtaposed with a thin silver cross and a swirling red rose, bordered in black. In the photo, bald-headed, fit, and strong, Christian gazes fiercely but eagerly at his next challenge. Signed by his parents, his sis-ter, his friends, and his climbing partners, a brief and poignant poem com-memorates his passing:

> *wir sind nicht tot,*
> *wir tauschen nur die Räume*
> *wir leben fort*
> *in euch und euren Träumen.*

> we aren't dead,
> we're only changing places
> we live away from here
> in you and in your dreams.

There was a fair amount of fuss in the American media when news got out that I'd climbed Annapurna and finished the cycle of the fourteen 8,000ers. The *New York Times* ran a sizable piece about me, as did many other papers around the country, including the *Los Angeles Times.* The *Seattle Times,* the

Seattle Post-Intelligencer, and our own local *Bainbridge Island Review* put me on the front page of their papers several issues running. As I sat in the plane flying home from Nepal, I was featured on *World News Tonight with Peter Jennings* as the Person of the Week. From Seattle via satellite feed, I appeared on the *Today* show and *CNN Morning News,* and I flew to New York for CNN's *Paula Zahn Now* and the ESPN sports show *Cold Pizza.* In subsequent months, the three leading American adventure magazines, *Outside, Men's Journal,* and *National Geographic Adventure,* all ran feature articles, and the latter publication elected me Adventurer of the Year in its December 2005 issue. And—talk about a billboard!—Starbucks asked me to supply a personal motto or quotation that the company would print on eight million coffee cups the next August. After long deliberation, I chose the following statement of my philosophy: "I've learned in climbing that you don't 'conquer' anything. Mountains are not conquered and should be treated with respect and humility. If we take what the mountain gives, have patience and desire, and are prepared, then the mountains will permit us to reach their highest peaks. I believe a lot of things are like that in life."

There was a whole array of honorary tributes in and around Seattle. I was chosen to throw out the first ball at a Mariners baseball game, and introduced at halftime at a Supersonics basketball game. And in 2005, I developed a special relationship with the Seahawks, the NFL football team.

Sometime before the season started, the team's president, Tim Ruskell, and its CEO, Tod Leiweke, were sitting around the fireplace in Leiweke's cabin, brainstorming. Ruskell said, "We need a local celebrity to connect the fans to the team, and maybe even to motivate the players." Leiweke had been to a fund-raising talk I'd given a couple of years earlier, for the local Boys and Girls Club. "How about Ed Viesturs?" he suggested. To my great surprise, in the summer of 2005, Ruskell and Leiweke approached me about talking to the team.

So, after the Seahawks' last preseason practice, as the fifty-odd players, still sweaty and in uniform, gathered in the locker room, coach Mike Holmgren brought me in and introduced me. I spoke for fifteen minutes on the themes of "teamwork" and "one step at a time." I talked about how on an

8,000-meter peak, you have to trust your partner—your teammate—implicitly. In climbing, the rope ties you to your partner in a life-or-death linkage of trust. I also talked about plugging away, taking some steps forward, some backward, while staying focused on the final goal, no matter how far away it seemed. For the team, the Super Bowl was the summit.

I felt a bit intimidated, standing there pontificating to these three-hundred-pound athletes who had—to say the least—been around the block. In high school, college, and now the NFL, they'd listened to every motivational speech known to man. And I knew that the outdoors and pro sports were two realms that had very little overlap. Mountain climbing, I thought, would seem just plain weird to a dude who made his living intercepting passes or tackling fullbacks. But I went ahead with my spiel. I had a few ideas in my head about what I wanted to convey, but the speech was spontaneous and off-the-cuff.

As I looked at my audience, I noticed that, yes, some of the guys were studying their fingernails, wondering how soon they could take a shower, but a lot of the players were listening and even looked rapt. When I was done, Holmgren suddenly asked, "What about that movie *Touching the Void*, where the guy cuts the rope?"

In *Touching the Void*, a true story based on the book of the same name by Joe Simpson, the author and his good friend Simon Yates are making a desperate descent of a big mountain wall in the Andes, after Simpson has broken his leg. Trying to lower Simpson, Yates accidentally lets him slip over an overhang, leaving his partner dangling helplessly in midair. With only a hip bucket seat punched in the snow for his anchor, Yates feels himself slowly starting to be pulled off the wall himself. As a last resort, Yates cuts the rope. I explained all of this to the players.

"Man, that's pretty fucked up!" one of the guys exclaimed. Murmurs of agreement traveled around the locker room.

"It was the only thing he could do," I commented. "If Yates didn't cut the rope, both guys would have died."

Simpson plummets into a crevasse, I went on to explain, but he's still alive. Yates rappels off the wall, leaving his rope, then staggers back to base camp. At first thinking he's condemned to a certain death, Simpson gradually rallies, extricates himself from the crevasse, and crawls, shattered leg and all, back to base camp. It takes him two days to perform this self-rescue. He arrives just as Yates is packing up to go home.

Another player couldn't resist blurting out, "Man, I'd a been pissed!" The whole team broke up.

After my pep talk, several players came up and shook my hand. One said, "Hey, I'm heavy into snowboarding. I'd like to climb Rainier someday."

The upshot of my little visit was that after every victory during the season, each player was rewarded with a miniature carabiner—the key piece of gear, as I'd pointed out, that links the roped climbers to each other while on a mountain. One side of the biner was engraved with the word TEAM-WORK, the other with the phrase ONE STEP AT A TIME. I thought the players would chuck these little souvenirs, but sportswriters started noticing chains of baby carabiners dangling from players' lockers, and they asked about them.

There's an old Seahawks tradition called the Twelfth Man, signifying the fans' support. Before one of the home games, I was chosen, as representative of the fans, to raise the Twelfth Man banner on a flagpole overlooking one end zone. And at the end of what would prove to be a conference-winning season for the Seahawks, I was given the game ball from the contest that clinched the NFC West division title, and was chosen once again to raise the Twelfth Man flag—this time at the top of the six-hundred-foot-tall Space Needle. In a fifty-mile-an-hour gale, I hoisted the thirty-five-foot-long flag. During the following weeks, all of Seattle watched it fly proudly in the sky as the Seahawks advanced to the Super Bowl.

I'd like to think that my fifteen-minute inspirational talk was the main reason for the Seahawks going thirteen and three during the 2005 season, winning a playoff game for the first time since 1984, and getting all the way to the Super Bowl, which a lot of us in the Seattle area think they might have won with better officiating. But I suspect that Shaun Alexander's NFL record twenty-eight touchdowns as he won the league's MVP trophy may have had a little more to do with it. It was a stellar year for the whole Seahawks organization.

Personally, the main feeling I had on getting home was an overwhelming sense of relief that after eighteen years, the whole campaign was over. I was content and relaxed. Ever since my first attempt in 2000, and especially through the previous year, the daunting and somewhat frightening prospect of climbing Annapurna had hung over me. That specter had finally vanished. I had spent many sleepless nights brooding about that mountain. Now I slept like a baby.

My sponsors and many of my friends confessed how relieved they were that I was back, safe and sound, having slain the monster. No one had said anything anxious or pessimistic before I'd left for Nepal; for my sake, they'd maintained an upbeat facade. It was as if I'd been dating someone whom my friends didn't really approve of, but they'd kept their silence. Now that I'd broken up with her, they could admit that they'd always felt I'd made the wrong choice.

For the first time since I could remember, I didn't need to take a few weeks off, then get back into training and preparation for my next 8,000er. For a while, at least, I could do whatever I wanted. Lots of friends, as well as Paula, told me, "Ed, just relax—take it easy for a while." I thought, Sure, why not? But I was completely out of practice for relaxing. I couldn't remember the last time I'd goofed off for any extended period of time—was it in grade school, when my pal and I had prowled through the underground street-runoff drainpipes in Rockford, before I'd gotten into competitive swimming?

Anabel and Ella were too young to appreciate what the milestone of my fourteenth 8,000er meant, in terms of how it would affect our life as a family. Gil, at seven, had a better idea. As he said to me when I got home that May, "Now you don't have to go away again for such a long time!" Mostly the kids were just happy to have their dad home after a seven-week absence. I was overjoyed to be around them and Paula, and to note all the changes that Anabel had gone through. I like to say that coming home is the best part of any expedition.

Lots of people asked me if, along with a sense of profound satisfaction, I didn't feel a certain letdown on finishing the quest. After all, for more than eighteen years the passion to get to the top of high mountains had organized my life. For most of that time, it had *been* my life, once I'd turned my back on my veterinary career.

My honest answer would be to borrow one of Gil's favorite phrases: "It's bittersweet." In the summer of 2004, I took Gil on a fishing trip to Alaska. He had the time of his life, loved every minute of it, but toward the end, he really started missing Paula. As we were standing at the ferry dock in Craig, waiting for our flight out to Ketchikan, he said, "Dad, I'm feeling melancholy right now. I want this to end and to go home, but then again, I don't." (Precocious since he started talking, Gil loves to use words like *bittersweet* and *melancholy*.)

So, yes: bittersweet. Climbing the 8,000ers had been the biggest thing in my life. I was consumed by it, and all of a sudden, it was over.

Perhaps the single aspect of Endeavor 8000 that I'm proudest of is that I did it as safely and as prudently as I did. On thirty expeditions to 8,000-meter peaks, I never once got frostbite. I was never seriously injured. On 8,000ers, I've gotten closer to exhaustion than at any other time in my life, but I've never suffered (thank God) from either pulmonary or cerebral edema, or even from a bad case of acute mountain sickness. I've never had to be rescued. I've helped plenty of other climbers down 8,000ers, but I've never had to be helped down myself. Most importantly, I've never lost a partner in the mountains.

I'm also proud of the fact that I started Endeavor 8000 as a challenge to myself and that it remained that way throughout. I never sought out media attention, nor was I swayed on the mountain by peer or sponsor pressure. The only time I ever wrote about any of my climbs was when Ad Carter coaxed an account of our 1992 K2 expedition out of me for the *American Alpine Journal*. One Sunday afternoon just after I got home, I banged out a rough report on my typewriter, thinking Ad would edit the hell out of it and print it somewhere in the back of the journal with the scores of other climbers' brief reports of their ascents. "Nope," Ad said over the phone, "I'm printing the whole damn thing as is, and it will be one of the feature arti-cles in the front."

Interestingly, my experiences in the Death Zone could hardly be more different from those reported by Reinhold Messner, the first man ever to climb all the 8,000ers and one of my heroes. Again and again above 25,000 or 26,000 feet, Messner talks about having wild hallucinations. He hears voices; he talks to his ice ax as if it were a companion when he's on a solo expedition. When he climbs with a partner, sometimes he's convinced that a shadowy third companion ascends with him, always just out of sight be-hind his shoulder—a phenomenon also reported by several of the Antarctic explorers during the heroic age from 1890 to 1920. On the tragic descent from Nanga Parbat after he'd lost his brother in 1970, Messner became con-vinced that Günther was still with him, chatting away about such inconse-quential matters as a loose crampon.

If I'd ever had such hallucinations or visions on a high mountain, I'd have known it was time to head down.

Among my thirty expeditions, I've reached the summits of 8,000ers an even twenty times. But that means that I had to—or decided it was only safe to—turn back ten times: four times on Everest, twice on Annapurna, once each on Shishapangma, Broad Peak, Dhaulagiri, and Nanga Parbat. And four of those ten turnarounds came when I was within 350 vertical feet of the top. I'm also proud of the fact that I never turned around because of lack of preparation, strength, or desire. It was always the conditions that caused me to pause and retreat.

About safety, I have a real pet peeve. Countless times—as I'm being in-troduced to give a slide show, for instance—someone will refer to me as a "risk taker." I always correct him or her: "I'm not a risk taker. I'm a risk man-ager."

Because of this attitude, I've been accused of being a rationalizer, in de-nial about risk in the mountains. In 1996, I had a provocative exchange with the writer who interviewed me for *Men's Journal* over this issue, when he tried to ensnare me in a statistical analysis of the risks I'd run in the Hi-malaya and Karakoram. He'd been a math major in college, and he thought probability theory could be applied to climbing in the great ranges. He cited a rigorous study conducted by a German historian of mountaineering who had counted up all the members of all the expeditions that had gone to 8,000-meter peaks and divided them by the number of deaths on those expeditions. His conclusion was that on any given expedition to an 8,000er, you stand a 1 in 34 chance of getting killed. By the time the writer interviewed me, I'd been on seventeen such expeditions. To the former math major, the odds I'd run of buying the farm were a simple equation in dependent probability.

It was like Russian roulette, he explained. If the gun has six chambers and one bullet, when you spin the cylinder and pull the trigger, you stand a 1 in 6 chance of shooting yourself. If you do it twice, the odds of dying obviously go up. Mathematicians calculate the exact odds by multiplying 5/6 by 5/6—that ratio represents the necessary interlinked chances of *not* shooting yourself and is known as dependent probability. Those fractions multiply out to 25/36, or about 0.69. In other words, after you've played Russian roulette twice, you've incurred a 69 percent chance of not killing yourself, or a 31 percent chance of doing the fatal deed.

Most people think intuitively that if you spin the cylinder and pull the trigger six times, you've run about 50-50 odds of committing suicide, but it's actually much worse. Five to the sixth power divided by six to the sixth comes out around 0.33. After six clicks of the trigger, you've stood only a 1 in 3 chance of staying alive.

I could follow—and buy—this argument fine so far. After all, I'd taken plenty of statistics in undergrad and vet school. But now the writer tried to apply the same reasoning to my expeditions. He calculated 33 to the seventeenth power divided by 34 to the seventeenth and came out around 0.60. Thus, he insisted, by 1996 I'd actually run a 40 percent chance of killing myself on the high peaks.

As he unfolded this cute little theory, I stared at the guy, incredulous. "That's ridiculous," I said. "That doesn't apply to me."

"Why not?"

I explained that the 1 in 34 stat included all kinds of poorly trained or inexperienced climbers on their first expeditions to an 8,000er (like some of the guided clients on Everest in '96), whereas I prided myself on my training, expertise, and caution.

"Yeah," the writer shot back, "but the stat also includes chubbers who do no more than go once from base camp to Camp I. You're always going for the summit—without oxygen."

"It's still ridiculous," I repeated. "It just doesn't apply."

The guy had a smirk on his face. "So, Ed," he needled, "subjectively, what chance do you think you've run on the 8,000ers?"

"I don't go to the Himalaya with the thought of taking a chance of dying," I answered. "Maybe one in a hundred." I thought for a moment. "No, not even that much."

"But Ed," he hammered away, "you nearly died on K2!"

We never did see eye to eye on the question. But the writer had the gall to publish our exchange, without giving me the chance to explain my case. Instead, he presented my responses as a classic case of denial.

Despite that cheap shot, the writer and I have stayed friends over the years. In the spring of 2005, after I got back from Annapurna and telephoned him with the news of our successful climb, he congratulated me heartily, then asked how many expeditions to 8,000-meter peaks I'd undertaken by now.

"Thirty," I answered.

He called me back a day or two later. "Forty-one percent, Ed," he said, out of the blue.

"What?"

"By now, you've run a fifty-nine percent chance of killing yourself. Only a forty-one percent chance of staying alive." The smug bastard had run his calculator again, dividing 33 to the thirtieth power by 34 to the thirtieth.

Since my writer friend never really gave me a fair chance to explain in print my own calculus of the odds I've run on the 8,000ers, here's my opportunity to do so. This is why I think his pat little statistical exercise is completely out of whack.

What this guy could not fathom was that after thirty expeditions to 8,000-meter peaks, I wasn't playing the odds—I was beating the odds. I believe that most accidents and deaths on the high peaks are due to human error. Using up all your energy getting to a summit, for instance, or going too late to a summit, without sufficient thought about what it will take to get down. Ambition and desire overpowering common sense have killed many a Himalayan climber.

Our instincts have evolved over millions of years, instincts that kept our remote ancestors alive. Humans with poor survival instincts got weeded out long ago, through natural selection. The fight-or-flight instinct is a perfect example, passed down to us in our very genes.

I've learned that I need to listen to my instincts. The signals we receive from them are not imaginary. On K2 in 1992, I committed a nearly fatal error when I failed to acknowledge those signals and kept pushing on toward the summit. Yet even at the time, I *knew* I was making a mistake. There's a big difference between realizing that you can get yourself into trouble and just blindly stumbling along without a clue. "Ignorance is bliss" means that you don't even know what you don't know.

Inexperience inevitably leads to accidents. If you get away with making mistakes, it's crucial to learn from them. I've seen too many climbers who seem instead to have the blind conviction that "It won't happen to me."

One of my favorite sayings is "You don't just pick up a hammer and build a house." In the same sense, you don't just pick up an ice ax and climb an 8,000-meter peak. You need to start with the basics and work your way up the ladder. That means surrounding yourself with people who have more experience than you do. From the very start, I knew I faced a long road to learn all I needed to go safely to the Himalaya.

From Curt Mobley, my first climbing mentor, way back in 1977, through senior RMI guides such as Eric Simonson, Phil Ershler, and George Dunn, I was fortunate to be tutored by some of the best and the most careful. And my own decade-long tenure as a Rainier guide in turn made me a safer climber, because when you have novice clients under your supervision, you're constantly thinking, *If this happens, then what do I do?*

Russian roulette is far too simplistic a model to apply to something as complex as Himalayan climbing. A gun is a mechanical device: as the cylinder rotates, it's a matter of sheer luck whether it stops at an empty chamber or at the loaded chamber. Expedition climbing involves scores of variables besides random chance.

If I train harder than the next guy, I'll be faster and stronger, and at the end of the day, I'll have more endurance left. By being quicker, I can expose myself for a much shorter time to the true objective hazards, where chance comes into play—like the Gauntlet on Annapurna, which took Christian Kuntner's life.

It's critical to make your own decisions and not be swayed by the crowd. I've seen how summit fever operates on Everest: at base camp, I've had to hold back clients who act like runaway horses when they spot others heading off on summit bids. At that moment, above all, you need to trust your own judgment, not someone else's, and listen to your instincts. If it feels wrong, it is wrong.

Luck, I will admit, has played a certain part in my mountaineering career. I don't assume that I have some kind of Teflon coating that's kept me alive. A stray falling stone or avalanche could always have taken me out. But on all those expeditions, something worked in the right way. Some combination of training, skills, instinct, and a dash of luck saw me through.

At the same time, you need to be wary at all times and never let down your guard or become complacent. No matter how experienced you are or how famous you are, you can still get killed in the mountains. As Paula constantly reminds me, "Even though you think you've got it figured out, you don't." And I've often recalled the motto Lou Whittaker taught me on Rainier: "Just because you love the mountains doesn't mean the mountains love you."

Finally, there's another crucial flaw with the analogy to Russian roulette. In mountaineering, I believe, the odds do not accumulate after each climb, as they do for a set of successive pulls of a trigger. Each expedition is separate from the previous one. If I learn something from a previous climb, and become a better mountaineer—smarter, faster, stronger, more efficient—

then the next climb will be safer. The risk actually goes down! I know that to some mathematicians, this may sound irrational, but in mountaineering, everything changes from one climb to the next. With a gun and a random spinning of the cylinder, nothing changes. You learn absolutely nothing from surviving the previous click of the empty chamber.

No, sorry. The analogy doesn't hold. Climbing is not Russian roulette. I'll believe in this article of faith—which, after all, has been at the center of everything I've ever done in the mountains—until my dying day.

And yet...

In late January 2006, eight months after I returned from Annapurna, I got a frantic e-mail from Katia Lafaille. By then, J.-C. had been on Makalu for almost fifty days. In several separate pushes, he'd worked his solitary way slowly up the mountain, establishing camps and acclimatizing. The weather had been horrendous—weeks and weeks of hurricane winds at a steady 55 miles per hour, with gusts up to 110. Meanwhile, relations with his cook staff at base camp had so deteriorated that the three Sherpas and J.-C. were not even on speaking terms. His sole contact with the outside world was via sat phone calls to Katia, with whom he talked three times a day.

On the afternoon of January 26, J.-C. had finally pitched his Camp II at 25,000 feet—about 2,800 feet below the summit. The next morning, just before setting off for the top, he phoned Katia around five A.M. He was in great spirits despite the ordeals he had undergone in the previous weeks. He promised to call her again soon, perhaps in only three hours, when he reached the foot of the French Couloir.

Katia waited and waited for the call that never came. As night fell in Nepal, she e-mailed me, her words fraught with anxiety and fear. Yet Katia knew all about Paula's vigil through the night in May 2005, when I had summited on Annapurna but had been unable to call her with the news, thanks to my malfunctioning sat phone. I e-mailed Katia back, "There is always hope. Please give him time to come down."

As day after day passed, and there was only silence from Makalu, not only Katia but the whole climbing world succumbed to resignation and despair. On January 31, the headline in *Le Monde* confirmed what everybody knew: "No More Hope for Jean-Christophe Lafaille." Above Camp II, something had gone far more wrong than a broken sat phone.

There was no hope of launching a rescue or even a search. At the time, not a single other mountaineer in the world was acclimatized to 25,000 feet. There was no way to communicate with the three Sherpas at base camp, who in any event were incapable of climbing up to look for J.-C. As it turned out, they had no idea what was going on higher on the mountain.

The rest of us were left to imagine what might have gone wrong. I was inclined to think J.-C. might have fallen into a crevasse from which he couldn't extricate himself. When Veikka and I had crossed that high plateau in 1995, we had weaved our way, roped together, through a maze of crevasses, and three times Veikka had punched a leg through a snow bridge hiding a deep crevasse. Yet there were so many other ways that J.-C. could have died: in an avalanche or crushed by a serac, getting blown off the summit ridge, or simply succumbing to the cold or even to a recurrence of the pulmonary edema that had stricken him on Broad Peak in 2003. We may never know J.-C.'s fate, for many a mountaineer has vanished in the high Himalaya, never to be seen again.

Katia flew with her brother and Veikka to Nepal by helicopter to Makalu base camp on February 4. There she performed a ceremony based on the Sherpa *puja*; then she added photos and personal mementos to a small *chorten* built by previous climbers, including her farewell note: "Goodbye, my love, forever. We'll meet again up there."

J.-C.'s death shook me every bit as badly as Scott's and Rob's deaths on Everest in 1996 had. Of all the climbers I'd ever met, J.-C. was the one who I thought wouldn't die in the mountains. On the one hand, I felt a huge relief that by then I'd finished my campaign among the 8,000ers. On the other hand, it forced me to reassess.

What if, after all, I had been killed on one of my 8,000-meter peaks?

What if it had been me instead of Christian Kuntner who had had the bad luck to be struck by the ice block in that gully on the north face of Annapurna? Could all the joy and satisfaction I'd gained during my eighteen years of campaigning in the Himalaya and Karakoram even begin to balance the lasting grief and loss my death would have caused Paula, Gil, Ella, and Anabel? Of course not!

I could rationalize that, by his own admission, J.-C. was willing to push himself far closer to the limits of acceptable risk than I was. In the wake of the tragedy, Veikka summed up his own feelings in a statement I agree with: "I don't know if Makalu solo in winter is too extreme. It's way too extreme for me." Yet I'd never second-guess J.-C. If anybody could have pulled off such an ultimate ascent, it was he.

In the last analysis, I still believe in my own notion of risk management. And I also believe that the logical antithesis of the life I've led as a mountaineer would be to go through your days avoiding every activity that could possibly be dangerous. You can live a life so sheltered that when you're old and gray, all you can claim is to have lived long enough to become old. That's not my way.

I used to believe that mountaineering was inherently selfish. That it didn't do anybody else any good—it didn't change the world, it didn't save the planet. The same, to be sure, could be said of most human endeavors. Being a pro quarterback or a movie star or the CEO of an insurance company doesn't save the planet either. Unless you're a firefighter, an EMT, a crisis worker in a natural catastrophe, a research scientist looking for cures for intractable diseases, or the like, you're not doing much to improve the world or other people's lives.

When I first voiced these feelings to Paula, however, she strenuously disagreed. She said, "Eddie, I've seen you speak and give slide shows. I've seen you inspire whole crowds of people. What you do when you do that isn't selfish at all. You're taking what you excel at and spreading it as a gift among countless others."

Over the years, as I've gotten more comfortable with the limelight, I've taken those public performances more and more seriously. By the year

2000, I was giving some thirty to forty talks with slides each year. And as I closed in on Endeavor 8000, the audiences grew. The average man or woman on the street doesn't have a clue what an 8,000-meter peak really is, so perhaps something in my talks clicks with folks who have no ambition of ever going to the Himalaya themselves. A few years ago, I sold out all twenty-five hundred seats at Benaroya Hall, the handsome new opera house in Seattle, at something like twelve bucks a ticket. As I walked up to the front door that evening, I was taken aback to see dozens of people on the street, searching for scalpers to sell them tickets.

Only three months after I got home from Annapurna in the spring of 2005, I went on the most grueling lecture tour I'd yet undertaken, showing slides and giving talks at ten cities in three weeks. And the venues were almost all sold out. Always before, I'd felt that my talk ended ambiguously, with the question mark hanging in the air as to whether I'd ever finish all fourteen 8,000ers. Now, with Annapurna, I had the perfect ending. The story began with my reading Herzog's book about Annapurna, and though I never intended to keep Annapurna as my last and hardest 8,000er, that's how it worked out.

I give both public shows for general audiences and private shows for corporations. The revenue from the latter goes into my pocket—it's part of the livelihood I've managed to stitch together over the years. But I give most of the profits from my public shows to charity. Typically, such a show will be part of my yearly obligation to one of my sponsors. The company has already budgeted in my travel and production costs, so it doesn't require reimbursement from ticket sales. Together, the company and I choose charities to which to donate the profits. It's a win-win situation all around. This year we made donations to local kids' groups, whereas in the past I have also raised money for international organizations such as the Himalayan Trust, the charity founded by Sir Edmund Hillary to build schools and hospitals in remote parts of Nepal.

One of my favorite beneficiaries is an outfit called Big City Mountaineers, which takes inner-city kids who have done well in school to places like Yosemite or Wyoming, where they can hike or fish for the first time in their lives. Most inner-city youths have never been in anything like a wilderness, never paddled a canoe or camped in the woods. If only one out of ten kids is affected enough by that experience to change his or her life, it's well worth it.

I take the corporate events just as seriously as I do the public ones. Giving a public show, I'm free to talk about whatever I like, but for a corporate lecture, there's usually a message that I'm asked to convey. As my own worst critic, I feel more pressure at a corporate event than at a public slide show: I'm being paid to fulfill some company's expectations, and I want to give value for the money. The kind of specific theme I'm asked to address might be "teamwork" or "overcoming difficult obstacles" or "producing better results than the year before."

I know that a lot of climbers are cynical about whether the lessons learned in the mountains can be applied to how you conduct your business or your personal life, but I'm a firm believer in such translations. The business audiences eat it up. At first they may just ooh and aah at the slides, but I find that it comes naturally for me to draw out the underlying principles of hard-earned success. I may say, "Look, it took me eighteen years to complete a very difficult endeavor. Viewed as a whole, climbing all fourteen 8,000ers would have seemed almost impossible, but I took it one day at a time, one step at a time. I was passionate about what I did, and I never gave up.

"Whatever challenge you have before you can be accomplished in the same fashion—whether it takes a week, two months, or a year. If you look at the challenge as a whole, it may seem insuperable, but if you break it down into tangible steps, it can seem more reasonable, and ultimately achievable." The model for that strategy comes from the way I learned to break up the "impossible" 4,000-foot climb to a summit into tiny, manageable pieces: just get to that rock outcrop there, then focus on the ice block up ahead, and so on.

For the general public, the "lessons" are less pragmatic, more emotional and spiritual. The famous last line of Herzog's book is "There are other Annapurnas in the lives of men." That ringing affirmation was emblazoned on my brain the very day I first read it. Giving a talk or a slide show, however, I modify the formula and I say, "Every person has his or her own Annapurna." I go on to explain that there were many Annapurnas in my life— challenges I wasn't sure I could meet—but that "the real Annapurna was my last one." For each of you out there, your Annapurna might be a tough project at work, a bad illness, or the breakup of a marriage, but the trick is to find a way of converting adversity into something positive, a challenge to look forward to.

As I said, this message seems to resonate with scores of people who hear my talk. They come up afterward and tell me so. Recently I talked to a woman who'd had a really rough struggle with cancer. "You inspired me to take the disease on as my Annapurna," she said.

I've had other people come up to tell me they had heard me speak sometime before and had taken my example to heart. When confronted with some seemingly impossible task or challenge, they'd ask themselves, "What would Ed do?"

I may be done with my own 8,000ers, but I hope I can continue to use the example of my expeditions to inspire and motivate others. If that, as Paula insists, contributes some small good to the world, then maybe mountaineering needn't be quite as selfish as I used to think it was.

Just two months after I got back from Annapurna, Paula and I watched in awe as, on television, Lance Armstrong won his seventh Tour de France, then announced his retirement from competitive cycling. I wondered if his feelings at the moment were similar to mine. Although I had no intention of retiring from climbing myself, I had told everybody who'd asked that I no longer had any desire to return to the 8,000-meter peaks. (The sole exception might be some innovative project that took me back to Everest, perhaps in conjunction with making another film.) I regard that chapter in my life, that quest, as over. But the media often misconstrued what I was saying. "Viesturs retires!," a headline would proclaim. *Outside* ran a set-up photo of me selling all my climbing gear in a yard sale. It was meant tongue-in-cheek (I found it hilarious), but far too many people took it literally.

The truth is, I'm not about to quit climbing for good at age forty-seven. There are mountains all over the world that don't happen to reach the magical altitude of 8,000 meters that still intrigue me. Way back in 1988, I failed on an attempt on Mount Saint Elias, on the border of Alaska and the Yukon. I'd love to go back. At 18,008 feet, it's a truly majestic giant of a peak, the fourth-highest in North America. Surging in one dramatic thrust out of the sea only forty miles north of Yakutat Bay, it's the highest mountain in the world so close to an ocean. The route I tried was first climbed in the astonishingly early year of 1897, by an Italian team led by the Duke of the Abruzzi, who also made the first serious attempt on K2, and for whom the Abruzzi Ridge is named. The climb of Saint Elias marked the first major ascent ever made in Alaska or subarctic Canada.

Another peak that appeals to me is Nanda Devi, in India. Although currently off-limits to foreign climbers, it's a beautifully shaped mountain, standing in relative isolation, and at 25,645 feet it's not far short of 8,000 meters. Its first ascent in 1936 was also a landmark, for Nanda Devi would remain the highest peak climbed anywhere in the world for another fourteen years, until the French succeeded on Annapurna. The expedition, a model of teamwork, blended four young American upstarts with four of the most experienced British alpinists of the day. At the end of August, Noel Odell and H. W. Tilman reached the top, later inspiring—in Tilman's classic account of the climb, *The Ascent of Nanda Devi*—perhaps the finest understatement of the joy of standing on an untrodden summit ever committed to print: "I believe we so far forgot ourselves as to shake hands on it."

I can also imagine going on laid-back trips to remote ranges with a small group of friends, not bound for any particular summit but with the goal of simply poking our way through little-known wildernesses. There are mountains in central Tibet, for instance, that have seen few or no Westerners. To wander through those ranges, beneath unclimbed and unnamed peaks, would be the utter antithesis of hanging out at Everest base camp.

Upon my return from Annapurna, the single question that I got asked ad nauseam was "What next?"—occasionally cast in a more aggressive and skeptical phrasing: "So, what are you going to do with the rest of your life?" Sometimes, in exasperation, I was tempted to fire back, "What do I *need* to do? I've just done something that only five other people have ever done!" But, of course, I kept silent.

Quite aside from climbing, there are other kinds of travel and adventure that appeal to me. I've never been to Antarctica, despite having been inspired as a teenager by Shackleton, Scott, Amundsen, and other polar heroes of the early twentieth century. I can imagine reveling in some sort of exploratory journey in the far south. And I love scuba diving. Beneath the surface of the ocean is another whole world I've only begun to learn about.

A new wrinkle in this sport, which goes far beyond scuba, is called "free diving." Without scuba tanks, divers now reach depths beyond 300 feet, surviving on a single breath held for as long as three minutes. Free diving is like mountaineering in that you need to weigh very carefully how deep and long you can descend and still safely return to the surface. Go too long and too deep, and you'll never make it back alive. Although I've never tested myself like this in the depths, the sport has the kind of mental and physical challenges that appeal to me.

When people who know what I've done among the 8,000-meter peaks meet Paula, a lot of them assume she must be a serious climber, too. But that's a bizarre conclusion. Sometimes I say (or am tempted to say), "You're an attorney. Does that mean your wife has to be an attorney? Paula has her own life."

At the same time, should Gil or Ella or Anabel, as they grow up, get interested in climbing, I'd be delighted to go climbing with them. If they want to do it, great; if not, great. It's got to be their own decision, but I wouldn't dissuade them. I have friends who are serious mountaineers who freak out at the thought of their own children taking up climbing. On the other hand, I look at the example of John Roskelley, my partner on Kangchenjunga in 1989. John was the strongest American high-altitude mountaineer in the early 1980s, but by the mid-'90s, he'd quit the game of serious climbing. A Spokane native, he got involved in local politics and was elected county commissioner. Then, when his son, Jess, showed a keen interest in becoming a mountaineer himself, John took his gear out of mothballs and started climbing again with Jess. This father-and-son duo reached the summit of Everest in 2003. At fifty-four, John had finally succeeded on the only high peak that had defeated him several times in his salad days. Jess, at twenty, became the youngest American ever to climb Everest. Since then, father and son have paired up to climb a hard new route on Menlungtse, a stunning peak in Tibet.

Still, in the wake of completing Endeavor 8000, I have to admit that at times I've felt at loose ends. For eighteen years, every year I knew what I'd be doing the next year. After only a few weeks at home after one expedition, I'd start planning and training for the next. Now, suddenly, there was no "next expedition" demanding my attention.

In the fall of 2005, a friend visiting us on Bainbridge Island said to Paula, "It must be a great relief, knowing Ed'll be here next spring, not off on another mountain."

Paula cast a slightly jaundiced look his way. "I still think he'll be gone next spring," she answered. "Yes, he's finally caught the carrot—but there's always another carrot out there."

In the spring of 2006, as Veikka was planning to go to Kangchenjunga with the Germans he'd teamed up with on Nanga Parbat, I jokingly told him, "Maybe I'll come to base camp and watch you through binoculars." That whimsy would have represented a certain coming full circle in my life, from 1989, when Lou Whittaker had watched us from base camp on Kangchenjunga as I climbed my first 8,000er.

As it turned out, Veikka reached the summit of Kangchenjunga, his eleventh 8,000er, on May 14, 2006, with two of his German teammates. It was a grueling climb, and the trio topped out only at 4:30 P.M. in bad weather, then regained their highest camp after dark. Veikka suffered minor frostnip on his fingers, and when I first talked to him, by sat phone from his base camp, he told me that he'd lost a few brain cells on the world's third-highest peak, but that the remaining cells were smarter.

Having worked so hard to develop relationships with my sponsors, I'd like to keep up those important liaisons. For me, it was always about more than sponsorship. I never endorsed a product I didn't believe in. I was thoroughly integrated with the companies who sponsored me, constantly helping them design and field-test their gear. I can envision a future in which I take a position at one of those companies.

The flip side of that speculation is the nagging fear that now that I've finished my quest, the sponsors might slowly drift away. Some sponsors really "get it," not only understanding who I am and what I've done, but the value of that for their own marketing and design work. For other sponsors, it's a bit of a struggle. It's like dating versus marriage. For some of those eighteen years, I've dated this sponsor or that. Now I want to talk about marriage? I've seen this happen to other mountaineers. One outdoor company, for instance (not one of my sponsors), maintains its chosen team of several dozen sponsored climbers; they appear in advertisements, give slide shows, show up at company events—and, meanwhile, are supposed to perform cutting-edge deeds in the mountains. No clique in the outdoor world has a sexier cachet than the company's "Dream Team," as outsiders sardonically call it. But I've watched as mountaineers with two solid decades of achievement in rock climbing or big-range mountaineering get dropped from the team, to be replaced by the latest nineteen-year-old phenom.

What if the sponsors, I sometimes think in my down moments, slowly lose interest just because I don't have another 8,000er to pursue? I'm realistic enough to know I can't bask in the limelight forever. Someone younger will come along, with new goals and ideas that may seem more relevant to sponsors. When that time comes, I'll accept it. But in such down moments, I'll wonder, How can I reinvent myself at forty-seven? Sometimes I say to Paula, only half-jokingly, "Jeez, I might just have to get a regular job."

As we walked away from Annapurna, I felt as though an angel had been watching over us. Often, in the mountains, I've had a certain intimation that someone or something was watching over me as I climbed.

People frequently ask me if I'm religious. It's a hard question. I guess I believe in something less tangible, not a single omnipotent deity ruling the universe.

I have, if not a deeply religious bent, at least a spiritual one. In this respect, I've learned an immense amount from Sherpa culture and its Buddhist faith. On my expeditions, I've always noticed that as early as the first days at base camp, the Sherpas can tell which Westerners are there for the right reasons. Climbers who simply love being in beautiful places and relish the joy of climbing for its own sake win their approbation; those who just want to get it over with and go home boasting of reaching the top, don't.

The Sherpas have taught me to tread lightly and gently while climbing these magnificent peaks. To climb with humility and respect. And that mountains are not conquered: they simply do or do not allow us to climb them.

Although I remain uncertain about God or any particular religion, I believe in karma. What goes around, comes around. How you live your life, the respect that you give others and the mountain, and how you treat people in general will come back to you in kindred fashion. I like to talk about what I call the Karma National Bank. If you give up the summit to help rescue someone who's in trouble, you've put a deposit in that bank. And sometime down the road, you may need to make a big withdrawal.

People sometimes describe me as a "nice guy." While that's flattering in a sense, I think it slightly misses the point. What drives my life is not the desire to get along with other people or make friends so much as a moral obligation to give back as much as—no, more than—I take. That's karma. It's really not so far from the Golden Rule: "Do unto others as you would have them do unto you."

Some three decades ago, I was a naive kid growing up in Rockford, Illinois. One day I read a book—Maurice Herzog's *Annapurna*—and it completely changed the direction of my life. Eventually, it turned me toward a quest that no one else in the United States had accomplished, or even tried to accomplish—to climb the fourteen highest mountains in the world, in as pure a style as I could muster.

Many were the days and nights in the middle of my campaign when I told myself, What the hell do you think you're doing? Many were the moments when I felt a kind of panicky despair: how can I possibly support myself and make a living while I climb the 8,000ers? Somehow, I figured out how to do it. I never stopped believing in myself. Throughout those eighteen years, I've been blessed with relatives and friends who stood by me through times of struggle and defeat, who never doubted that I would manage to finish what I'd started. And during the last decade of that quest, beginning when I met Paula, I've enjoyed the unfathomable further blessing of being supported by a family I love more than anything in the world.

No matter what the future holds in store, I can say now—out loud, without hesitation—something that, sadly, all too few men and women can ever say: I have lived my dream.

ACKNOWLEDGMENTS

There are many people I would like to thank, for all their support, love, and encouragement throughout this amazing journey in the mountains and through life. Without them, my road would have been a tougher one to travel, and I am truly grateful to them for believing in me. To list them all would take many pages; if I omit some of them here, that lapse is inadvertent. Among my family, friends, and sponsors, there are scores of people who will know, whether or not I say so here, that I honor their friendship and thank them for everything they have contributed.

First and foremost, I want to thank my wife, Paula, for her love, patience, and encouragement. Her words and support have given me tremendous strength and inspiration during the past dozen years, as they will, I'm sure, for many years to come.

My children, Gilbert, Ella, and Anabel, for giving me unconditional love, joy, and laughter, as well as the best reasons in the world for coming home.

My parents, Ingrid and Elmars, for showing me what's possible and for allowing me to seek my own path.

My sister, Velta, who always believed in my dream.

My great friend, partner, tentmate, and confidant in the mountains for over a decade, Veikka Gustafsson. I look forward to many more great adventures with him. May he also accomplish his own goals.

My earliest climbing partners: Richard King, with whom I learned the basics of rockcraft, and Curt Mobley, my first true climbing partner and friend in the Northwest.

Those who showed me the art of mountaineering, taught me the management of risk, and brought me to the greater mountain ranges of the world: George Dunn, Eric Simonson, Phil Ershler, and Lou and Jim Whittaker.

Tracey Roberts, who trusted me enough to let me lead my first guided ascent of Mount Rainier.

My staunch and loyal friends who in some way or another helped me stay afloat when times were tough: Dave Magee, Dan Hiatt, and Steve Swaim.

My great friend, adviser, and partner on three successful Everest expeditions: David Breashears, who gave me the opportunity to challenge myself in unique ways, entrusted me with responsibilities that required me to do my best, and by example showed me the meaning of leadership.

Robert Schauer, for his compassion and intelligence in the face of hardship and tragedy in 1996. It was a joy to climb with him again in 2004.

My climbing partner, scuba buddy, sailing mate, and great friend Hall Wendel, with whom I continue to share laughter and memories.

Other climbing partners and friends with whom I shared moments of joy and laughter with in the mountains: Andy Politz, Jim Wickwire, John Roskelley, Greg Wilson, Jimmy Hamilton, Robert Link, Craig Van Hoy, Dave Carter, Charley Mace, Guy Cotter, Carlos Carsolio, Krzysztof Wielicki, Simone Moro, Denis Urubko, Jan Arnold, Jason Edwards, Charlie Kittrell, Steve Gall, Tashi Tenzing, Jamling Norgay, Araceli Segarra, Peter and Erica Whittaker, Larry Nielson, Jon Krakauer, Steve and Mike Marolt, Neal Beidleman, Michael Kennedy, Joe Horsikey, Paul Maier, Steve Connolly, and Rick Hanners.

John Cumming, who, during one of my darkest days, had the magnanimity to invite me to join with Mountain Hardwear, which gave me the support and strength to pursue my goal of all 8,000ers.

Ian Cumming and Jack Gilbert for their infinite wisdom and advice.

Gil Friesen, who, sight unseen, became one of my greatest advocates and mentors. Now I am honored to consider him one of my dearest friends. The world needs more generous people like him.

Jodie and John Eastman: friends who believed in me, stepped up to the plate, and gave me invaluable support and advice.

Ubbe Liljeblad, who taught me how to train harder and be stronger.

Michael and Alexa Rosenthal of Island Fitness, for their thoughtful and gracious support.

Peter Potterfield, who documented some of my expeditions, helped write my first book, and originally brought my adventures to the general public via the Internet.

Jimmy Chin, for his companionship, sense of humor, and professionalism as a photographer and videographer on Everest in 2004 and Cho Oyu and Annapurna in 2005.

Doctors Robert ("Brownie") Schoene, Tom Hornbein, Kurt Papenfus, and Peter Hackett, for their friendship and invaluable medical advice throughout my career.

Ron Judd of the *Seattle Times,* a great advocate and friend who kept me in the paper regularly, and who gave Paula solace while I was climbing Annapurna.

Elizabeth Hawley, for her insight and support, and for keeping me honest.

My friend Norkyel of the Garuda Hotel in Kathmandu, who always welcomed us with open arms.

Chris Mathius, for his instant friendship, and for showing me that working hard and having fun can be a lifestyle, with the latter being the priority. May his feet be tanned forever!

Other friends who in some unique way gave support or imparted wisdom and advice during my campaign: Rick Ridgeway, Jess Kraus, Gerald Lynch, Roland Puton, Jim Wagner, and Nawang Gombu.

All of my sponsors, past and present; their support has been invaluable and tremendously appreciated. My multiyear endeavor would have been impossible without their financial and emotional backing. Specifically, I wish to thank everyone at Mountain Hardwear. If there was ever a feeling of solidity and family with any sponsor, it was with them, for which I am forever grateful.

My other sponsors, who stayed with me to the summit of Annapurna and beyond: Rolex, Timberland, Sole Custom Footbeds, Outdoor Research, Leki, Princeton Tec, and Island Fitness.

A heartfelt thanks to our Italian friends on Annapurna: Silvio "Gnaro" Mondinelli, Christian Gobbi, Mario Merelli, Mario Panzeri, and Daniele Bernasconi, who selflessly invited us to climb with them on the route they had so carefully prepared, plied us with freshly brewed espresso, showered us with gifts of prosciutto and parmesan cheese, and allowed us to join them on their summit attempt of Annapurna. The bear hug I received from Silvio upon my return from the summit epitomized the generosity that these fellow climbers demonstrated during our entire expedition.

A special thanks to others who contributed to my successful Annapurna expedition: Jimmy Chinn; my friends at Cisco Systems; Franz Schmadl and Fred Gatling of OSV Partners; Jason Kintzler of Brunton; Richard Bangs and staff at MSN; Lindsey Yaw; Didrick Johnck; Wongchu Sherpa and staff at Peak Promotion; Claire Martin and staff at *Men's Journal;* and Justin Sugiyama of Thuraya Satellite phones.

Sponsors and supporters along the way who gave their support: MZH sleeping bags, Kelty, JanSport, Petzl, McNett, Wapiti Woolies, Thule, MTV, Polo Ralph Lauren, Trango, Smartwool, Greatoutdoors.com, Mountain zone.com, National Geographic Society, Microsoft, Cascade Designs, Creative Revolution, Bruce Franks and everyone at Asolo, Sterling Ropes, Julbo, L. L. Bean, Yukon Trading Company, Jetboil, Adventure Medical Kits, Dermatone, Mars, Eureka Tents, Sun Catcher, Clif Bar, AIG, Orvis, and Kokatat.

All of the wonderful people of Nepal, Pakistan, and Tibet who warmly welcomed me as a traveler and mountaineer and allowed me to fill my life with wonderful experiences and lasting memories in their beautiful countries.

Upon the return from my ascent of Annapurna, those organizations that valued my thirty years of climbing experience, achieving goals and risk management to speak on their behalf and represent them—the Thermos Corporation, the Seattle Seahawks, and the numerous other corporations and individuals that have had me speak to their employees, teams, and customers.

David Roberts, who tirelessly helped me craft this book and organized a long history of expeditions into something that made sense. From our first meeting in 1996, we have become good friends; I was his subject for several articles, and his sparring partner in our never-ending debate concerning odds and risk in mountaineering. His wisdom, insights, and talents as a writer are much appreciated. Thanks to him I have told my tale in a way that I hope touches many readers.

Stacy Creamer, our editor at Broadway Books, first for showing such enthusiasm about the book, and then for her diligent and knowledgeable editing.

Stuart Krichevsky, my literary agent, who helped make this book a viable and enjoyable endeavor for all involved.

I would also like to remember friends lost along the way. These people were an inspiration to everyone they met. Some I knew intimately, and some I crossed paths with in the mountains for only a short time. I feel privileged to have known them in some capacity, and we shall all miss them: Rob Hall, Scott Fischer, Alex Lowe, Anatoli Boukreev, Doug Hansen, Chantal Mauduit, Göran Kropp, and Christian Kuntner. May we all strive to live life as passionately and completely as they did.

Tragically, just now, as I write this final section of this book, we have lost the incomparable Jean-Christophe Lafaille, who in my opinion epitomized greatness and perfection in the mountains. As we shared a rope, his insights and companionship were deeply rewarding and satisfying for me. J.-C. cherished not only his time in the mountains but also his wife, Katia, his children, and the other joys of his too short life. We had much in common in these respects, and I had looked forward to more time with this strong yet gentle man. Now I have only the memories.

▲
▲
▲

In addition to all those acknowledged above, David Roberts would like to express his gratitude for the able assistance, unflagging encouragement, and shrewd criticism of agent Stuart Krichevsky and his two assistants, Shana Cohen and Elizabeth Kellermeyer; editor Stacy Creamer and her assistant, Laura Swerdloff; copy editor Bonnie Thompson; Sharon Roberts; Greg Child; Jon Krakauer; John Rasmus; and Paula Viesturs.

Finally, my ultimate gratitude goes to Ed Viesturs, an extraordinary human being as well as an astoundingly good and safe climber. Working on this book together has considerably deepened not only our friendship but my admiration for the man—for his compassion for others, his unflinching sense of responsibility to his teammates, his loving role as father and husband, his modesty, and his generosity. As different as he and I are in temperament, this collaboration could have been a vexatious locking of horns. Instead, it was like an endlessly fascinating conversation, a dialogue that was equal rather than Socratic, and if some of the quality of that interaction emerges on the printed page, I will be gratified.

May 21, 1987: Everest—north face summit attempt

October 1988: Everest—east face attempt

MAY 18, 1989: KANGCHENJUNGA

MAY 8, 1990: EVEREST

MAY 15, 1991: EVEREST

AUGUST 16, 1992: K2

May 15, 1993: Shishapangma—summit attempt
October 1993: Everest—north face solo attempt

MAY 9, 1994: EVEREST
MAY 16, 1994: LHOTSE
OCTOBER 6, 1994: CHO OYU

May 7, 1995: Everest—summit attempt
MAY 18, 1995: MAKALU
JULY 4, 1995: GASHERBRUM II
JULY 15, 1995: GASHERBRUM I

MAY 23, 1996: EVEREST
SEPTEMBER 29, 1996: CHO OYU

MAY 23, 1997: EVEREST
July 9, 1997: Broad Peak—summit attempt

May 16, 1998: Dhaulagiri—summit attempt

APRIL 22, 1999: MANASLU
MAY 4, 1999: DHAULAGIRI

May 2000: Annapurna—north face attempt

APRIL 30, 2001: SHISHAPANGMA
June 2001: Nanga Parbat—attempt

May 2002: Annapurna—east ridge attempt

JUNE 23, 2003: NANGA PARBAT
JULY 15, 2003: BROAD PEAK

MAY 17, 2004: EVEREST

MAY 12, 2005: ANNAPURNA

8,000ER.

A mountain whose summit exceeds 8,000 meters (26,247 feet) above sea level. There are fourteen such peaks in the world, all lying in Nepal, Pakistan, and Tibet.

ACUTE MOUNTAIN SICKNESS (AMS).

Any of several forms of illness brought on by high altitude. Usually distinguished from PULMONARY EDEMA or CEREBRAL EDEMA. See discussion, page 193.

ALPINE-STYLE.

The technique of going light and fast on a big mountain, eschewing FIXED ROPES, established camps, and LOAD CARRIES. Considered better form than the slower, more gear-intensive traditional EXPEDITION-STYLE.

ANAEROBIC THRESHOLD.

The percentage of VO_2 MAX at which an athlete starts operating in an oxygenless state. See discussion, page 191.

ANCHOR.

Any combination of PITONS, NUTS, CAMS, ICE SCREWS, and the like that secures a stance from which a climber can belay his partner. The anchor can also be used as a RAPPEL station.

AVALANCHE.

Any prolonged slide down a mountain face of massive quantities of snow and ice. Can be triggered by natural causes of collapse (warm temperatures, especially) but also by the passage of a climber. See also SLAB CONDITIONS, WIND SLAB.

BELAY.

To secure one's partner by feeding the rope in or out as he climbs, with the shock of a potential fall absorbed either by a mechanical device attached to one's WAIST HARNESS or by passing the rope around one's back.

BIVOUAC.

To spend the night on a mountain, usually without sleeping bag or tent. A bivvy tent is a lightweight, minimalist structure with barely enough room for two recumbent climbers.

BOLLARD.

A knob or horn of ice or hard snow, carved to serve as a RAPPEL anchor.

BUTTRESS.

A broad protruding bulge or rib on a mountain.

CAM.

A kind of NUT that can be flexed by a trigger handle to expand or contract in size. Invented in 1973, this ingenious device has revolutionized climbing, because it works in cracks that refuse to accept traditional NUTS.

CARABINER, BINER.

An oval snap link made of light but strong metal, used to attach the rope to any piece of PROTECTION or part of an ANCHOR.

CEREBRAL EDEMA (HACE).

Leakage of fluid into the brain causeed by HYPOXIA. See discussion, page 193.

CIRQUE.

A basin formed by steep cliffs and peaks at the head of a valley.

CLIP, CLIP IN, UNCLIP.

To attach or detach a CARABINER from a piece of PROTECTION or a rope.

COL.

A narrow mountain pass, usually between steep COULOIRS or faces and/or sharp ridges.

CORNICE.

A curling plume of snow and ice, formed by strong recurrent winds, that overhangs the leeward face of the mountain. Especially treacherous, for a cornice can be mistaken for the ridge crest itself, and a climber can all too easily break through its insubstantial crust and plunge down the wall beneath.

COULOIR.

A steep snow gully, usually found high on a mountain.

CRAMPONS.

Sets of metal spikes strapped to the bottoms of one's boots to enable climbing or hiking on ice and hard snow. Modern crampons typically have twelve points—ten pointing directly downward to give purchase while walking and two pointing forward at the toe, used when climbing steep or vertical snow and ice. See discussion, page 122.

CREVASSE.

A major crack or fissure in the surface of a glacier created by the glacier's flow over steep or uneven ground. If the ground below is concave, the crevasse is typically narrow at the surface but bulges to greater widths below. If the ground below is convex, the crevasse is typically wider at the surface and narrows with increasing depth. A hidden crevasse is one rendered all but invisible (and thus treacherous) after storms build a thin bridge of snow that closes the surface crack and disguises the crevasse's very existence.

DEATH ZONE.

Originally used by climbers to refer to altitudes above 17,000 feet, at which the body inevitably deteriorates. Now more commonly used to allude to the especially dangerous regions above 26,000 feet.

DEXAMETHASONE.

A steroid temporarily effective in treating high-altitude illnesses.

DIAMOX.

A diuretic drug temporarily effective in treating high-altitude illnesses.

EXPEDITION-STYLE.
The traditional means of climbing a big mountain, involving stocked tent camps, LOAD CARRIES, and FIXED ROPES. In the Himalaya and the Karakoram, quite often Sherpas or other local high-altitude porters are employed to assist with the load carrying. See ALPINE-STYLE.

FIGURE-EIGHT DEVICE.
A metal device shaped like the number 8 through which the rope is threaded to distribute pressure while RAPPELLING or BELAYING.

FIXED ROPE.
A thin rope left in place on a mountain pitch to facilitate subsequent ascents, descents, and LOAD CARRIES.

FROSTBITE.
The freezing of tissue (usually toes and fingers) to a deeper than superficial level, often necessitating amputation.

GAITERS.
Leggings that cover from boot top to lower calf, keeping snow out of the boots and providing warmth.

GAMOW BAG.
A coffinlike nylon capsule into which an acutely ill victim of PULMONARY EDEMA or CEREBRAL EDEMA can be placed; teammates then pump pressure into the interior, artificially reducing the effects of altitude. Has saved quite a few lives in the Himalaya and Karakoram. See discussion, page 194.

GLISSADE.
To slide under control down a steep snow slope, usually by digging the edges of one's boots into the slope and slipping sideways like a skier. Can also be performed on the seat of one's pants.

HACE.
See CEREBRAL EDEMA.

HANGING GLACIER.

A small glacier or part of a larger one that sits unstably perched above a cliff. Particularly dangerous to climb beneath.

HAPE.

See PULMONARY EDEMA.

HARDWARE.

Collective term for a climber's various pieces of PROTECTION, ranging from PITONS to CAMS to ICE SCREWS and the like.

HYPOXIA.

Oxygen deprivation at high altitude. See discussion, page 193.

ICE AX.

One of the mountaineer's most essential pieces of gear. In its classic form, it consists of a metal head with an adze on one side and a sharpened pick on the other, a two-and-a-half-foot-long metal shaft, and a sharpened metal point on the end of the shaft. Used for chopping steps in ice and snow, for BELAYING, for SELF-ARRESTS in a fall or AVALANCHE, for probing for hidden CREVASSES, and simply for balance (when used like a cane) while hiking. See also ICE TOOLS.

ICEFALL.

A steep, extremely crevassed section of a glacier where the ice flows over contorted ground.

ICE SCREW.

A kind of PITON for hard ice, threaded like a screw; it is rotated home as one hammers it directly into the ice.

ICE TOOLS.

Any of a number of modern devices evolved from the traditional ICE AX; used directly for climbing steep ice and mixed ice and rock, rather than for balance or chopping steps.

JUMAR.

To use a sliding and locking mechanism to climb ropes fixed in place. The word derives from the brand name of the most popular mechanical ascender, introduced in the late 1960s. A jumar is a metal device that grips the rope under a downward pull but slides easily upward.

LEAD.

To climb a PITCH first on the rope. A LEAD is a PITCH so climbed.

LIAISON OFFICER.

A native intermediary, officially assigned by the local government to ensure that the expedition follows the rules of the permit. See SIRDAR.

LINE.

Route on a rock wall or mountain. Also synonymous with rope, as in "fixed lines."

LOAD CARRY.

A ferry of supplies across a part of a mountain or of an approach route that has previously been climbed or TRAVERSED.

MONSOON.

In the Himalaya, the recurrent and predictable three- to four-month summer season of nearly constant snowfall and thick clouds. Effectively prevents climbing during that time.

MORAINE.

Any ridge or mound of rock and gravel deposited by a flowing glacier.

NÉVÉ.

A crust of hard snow.

NUT.

A trapezoidal or hexagonal piece of metal, attached to a SLING or wire and slotted into a crack in the rock so that it holds under a downward pull, affording protection to the leader or serving as part of an ANCHOR. A hex nut is a nut formed from a piece of hollow hexagonal tubing and is used in wide cracks.

OXYGEN, BOTTLED OR SUPPLEMENTAL.

A system used at high altitude consisting of bottles of pressurized oxygen carried on one's back, connected by tubing to a face mask and controlled by a regulator. Flow ranges from two liters a minute to upward of four. Effectively reduces the apparent altitude by several thousand feet.

PITCH.

A rope length or partial rope length; also, the terrain climbed by the leader.

PITON.

A metal spike. driven into a crack in the rock, used either as part of an ANCHOR or to shorten the leader's potential fall. The piton has an eye, through which it is attached by a CARABINER to the free-running rope.

PROTECTION.

A collective term for all the PITONS, NUTS, and CAMS placed by the leader to shorten a potential fall.

PUJA.

A Sherpa ceremony of propitiation of the mountain gods, usually performed at base camp near the beginning of an expedition.

PULMONARY EDEMA (HAPE).

Leakage of fluid into the lungs caused by HYPOXIA. See discussion, page 193.

PUT UP, PUT IN.

Jargon: to make the first ascent of a route on a cliff or a mountain.

RAPPEL.

To descend a cliff by sliding down a rope that is doubled and attached at the midpoint to an ANCHOR. From the bottom of the rappel, the climber retrieves the rope by pulling one end, so that it slides through the anchoring SLINGS or CARABINERS and comes loose.

ROPE UP.

To tie in with a partner or partners preparatory to climbing on TECHNICAL ground or through CREVASSE fields.

SECOND.

To follow a PITCH led by one's partner, secured with a BELAY from above.

SELF-ARREST.

To stop oneself in a fall or an AVALANCHE by lying facedown on top of one's ICE AX and digging the pick into the slope.

SERAC.

A plume, tower, or lump of ice on the surface of a glacier or mountain slope. Particularly dangerous because it can collapse without warning.

SEVEN SUMMITS.

The campaign of climbing to the top of the highest peak on each continent, first accomplished by Texas oilman Dick Bass in 1985.

SHERPA.

A native of any of several mountainous regions in Nepal and a member of a Buddhist culture. For the last eighty years, Sherpas have been matchless comrades to climbers on the highest mountains, as they carry loads, fix ropes, establish camps, rescue mountaineers in trouble, and perform ascents of their own.

SHORT-ROPE.

To safeguard an exhausted, ill, or injured climber by tying in to his rope at a very close interval, then descending just behind the weakened mountaineer, ready to catch a fall or even assist in lowering him.

SIRDAR.

A leader, of local origin, assigned and paid to negotiate between climbers and porters and villagers; he also facilitates progress during approach marches and at base camp. In addition, the sirdar often manages the high-altitude load carriers on a large-scale expedition.

SLAB CONDITIONS.

The state in which a surface snow layer has been deposited by wind, creating a very hard, Styrofoam-like consistency. When the crust is broken by passing climbers or by a natural trigger, such as a falling rock, large sections can release in an AVA-LANCHE. See also WIND SLAB.

SLEDGE.
A sled, improvised from the materials at hand, used to lower a stricken climber.

SLIDE, SNOWSLIDE.
An AVALANCHE.

SLING.
A loop of nylon webbing, useful for many different tasks.

SNOW BLINDNESS.
Burning of the cornea caused by ultraviolet rays, usually at high altitude when one removes one's goggles for too long. Very painful; can cause temporary loss of vision.

SOLO.
To climb without a partner and, usually, without a rope or any means of self-protection.

SPINDRIFT.
Especially fine clouds of snow particles, either falling as precipitation or driven in front of or on the edges of an AVALANCHE.

TECHNICAL CLIMBING.
Any climbing difficult enough to require a rope and PROTECTION.

TOP-ROPE.
To belay a climber from above, rendering falls harmless. Top-rope climbing on small cliffs allows one to push one's skills to the limit.

TRAVERSE.
To climb a PITCH by moving sideways or diagonally upward. Also, to cross a mountain or even a range by ascending one side and descending the opposite side.

TREKKER.
A commercial client who hikes, aided by guides and porters, along multiday circuits among the foothills and approaches of high mountains.

VO$_2$ MAX.
A measure of how much oxygen an athlete can take in and effectively use. See discussion, page 191.

VOIE NORMALE.
The "normal," or easiest, route on a mountain, usually that of the first ascent.

WAIST HARNESS, HARNESS.
A device worn around the waist and upper thighs, to which the climbing rope is tied. The harness distributes the load (and the shock of a fall) in a far more comfortable—and, ultimately, far safer—fashion than does the traditional technique of tying the rope directly around one's waist.

WHITEOUT.
A weather condition in which fog, mist, or snow renders visibility almost nil.

WILLOW WANDS.
Thin wooden or bamboo stakes, usually painted green, with red tape affixed to one end to make a small flag; stuck upright in the surface of a glacier every few dozen yards or more, they mark a trail and ensure routefinding in storms and WHITEOUTS. See discussion, page 27.

WINDBLAST.
The unique mini-hurricane caused by air ahead of an AVALANCHE being violently and suddenly displaced.

WIND SLAB.
Plates of frozen snow poorly attached to softer snow beneath, the precipitating agent in slab AVALANCHES. See SLAB CONDITIONS.

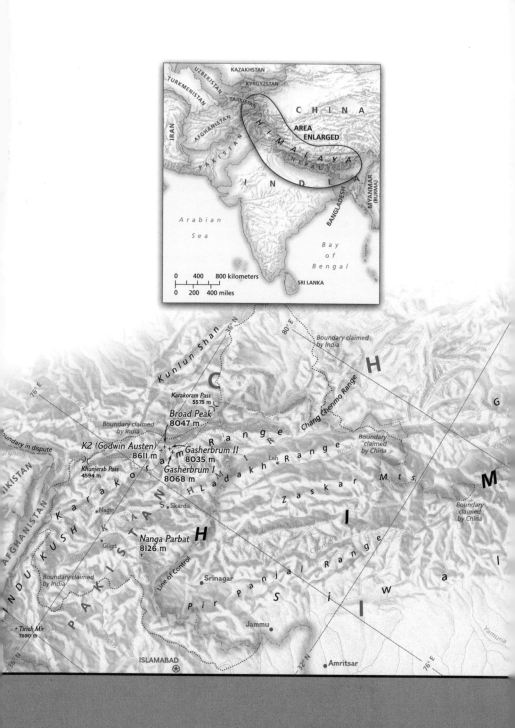